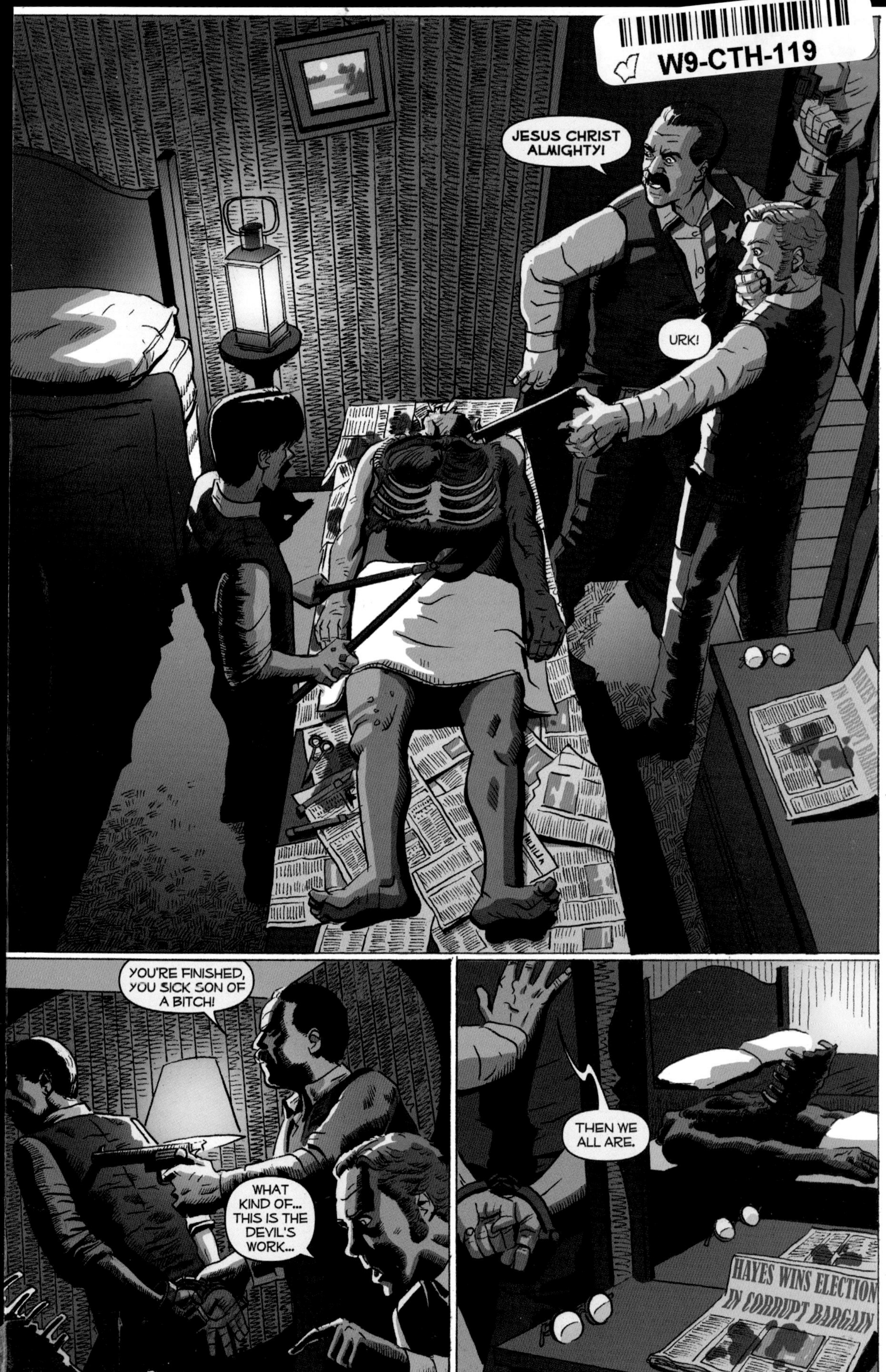
JESUS CHRIST ALMIGHTY!
URK!
YOU'RE FINISHED, YOU SICK SON OF A BITCH!
WHAT KIND OF... THIS IS THE DEVIL'S WORK...
THEN WE ALL ARE.
HAYES WINS ELECTION IN CORRUPT BARGAIN

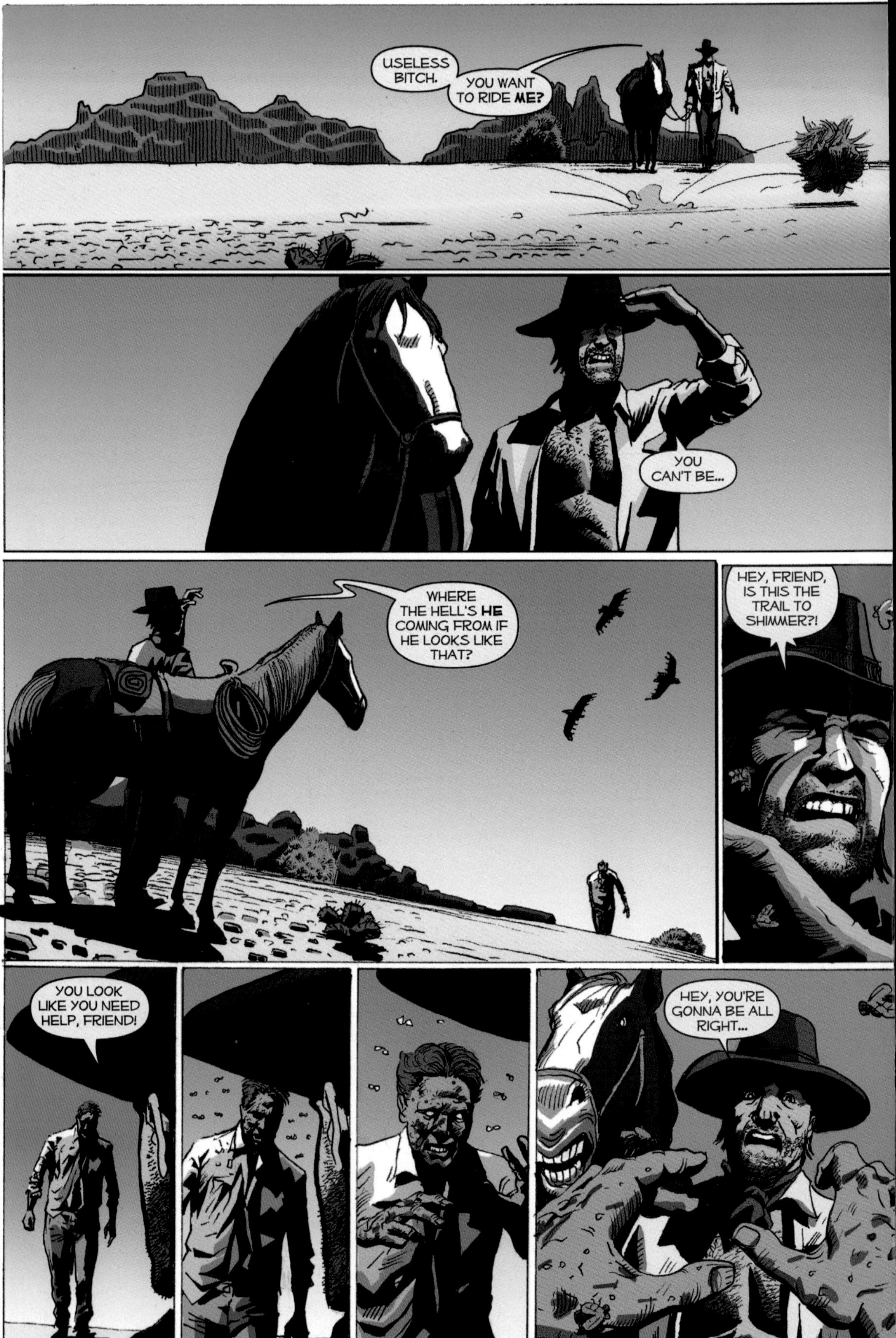
USELESS BITCH.
YOU WANT TO RIDE ME?
YOU CAN'T BE...
WHERE THE HELL'S HE COMING FROM IF HE LOOKS LIKE THAT?
HEY, FRIEND, IS THIS THE TRAIL TO SHIMMER?!
YOU LOOK LIKE YOU NEED HELP, FRIEND!
HEY, YOU'RE GONNA BE ALL RIGHT...

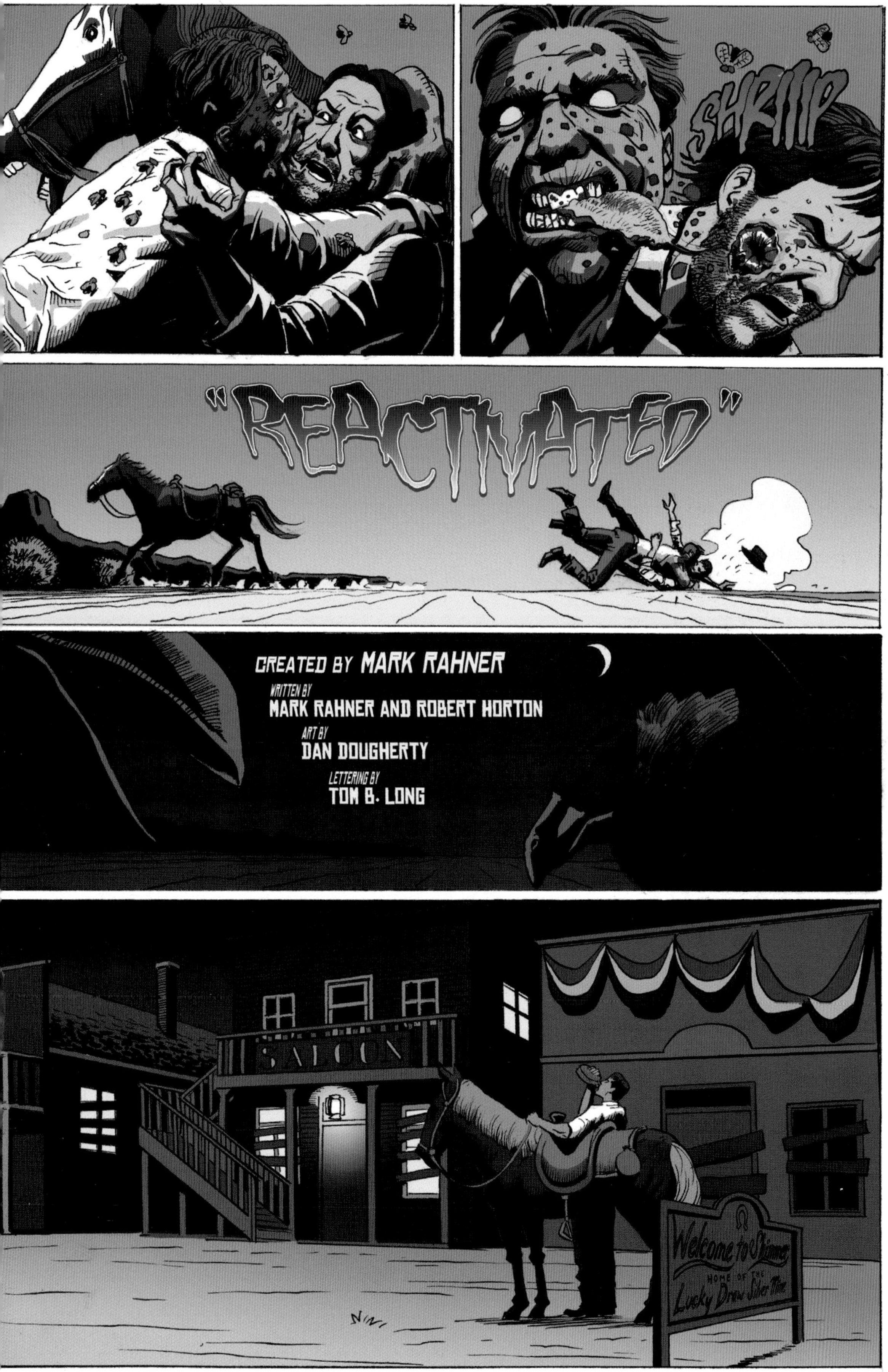
SHRIIP
"REACTIVATED"
CREATED BY MARK RAHNER
WRITTEN BY
MARK RAHNER AND ROBERT HORTON
ART BY
DAN DOUGHERTY
LETTERING BY
TOM B. LONG
SALOON
Welcome to Shimmer
HOME OF THE
Lucky Draw Silver Mine

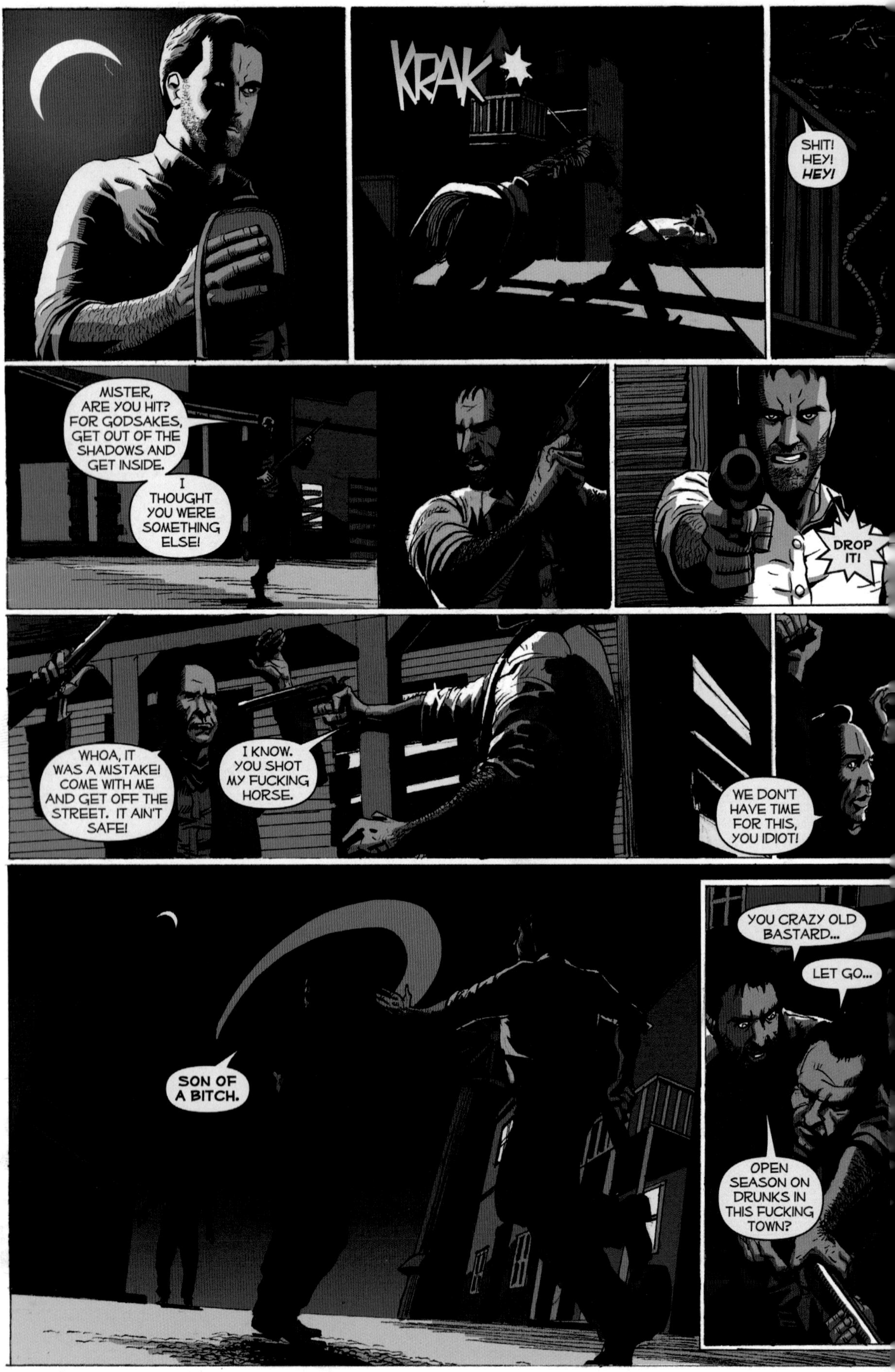
KRAK
SHIT! HEY! HEY!
MISTER, ARE YOU HIT? FOR GODSAKES, GET OUT OF THE SHADOWS AND GET INSIDE.
I THOUGHT YOU WERE SOMETHING ELSE!
DROP IT!
WHOA, IT WAS A MISTAKE! COME WITH ME AND GET OFF THE STREET. IT AIN'T SAFE!
I KNOW. YOU SHOT MY FUCKING HORSE.
WE DON'T HAVE TIME FOR THIS, YOU IDIOT!
SON OF A BITCH.
YOU CRAZY OLD BASTARD...
LET GO...
OPEN SEASON ON DRUNKS IN THIS FUCKING TOWN?

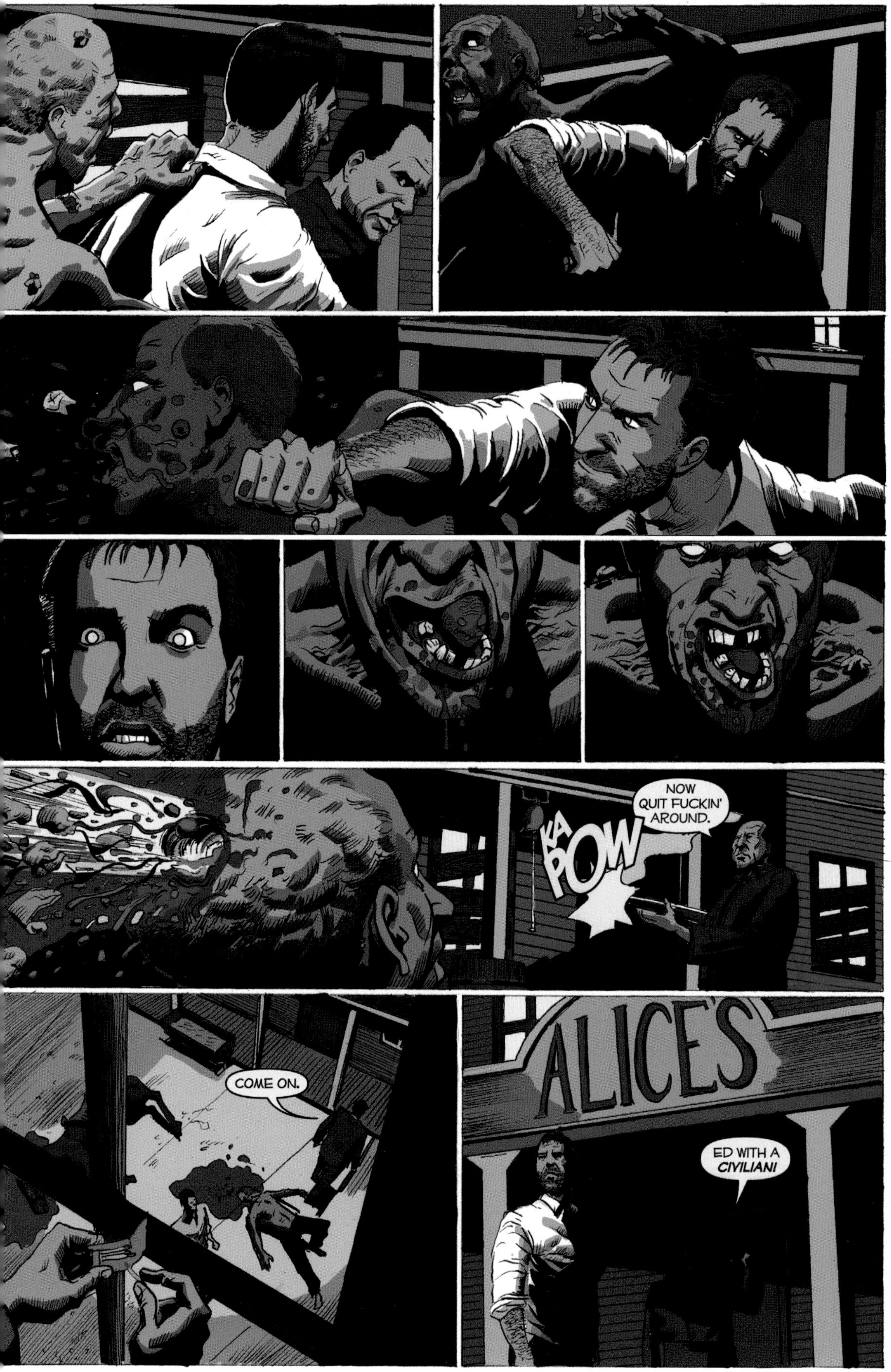
KA POW
NOW QUIT FUCKIN' AROUND.
COME ON.
ALICE'S
ED WITH A CIVILIAN!

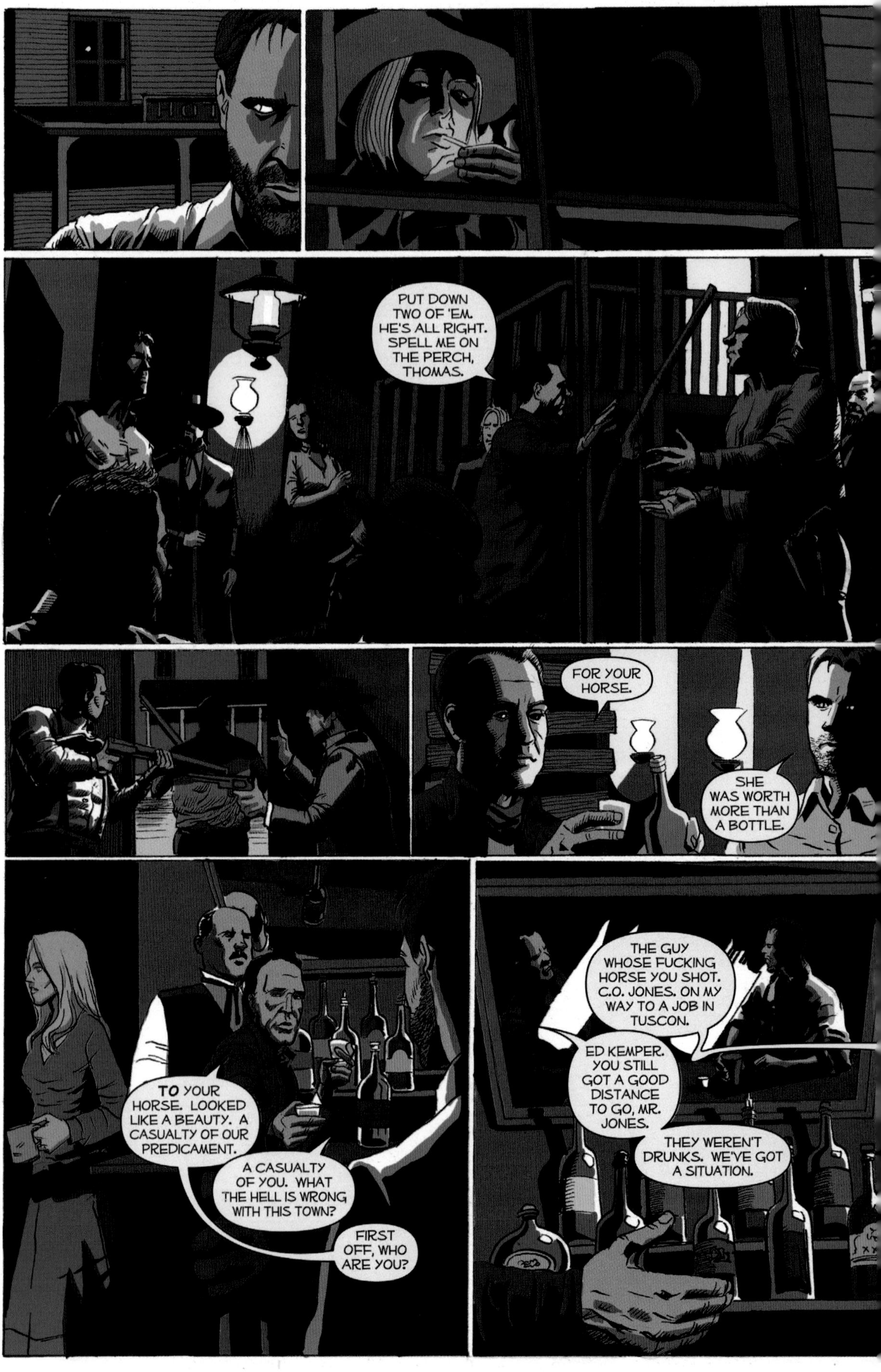
PUT DOWN TWO OF 'EM. HE'S ALL RIGHT. SPELL ME ON THE PERCH, THOMAS.
FOR YOUR HORSE.
SHE WAS WORTH MORE THAN A BOTTLE.
TO YOUR HORSE. LOOKED LIKE A BEAUTY. A CASUALTY OF OUR PREDICAMENT.
A CASUALTY OF YOU. WHAT THE HELL IS WRONG WITH THIS TOWN?
FIRST OFF, WHO ARE YOU?
THE GUY WHOSE FUCKING HORSE YOU SHOT. C.O. JONES. ON MY WAY TO A JOB IN TUSCON.
ED KEMPER. YOU STILL GOT A GOOD DISTANCE TO GO, MR. JONES.
THEY WEREN'T DRUNKS. WE'VE GOT A SITUATION.

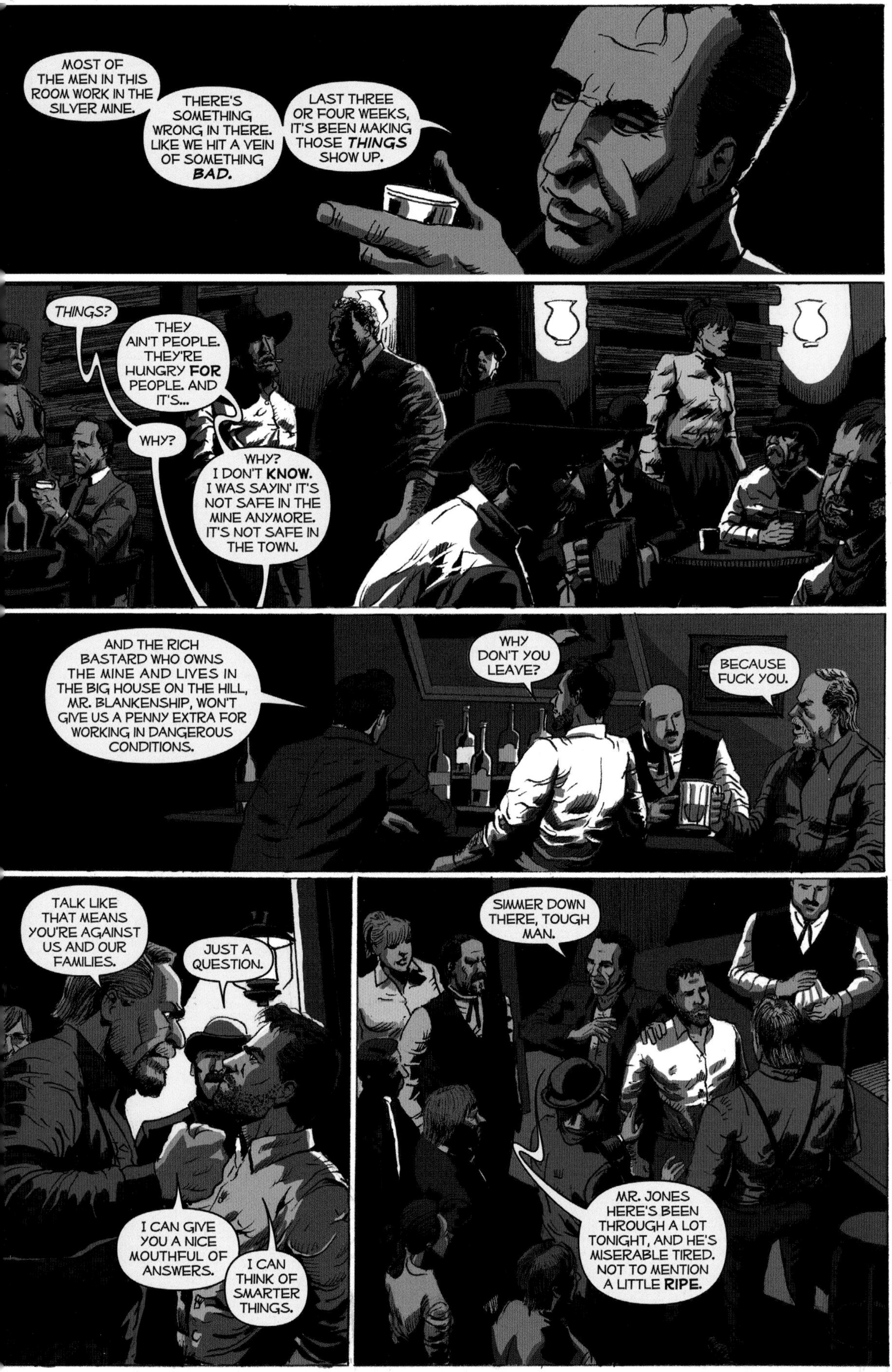
MOST OF THE MEN IN THIS ROOM WORK IN THE SILVER MINE.
THERE'S SOMETHING WRONG IN THERE. LIKE WE HIT A VEIN OF SOMETHING **BAD.**
LAST THREE OR FOUR WEEKS, IT'S BEEN MAKING THOSE **THINGS** SHOW UP.
THINGS?
THEY AIN'T PEOPLE. THEY'RE HUNGRY **FOR** PEOPLE. AND IT'S...
WHY?
WHY? I DON'T **KNOW.** I WAS SAYIN' IT'S NOT SAFE IN THE MINE ANYMORE. IT'S NOT SAFE IN THE TOWN.
AND THE RICH BASTARD WHO OWNS THE MINE AND LIVES IN THE BIG HOUSE ON THE HILL, MR. BLANKENSHIP, WON'T GIVE US A PENNY EXTRA FOR WORKING IN DANGEROUS CONDITIONS.
WHY DON'T YOU LEAVE?
BECAUSE FUCK YOU.
TALK LIKE THAT MEANS YOU'RE AGAINST US AND OUR FAMILIES.
JUST A QUESTION.
I CAN GIVE YOU A NICE MOUTHFUL OF ANSWERS.
I CAN THINK OF SMARTER THINGS.
SIMMER DOWN THERE, TOUGH MAN.
MR. JONES HERE'S BEEN THROUGH A LOT TONIGHT, AND HE'S MISERABLE TIRED. NOT TO MENTION A LITTLE **RIPE.**

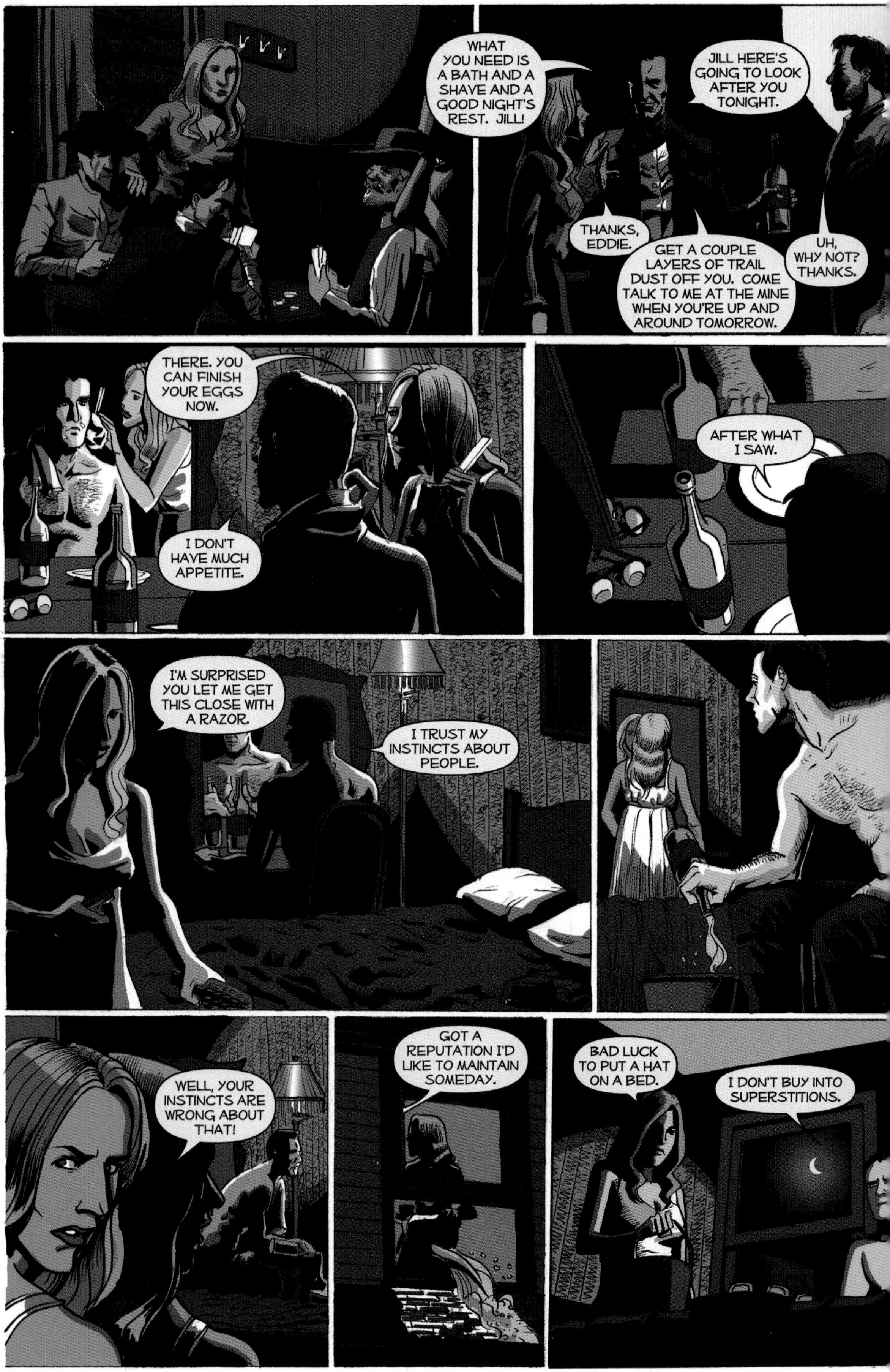
WHAT YOU NEED IS A BATH AND A SHAVE AND A GOOD NIGHT'S REST. JILL!
JILL HERE'S GOING TO LOOK AFTER YOU TONIGHT.
THANKS, EDDIE.
GET A COUPLE LAYERS OF TRAIL DUST OFF YOU. COME TALK TO ME AT THE MINE WHEN YOU'RE UP AND AROUND TOMORROW.
UH, WHY NOT? THANKS.
THERE. YOU CAN FINISH YOUR EGGS NOW.
I DON'T HAVE MUCH APPETITE.
AFTER WHAT I SAW.
I'M SURPRISED YOU LET ME GET THIS CLOSE WITH A RAZOR.
I TRUST MY INSTINCTS ABOUT PEOPLE.
WELL, YOUR INSTINCTS ARE WRONG ABOUT THAT!
GOT A REPUTATION I'D LIKE TO MAINTAIN SOMEDAY.
BAD LUCK TO PUT A HAT ON A BED.
I DON'T BUY INTO SUPERSTITIONS.

WELL, I BELIEVE IN BAD LUCK. NOT SO SURE ABOUT THE GOOD.

WHAT THE HELL IS GOING ON?

I'M A WHORE AND YOU'RE A MAN IN MY ROOM...

THAT'S NO ANSWER.

AND YOU DON'T LOOK MUCH LIKE A SEASONED PROFESSIONAL.

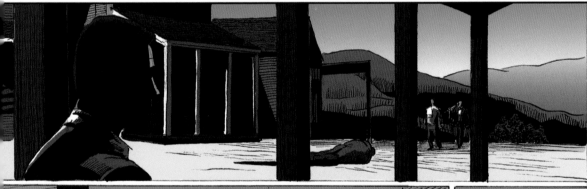

HEADING FOR THE MINE?

NOPE. WE GOTTA BURY SOME SHIT.

MINE'S THAT WAY.

THANKS.

DON'T THANK ME, YET.

SALO

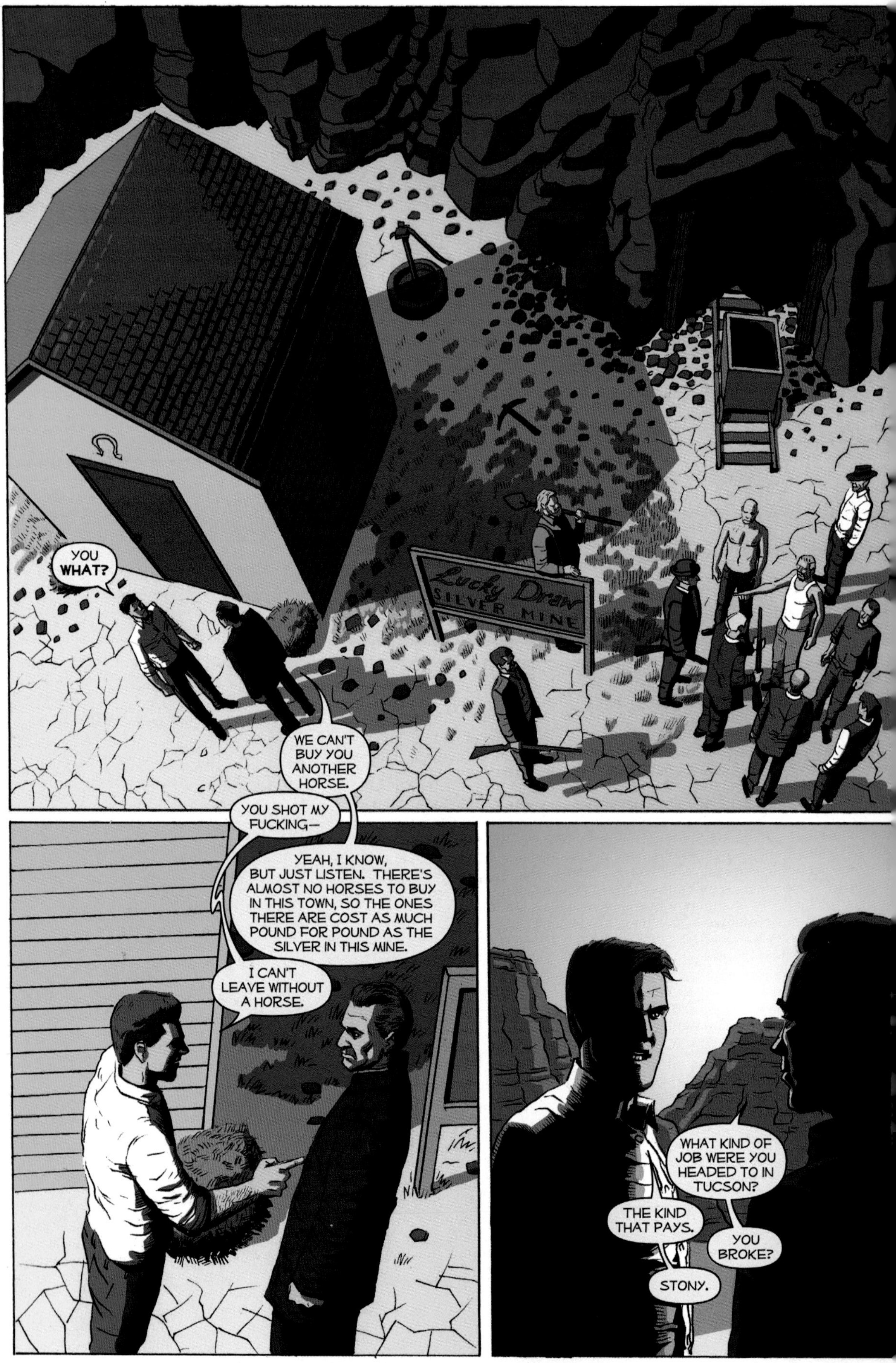
Lucky Draw
SILVER MINE
YOU WHAT?
WE CAN'T BUY YOU ANOTHER HORSE.
YOU SHOT MY FUCKING—
YEAH, I KNOW, BUT JUST LISTEN. THERE'S ALMOST NO HORSES TO BUY IN THIS TOWN, SO THE ONES THERE ARE COST AS MUCH POUND FOR POUND AS THE SILVER IN THIS MINE.
I CAN'T LEAVE WITHOUT A HORSE.
WHAT KIND OF JOB WERE YOU HEADED TO IN TUCSON?
THE KIND THAT PAYS.
YOU BROKE?
STONY.

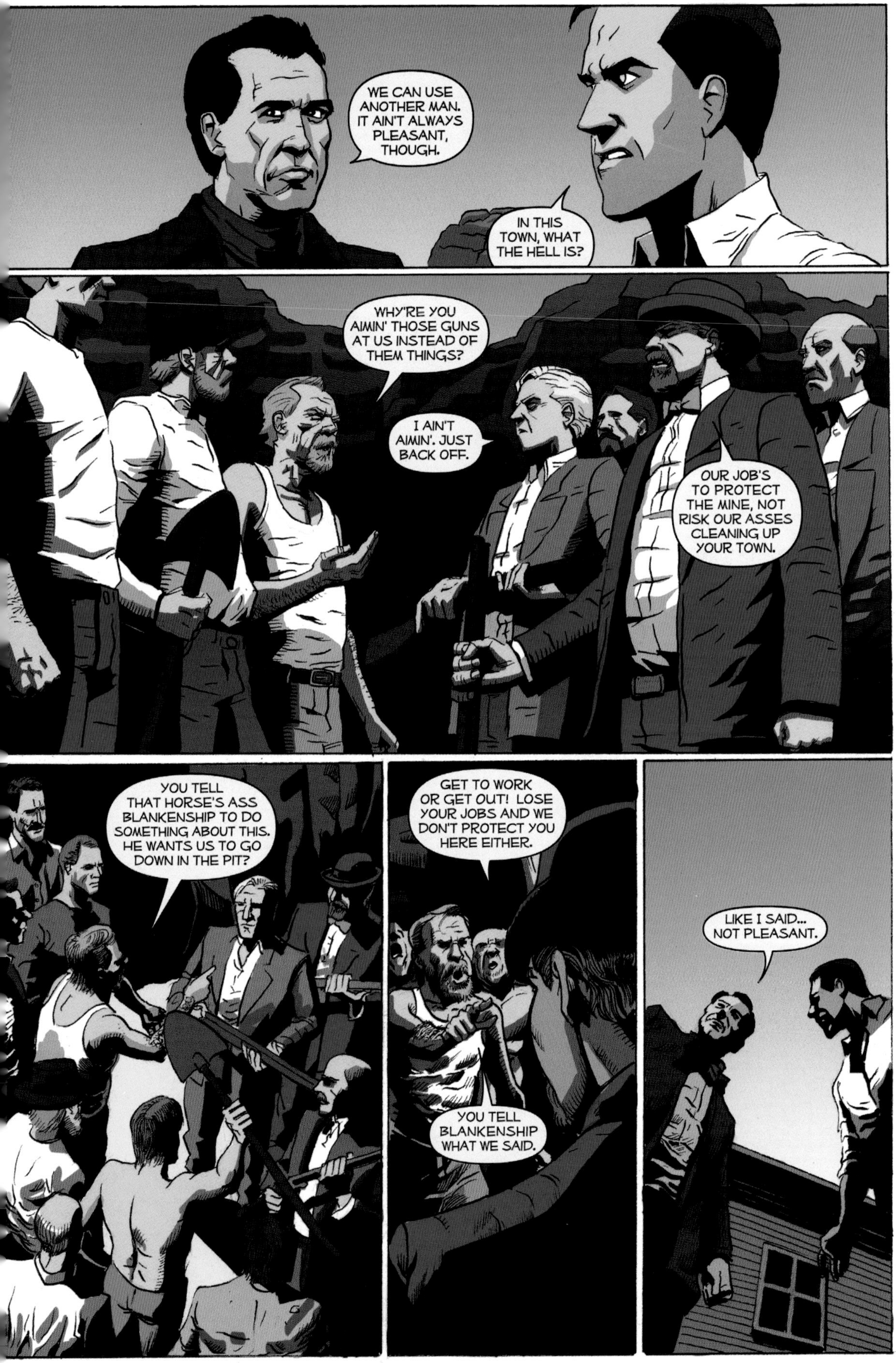
WE CAN USE ANOTHER MAN. IT AIN'T ALWAYS PLEASANT, THOUGH.
IN THIS TOWN, WHAT THE HELL IS?
WHY'RE YOU AIMIN' THOSE GUNS AT US INSTEAD OF THEM THINGS?
I AIN'T AIMIN'. JUST BACK OFF.
OUR JOB'S TO PROTECT THE MINE, NOT RISK OUR ASSES CLEANING UP YOUR TOWN.
YOU TELL THAT HORSE'S ASS BLANKENSHIP TO DO SOMETHING ABOUT THIS. HE WANTS US TO GO DOWN IN THE PIT?
GET TO WORK OR GET OUT! LOSE YOUR JOBS AND WE DON'T PROTECT YOU HERE EITHER.
YOU TELL BLANKENSHIP WHAT WE SAID.
LIKE I SAID... NOT PLEASANT.

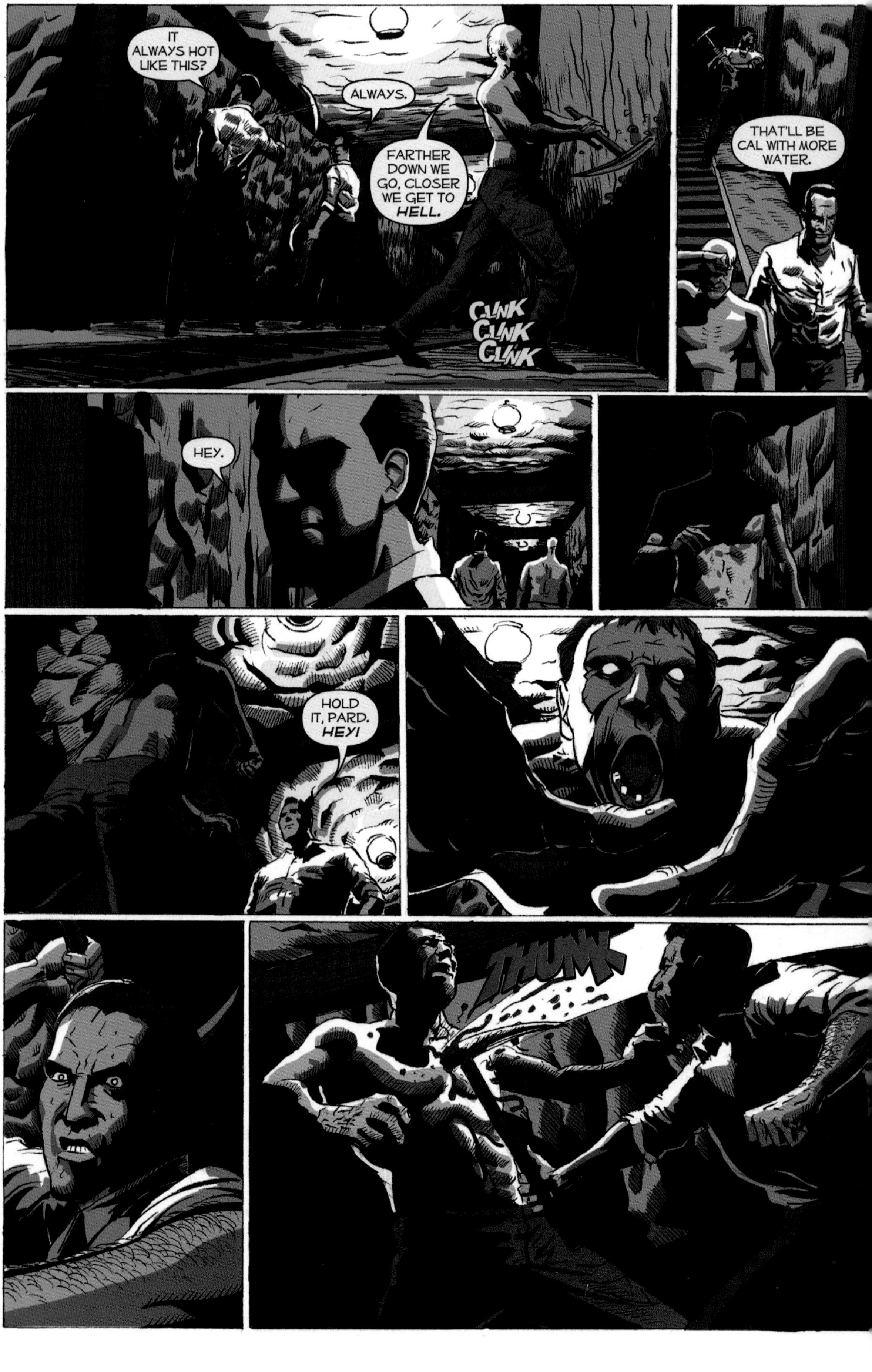
IT ALWAYS HOT LIKE THIS?
ALWAYS.
FARTHER DOWN WE GO, CLOSER WE GET TO **HELL.**
CLINK CLINK CLINK
THAT'LL BE CAL WITH MORE WATER.
HEY.
HOLD IT, PARD. **HEY!**
THUNK

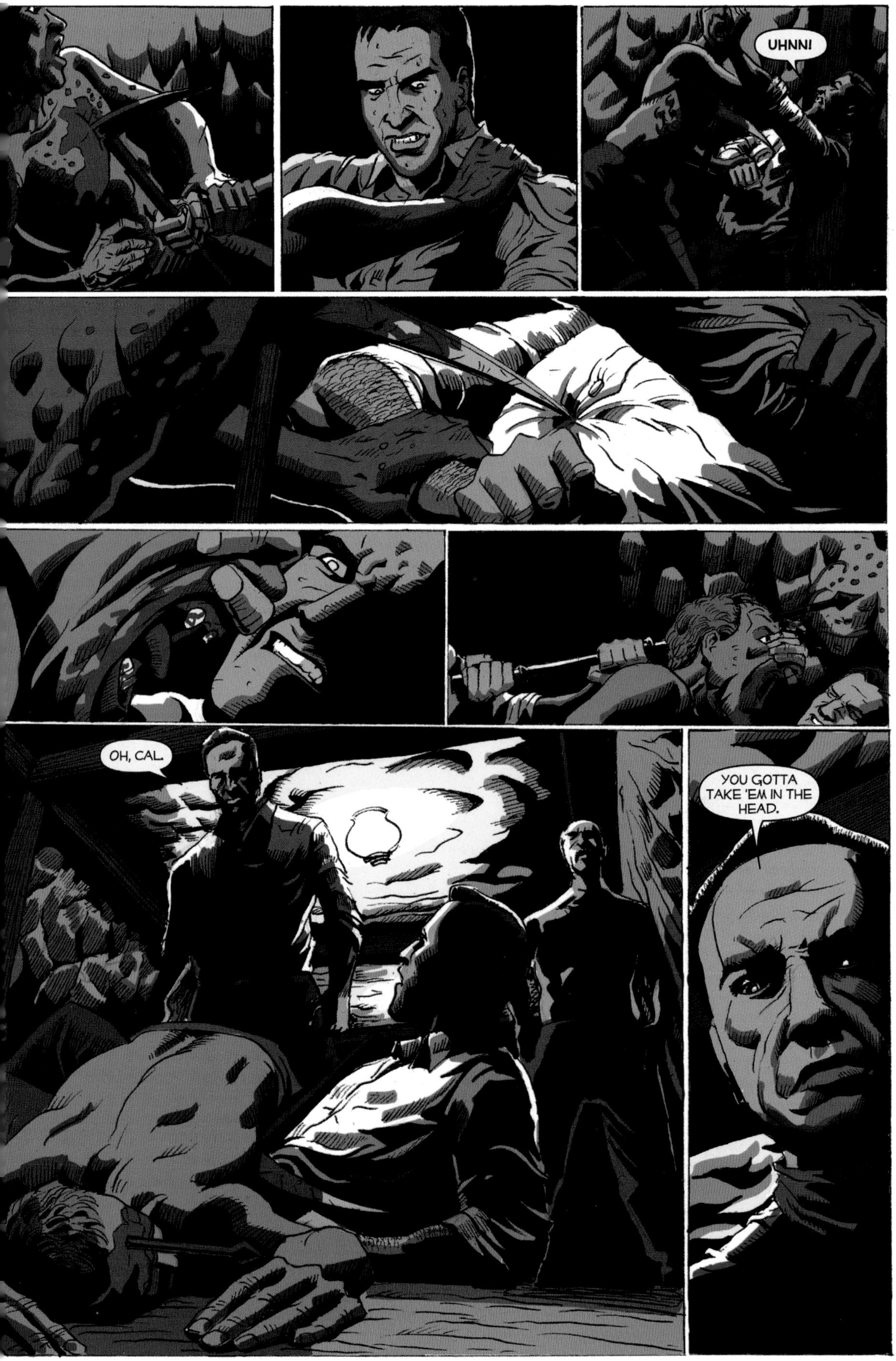
UHNN!
OH, CAL.
YOU GOTTA TAKE 'EM IN THE HEAD.

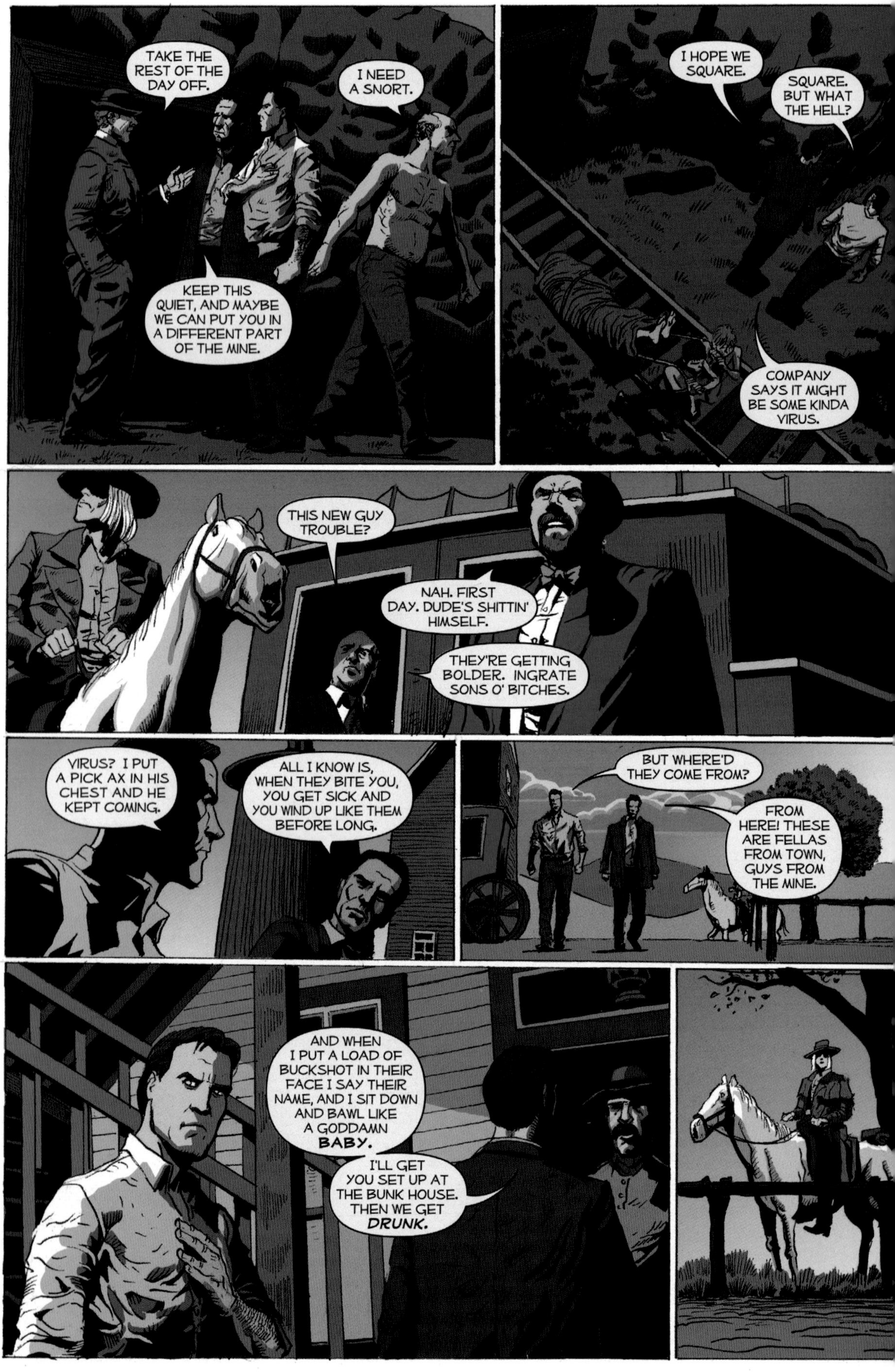
TAKE THE REST OF THE DAY OFF.
I NEED A SNORT.
KEEP THIS QUIET, AND MAYBE WE CAN PUT YOU IN A DIFFERENT PART OF THE MINE.
I HOPE WE SQUARE.
SQUARE. BUT WHAT THE HELL?
COMPANY SAYS IT MIGHT BE SOME KINDA VIRUS.
THIS NEW GUY TROUBLE?
NAH. FIRST DAY. DUDE'S SHITTIN' HIMSELF.
THEY'RE GETTING BOLDER. INGRATE SONS O' BITCHES.
VIRUS? I PUT A PICK AX IN HIS CHEST AND HE KEPT COMING.
ALL I KNOW IS, WHEN THEY BITE YOU, YOU GET SICK AND YOU WIND UP LIKE THEM BEFORE LONG.
BUT WHERE'D THEY COME FROM?
FROM HERE! THESE ARE FELLAS FROM TOWN, GUYS FROM THE MINE.
AND WHEN I PUT A LOAD OF BUCKSHOT IN THEIR FACE I SAY THEIR NAME, AND I SIT DOWN AND BAWL LIKE A GODDAMN BABY.
I'LL GET YOU SET UP AT THE BUNK HOUSE. THEN WE GET DRUNK.

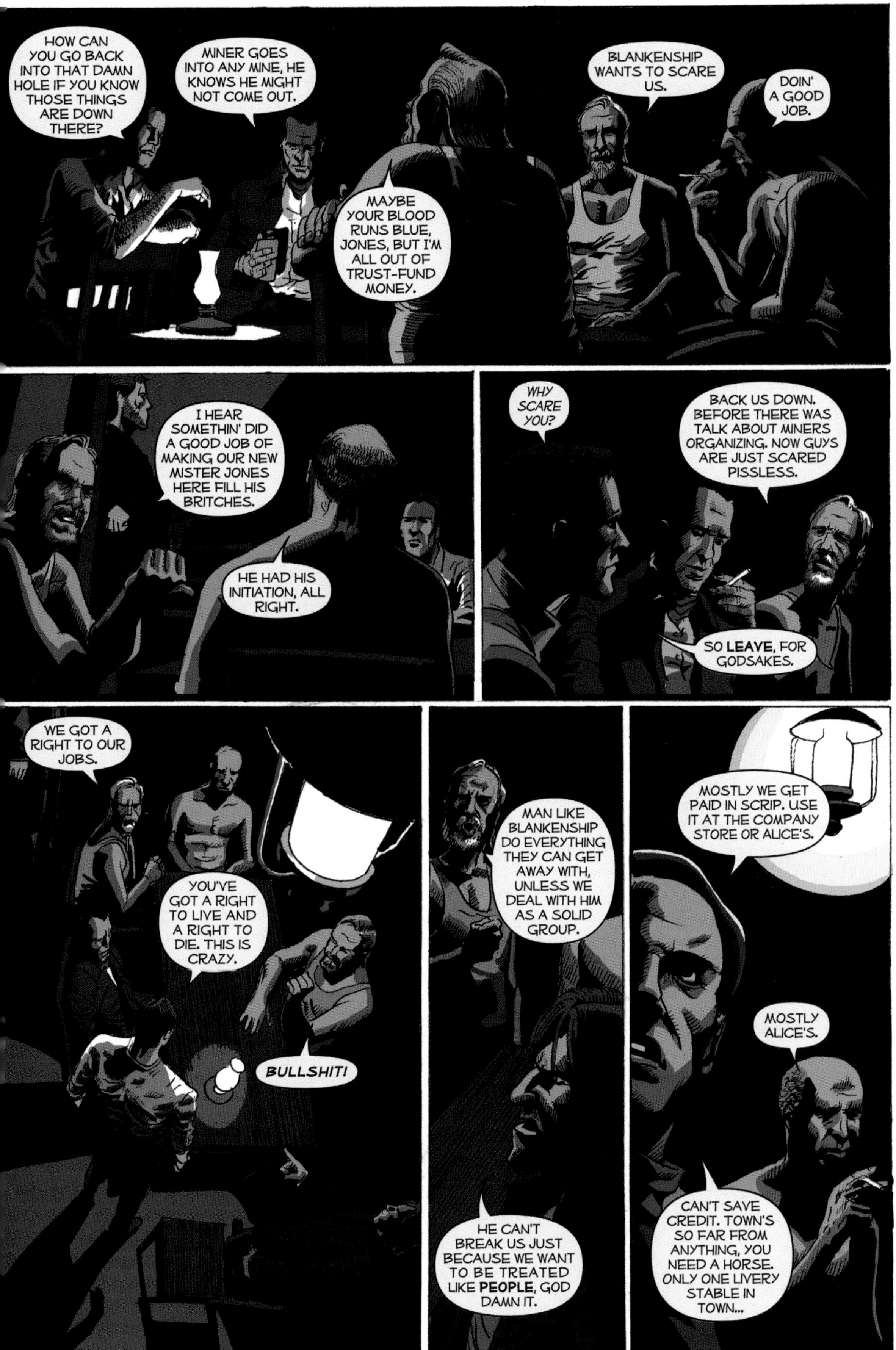
HOW CAN YOU GO BACK INTO THAT DAMN HOLE IF YOU KNOW THOSE THINGS ARE DOWN THERE?
MINER GOES INTO ANY MINE, HE KNOWS HE MIGHT NOT COME OUT.
MAYBE YOUR BLOOD RUNS BLUE, JONES, BUT I'M ALL OUT OF TRUST-FUND MONEY.
BLANKENSHIP WANTS TO SCARE US.
DOIN' A GOOD JOB.
I HEAR SOMETHIN' DID A GOOD JOB OF MAKING OUR NEW MISTER JONES HERE FILL HIS BRITCHES.
HE HAD HIS INITIATION, ALL RIGHT.
WHY SCARE YOU?
BACK US DOWN. BEFORE THERE WAS TALK ABOUT MINERS ORGANIZING. NOW GUYS ARE JUST SCARED PISSLESS.
SO **LEAVE**, FOR GODSAKES.
WE GOT A RIGHT TO OUR JOBS.
YOU'VE GOT A RIGHT TO LIVE AND A RIGHT TO DIE. THIS IS CRAZY.
BULLSHIT!
MAN LIKE BLANKENSHIP DO EVERYTHING THEY CAN GET AWAY WITH, UNLESS WE DEAL WITH HIM AS A SOLID GROUP.
HE CAN'T BREAK US JUST BECAUSE WE WANT TO BE TREATED LIKE **PEOPLE**, GOD DAMN IT.
MOSTLY WE GET PAID IN SCRIP. USE IT AT THE COMPANY STORE OR ALICE'S.
MOSTLY ALICE'S.
CAN'T SAVE CREDIT. TOWN'S SO FAR FROM ANYTHING, YOU NEED A HORSE. ONLY ONE LIVERY STABLE IN TOWN...

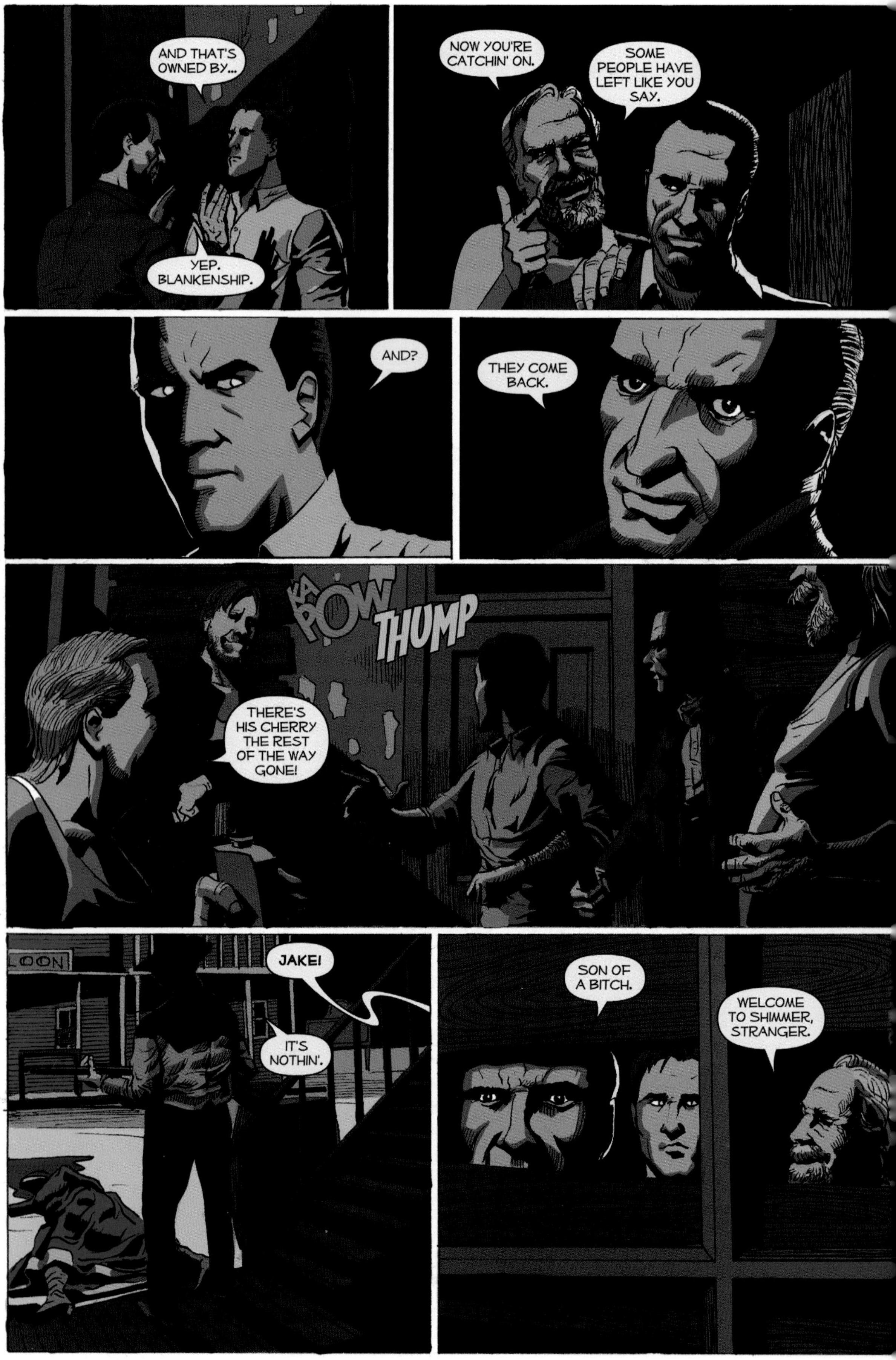
AND THAT'S OWNED BY...
YEP. BLANKENSHIP.
NOW YOU'RE CATCHIN' ON.
SOME PEOPLE HAVE LEFT LIKE YOU SAY.
AND?
THEY COME BACK.
KAPOW
THUMP
THERE'S HIS CHERRY THE REST OF THE WAY GONE!
LOON
JAKE!
IT'S NOTHIN'.
SON OF A BITCH.
WELCOME TO SHIMMER, STRANGER.

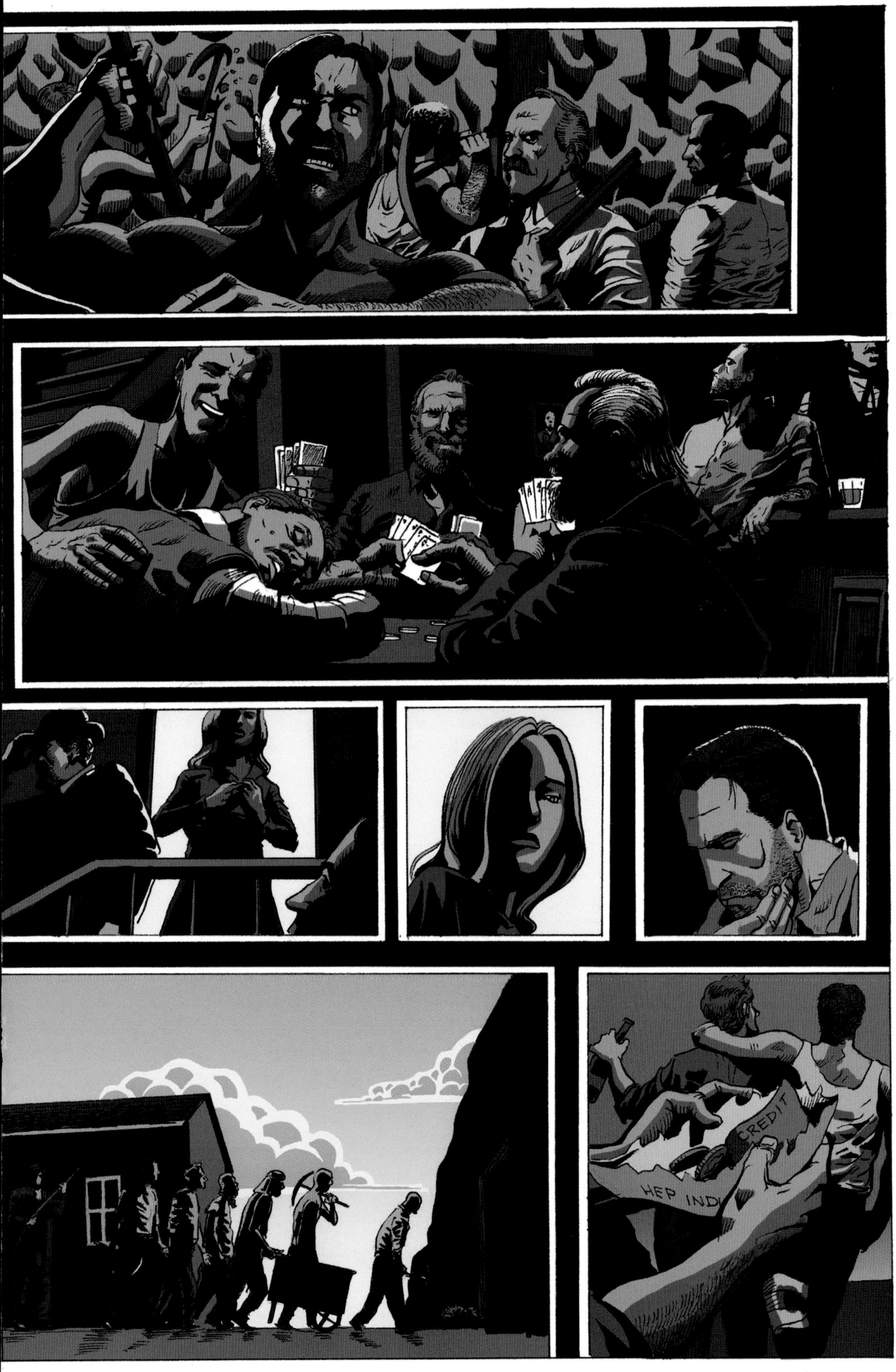
CREDIT
HEP IND

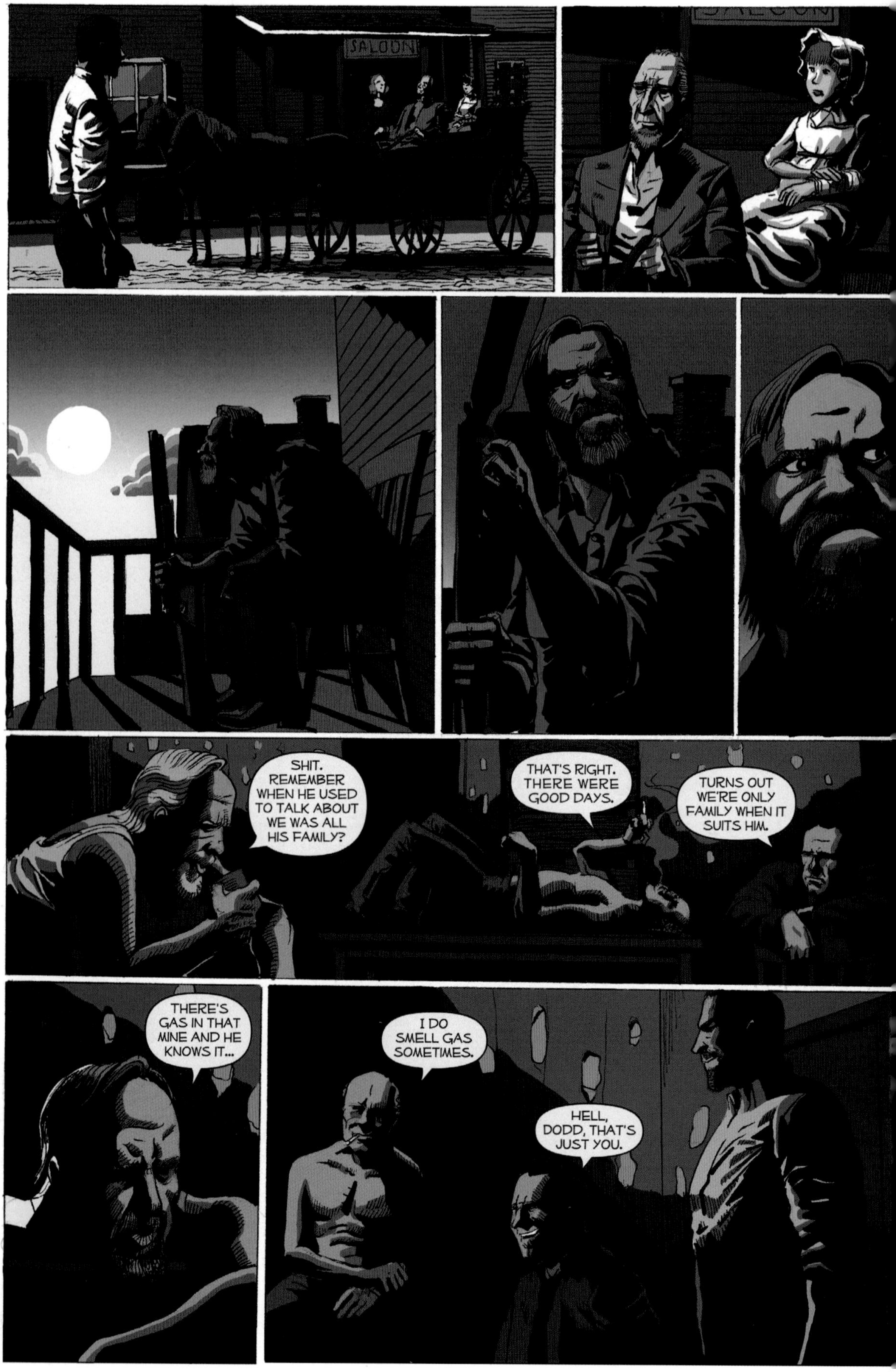
SALOON
SALOON
SHIT. REMEMBER WHEN HE USED TO TALK ABOUT WE WAS ALL HIS FAMILY?
THAT'S RIGHT. THERE WERE GOOD DAYS.
TURNS OUT WE'RE ONLY FAMILY WHEN IT SUITS HIM.
THERE'S GAS IN THAT MINE AND HE KNOWS IT...
I DO SMELL GAS SOMETIMES.
HELL, DODD, THAT'S JUST YOU.

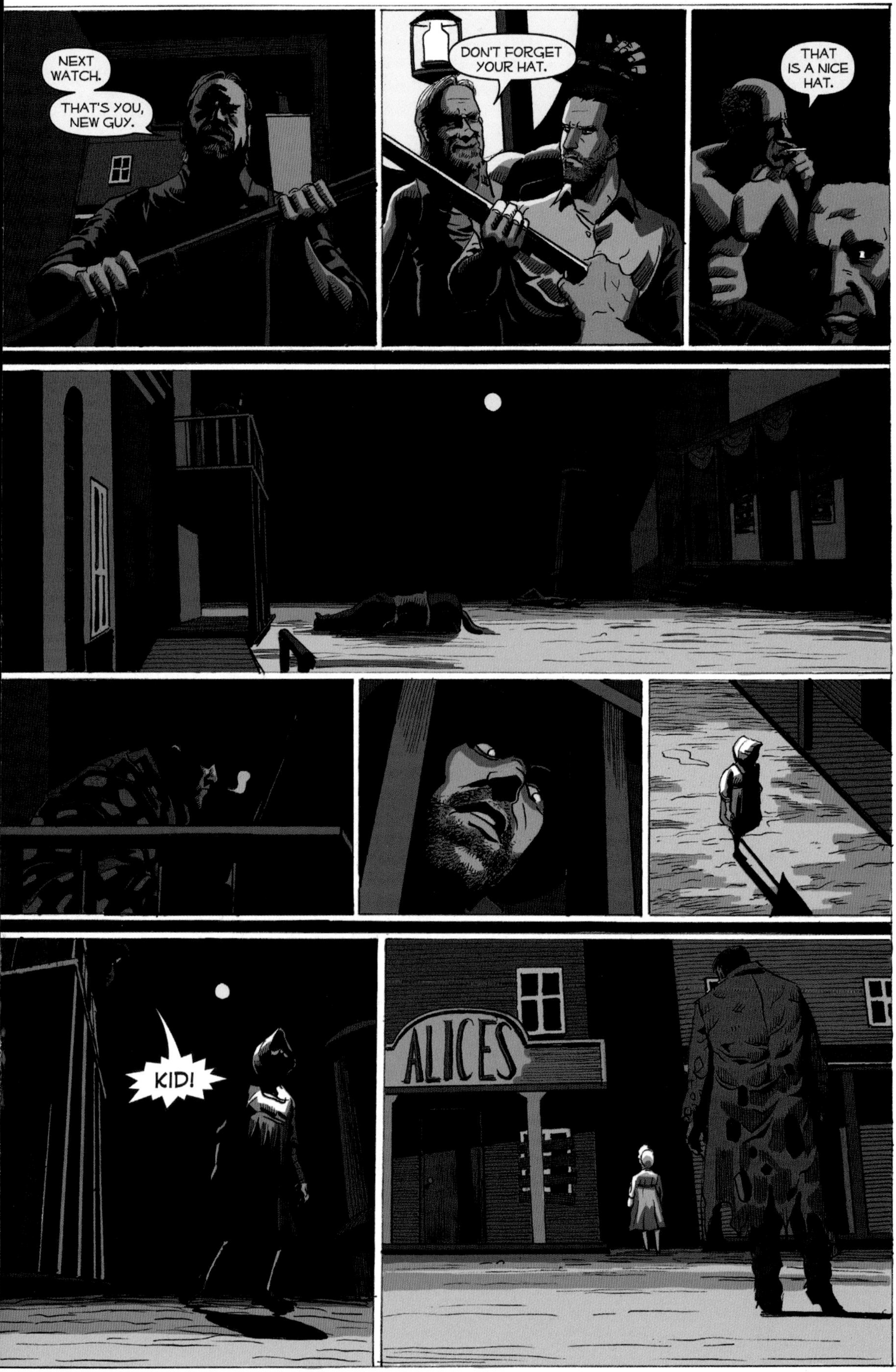
NEXT WATCH.
THAT'S YOU, NEW GUY.
DON'T FORGET YOUR HAT.
THAT IS A NICE HAT.
KID!
ALICES

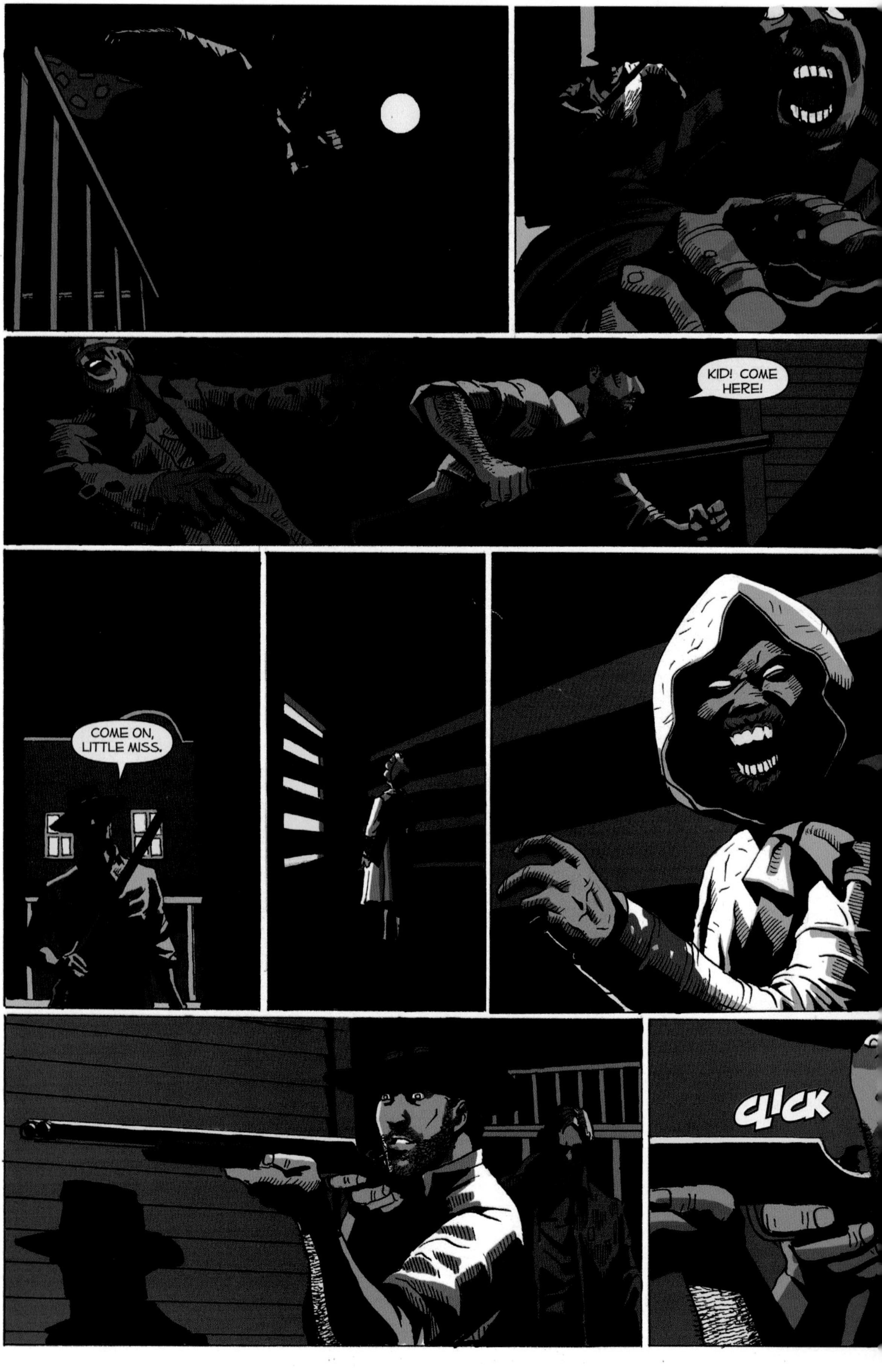
KID! COME HERE!
COME ON, LITTLE MISS.
CLICK

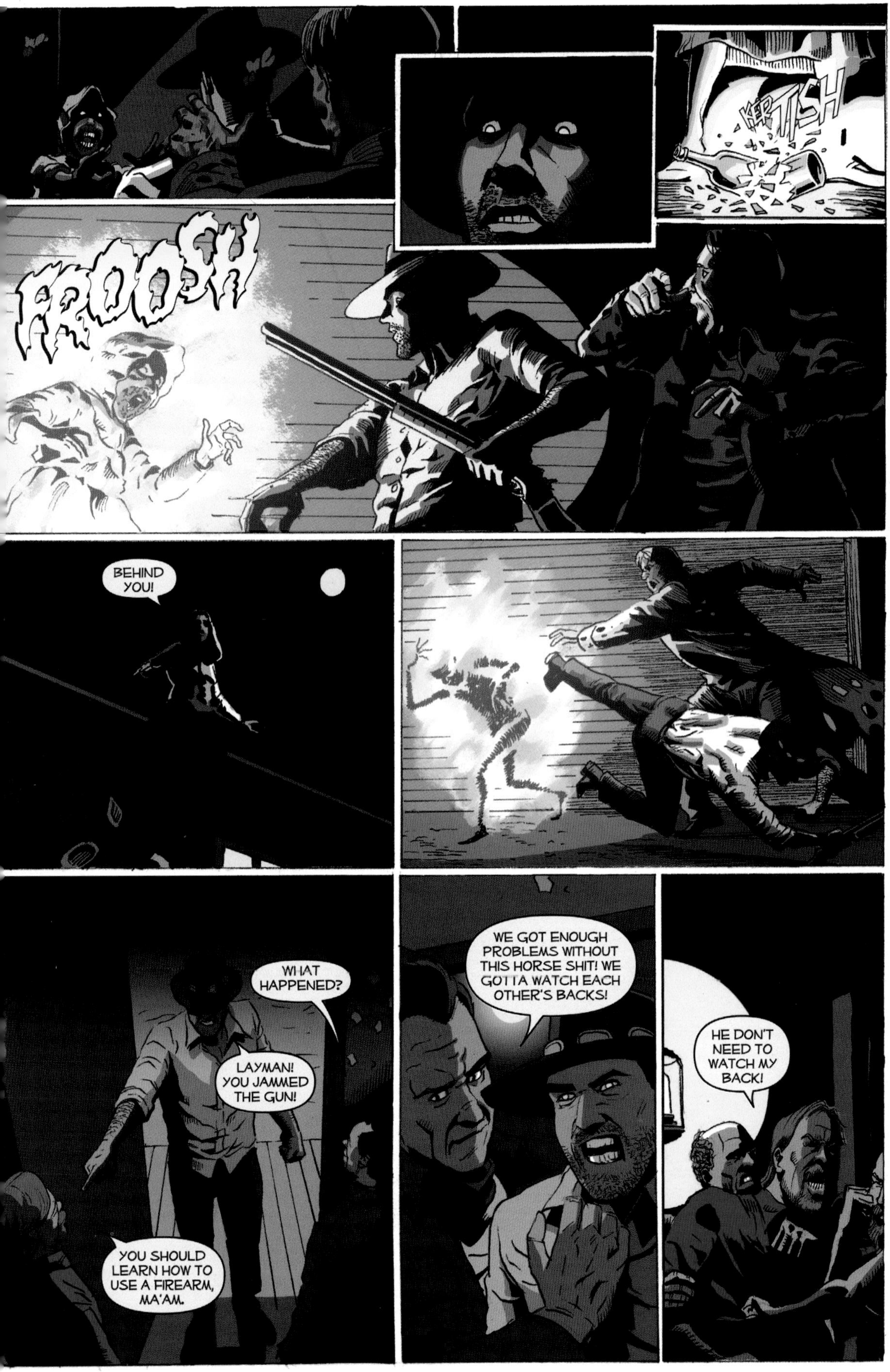
KER-TISH
FROOSH
BEHIND YOU!
WHAT HAPPENED?
LAYMAN! YOU JAMMED THE GUN!
YOU SHOULD LEARN HOW TO USE A FIREARM, MA'AM.
WE GOT ENOUGH PROBLEMS WITHOUT THIS HORSE SHIT! WE GOTTA WATCH EACH OTHER'S BACKS!
HE DON'T NEED TO WATCH MY BACK!

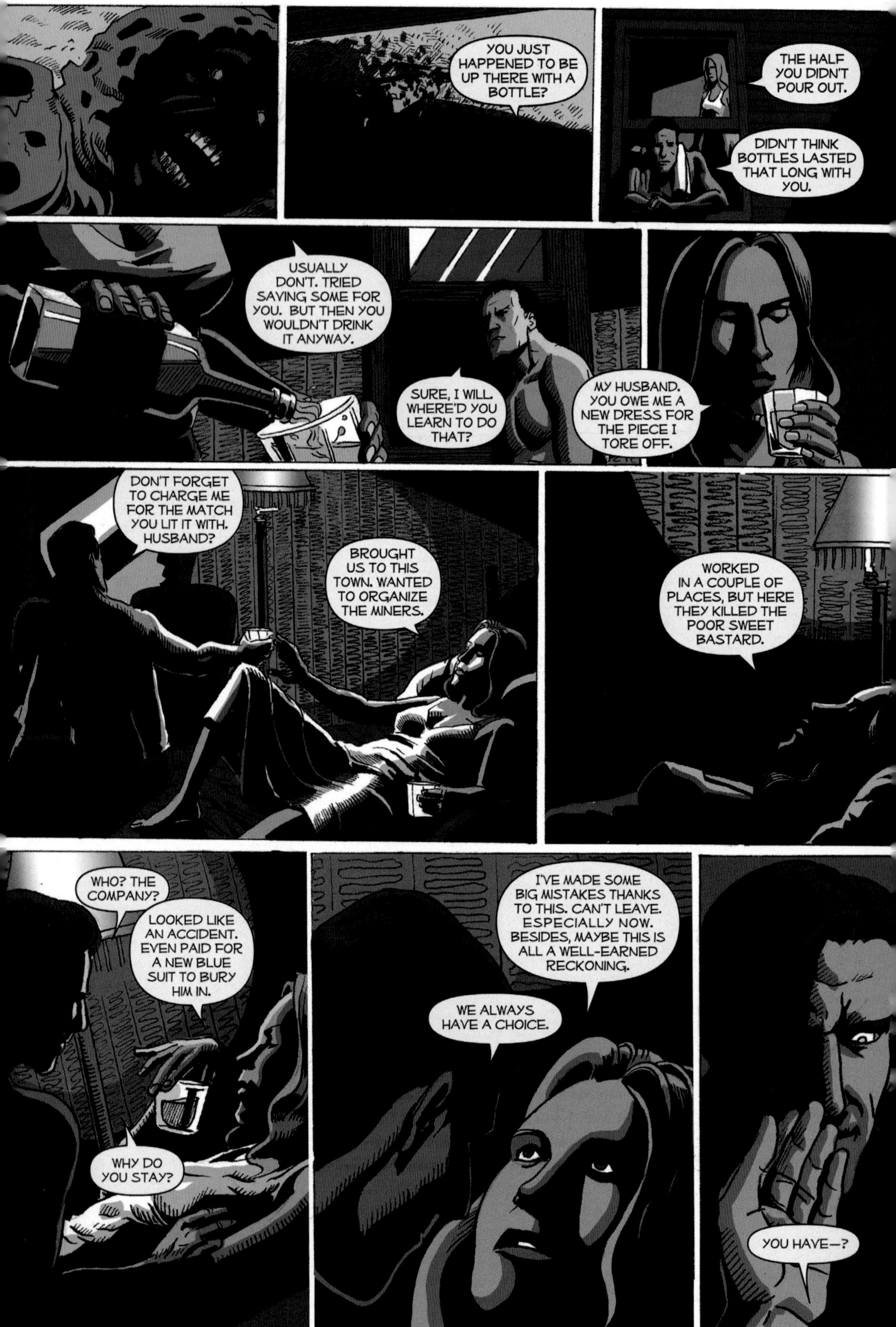
YOU JUST HAPPENED TO BE UP THERE WITH A BOTTLE?
THE HALF YOU DIDN'T POUR OUT.
DIDN'T THINK BOTTLES LASTED THAT LONG WITH YOU.
USUALLY DON'T. TRIED SAVING SOME FOR YOU. BUT THEN YOU WOULDN'T DRINK IT ANYWAY.
SURE, I WILL. WHERE'D YOU LEARN TO DO THAT?
MY HUSBAND. YOU OWE ME A NEW DRESS FOR THE PIECE I TORE OFF.
DON'T FORGET TO CHARGE ME FOR THE MATCH YOU LIT IT WITH. HUSBAND?
BROUGHT US TO THIS TOWN. WANTED TO ORGANIZE THE MINERS.
WORKED IN A COUPLE OF PLACES, BUT HERE THEY KILLED THE POOR SWEET BASTARD.
WHO? THE COMPANY?
LOOKED LIKE AN ACCIDENT. EVEN PAID FOR A NEW BLUE SUIT TO BURY HIM IN.
WHY DO YOU STAY?
I'VE MADE SOME BIG MISTAKES THANKS TO THIS. CAN'T LEAVE. ESPECIALLY NOW. BESIDES, MAYBE THIS IS ALL A WELL-EARNED RECKONING.
WE ALWAYS HAVE A CHOICE.
YOU HAVE—?

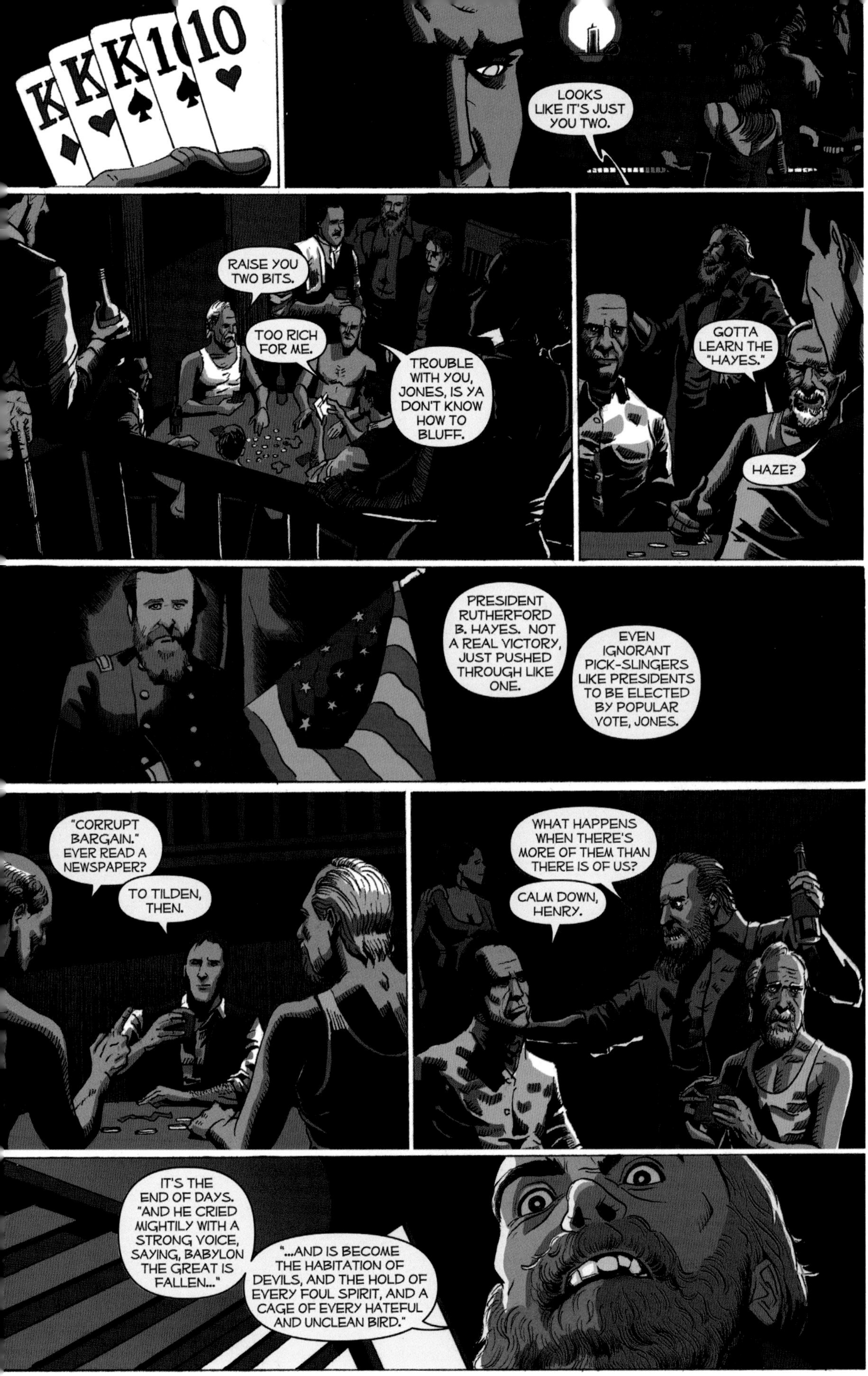
K K K 10 10
LOOKS LIKE IT'S JUST YOU TWO.
RAISE YOU TWO BITS.
TOO RICH FOR ME.
TROUBLE WITH YOU, JONES, IS YA DON'T KNOW HOW TO BLUFF.
GOTTA LEARN THE "HAYES."
HAZE?
PRESIDENT RUTHERFORD B. HAYES. NOT A REAL VICTORY, JUST PUSHED THROUGH LIKE ONE.
EVEN IGNORANT PICK-SLINGERS LIKE PRESIDENTS TO BE ELECTED BY POPULAR VOTE, JONES.
"CORRUPT BARGAIN." EVER READ A NEWSPAPER?
TO TILDEN, THEN.
WHAT HAPPENS WHEN THERE'S MORE OF THEM THAN THERE IS OF US?
CALM DOWN, HENRY.
IT'S THE END OF DAYS. "AND HE CRIED MIGHTILY WITH A STRONG VOICE, SAYING, BABYLON THE GREAT IS FALLEN..."
"...AND IS BECOME THE HABITATION OF DEVILS, AND THE HOLD OF EVERY FOUL SPIRIT, AND A CAGE OF EVERY HATEFUL AND UNCLEAN BIRD."

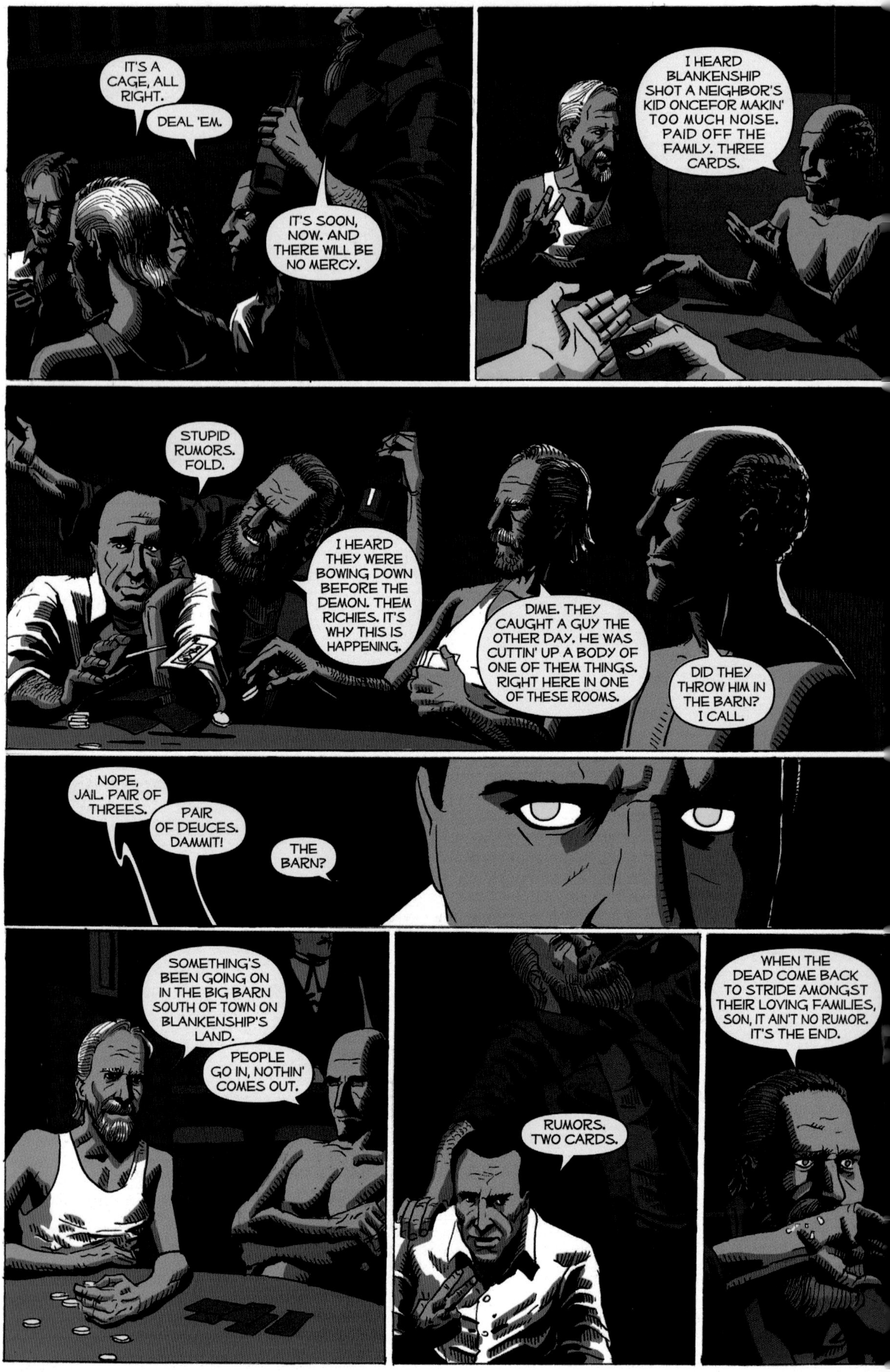
IT'S A CAGE, ALL RIGHT.
DEAL 'EM.
IT'S SOON, NOW. AND THERE WILL BE NO MERCY.
I HEARD BLANKENSHIP SHOT A NEIGHBOR'S KID ONCEFOR MAKIN' TOO MUCH NOISE. PAID OFF THE FAMILY. THREE CARDS.
STUPID RUMORS. FOLD.
I HEARD THEY WERE BOWING DOWN BEFORE THE DEMON. THEM RICHIES. IT'S WHY THIS IS HAPPENING.
DIME. THEY CAUGHT A GUY THE OTHER DAY. HE WAS CUTTIN' UP A BODY OF ONE OF THEM THINGS. RIGHT HERE IN ONE OF THESE ROOMS.
DID THEY THROW HIM IN THE BARN? I CALL.
NOPE, JAIL. PAIR OF THREES.
PAIR OF DEUCES. DAMMIT!
THE BARN?
SOMETHING'S BEEN GOING ON IN THE BIG BARN SOUTH OF TOWN ON BLANKENSHIP'S LAND.
PEOPLE GO IN, NOTHIN' COMES OUT.
RUMORS. TWO CARDS.
WHEN THE DEAD COME BACK TO STRIDE AMONGST THEIR LOVING FAMILIES, SON, IT AIN'T NO RUMOR. IT'S THE END.

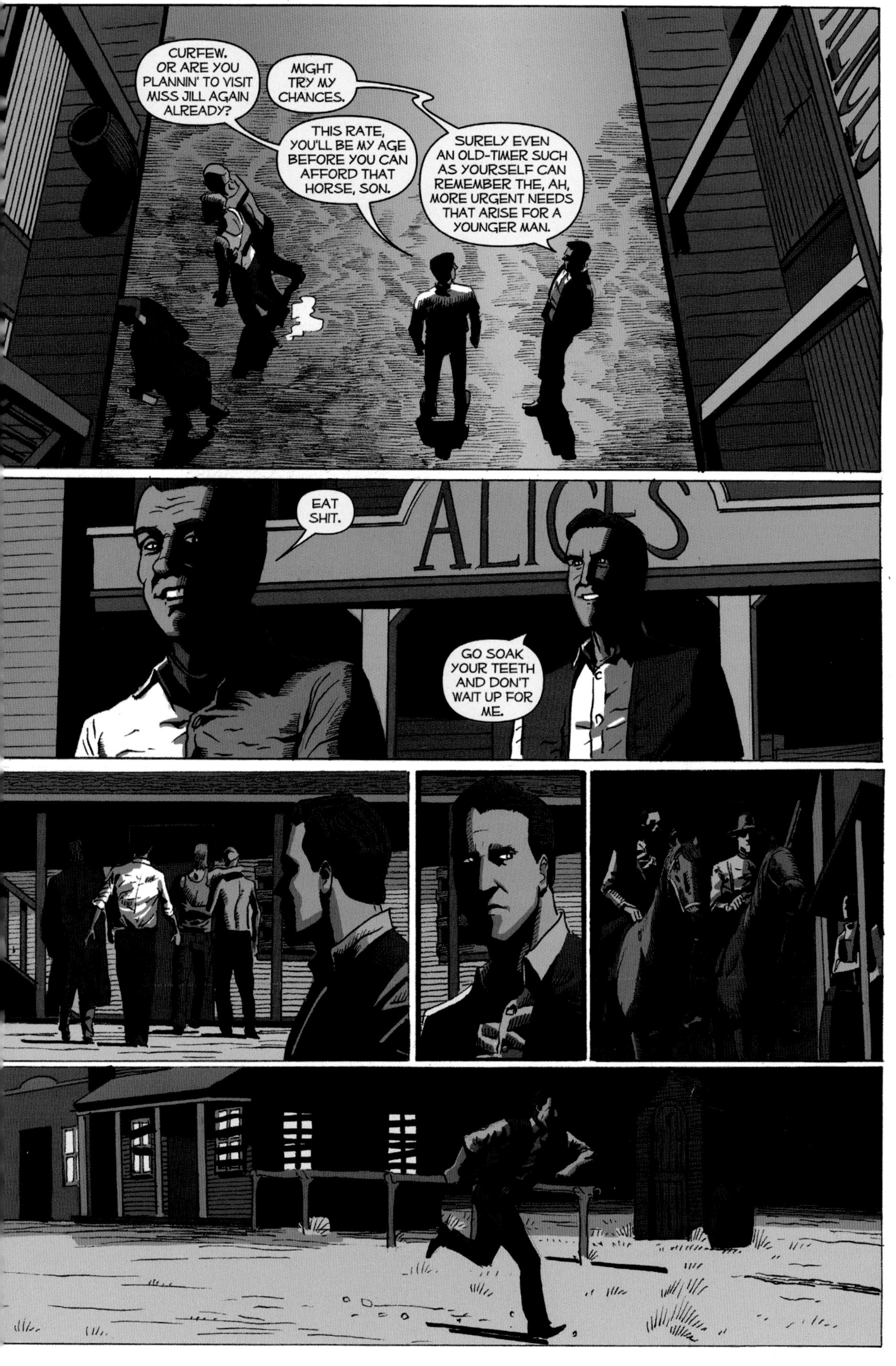
CURFEW. OR ARE YOU PLANNIN' TO VISIT MISS JILL AGAIN ALREADY?
MIGHT TRY MY CHANCES.
THIS RATE, YOU'LL BE MY AGE BEFORE YOU CAN AFFORD THAT HORSE, SON.
SURELY EVEN AN OLD-TIMER SUCH AS YOURSELF CAN REMEMBER THE, AH, MORE URGENT NEEDS THAT ARISE FOR A YOUNGER MAN.
ALICES
EAT SHIT.
GO SOAK YOUR TEETH AND DON'T WAIT UP FOR ME.

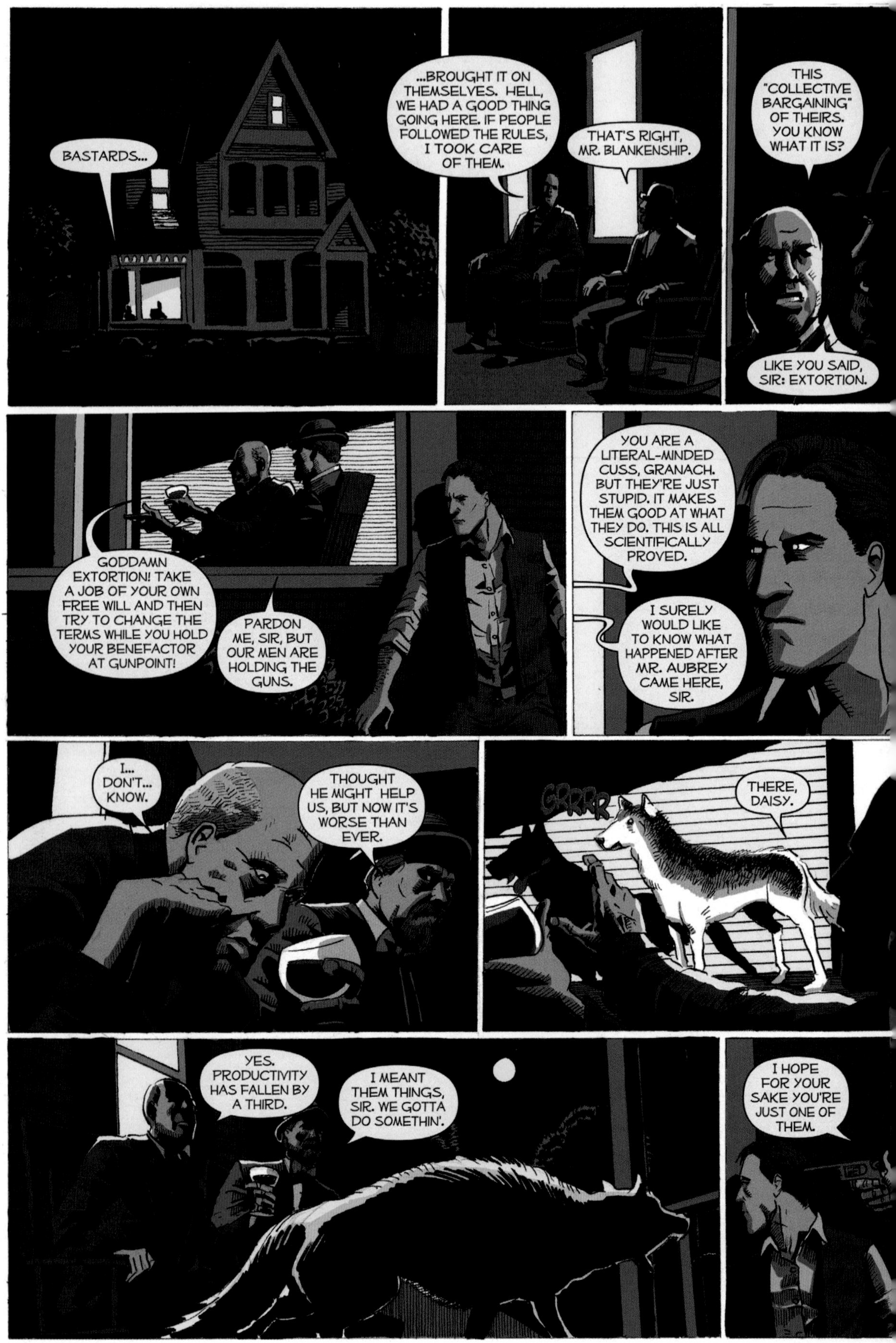
BASTARDS...
...BROUGHT IT ON THEMSELVES. HELL, WE HAD A GOOD THING GOING HERE. IF PEOPLE FOLLOWED THE RULES, I TOOK CARE OF THEM.
THAT'S RIGHT, MR. BLANKENSHIP.
THIS "COLLECTIVE BARGAINING" OF THEIRS. YOU KNOW WHAT IT IS?
LIKE YOU SAID, SIR: EXTORTION.
GODDAMN EXTORTION! TAKE A JOB OF YOUR OWN FREE WILL AND THEN TRY TO CHANGE THE TERMS WHILE YOU HOLD YOUR BENEFACTOR AT GUNPOINT!
PARDON ME, SIR, BUT OUR MEN ARE HOLDING THE GUNS.
YOU ARE A LITERAL-MINDED CUSS, GRANACH. BUT THEY'RE JUST STUPID. IT MAKES THEM GOOD AT WHAT THEY DO. THIS IS ALL SCIENTIFICALLY PROVED.
I SURELY WOULD LIKE TO KNOW WHAT HAPPENED AFTER MR. AUBREY CAME HERE, SIR.
I... DON'T... KNOW.
THOUGHT HE MIGHT HELP US, BUT NOW IT'S WORSE THAN EVER.
GRRRR
THERE, DAISY.
YES. PRODUCTIVITY HAS FALLEN BY A THIRD.
I MEANT THEM THINGS, SIR. WE GOTTA DO SOMETHIN'.
I HOPE FOR YOUR SAKE YOU'RE JUST ONE OF THEM.

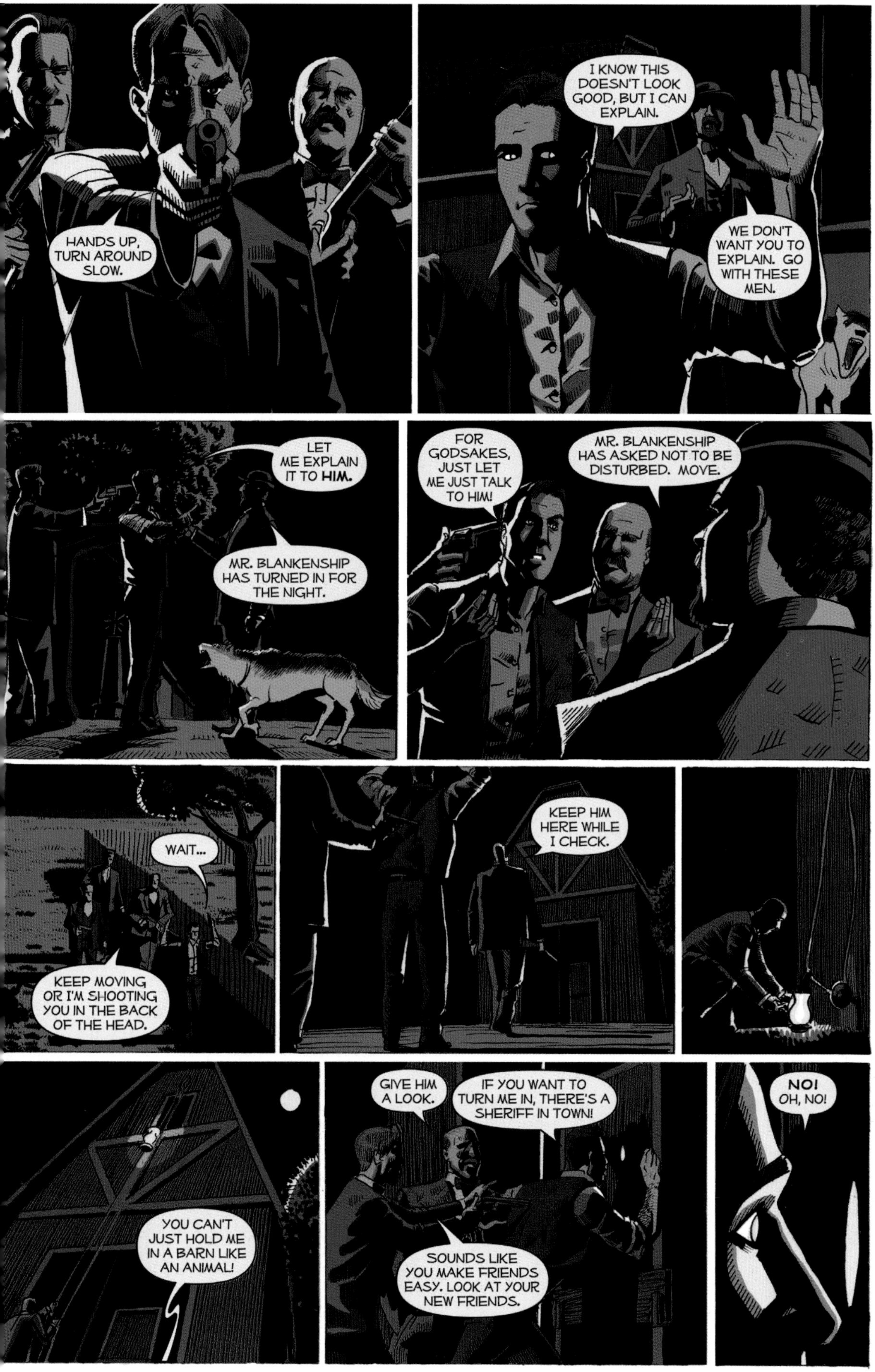
HANDS UP, TURN AROUND SLOW.
I KNOW THIS DOESN'T LOOK GOOD, BUT I CAN EXPLAIN.
WE DON'T WANT YOU TO EXPLAIN. GO WITH THESE MEN.
LET ME EXPLAIN IT TO **HIM.**
MR. BLANKENSHIP HAS TURNED IN FOR THE NIGHT.
FOR GODSAKES, JUST LET ME JUST TALK TO HIM!
MR. BLANKENSHIP HAS ASKED NOT TO BE DISTURBED. MOVE.
WAIT...
KEEP MOVING OR I'M SHOOTING YOU IN THE BACK OF THE HEAD.
KEEP HIM HERE WHILE I CHECK.
YOU CAN'T JUST HOLD ME IN A BARN LIKE AN ANIMAL!
GIVE HIM A LOOK.
IF YOU WANT TO TURN ME IN, THERE'S A SHERIFF IN TOWN!
SOUNDS LIKE YOU MAKE FRIENDS EASY. LOOK AT YOUR NEW FRIENDS.
NO! OH, NO!

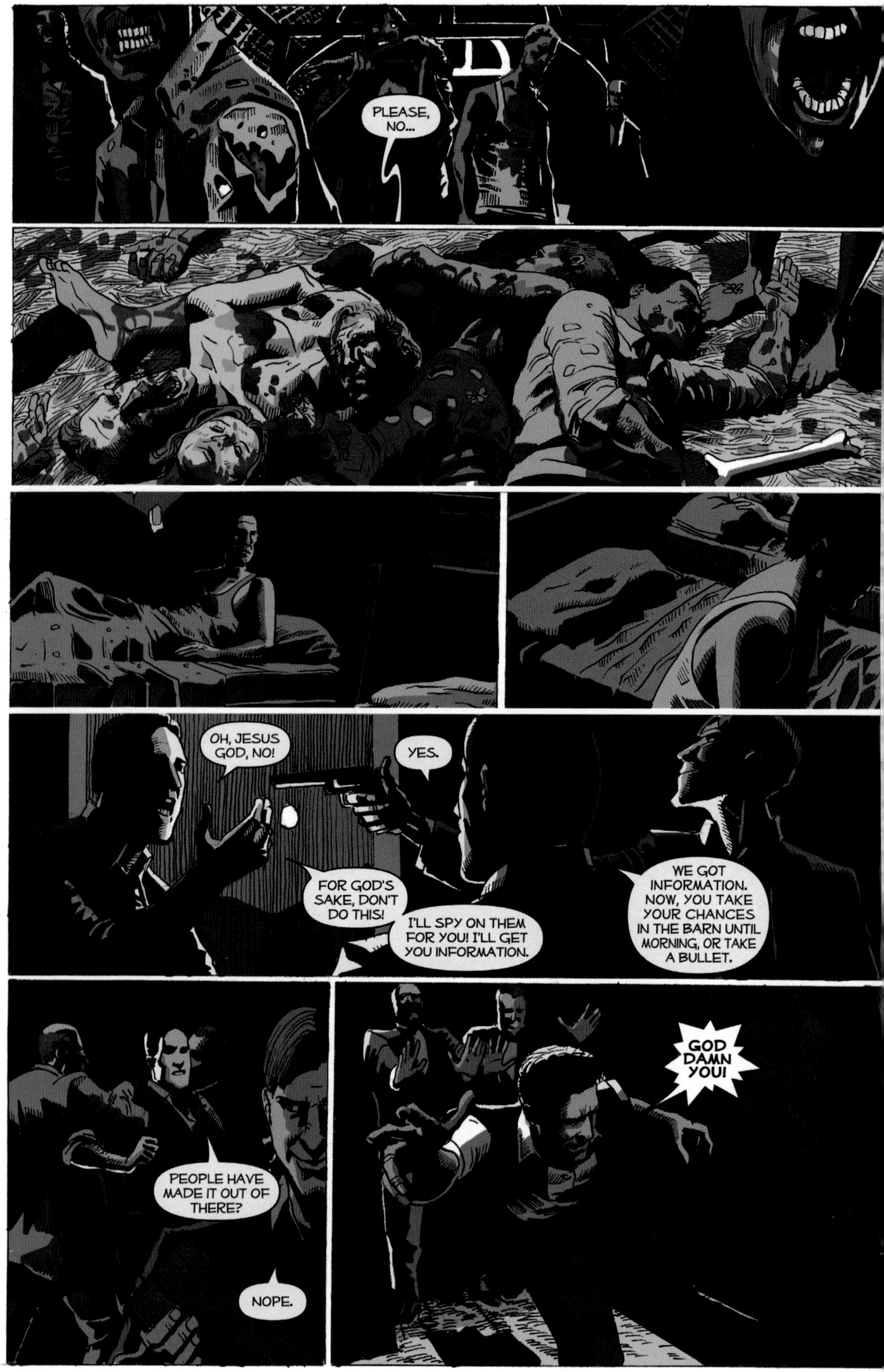
PLEASE, NO...
OH, JESUS GOD, NO!
YES.
FOR GOD'S SAKE, DON'T DO THIS!
I'LL SPY ON THEM FOR YOU! I'LL GET YOU INFORMATION.
WE GOT INFORMATION. NOW, YOU TAKE YOUR CHANCES IN THE BARN UNTIL MORNING, OR TAKE A BULLET.
PEOPLE HAVE MADE IT OUT OF THERE?
NOPE.
GOD DAMN YOU!

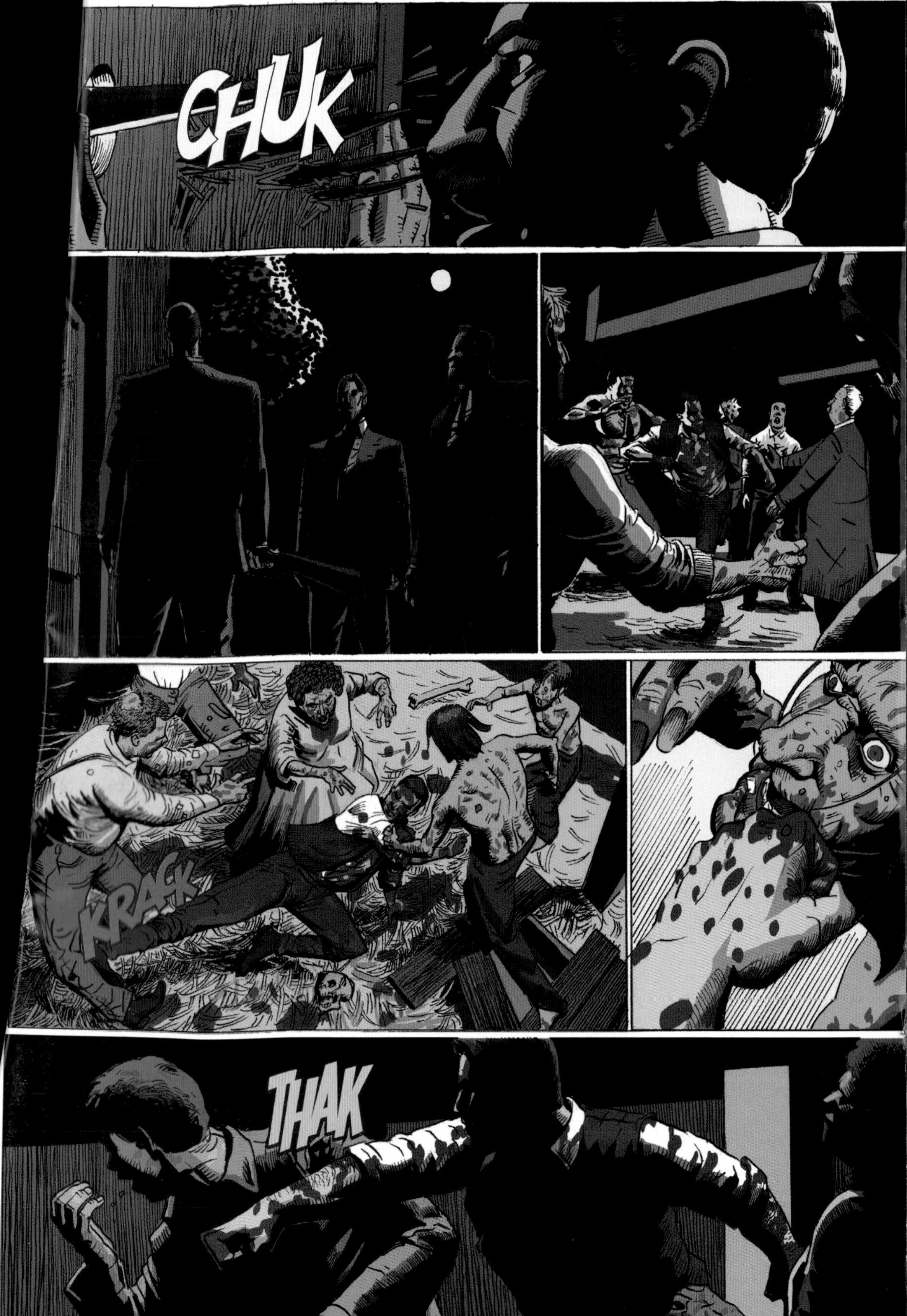
CHUK
KRACK
THAK

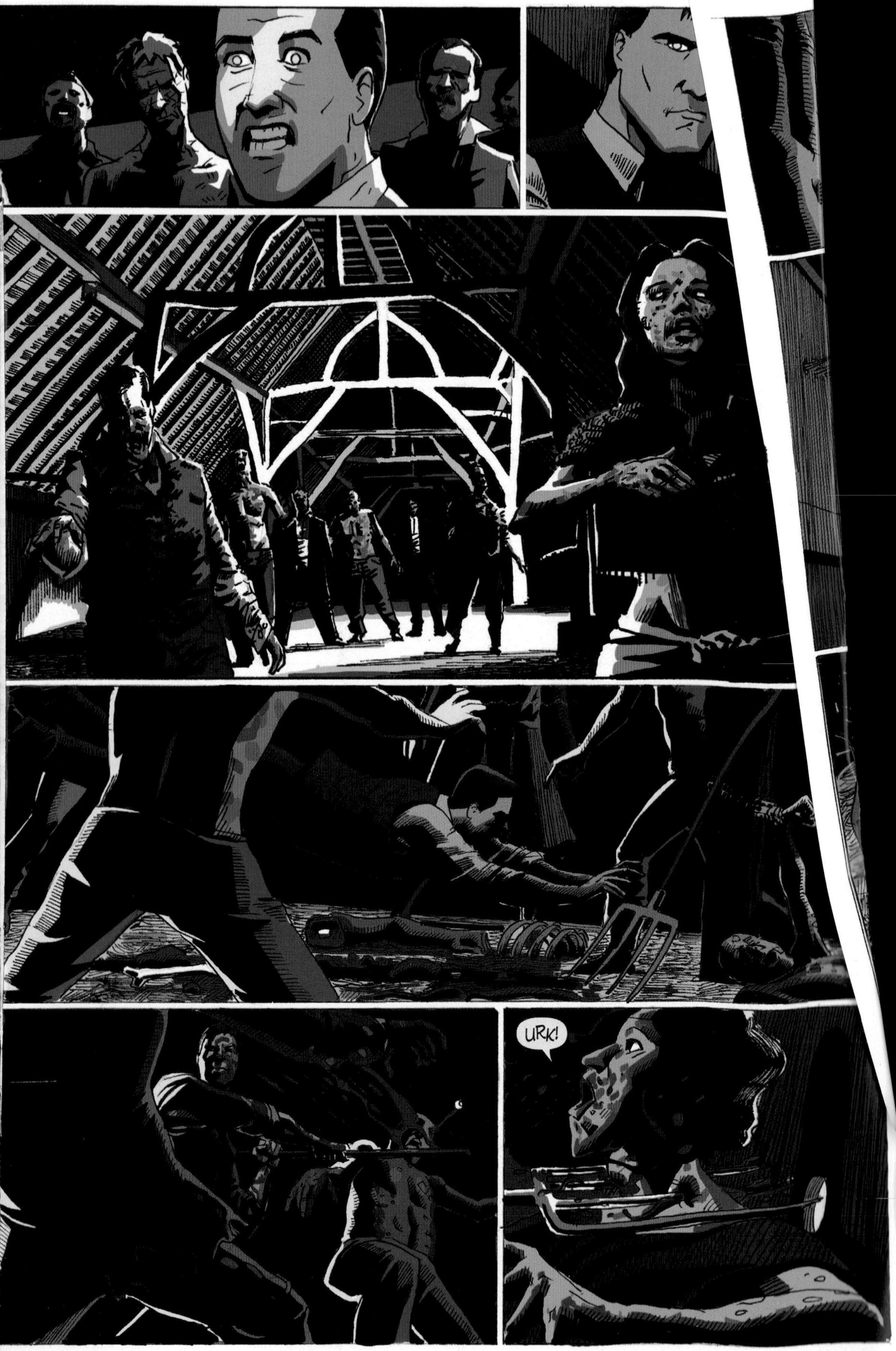
URK!

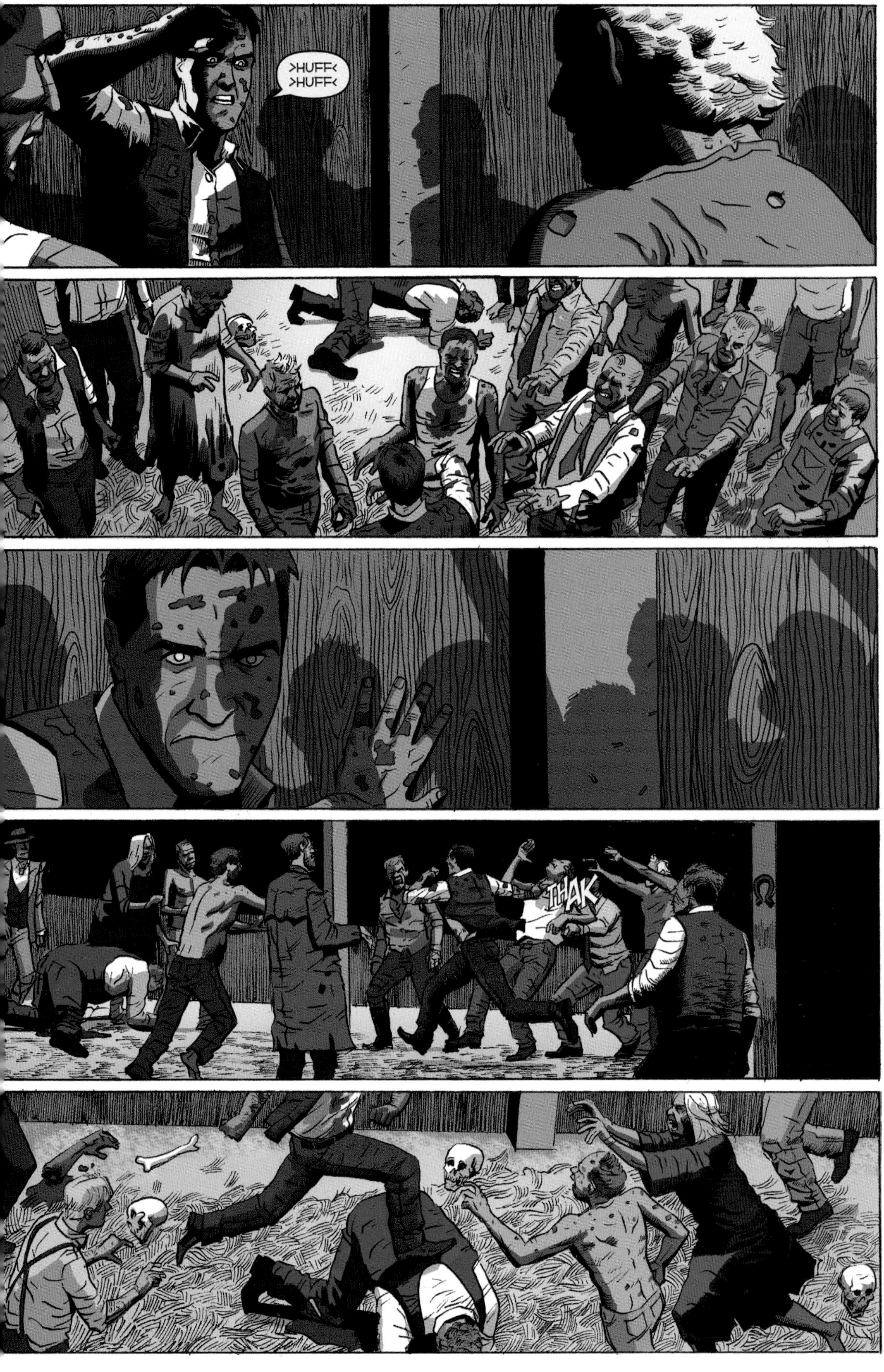
>HUFF<
>HUFF<
THAK

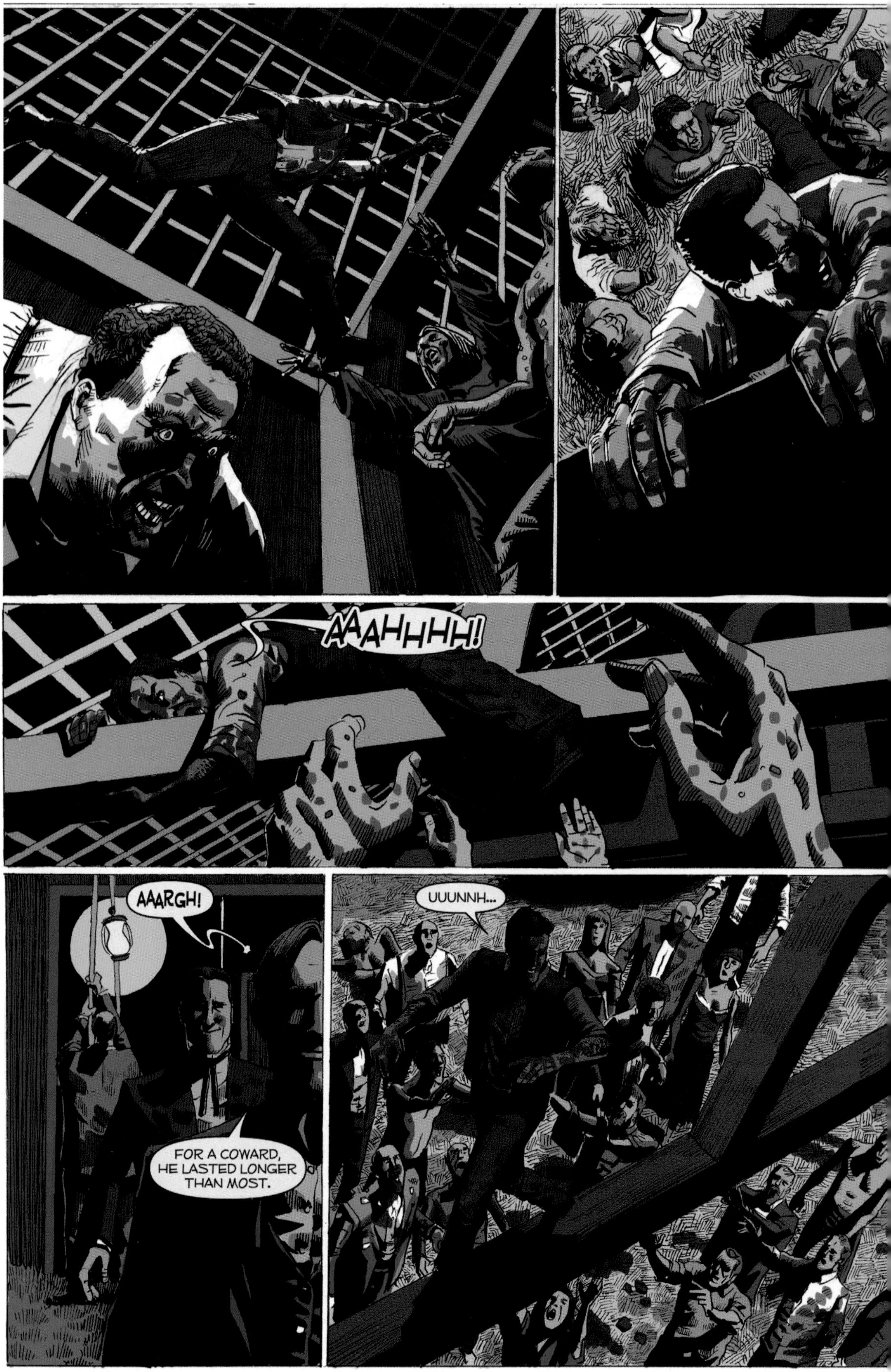
AAAHHHH!
AAARGH!
FOR A COWARD, HE LASTED LONGER THAN MOST.
UUUNNH...

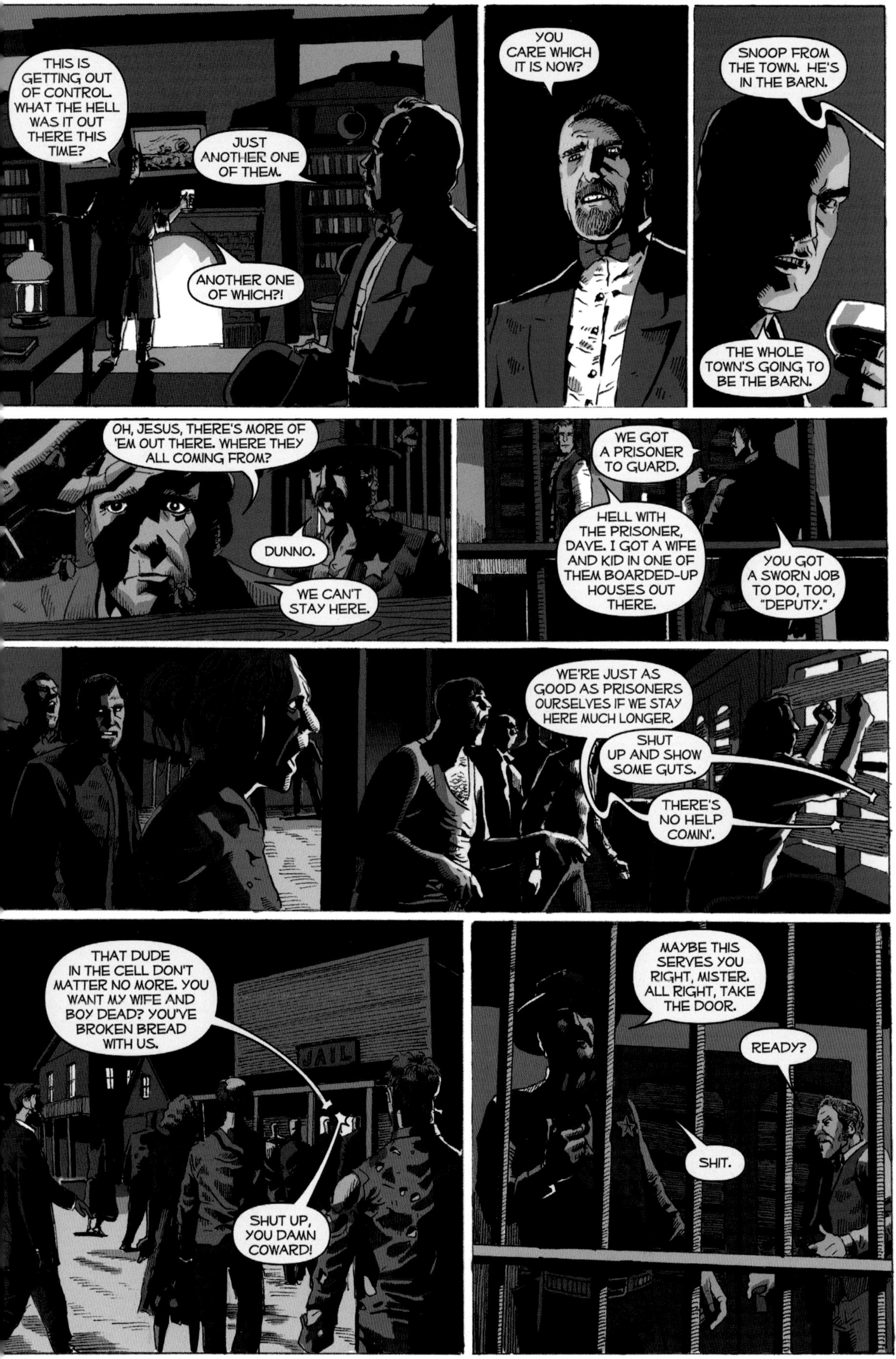
THIS IS GETTING OUT OF CONTROL. WHAT THE HELL WAS IT OUT THERE THIS TIME?
JUST ANOTHER ONE OF THEM.
ANOTHER ONE OF WHICH?!
YOU CARE WHICH IT IS NOW?
SNOOP FROM THE TOWN. HE'S IN THE BARN.
THE WHOLE TOWN'S GOING TO BE THE BARN.
OH, JESUS, THERE'S MORE OF 'EM OUT THERE. WHERE THEY ALL COMING FROM?
DUNNO.
WE CAN'T STAY HERE.
WE GOT A PRISONER TO GUARD.
HELL WITH THE PRISONER, DAVE. I GOT A WIFE AND KID IN ONE OF THEM BOARDED-UP HOUSES OUT THERE.
YOU GOT A SWORN JOB TO DO, TOO, "DEPUTY."
WE'RE JUST AS GOOD AS PRISONERS OURSELVES IF WE STAY HERE MUCH LONGER.
SHUT UP AND SHOW SOME GUTS.
THERE'S NO HELP COMIN'.
THAT DUDE IN THE CELL DON'T MATTER NO MORE. YOU WANT MY WIFE AND BOY DEAD? YOU'VE BROKEN BREAD WITH US.
JAIL
SHUT UP, YOU DAMN COWARD!
MAYBE THIS SERVES YOU RIGHT, MISTER. ALL RIGHT, TAKE THE DOOR.
READY?
SHIT.

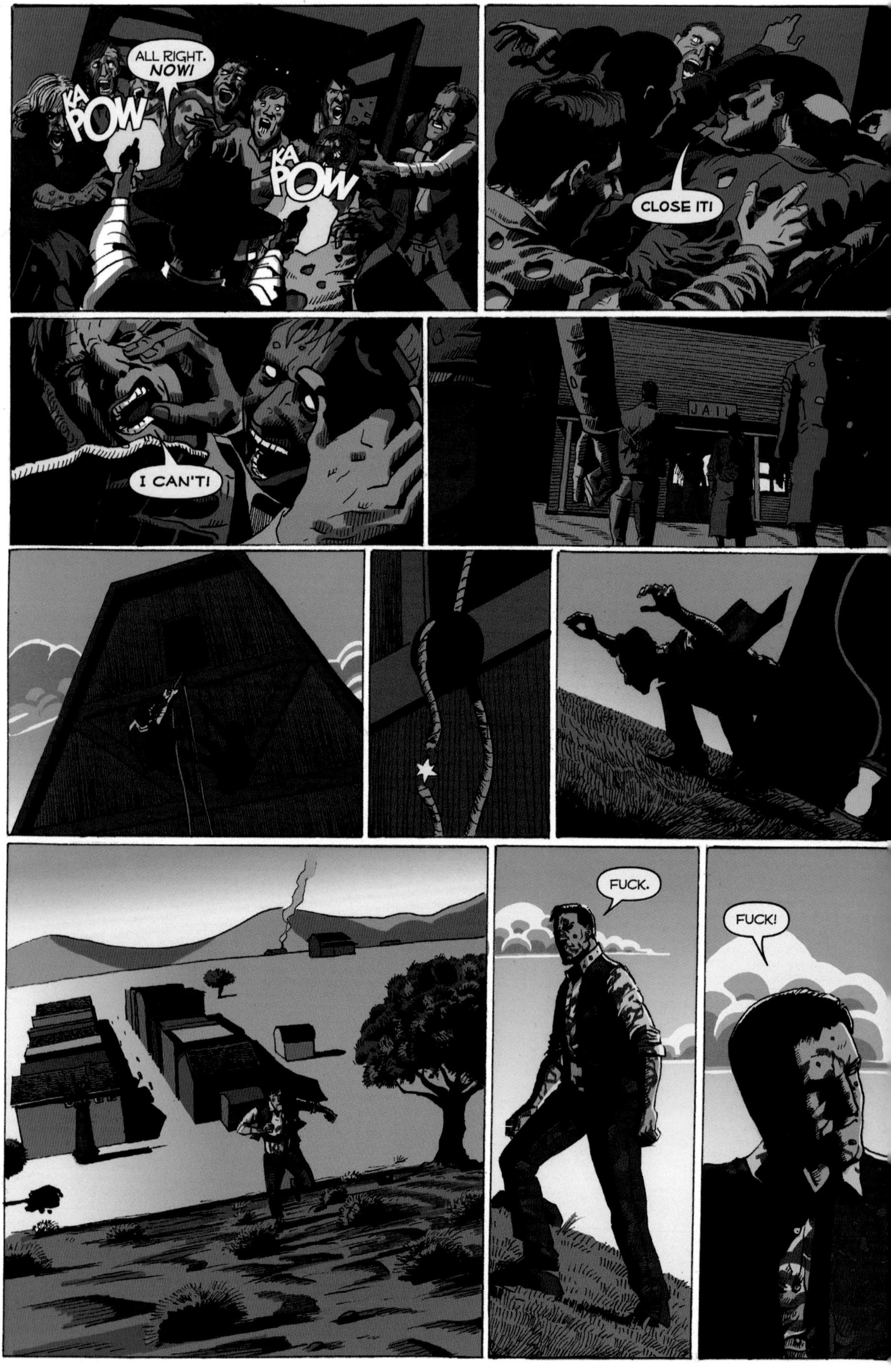
KA POW
ALL RIGHT. NOW!
KA POW
CLOSE IT!
I CAN'T!
JAIL
FUCK.
FUCK!

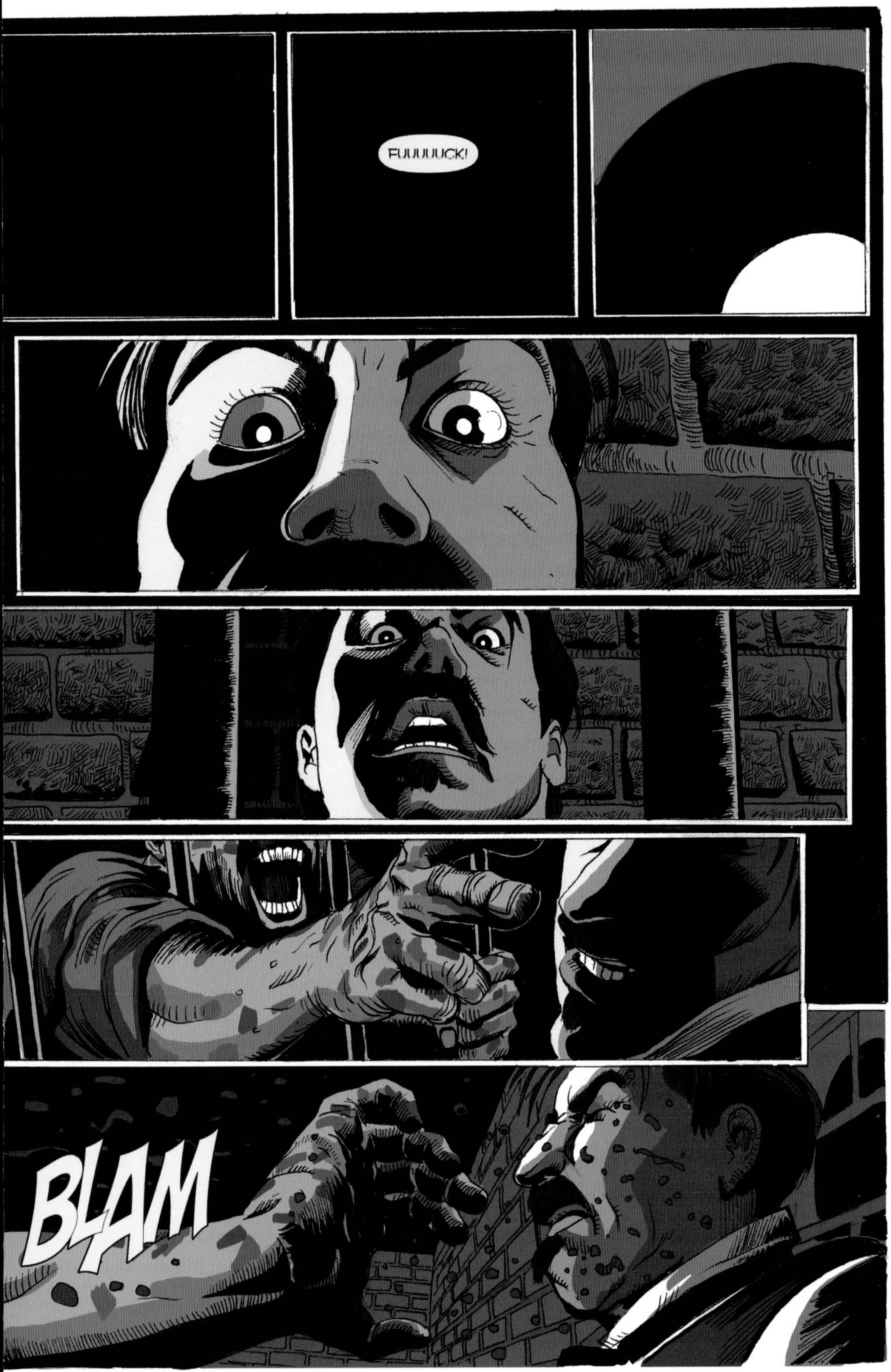
FUUUUUCK!
BLAM

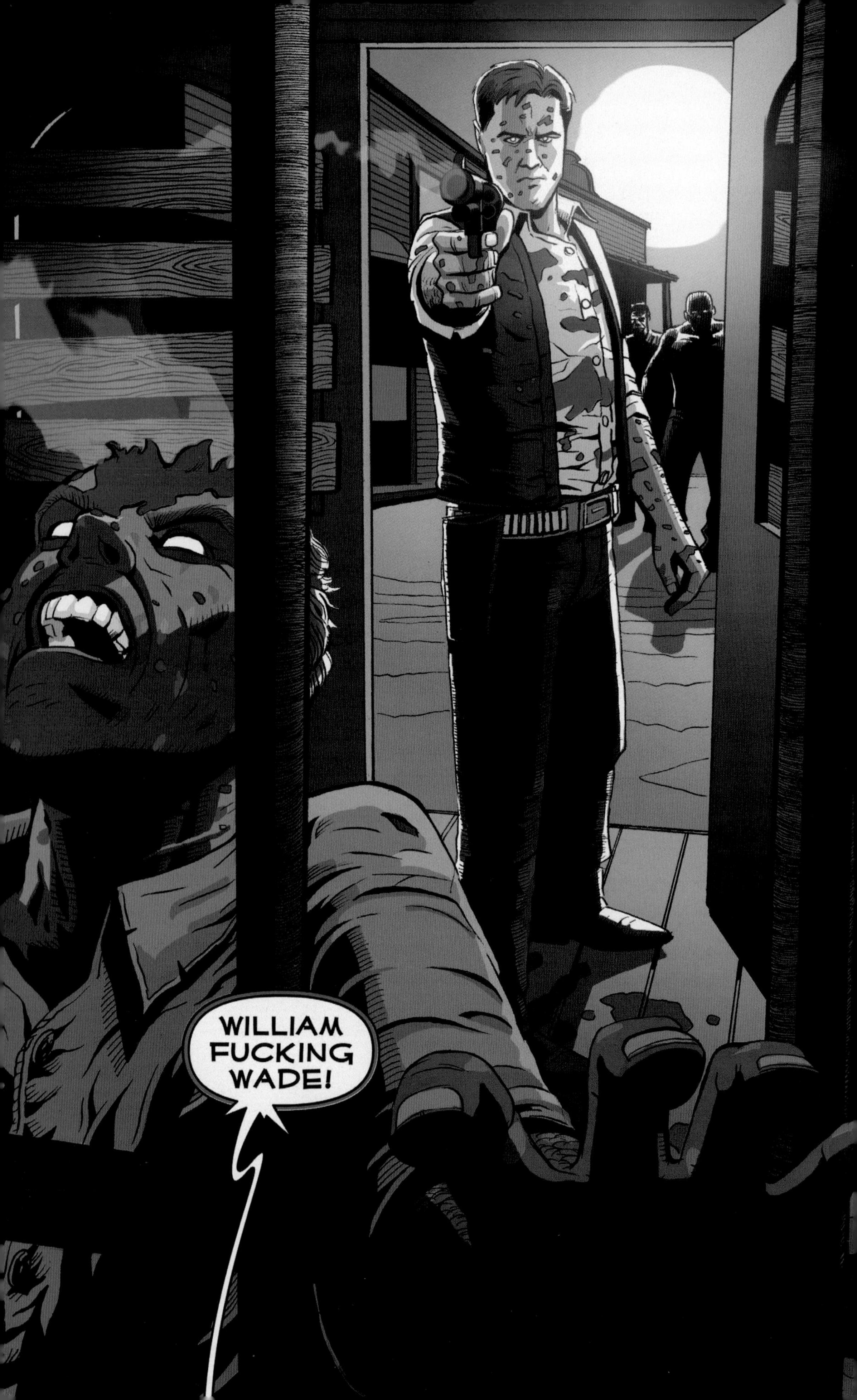
WILLIAM FUCKING WADE!

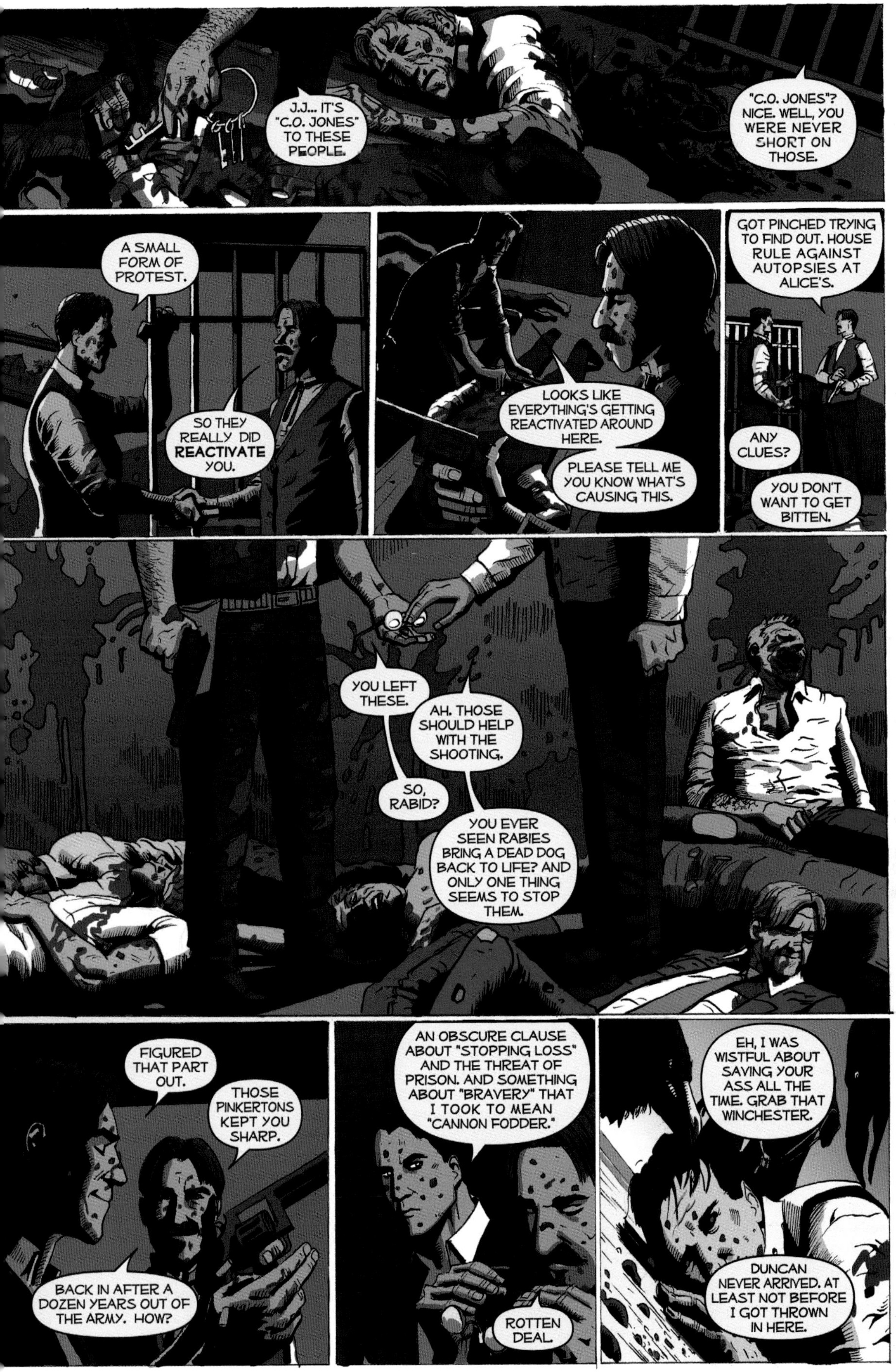
J.J... IT'S "C.O. JONES" TO THESE PEOPLE.
"C.O. JONES"? NICE. WELL, YOU WERE NEVER SHORT ON THOSE.
A SMALL FORM OF PROTEST.
SO THEY REALLY DID **REACTIVATE** YOU.
LOOKS LIKE EVERYTHING'S GETTING REACTIVATED AROUND HERE.
PLEASE TELL ME YOU KNOW WHAT'S CAUSING THIS.
GOT PINCHED TRYING TO FIND OUT. HOUSE RULE AGAINST AUTOPSIES AT ALICE'S.
ANY CLUES?
YOU DON'T WANT TO GET BITTEN.
YOU LEFT THESE.
AH. THOSE SHOULD HELP WITH THE SHOOTING.
SO, RABID?
YOU EVER SEEN RABIES BRING A DEAD DOG BACK TO LIFE? AND ONLY ONE THING SEEMS TO STOP THEM.
FIGURED THAT PART OUT.
THOSE PINKERTONS KEPT YOU SHARP.
BACK IN AFTER A DOZEN YEARS OUT OF THE ARMY. HOW?
AN OBSCURE CLAUSE ABOUT "STOPPING LOSS" AND THE THREAT OF PRISON. AND SOMETHING ABOUT "BRAVERY" THAT I TOOK TO MEAN "CANNON FODDER."
ROTTEN DEAL.
EH, I WAS WISTFUL ABOUT SAVING YOUR ASS ALL THE TIME. GRAB THAT WINCHESTER.
DUNCAN NEVER ARRIVED. AT LEAST NOT BEFORE I GOT THROWN IN HERE.

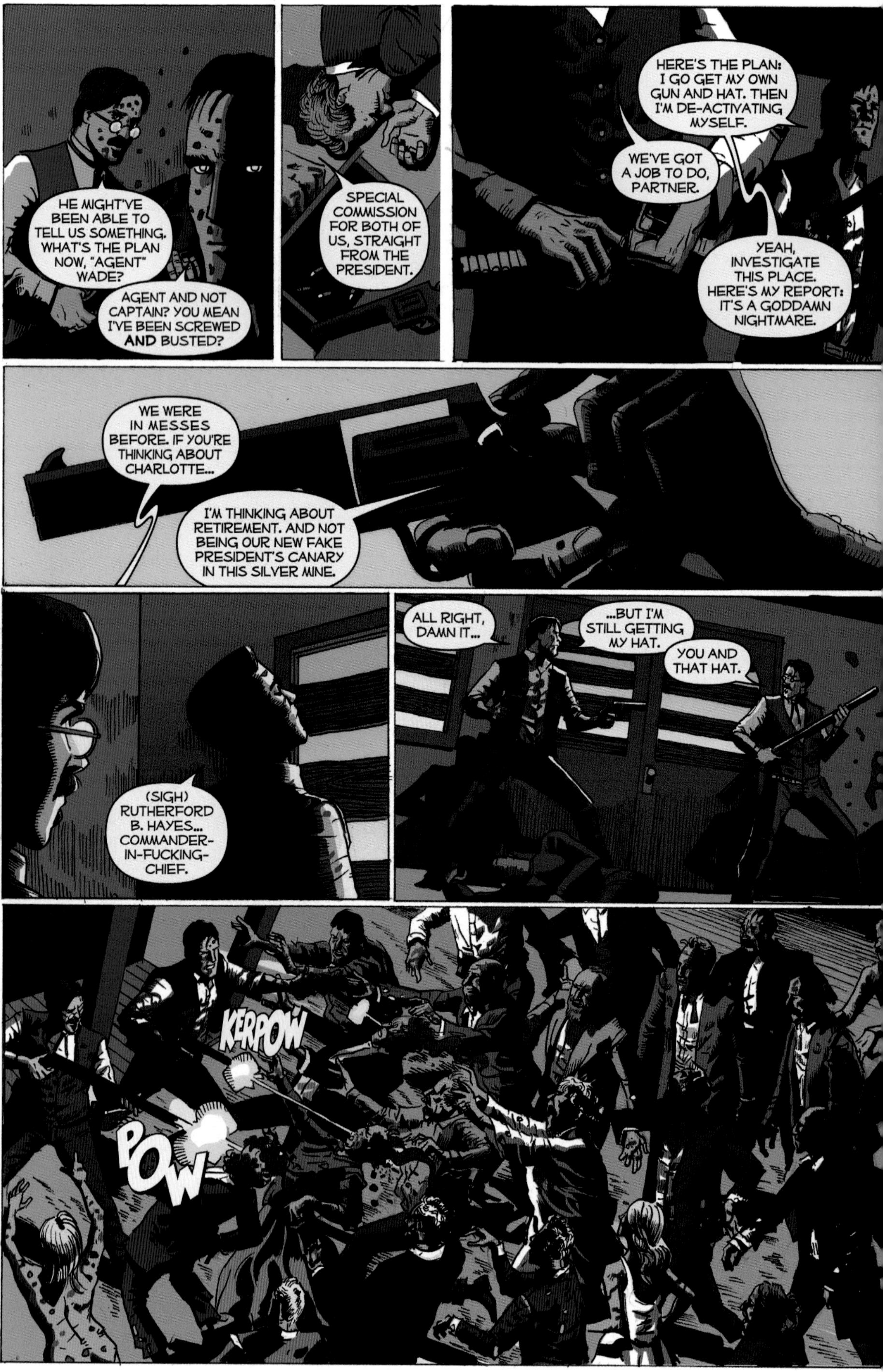
HE MIGHT'VE BEEN ABLE TO TELL US SOMETHING. WHAT'S THE PLAN NOW, "AGENT" WADE?
AGENT AND NOT CAPTAIN? YOU MEAN I'VE BEEN SCREWED **AND** BUSTED?
SPECIAL COMMISSION FOR BOTH OF US, STRAIGHT FROM THE PRESIDENT.
HERE'S THE PLAN: I GO GET MY OWN GUN AND HAT. THEN I'M DE-ACTIVATING MYSELF.
WE'VE GOT A JOB TO DO, PARTNER.
YEAH, INVESTIGATE THIS PLACE. HERE'S MY REPORT: IT'S A GODDAMN NIGHTMARE.
WE WERE IN MESSES BEFORE. IF YOU'RE THINKING ABOUT CHARLOTTE...
I'M THINKING ABOUT RETIREMENT. AND NOT BEING OUR NEW FAKE PRESIDENT'S CANARY IN THIS SILVER MINE.
(SIGH) RUTHERFORD B. HAYES... COMMANDER-IN-FUCKING-CHIEF.
ALL RIGHT, DAMN IT...
...BUT I'M STILL GETTING MY HAT.
YOU AND THAT HAT.
KERPOW
POW

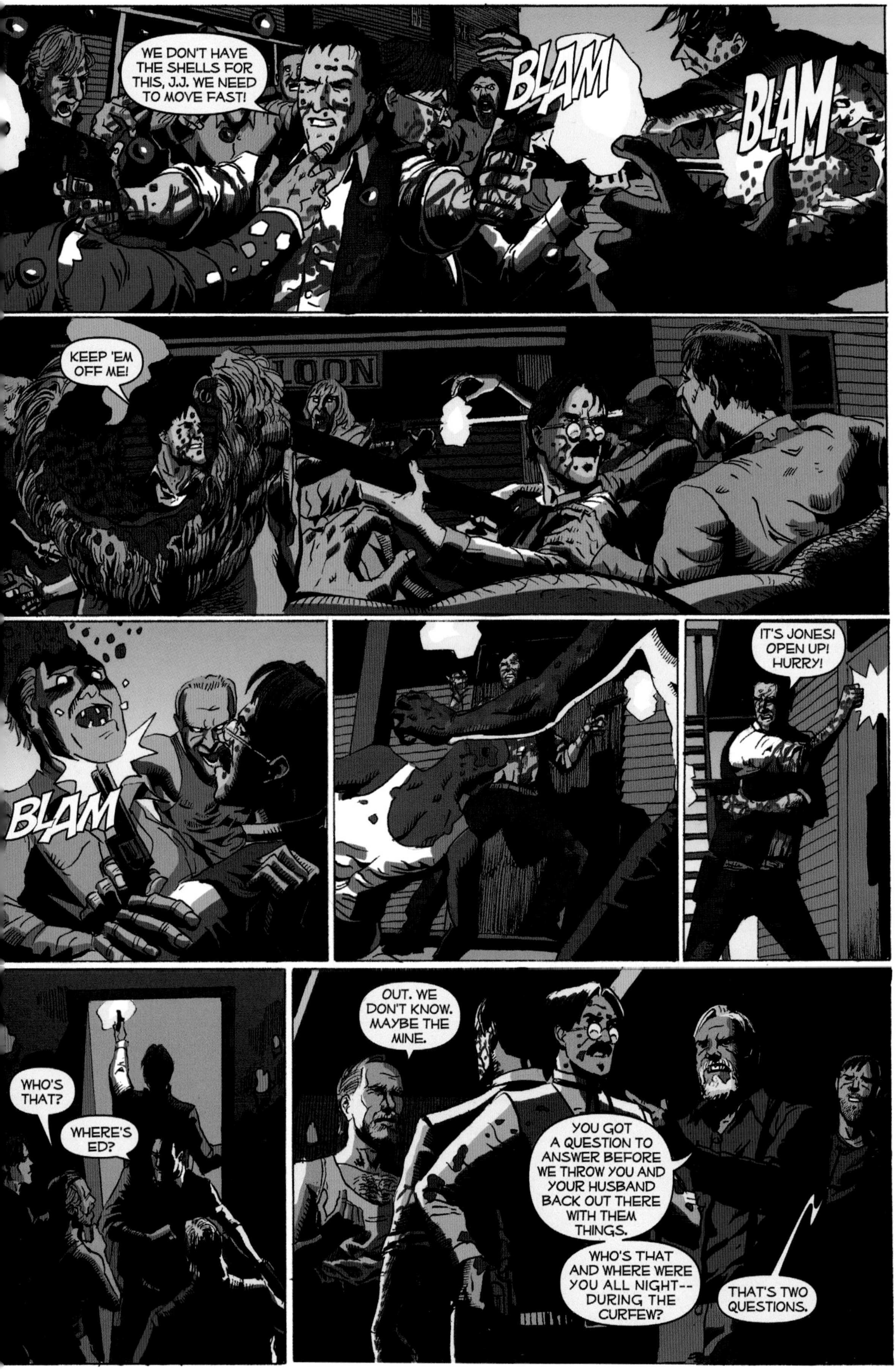
WE DON'T HAVE THE SHELLS FOR THIS, J.J. WE NEED TO MOVE FAST!
BLAM
BLAM
KEEP 'EM OFF ME!
LOON
BLAM
IT'S JONES! OPEN UP! HURRY!
WHO'S THAT?
WHERE'S ED?
OUT. WE DON'T KNOW. MAYBE THE MINE.
YOU GOT A QUESTION TO ANSWER BEFORE WE THROW YOU AND YOUR HUSBAND BACK OUT THERE WITH THEM THINGS.
WHO'S THAT AND WHERE WERE YOU ALL NIGHT-- DURING THE CURFEW?
THAT'S TWO QUESTIONS.

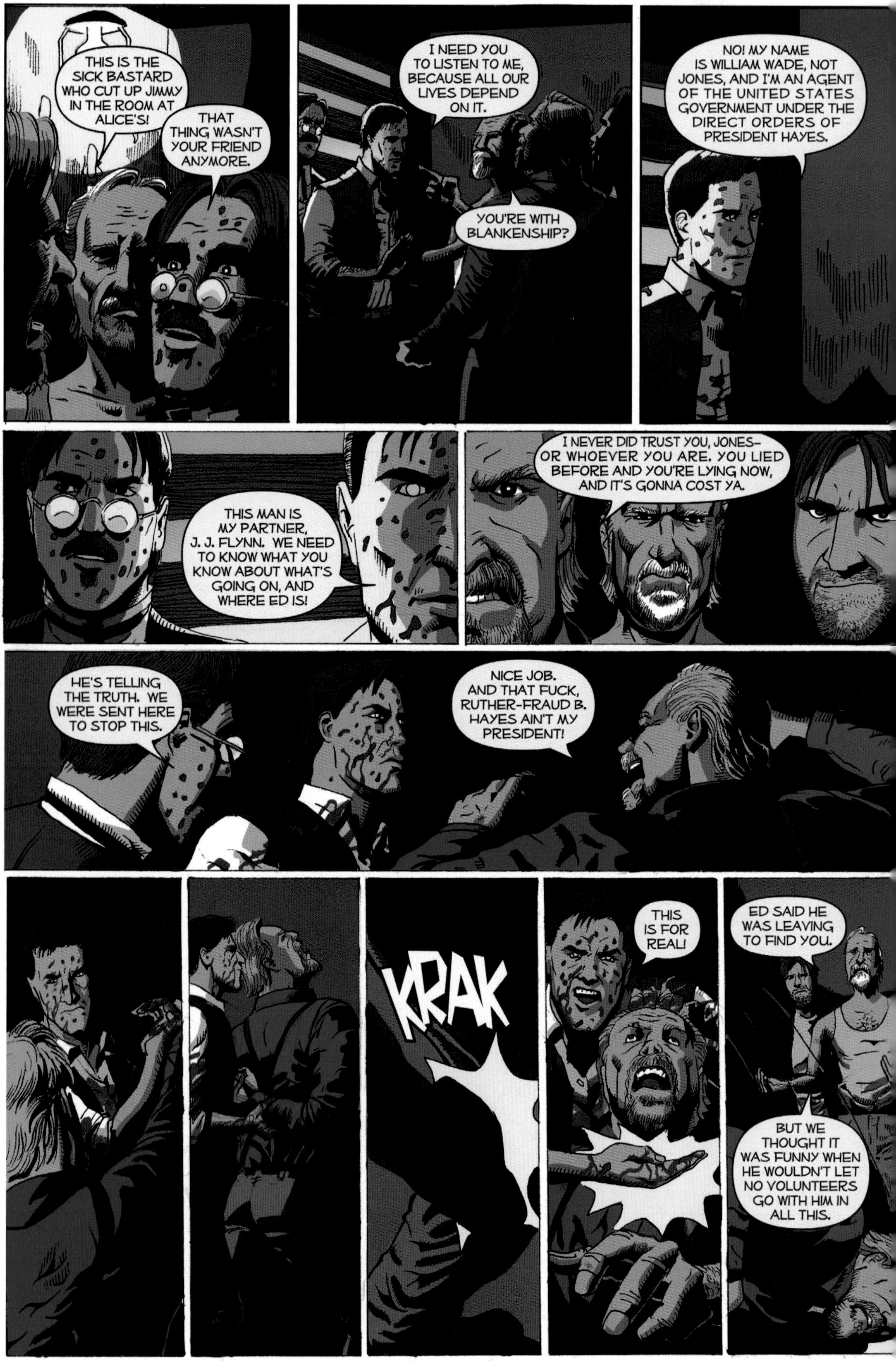
THIS IS THE SICK BASTARD WHO CUT UP JIMMY IN THE ROOM AT ALICE'S!
THAT THING WASN'T YOUR FRIEND ANYMORE.
I NEED YOU TO LISTEN TO ME, BECAUSE ALL OUR LIVES DEPEND ON IT.
YOU'RE WITH BLANKENSHIP?
NO! MY NAME IS WILLIAM WADE, NOT JONES, AND I'M AN AGENT OF THE UNITED STATES GOVERNMENT UNDER THE DIRECT ORDERS OF PRESIDENT HAYES.
THIS MAN IS MY PARTNER, J. J. FLYNN. WE NEED TO KNOW WHAT YOU KNOW ABOUT WHAT'S GOING ON, AND WHERE ED IS!
I NEVER DID TRUST YOU, JONES– OR WHOEVER YOU ARE. YOU LIED BEFORE AND YOU'RE LYING NOW, AND IT'S GONNA COST YA.
HE'S TELLING THE TRUTH. WE WERE SENT HERE TO STOP THIS.
NICE JOB. AND THAT FUCK, RUTHER-FRAUD B. HAYES AIN'T MY PRESIDENT!
KRAK
THIS IS FOR REAL!
ED SAID HE WAS LEAVING TO FIND YOU.
BUT WE THOUGHT IT WAS FUNNY WHEN HE WOULDN'T LET NO VOLUNTEERS GO WITH HIM IN ALL THIS.

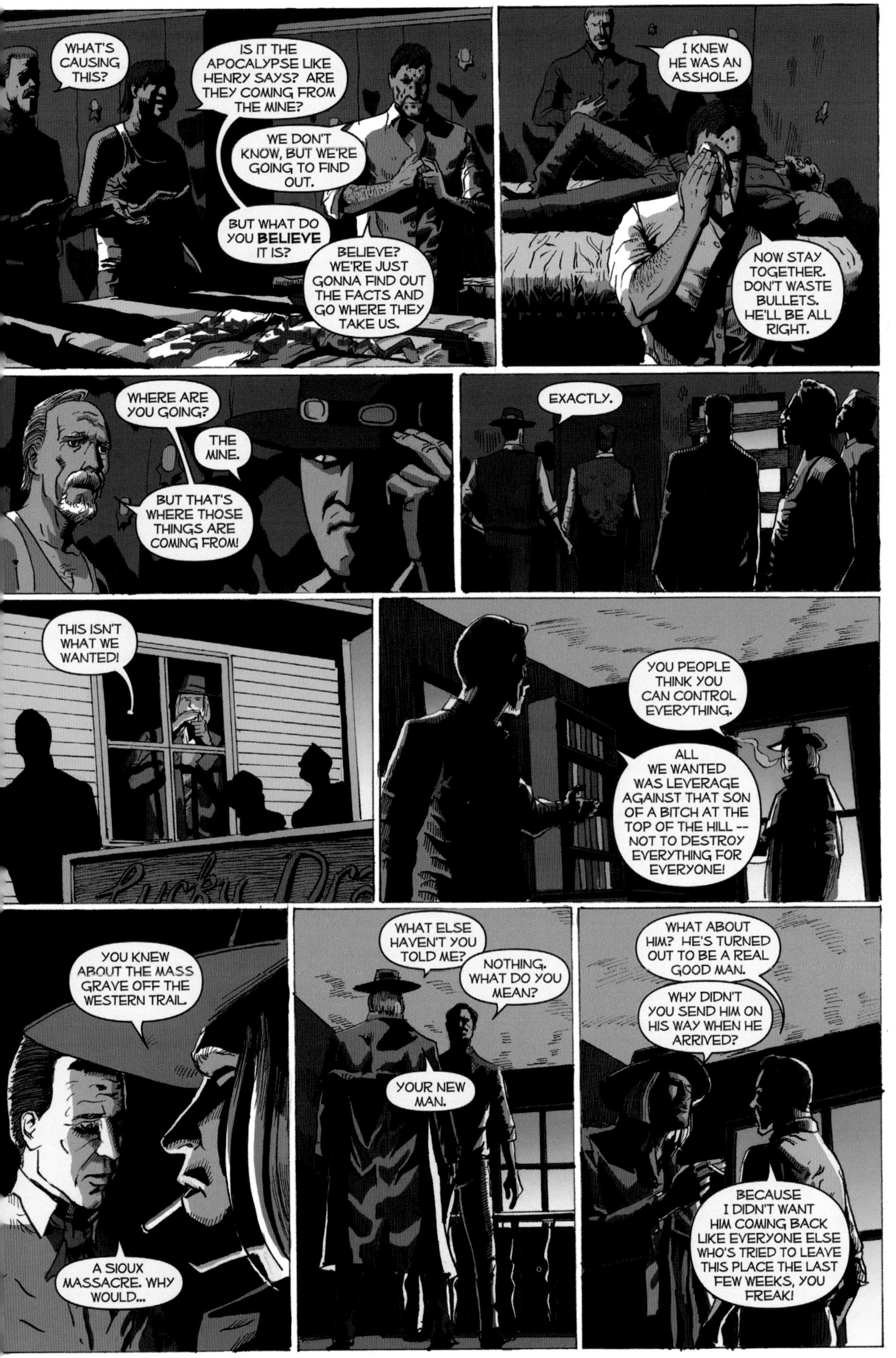
WHAT'S CAUSING THIS?
IS IT THE APOCALYPSE LIKE HENRY SAYS? ARE THEY COMING FROM THE MINE?
WE DON'T KNOW, BUT WE'RE GOING TO FIND OUT.
BUT WHAT DO YOU **BELIEVE** IT IS?
BELIEVE? WE'RE JUST GONNA FIND OUT THE FACTS AND GO WHERE THEY TAKE US.
I KNEW HE WAS AN ASSHOLE.
NOW STAY TOGETHER. DON'T WASTE BULLETS. HE'LL BE ALL RIGHT.
WHERE ARE YOU GOING?
THE MINE.
BUT THAT'S WHERE THOSE THINGS ARE COMING FROM!
EXACTLY.
THIS ISN'T WHAT WE WANTED!
YOU PEOPLE THINK YOU CAN CONTROL EVERYTHING.
ALL WE WANTED WAS LEVERAGE AGAINST THAT SON OF A BITCH AT THE TOP OF THE HILL -- NOT TO DESTROY EVERYTHING FOR EVERYONE!
YOU KNEW ABOUT THE MASS GRAVE OFF THE WESTERN TRAIL.
A SIOUX MASSACRE. WHY WOULD...
WHAT ELSE HAVEN'T YOU TOLD ME?
NOTHING. WHAT DO YOU MEAN?
YOUR NEW MAN.
WHAT ABOUT HIM? HE'S TURNED OUT TO BE A REAL GOOD MAN.
WHY DIDN'T YOU SEND HIM ON HIS WAY WHEN HE ARRIVED?
BECAUSE I DIDN'T WANT HIM COMING BACK LIKE EVERYONE ELSE WHO'S TRIED TO LEAVE THIS PLACE THE LAST FEW WEEKS, YOU FREAK!

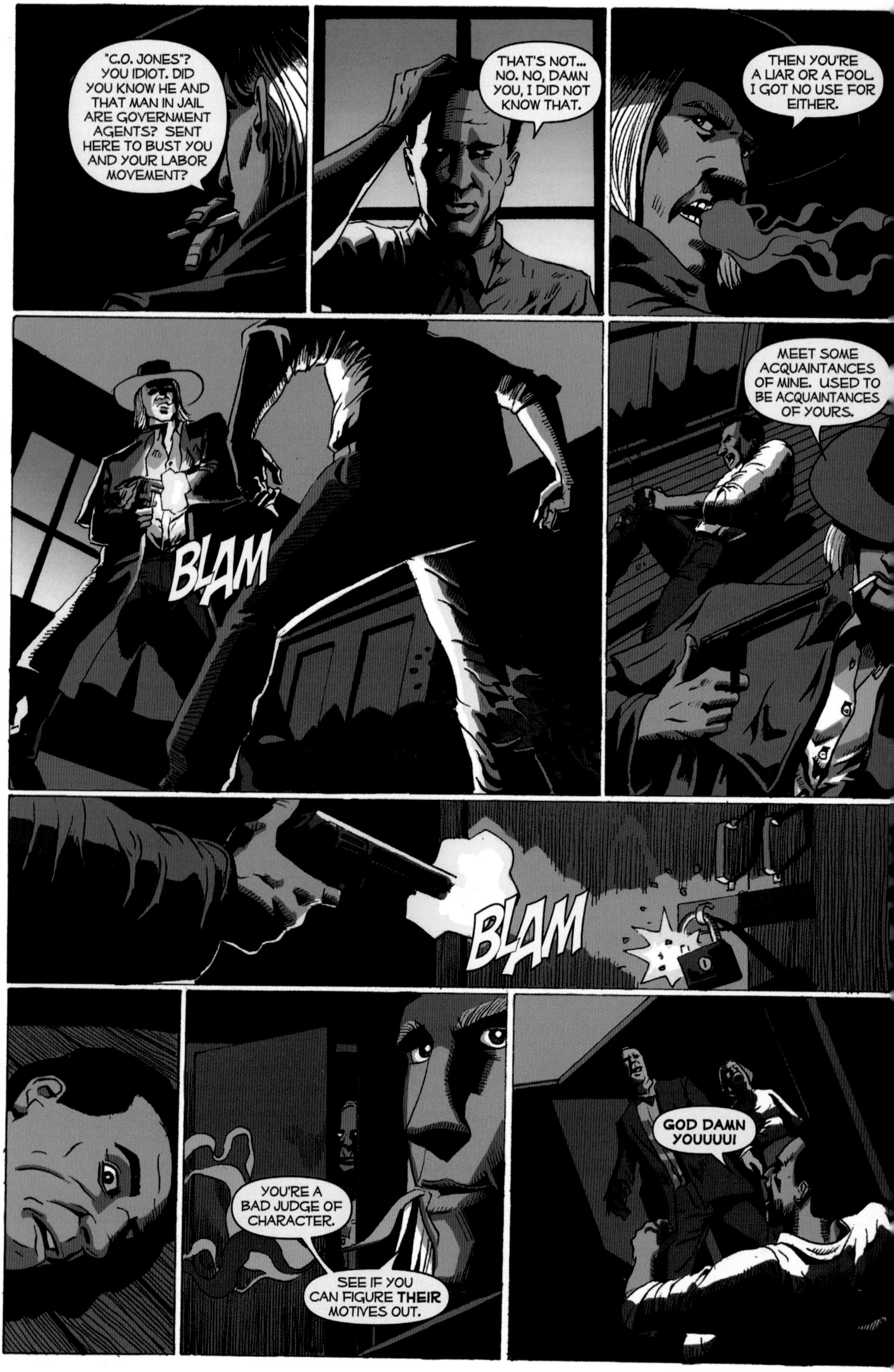
"C.O. JONES"? YOU IDIOT. DID YOU KNOW HE AND THAT MAN IN JAIL ARE GOVERNMENT AGENTS? SENT HERE TO BUST YOU AND YOUR LABOR MOVEMENT?
THAT'S NOT... NO. NO, DAMN YOU, I DID NOT KNOW THAT.
THEN YOU'RE A LIAR OR A FOOL. I GOT NO USE FOR EITHER.
BLAM
MEET SOME ACQUAINTANCES OF MINE. USED TO BE ACQUAINTANCES OF YOURS.
BLAM
YOU'RE A BAD JUDGE OF CHARACTER.
SEE IF YOU CAN FIGURE **THEIR** MOTIVES OUT.
GOD DAMN YOUUUU!

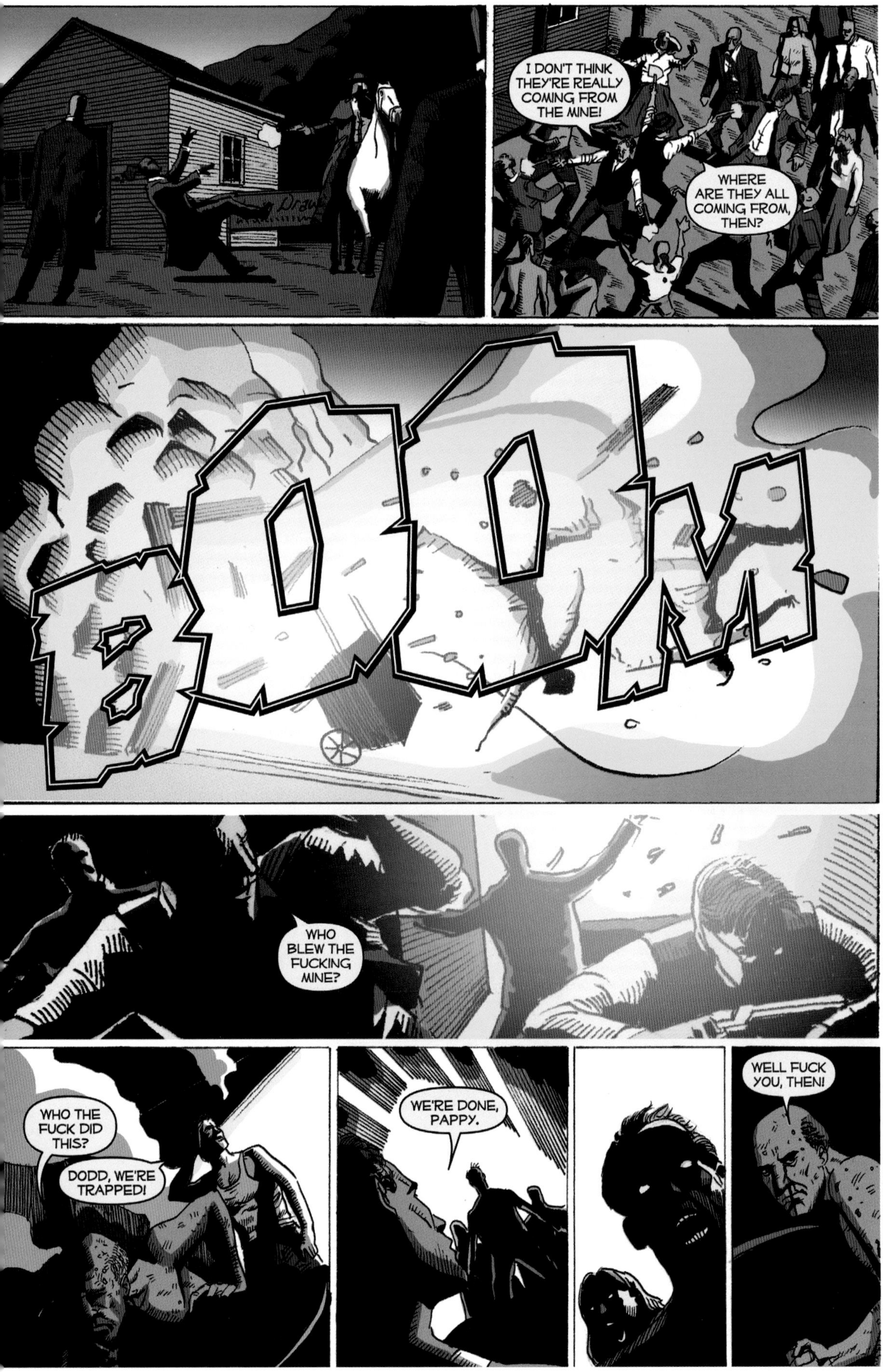
I DON'T THINK THEY'RE REALLY COMING FROM THE MINE!
WHERE ARE THEY ALL COMING FROM, THEN?
BOOM
WHO BLEW THE FUCKING MINE?
WHO THE FUCK DID THIS?
DODD, WE'RE TRAPPED!
WE'RE DONE, PAPPY.
WELL FUCK YOU, THEN!

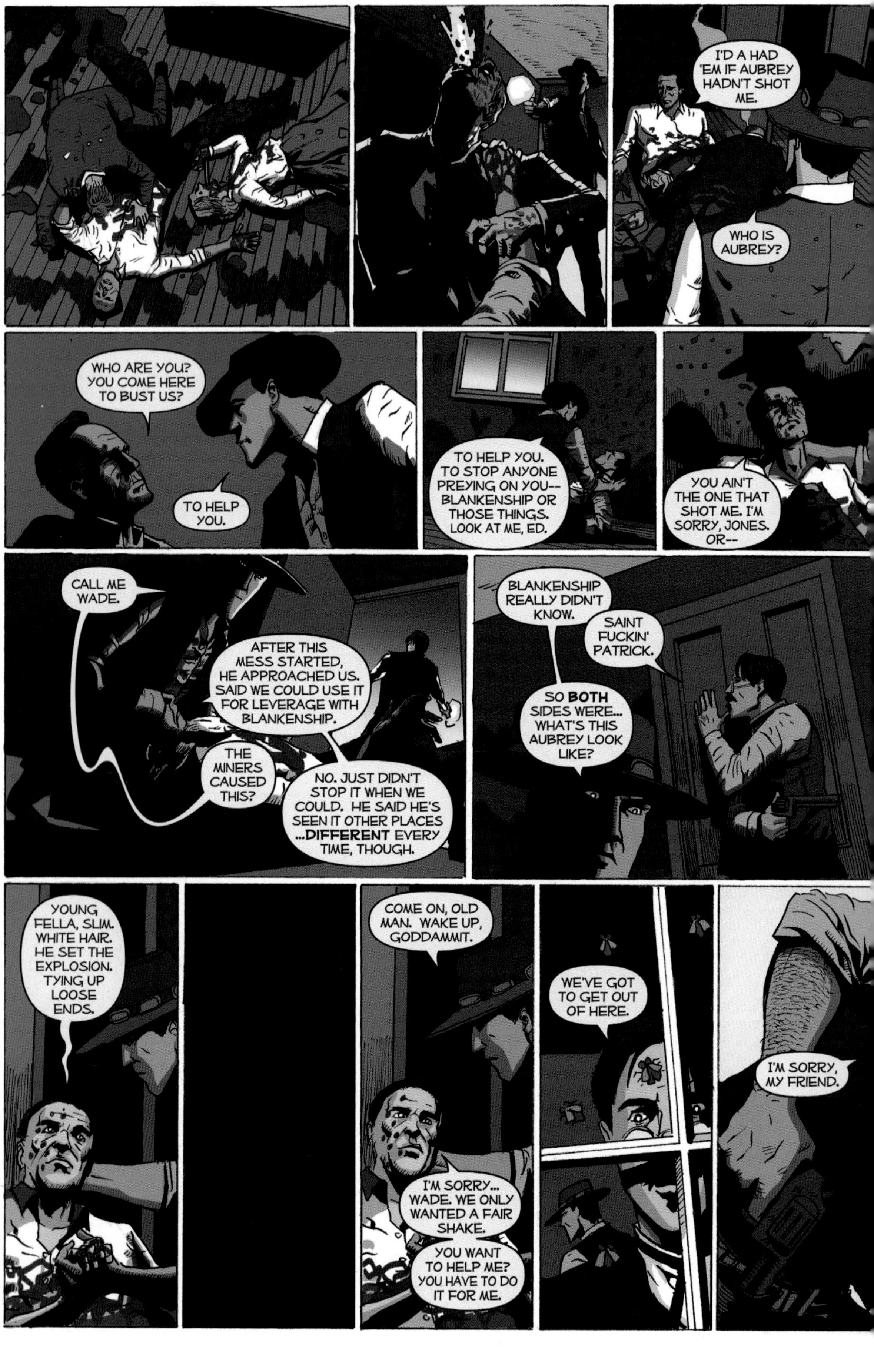

I'D A HAD 'EM IF AUBREY HADN'T SHOT ME.
WHO IS AUBREY?
WHO ARE YOU? YOU COME HERE TO BUST US?
TO HELP YOU.
TO HELP YOU. TO STOP ANYONE PREYING ON YOU-- BLANKENSHIP OR THOSE THINGS. LOOK AT ME, ED.
YOU AIN'T THE ONE THAT SHOT ME. I'M SORRY, JONES. OR--
CALL ME WADE.
AFTER THIS MESS STARTED, HE APPROACHED US. SAID WE COULD USE IT FOR LEVERAGE WITH BLANKENSHIP.
THE MINERS CAUSED THIS?
NO. JUST DIDN'T STOP IT WHEN WE COULD. HE SAID HE'S SEEN IT OTHER PLACES ...DIFFERENT EVERY TIME, THOUGH.
BLANKENSHIP REALLY DIDN'T KNOW.
SAINT FUCKIN' PATRICK.
SO BOTH SIDES WERE... WHAT'S THIS AUBREY LOOK LIKE?
YOUNG FELLA, SLIM. WHITE HAIR. HE SET THE EXPLOSION. TYING UP LOOSE ENDS.
COME ON, OLD MAN. WAKE UP, GODDAMMIT.
I'M SORRY... WADE. WE ONLY WANTED A FAIR SHAKE.
YOU WANT TO HELP ME? YOU HAVE TO DO IT FOR ME.
WE'VE GOT TO GET OUT OF HERE.
I'M SORRY, MY FRIEND.

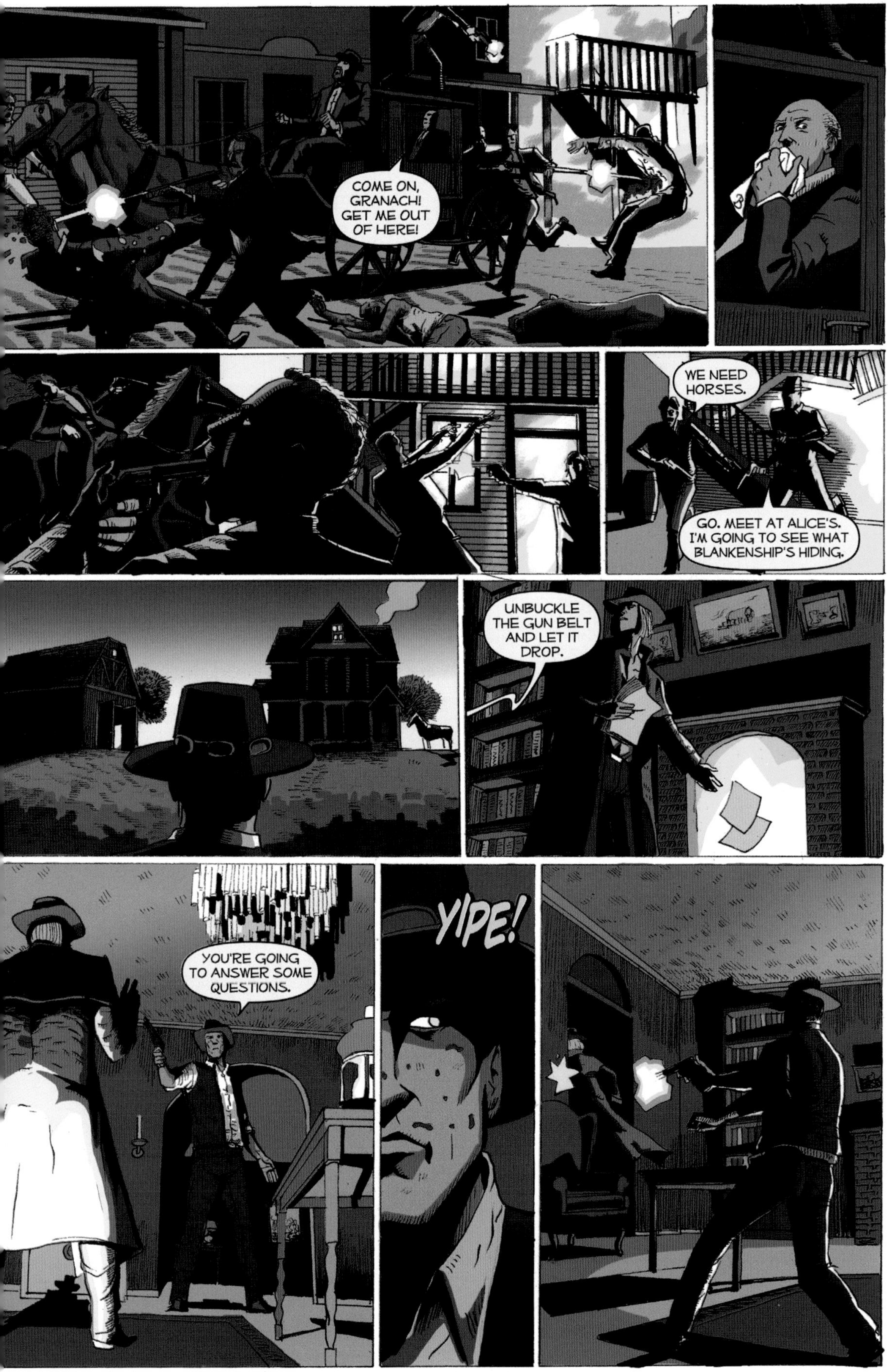
COME ON, GRANACH! GET ME OUT OF HERE!
WE NEED HORSES.
GO. MEET AT ALICE'S. I'M GOING TO SEE WHAT BLANKENSHIP'S HIDING.
UNBUCKLE THE GUN BELT AND LET IT DROP.
YOU'RE GOING TO ANSWER SOME QUESTIONS.
YIPE!

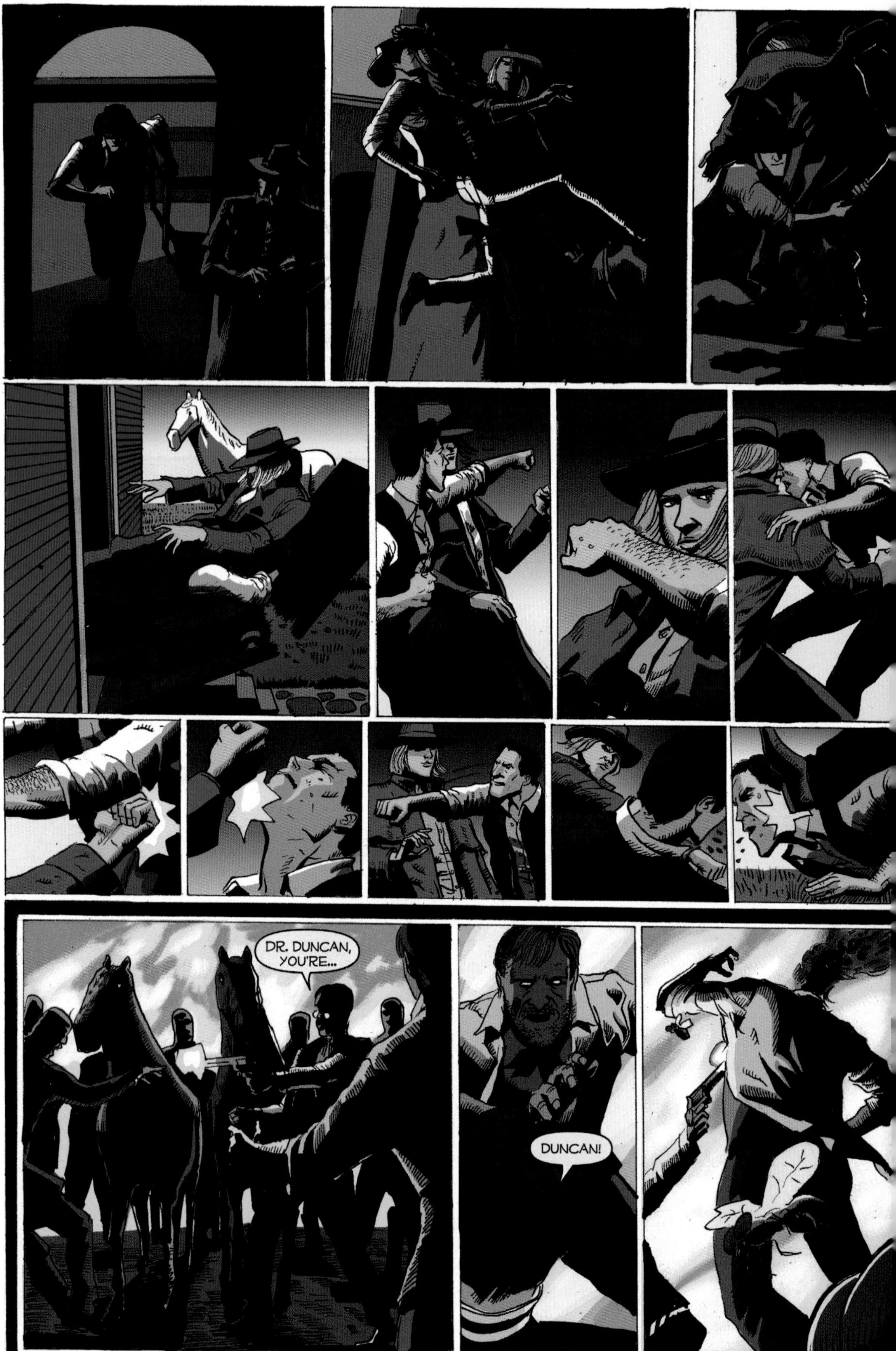
DR. DUNCAN, YOU'RE...
DUNCAN!

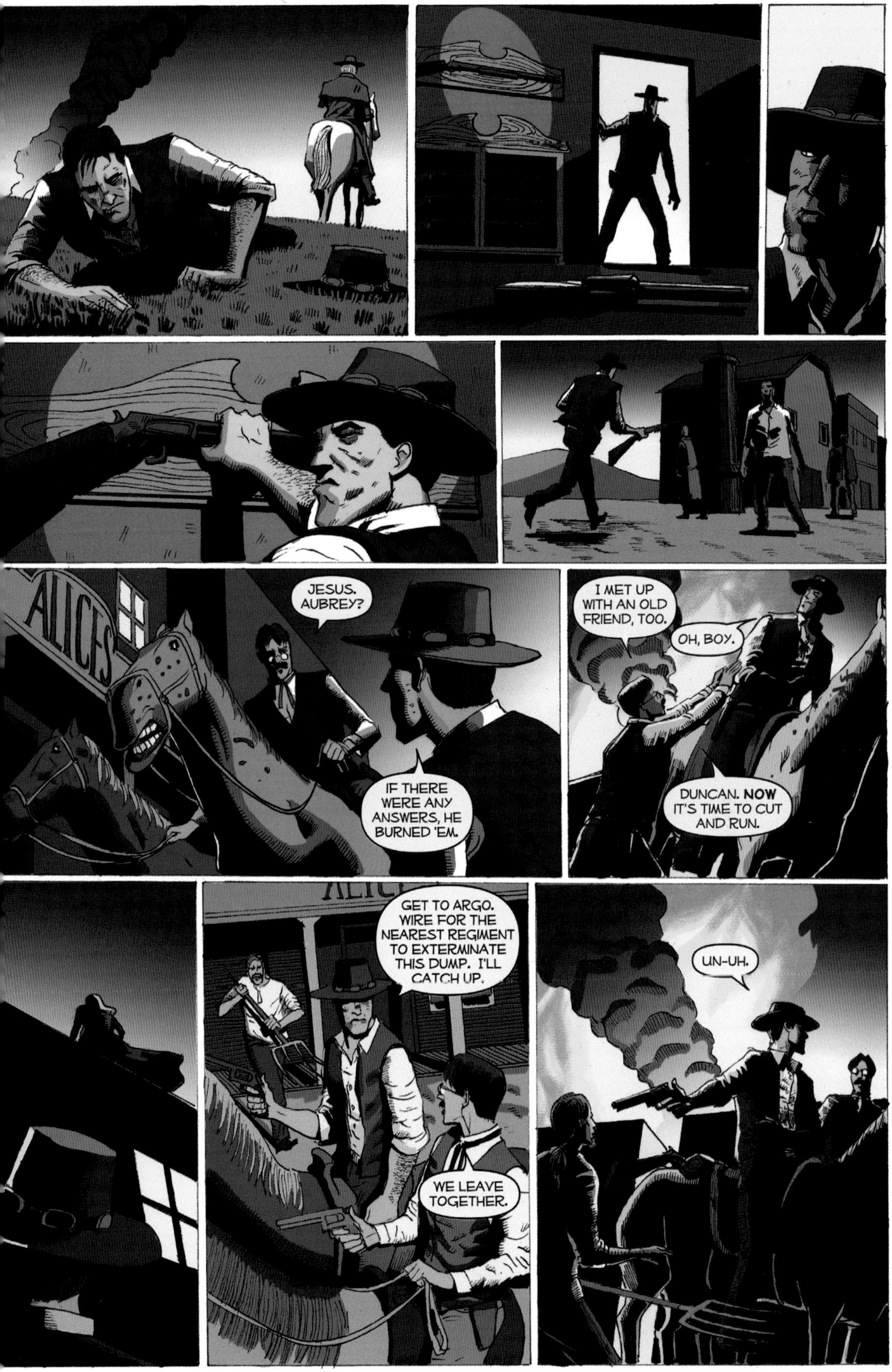
ALICES
JESUS. AUBREY?
IF THERE WERE ANY ANSWERS, HE BURNED 'EM.
I MET UP WITH AN OLD FRIEND, TOO.
OH, BOY.
DUNCAN. **NOW** IT'S TIME TO CUT AND RUN.
GET TO ARGO. WIRE FOR THE NEAREST REGIMENT TO EXTERMINATE THIS DUMP. I'LL CATCH UP.
WE LEAVE TOGETHER.
UN-UH.

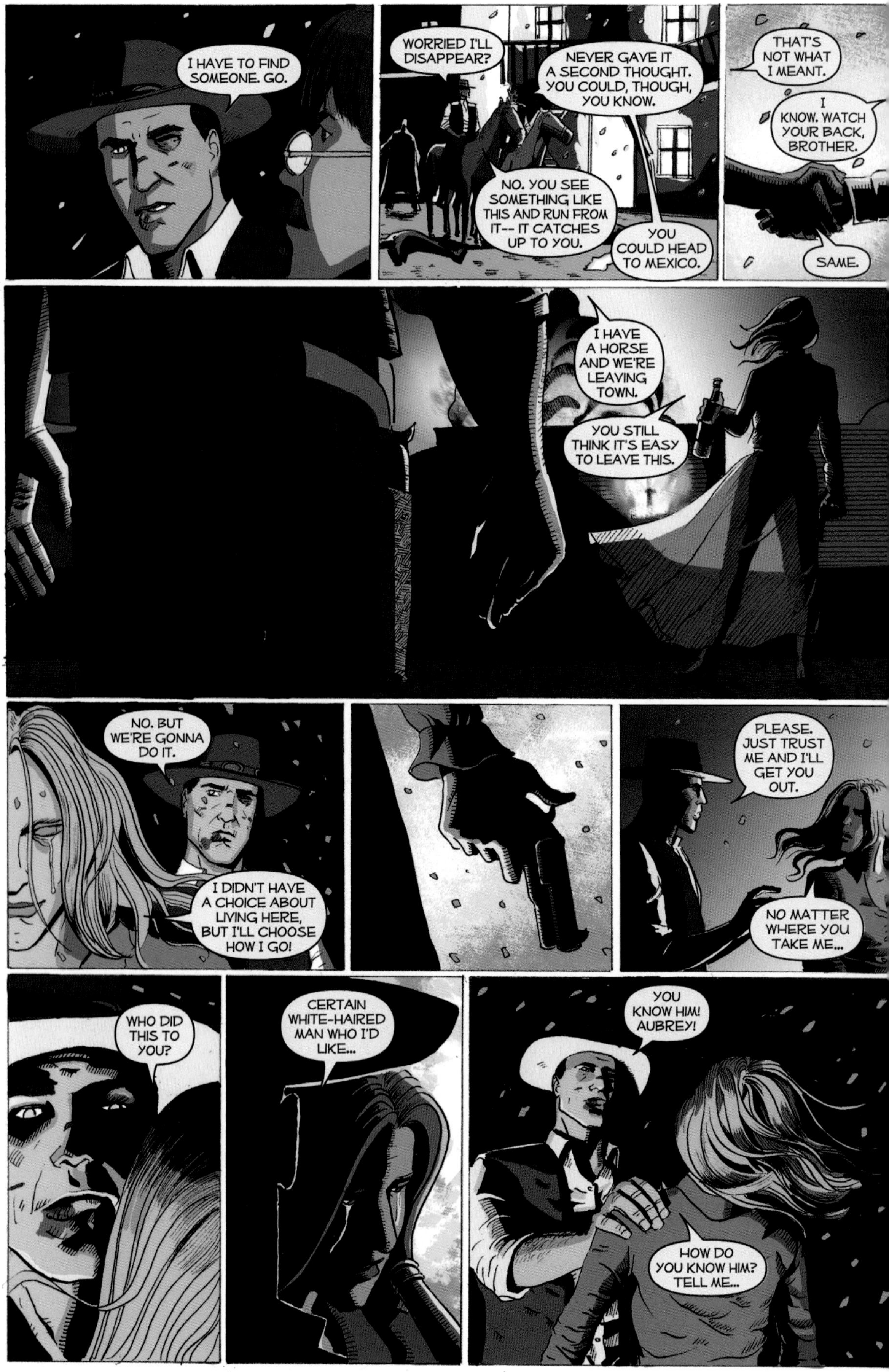
I HAVE TO FIND SOMEONE. GO.
WORRIED I'LL DISAPPEAR?
NEVER GAVE IT A SECOND THOUGHT. YOU COULD, THOUGH, YOU KNOW.
NO. YOU SEE SOMETHING LIKE THIS AND RUN FROM IT-- IT CATCHES UP TO YOU.
YOU COULD HEAD TO MEXICO.
THAT'S NOT WHAT I MEANT.
I KNOW. WATCH YOUR BACK, BROTHER.
SAME.
I HAVE A HORSE AND WE'RE LEAVING TOWN.
YOU STILL THINK IT'S EASY TO LEAVE THIS.
NO. BUT WE'RE GONNA DO IT.
I DIDN'T HAVE A CHOICE ABOUT LIVING HERE, BUT I'LL CHOOSE HOW I GO!
PLEASE. JUST TRUST ME AND I'LL GET YOU OUT.
NO MATTER WHERE YOU TAKE ME...
WHO DID THIS TO YOU?
CERTAIN WHITE-HAIRED MAN WHO I'D LIKE...
YOU KNOW HIM! AUBREY!
HOW DO YOU KNOW HIM? TELL ME...

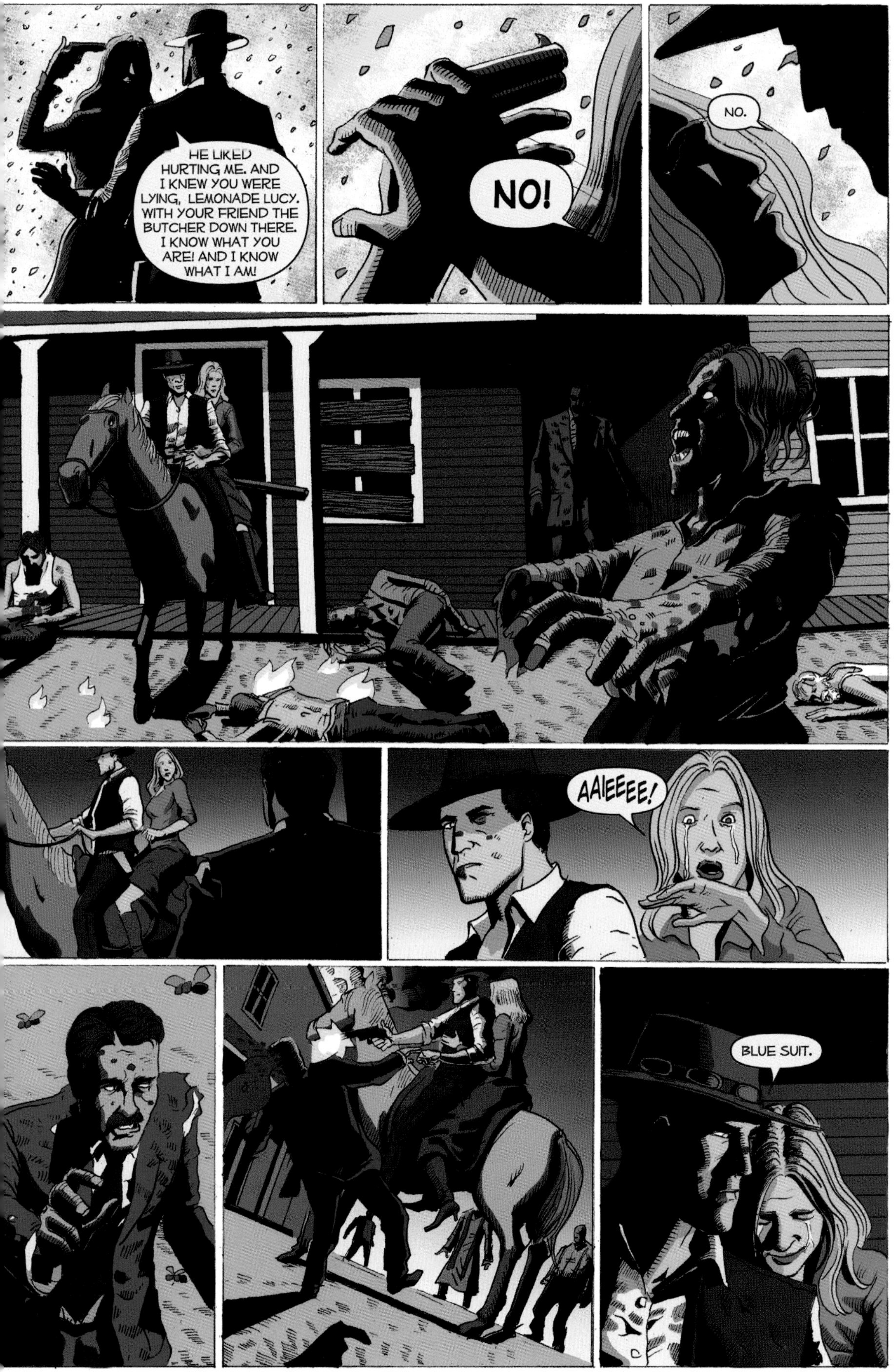
HE LIKED HURTING ME. AND I KNEW YOU WERE LYING, LEMONADE LUCY. WITH YOUR FRIEND THE BUTCHER DOWN THERE. I KNOW WHAT YOU ARE! AND I KNOW WHAT I AM!
NO!
NO.
AAIEEEE!
BLUE SUIT.

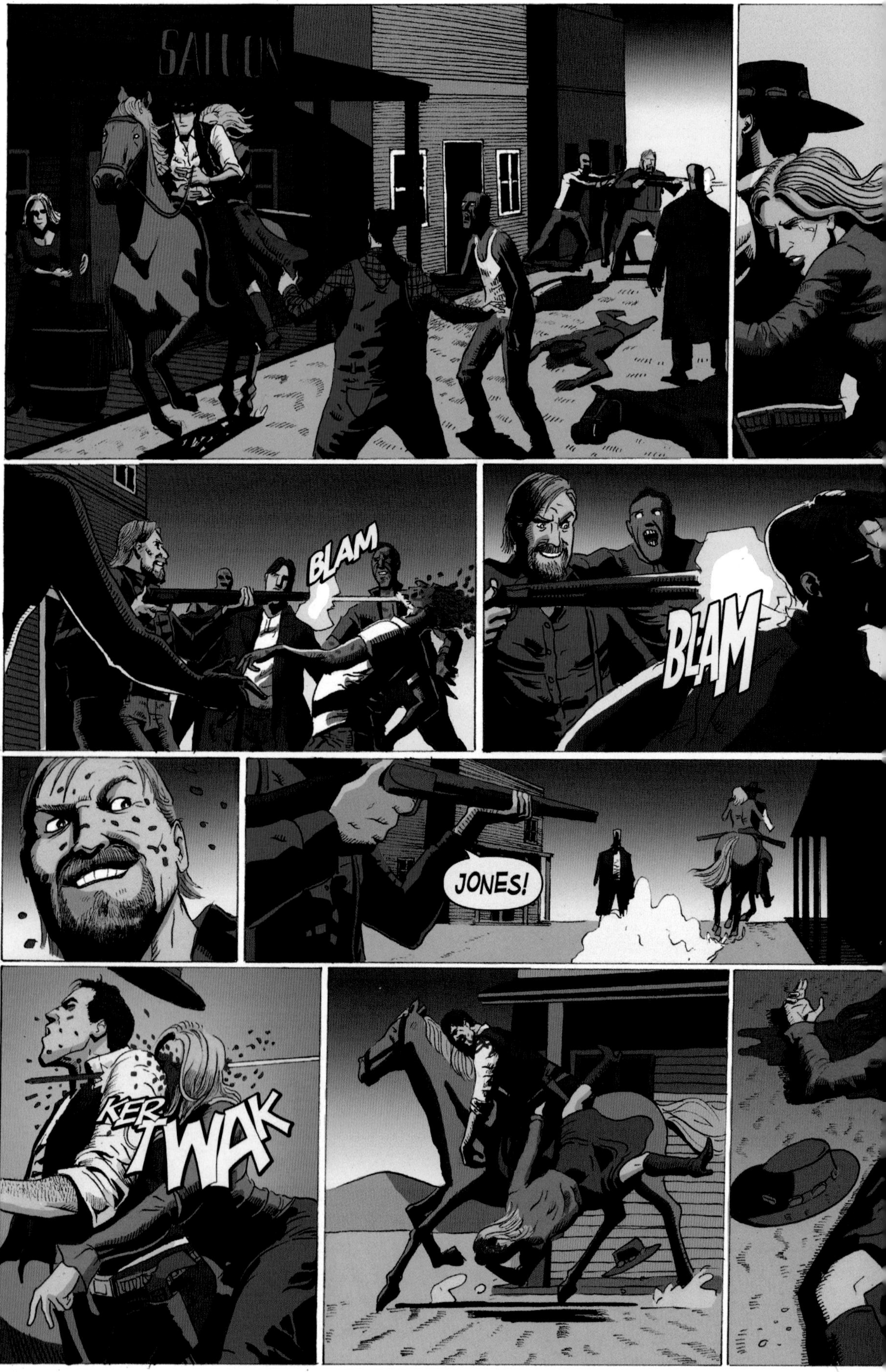
SALOON
BLAM
BLAM
JONES!
KER-TWAK

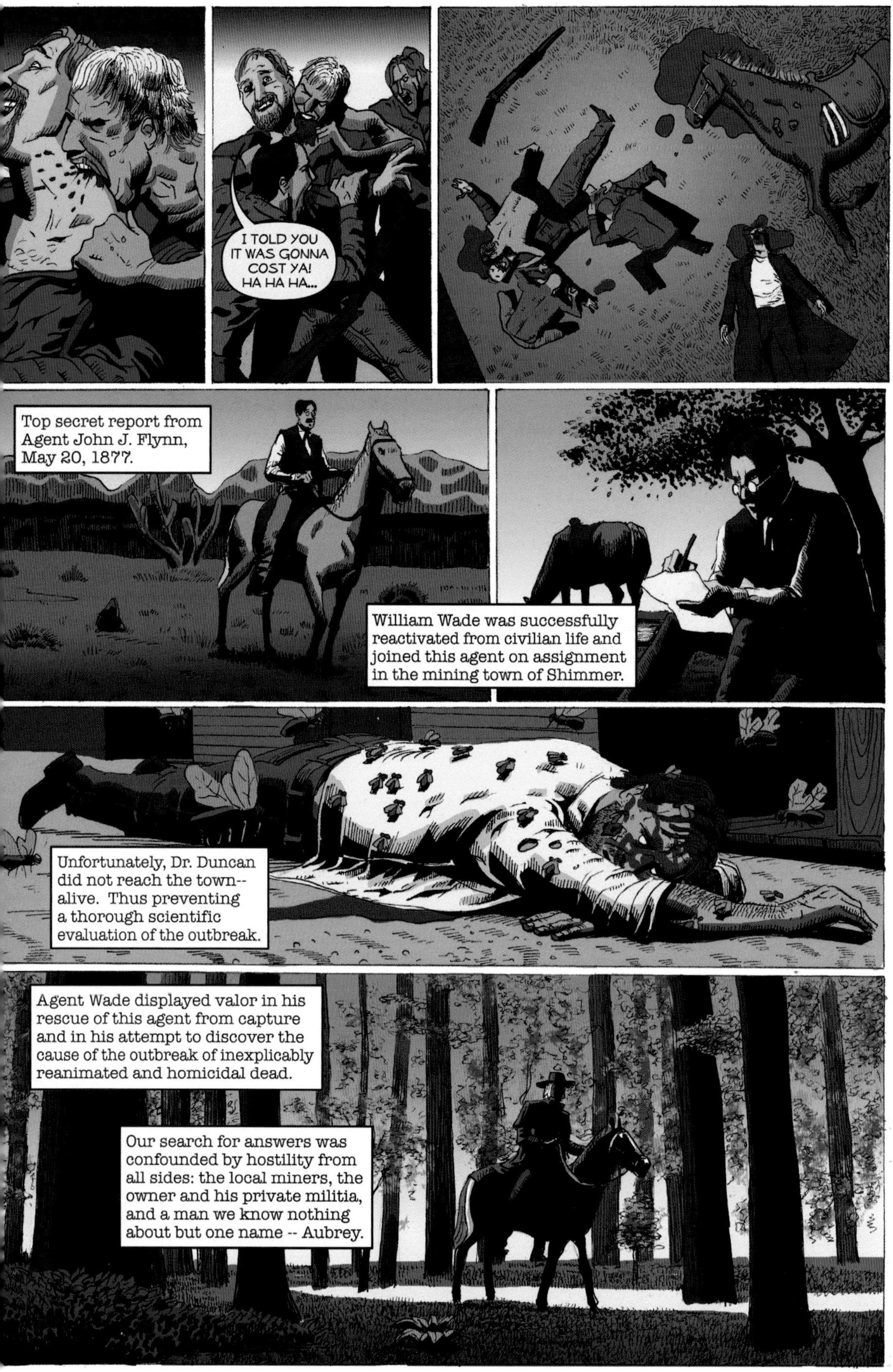
I TOLD YOU IT WAS GONNA COST YA! HA HA HA...
Top secret report from Agent John J. Flynn, May 20, 1877.
William Wade was successfully reactivated from civilian life and joined this agent on assignment in the mining town of Shimmer.
Unfortunately, Dr. Duncan did not reach the town-- alive. Thus preventing a thorough scientific evaluation of the outbreak.
Agent Wade displayed valor in his rescue of this agent from capture and in his attempt to discover the cause of the outbreak of inexplicably reanimated and homicidal dead.
Our search for answers was confounded by hostility from all sides: the local miners, the owner and his private militia, and a man we know nothing about but one name -- Aubrey.

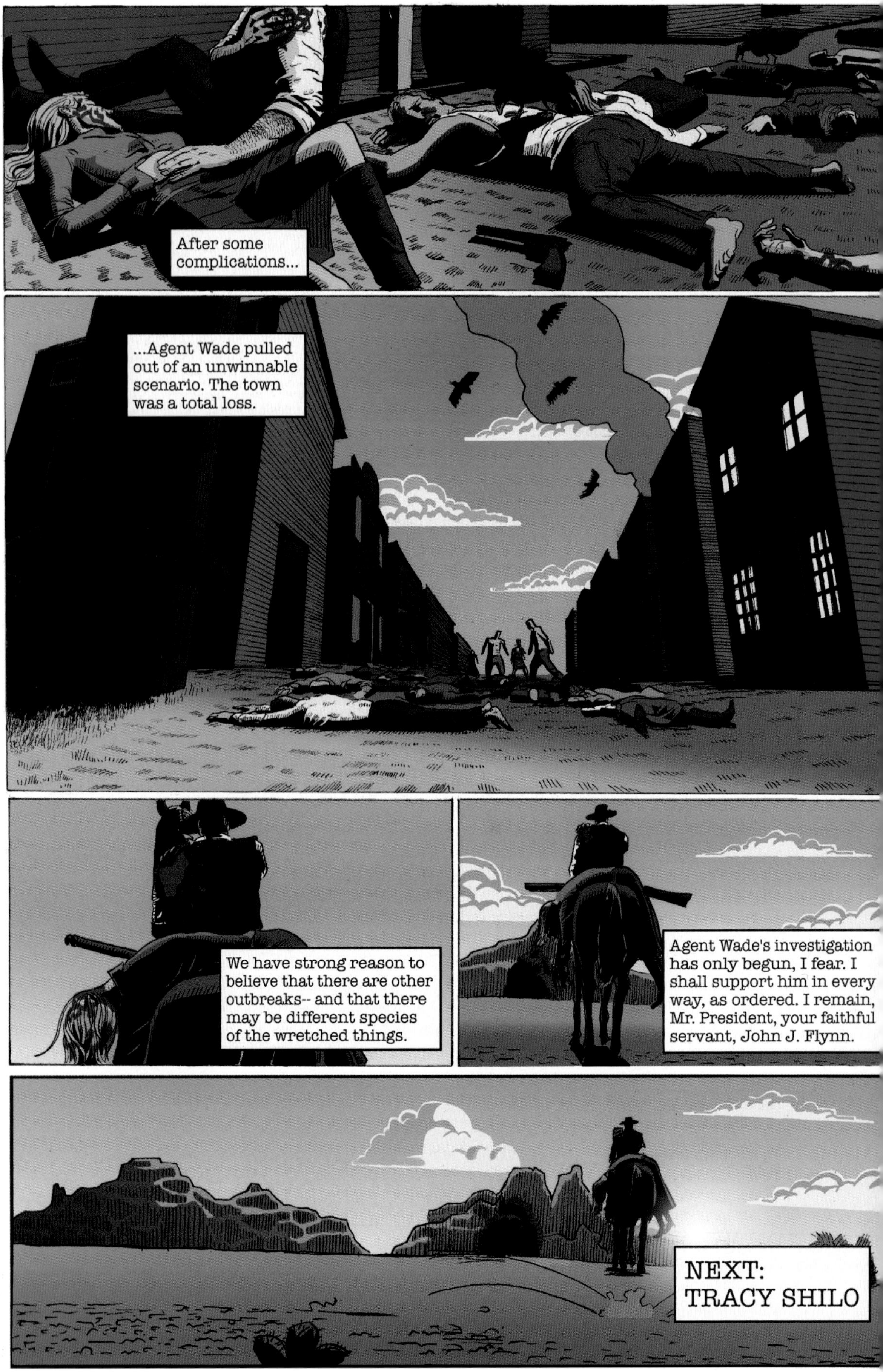
After some complications...
...Agent Wade pulled out of an unwinnable scenario. The town was a total loss.
We have strong reason to believe that there are other outbreaks-- and that there may be different species of the wretched things.
Agent Wade's investigation has only begun, I fear. I shall support him in every way, as ordered. I remain, Mr. President, your faithful servant, John J. Flynn.
NEXT: TRACY SHILO

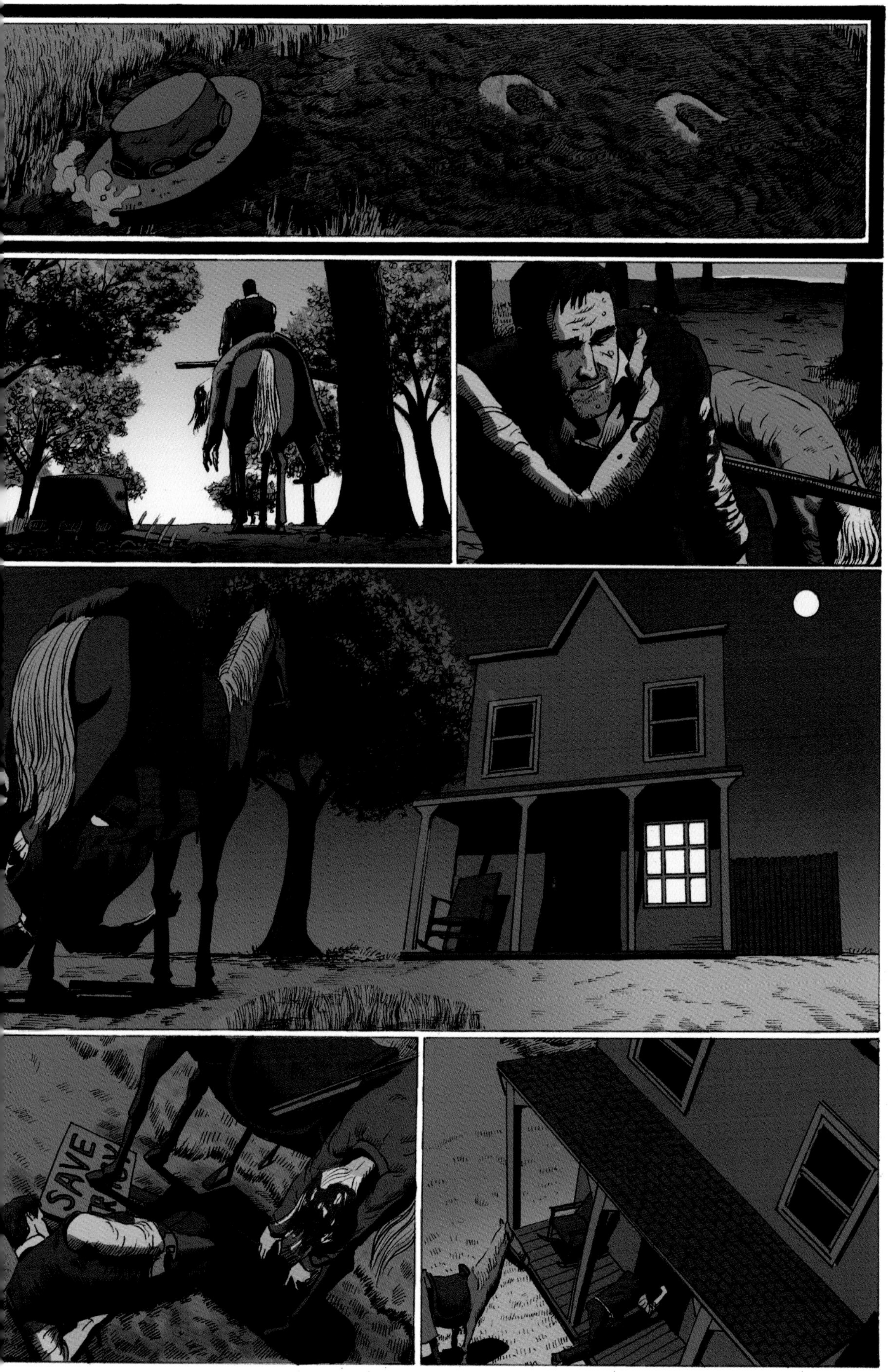
SAVE

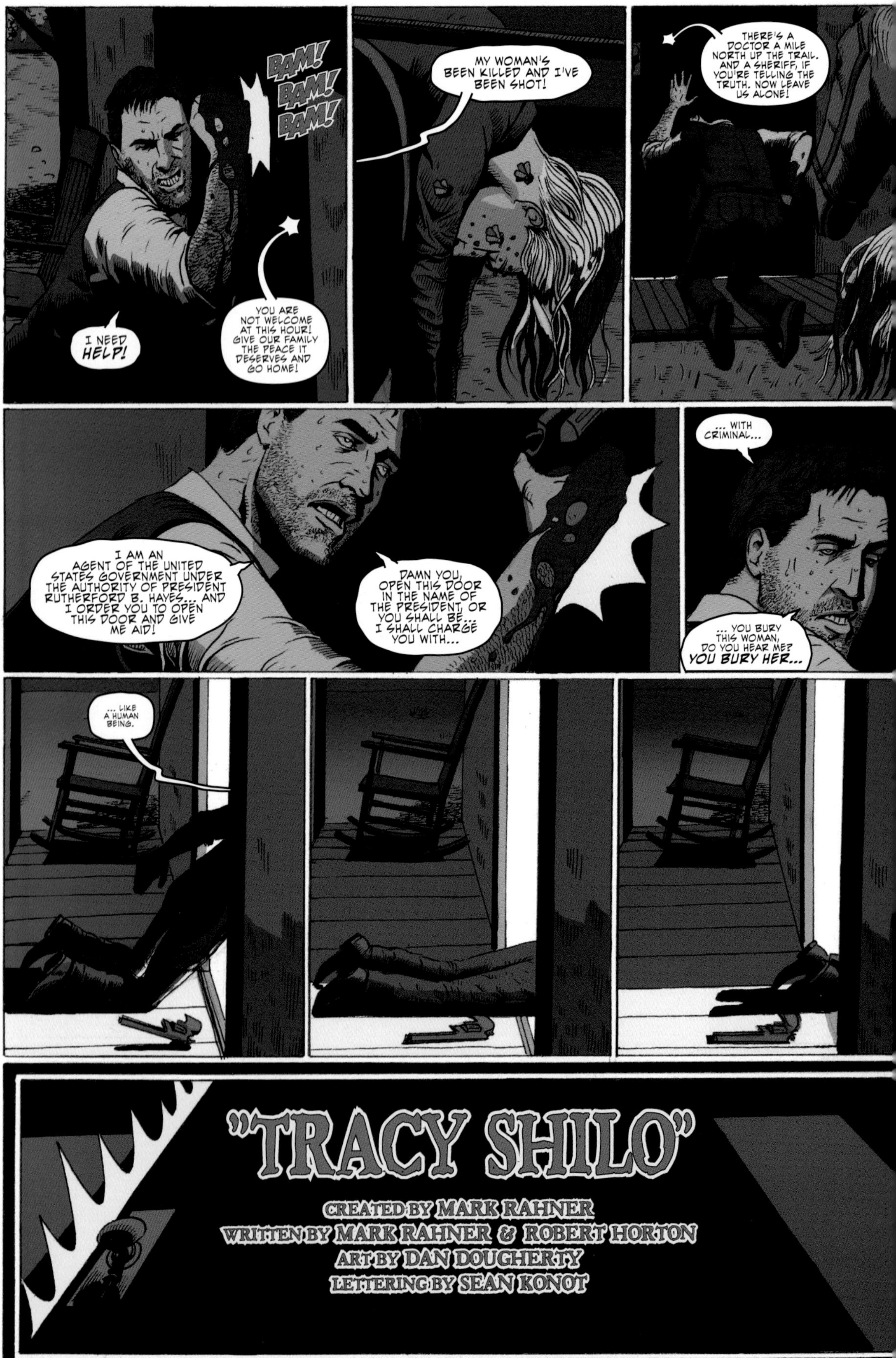
BAM! BAM! BAM!
I NEED HELP!
YOU ARE NOT WELCOME AT THIS HOUR! GIVE OUR FAMILY THE PEACE IT DESERVES AND GO HOME!
MY WOMAN'S BEEN KILLED AND I'VE BEEN SHOT!
THERE'S A DOCTOR A MILE NORTH UP THE TRAIL. AND A SHERIFF, IF YOU'RE TELLING THE TRUTH. NOW LEAVE US ALONE!
I AM AN AGENT OF THE UNITED STATES GOVERNMENT UNDER THE AUTHORITY OF PRESIDENT RUTHERFORD B. HAYES... AND I ORDER YOU TO OPEN THIS DOOR AND GIVE ME AID!
DAMN YOU, OPEN THIS DOOR IN THE NAME OF THE PRESIDENT, OR YOU SHALL BE... I SHALL CHARGE YOU WITH...
... WITH CRIMINAL...
... YOU BURY THIS WOMAN, DO YOU HEAR ME? YOU BURY HER...
... LIKE A HUMAN BEING.
"TRACY SHILO"
CREATED BY MARK RAHNER
WRITTEN BY MARK RAHNER & ROBERT HORTON
ART BY DAN DOUGHERTY
LETTERING BY SEAN KONOT

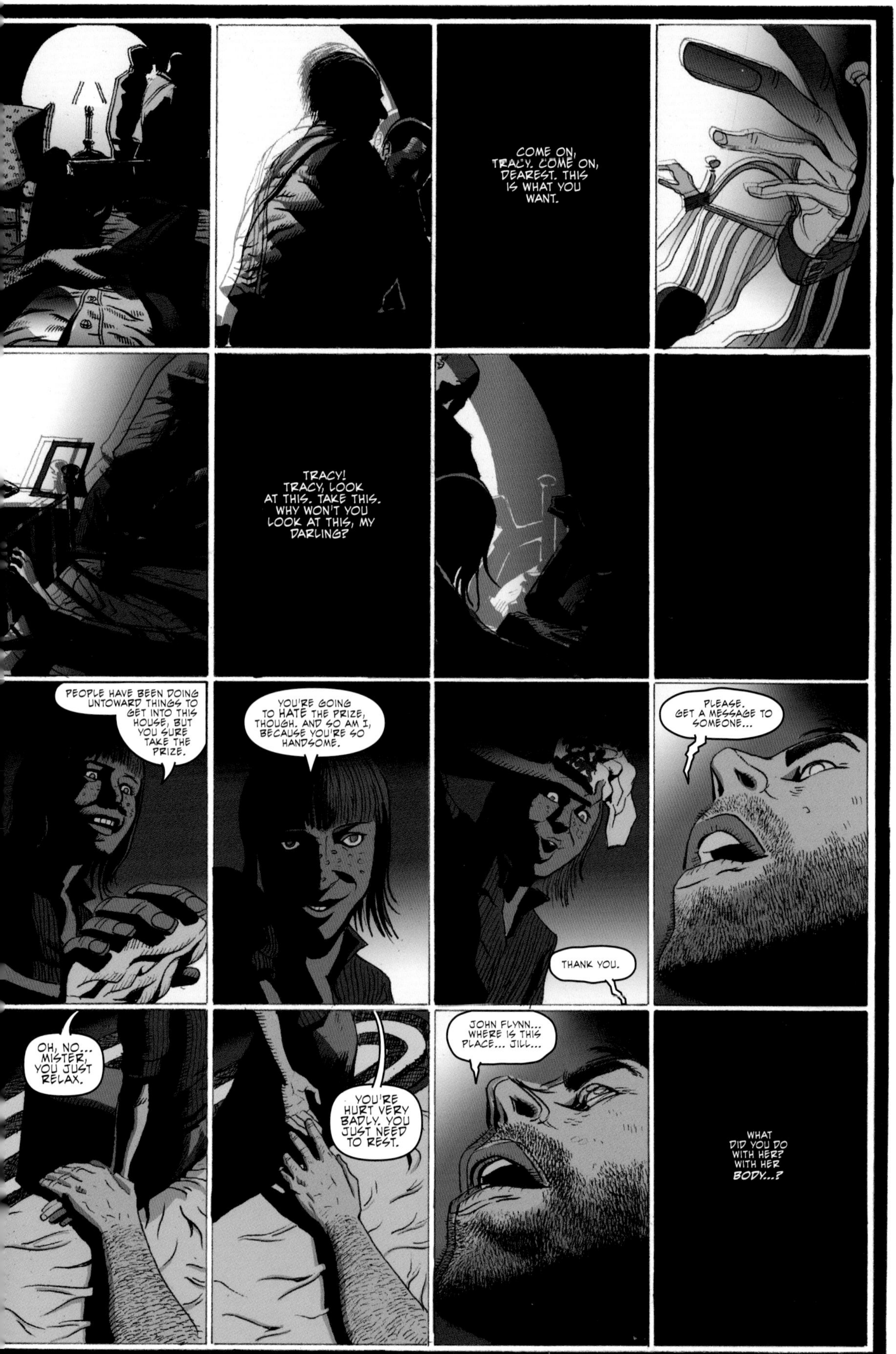
COME ON, TRACY. COME ON, DEAREST. THIS IS WHAT YOU WANT.
TRACY! TRACY, LOOK AT THIS. TAKE THIS. WHY WON'T YOU LOOK AT THIS, MY DARLING?
PEOPLE HAVE BEEN DOING UNTOWARD THINGS TO GET INTO THIS HOUSE, BUT YOU SURE TAKE THE PRIZE.
YOU'RE GOING TO HATE THE PRIZE, THOUGH. AND SO AM I, BECAUSE YOU'RE SO HANDSOME.
THANK YOU.
PLEASE. GET A MESSAGE TO SOMEONE...
OH, NO... MISTER, YOU JUST RELAX.
YOU'RE HURT VERY BADLY. YOU JUST NEED TO REST.
JOHN FLYNN... WHERE IS THIS PLACE... JILL...
WHAT DID YOU DO WITH HER? WITH HER BODY...?

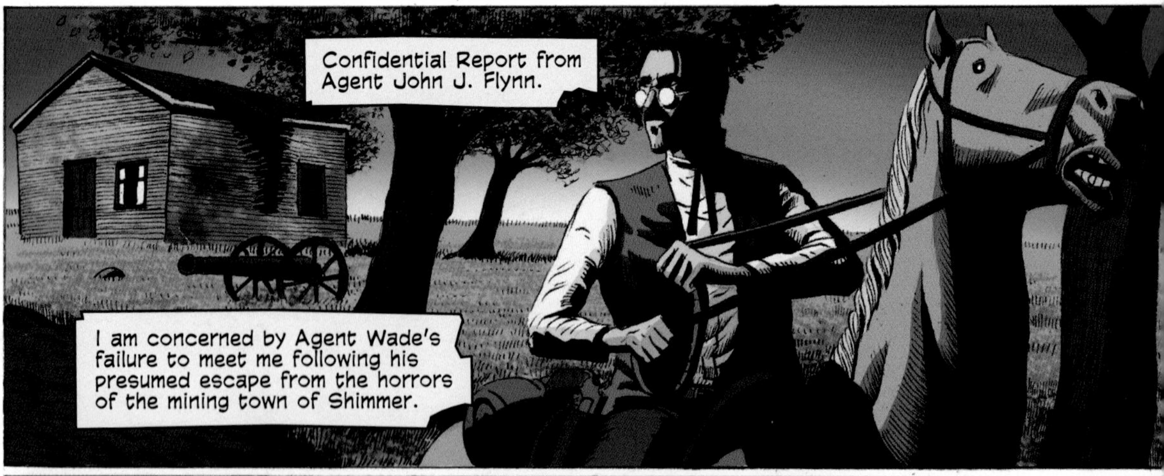
Confidential Report from Agent John J. Flynn.
I am concerned by Agent Wade's failure to meet me following his presumed escape from the horrors of the mining town of Shimmer.

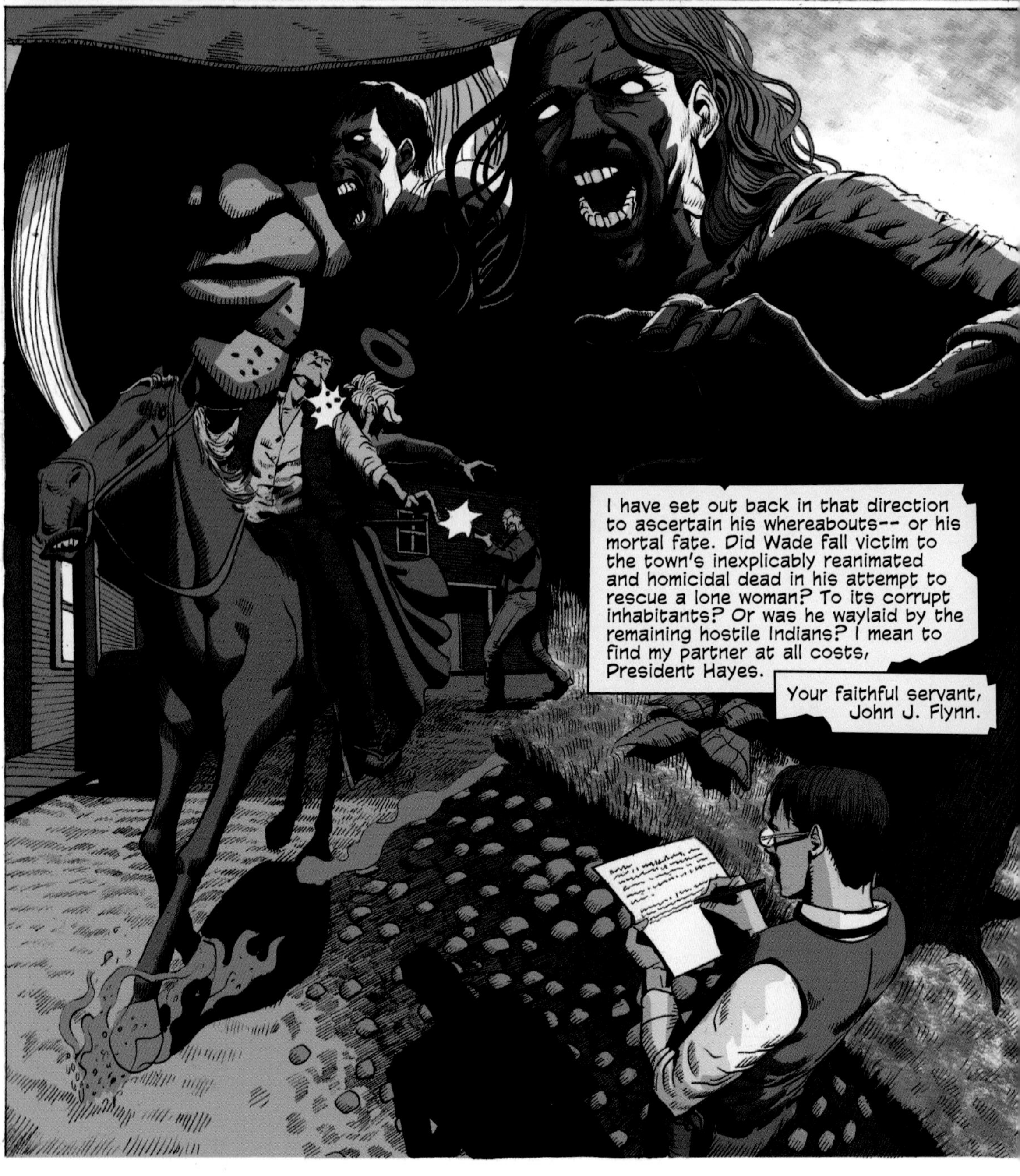
I have set out back in that direction to ascertain his whereabouts-- or his mortal fate. Did Wade fall victim to the town's inexplicably reanimated and homicidal dead in his attempt to rescue a lone woman? To its corrupt inhabitants? Or was he waylaid by the remaining hostile Indians? I mean to find my partner at all costs, President Hayes.
Your faithful servant, John J. Flynn.

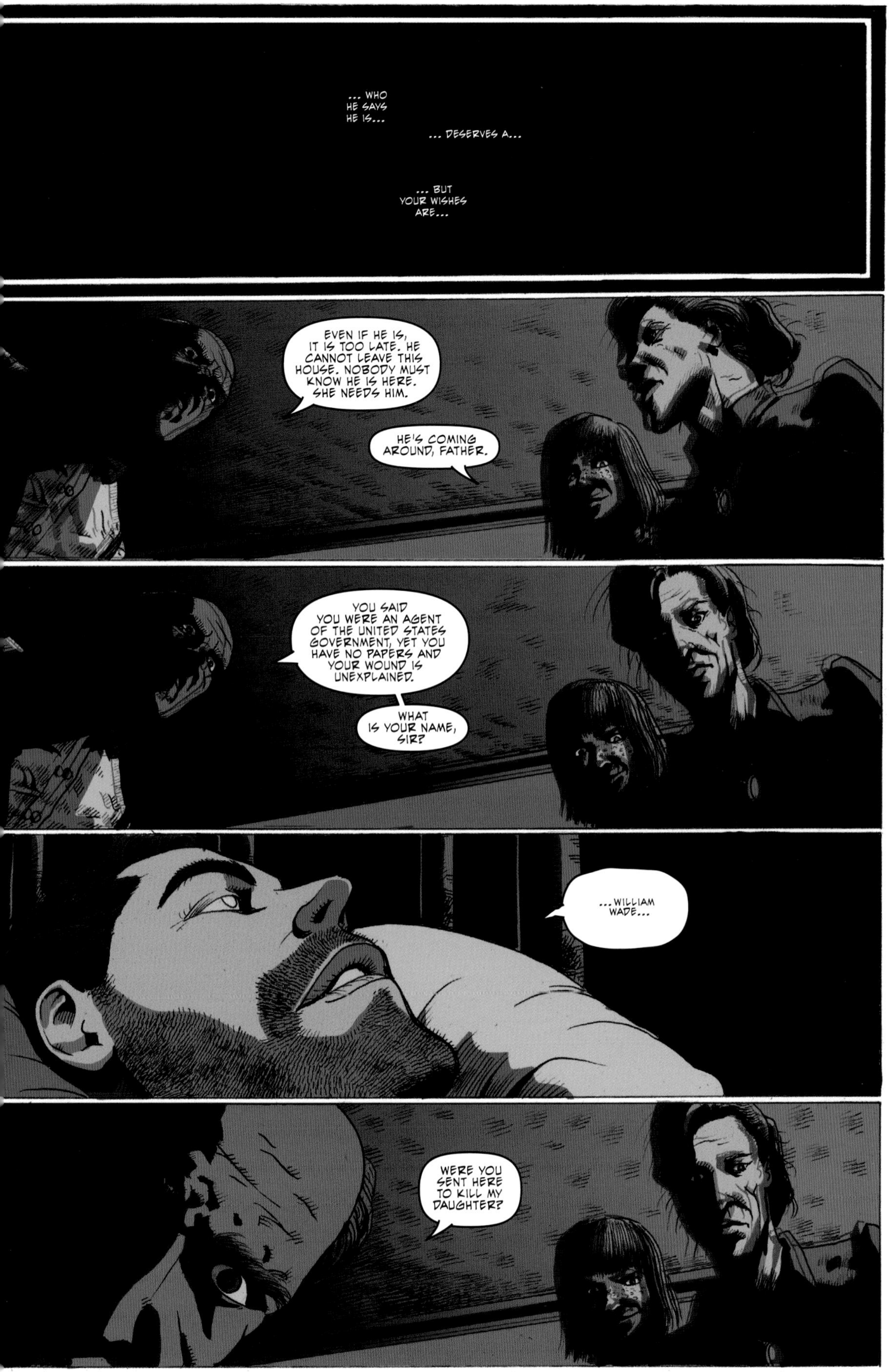
... WHO HE SAYS HE IS...
... DESERVES A...
... BUT YOUR WISHES ARE...
EVEN IF HE IS, IT IS TOO LATE. HE CANNOT LEAVE THIS HOUSE. NOBODY MUST KNOW HE IS HERE. SHE NEEDS HIM.
HE'S COMING AROUND, FATHER.
YOU SAID YOU WERE AN AGENT OF THE UNITED STATES GOVERNMENT, YET YOU HAVE NO PAPERS AND YOUR WOUND IS UNEXPLAINED.
WHAT IS YOUR NAME, SIR?
...WILLIAM WADE...
WERE YOU SENT HERE TO KILL MY DAUGHTER?

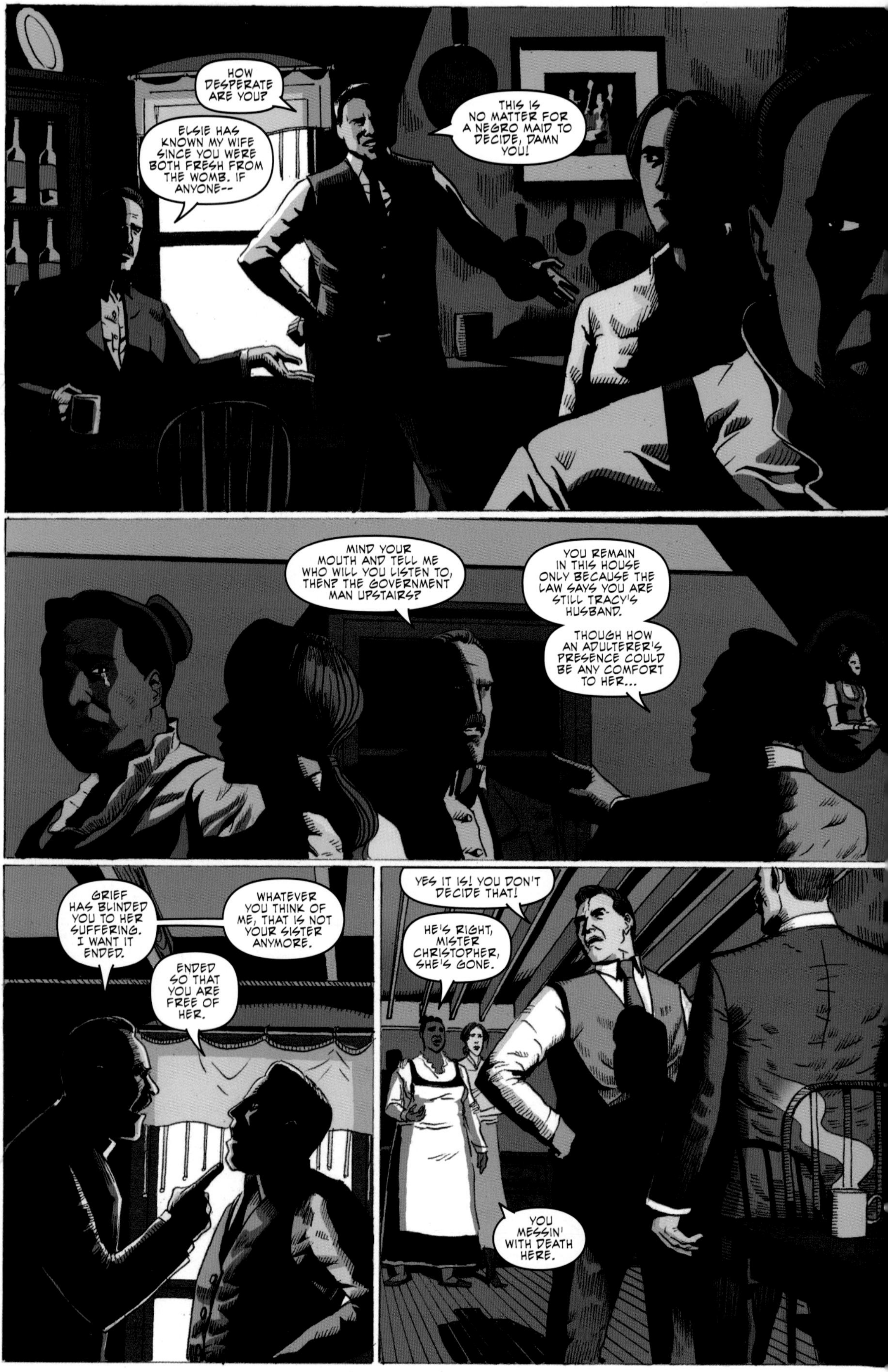
HOW DESPERATE ARE YOU?
ELSIE HAS KNOWN MY WIFE SINCE YOU WERE BOTH FRESH FROM THE WOMB. IF ANYONE--
THIS IS NO MATTER FOR A NEGRO MAID TO DECIDE, DAMN YOU!
MIND YOUR MOUTH AND TELL ME WHO WILL YOU LISTEN TO, THEN? THE GOVERNMENT MAN UPSTAIRS?
YOU REMAIN IN THIS HOUSE ONLY BECAUSE THE LAW SAYS YOU ARE STILL TRACY'S HUSBAND.
THOUGH HOW AN ADULTERER'S PRESENCE COULD BE ANY COMFORT TO HER...
GRIEF HAS BLINDED YOU TO HER SUFFERING. I WANT IT ENDED.
ENDED SO THAT YOU ARE FREE OF HER.
WHATEVER YOU THINK OF ME, THAT IS NOT YOUR SISTER ANYMORE.
YES IT IS! YOU DON'T DECIDE THAT!
HE'S RIGHT, MISTER CHRISTOPHER, SHE'S GONE.
YOU MESSIN' WITH DEATH HERE.

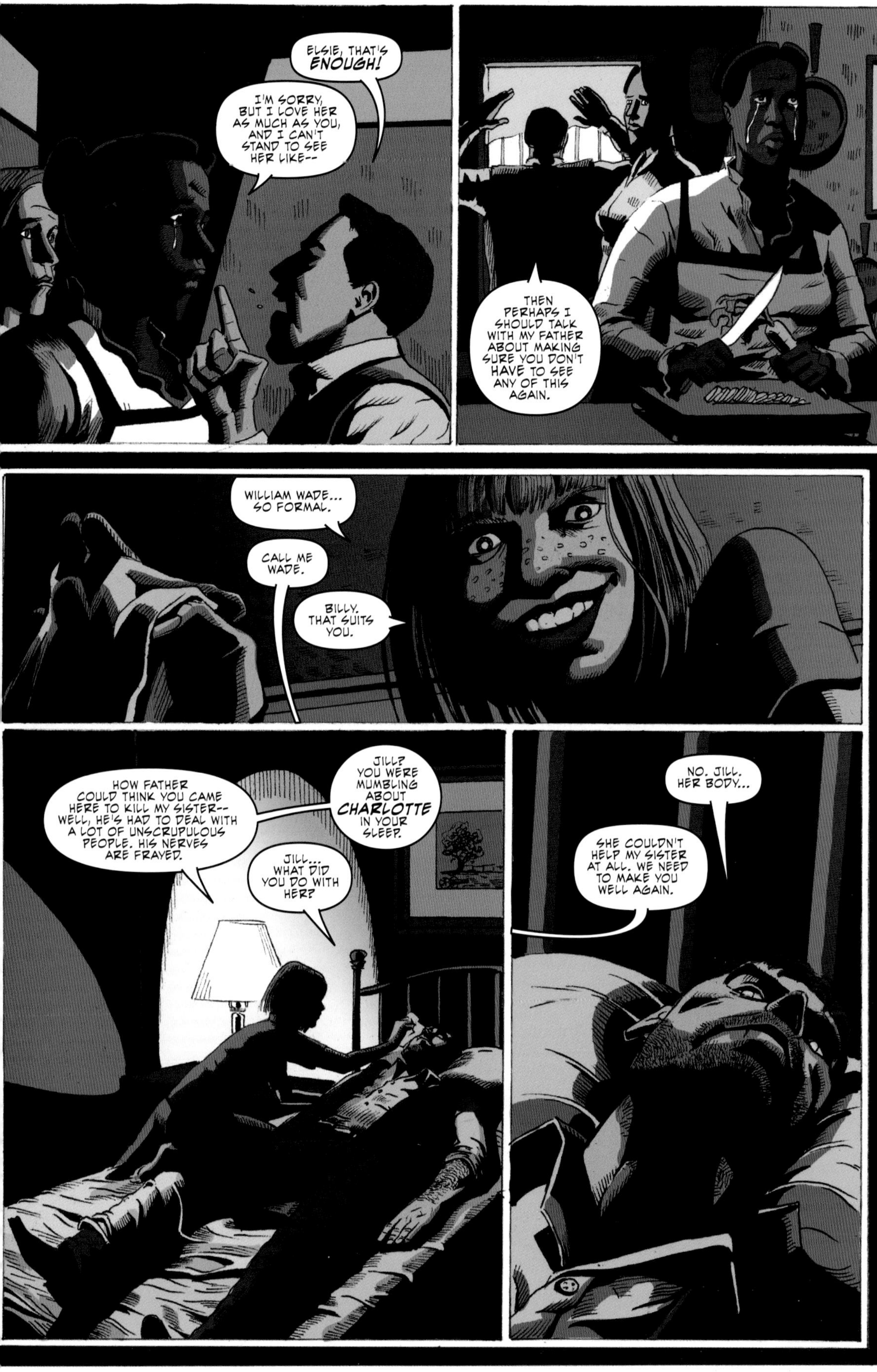

ELSIE, THAT'S ENOUGH!
I'M SORRY, BUT I LOVE HER AS MUCH AS YOU, AND I CAN'T STAND TO SEE HER LIKE--
THEN PERHAPS I SHOULD TALK WITH MY FATHER ABOUT MAKING SURE YOU DON'T HAVE TO SEE ANY OF THIS AGAIN.
WILLIAM WADE... SO FORMAL.
CALL ME WADE.
BILLY. THAT SUITS YOU.
HOW FATHER COULD THINK YOU CAME HERE TO KILL MY SISTER-- WELL, HE'S HAD TO DEAL WITH A LOT OF UNSCRUPULOUS PEOPLE. HIS NERVES ARE FRAYED.
JILL? YOU WERE MUMBLING ABOUT CHARLOTTE IN YOUR SLEEP?
JILL... WHAT DID YOU DO WITH HER?
NO. JILL. HER BODY...
SHE COULDN'T HELP MY SISTER AT ALL. WE NEED TO MAKE YOU WELL AGAIN.

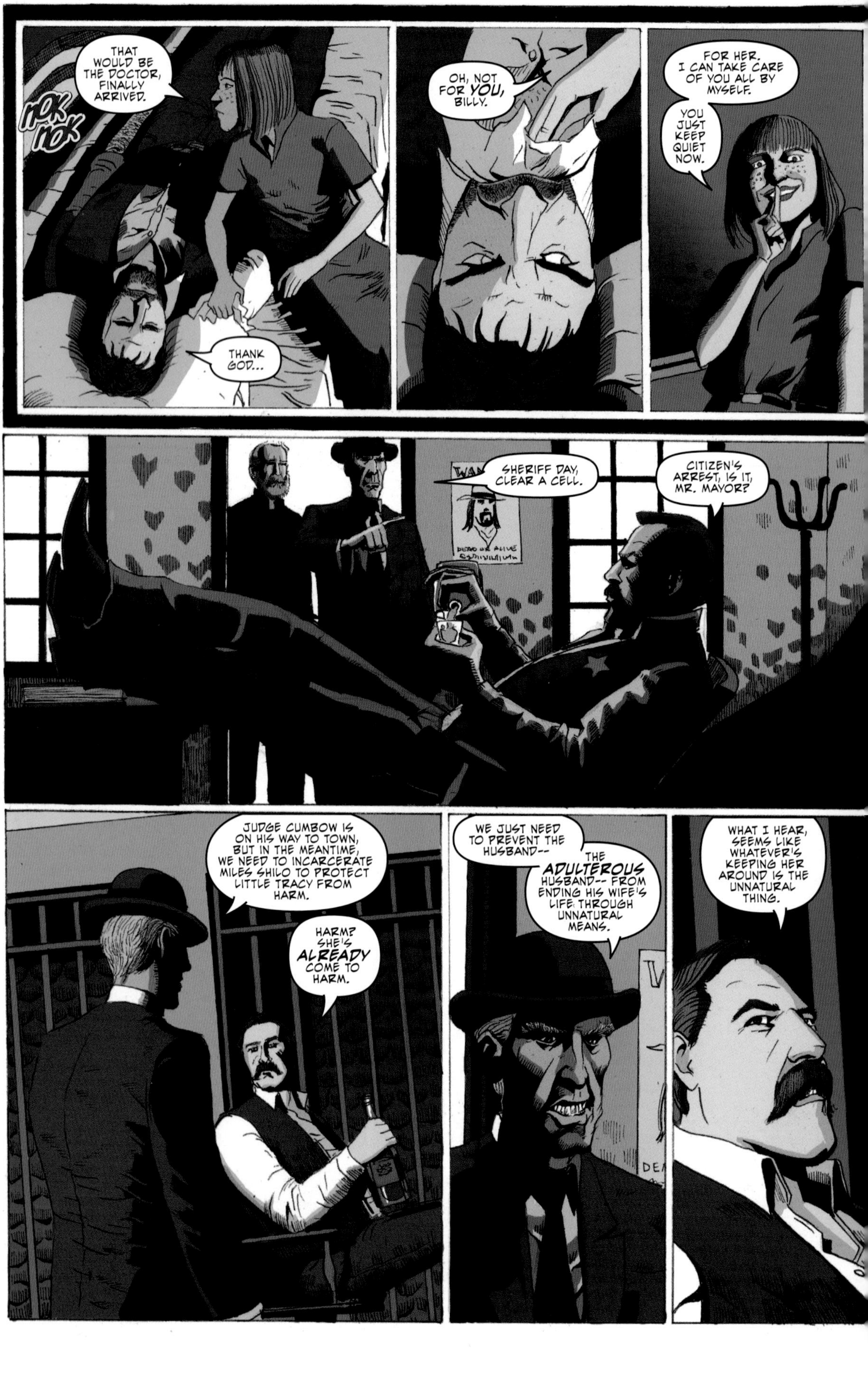

NOK NOK
THAT WOULD BE THE DOCTOR, FINALLY ARRIVED.
THANK GOD...
OH, NOT FOR YOU, BILLY.
FOR HER. I CAN TAKE CARE OF YOU ALL BY MYSELF.
YOU JUST KEEP QUIET NOW.
SHERIFF DAY, CLEAR A CELL.
CITIZEN'S ARREST, IS IT, MR. MAYOR?
DEAD OR ALIVE
JUDGE CUMBOW IS ON HIS WAY TO TOWN, BUT IN THE MEANTIME, WE NEED TO INCARCERATE MILES SHILO TO PROTECT LITTLE TRACY FROM HARM.
HARM? SHE'S ALREADY COME TO HARM.
WE JUST NEED TO PREVENT THE HUSBAND--
THE ADULTEROUS HUSBAND-- FROM ENDING HIS WIFE'S LIFE THROUGH UNNATURAL MEANS.
WHAT I HEAR, SEEMS LIKE WHATEVER'S KEEPING HER AROUND IS THE UNNATURAL THING.

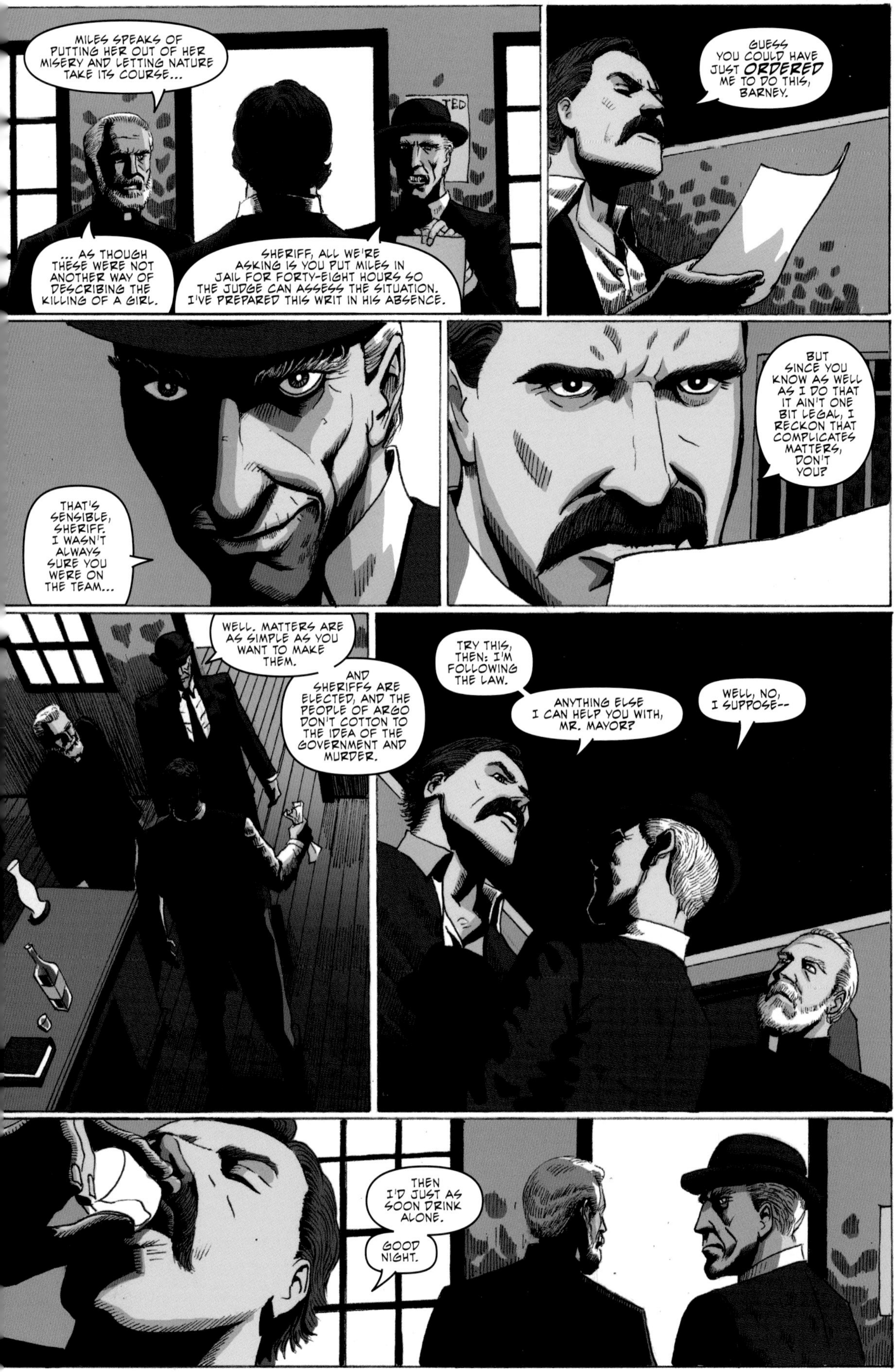
MILES SPEAKS OF PUTTING HER OUT OF HER MISERY AND LETTING NATURE TAKE ITS COURSE...
... AS THOUGH THESE WERE NOT ANOTHER WAY OF DESCRIBING THE KILLING OF A GIRL.
SHERIFF, ALL WE'RE ASKING IS YOU PUT MILES IN JAIL FOR FORTY-EIGHT HOURS SO THE JUDGE CAN ASSESS THE SITUATION. I'VE PREPARED THIS WRIT IN HIS ABSENCE.
GUESS YOU COULD HAVE JUST ORDERED ME TO DO THIS, BARNEY.
THAT'S SENSIBLE, SHERIFF. I WASN'T ALWAYS SURE YOU WERE ON THE TEAM...
BUT SINCE YOU KNOW AS WELL AS I DO THAT IT AIN'T ONE BIT LEGAL, I RECKON THAT COMPLICATES MATTERS, DON'T YOU?
WELL. MATTERS ARE AS SIMPLE AS YOU WANT TO MAKE THEM.
AND SHERIFFS ARE ELECTED, AND THE PEOPLE OF ARGO DON'T COTTON TO THE IDEA OF THE GOVERNMENT AND MURDER.
TRY THIS, THEN: I'M FOLLOWING THE LAW.
ANYTHING ELSE I CAN HELP YOU WITH, MR. MAYOR?
WELL, NO, I SUPPOSE--
THEN I'D JUST AS SOON DRINK ALONE.
GOOD NIGHT.

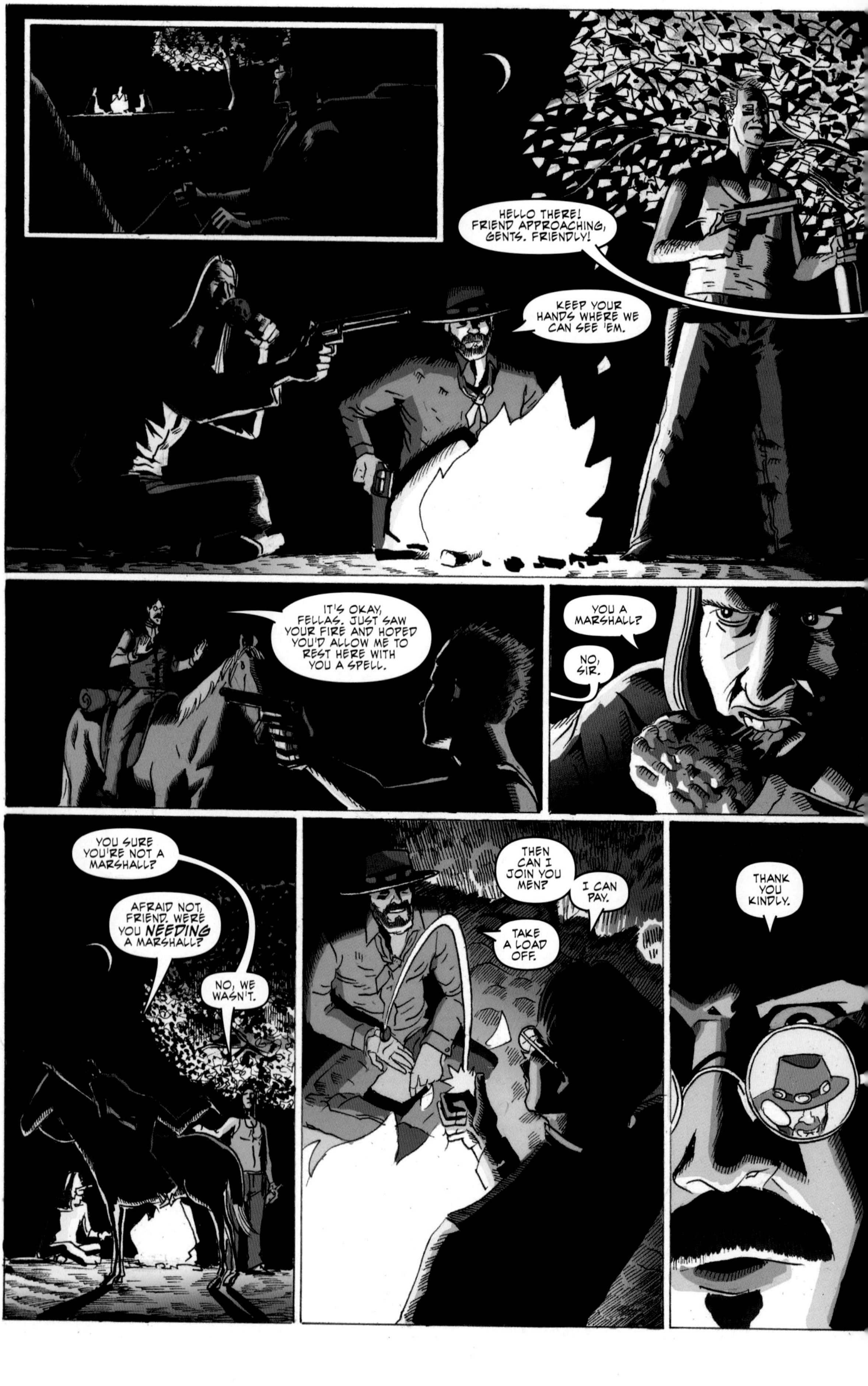
HELLO THERE! FRIEND APPROACHING, GENTS. FRIENDLY!
KEEP YOUR HANDS WHERE WE CAN SEE 'EM.
IT'S OKAY, FELLAS. JUST SAW YOUR FIRE AND HOPED YOU'D ALLOW ME TO REST HERE WITH YOU A SPELL.
YOU A MARSHALL?
NO, SIR.
YOU SURE YOU'RE NOT A MARSHALL?
AFRAID NOT, FRIEND. WERE YOU NEEDING A MARSHALL?
NO, WE WASN'T.
THEN CAN I JOIN YOU MEN?
I CAN PAY.
TAKE A LOAD OFF.
THANK YOU KINDLY.

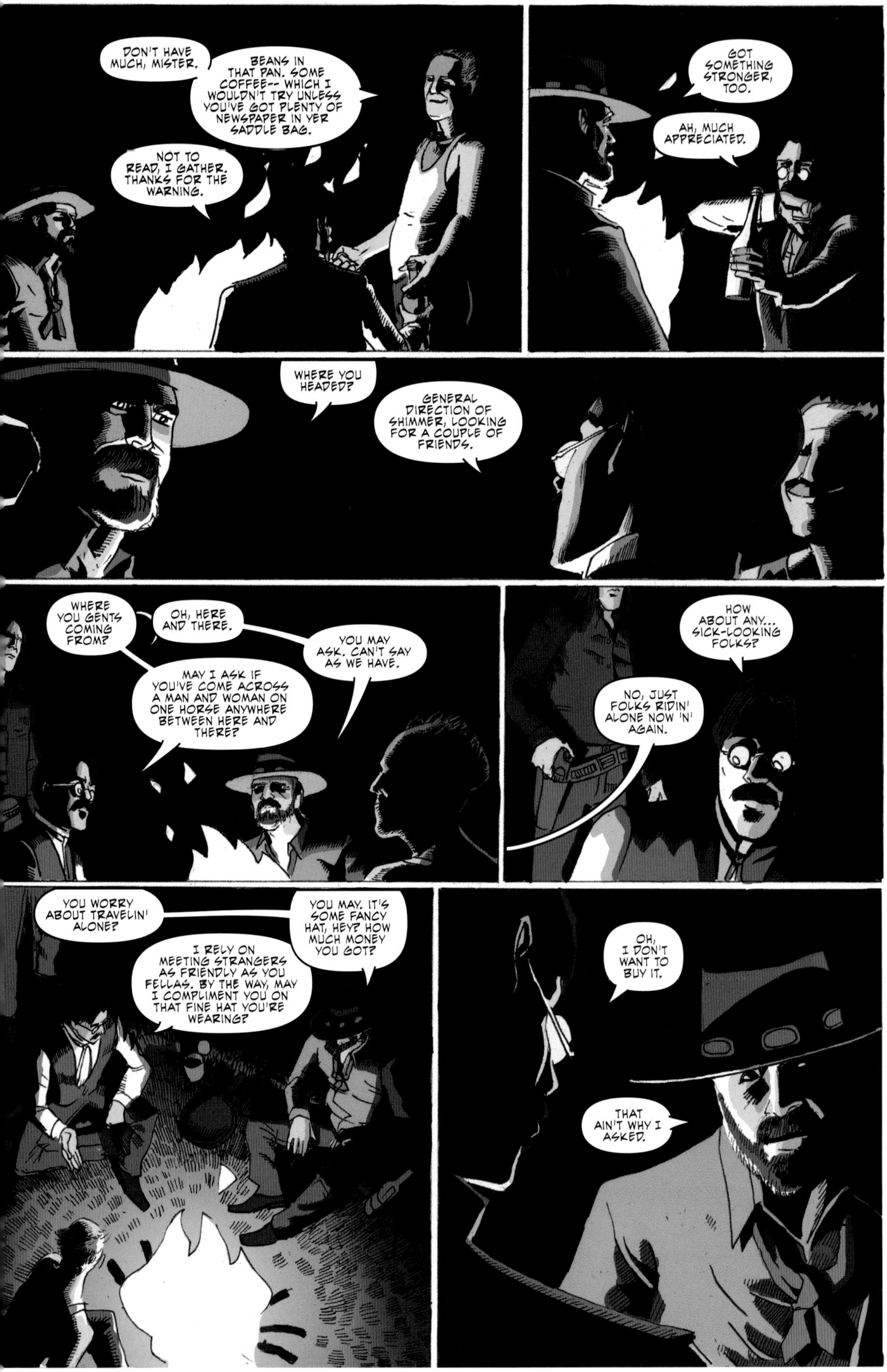
DON'T HAVE MUCH, MISTER.
BEANS IN THAT PAN. SOME COFFEE-- WHICH I WOULDN'T TRY UNLESS YOU'VE GOT PLENTY OF NEWSPAPER IN YER SADDLE BAG.
NOT TO READ, I GATHER. THANKS FOR THE WARNING.
GOT SOMETHING STRONGER, TOO.
AH, MUCH APPRECIATED.
WHERE YOU HEADED?
GENERAL DIRECTION OF SHIMMER, LOOKING FOR A COUPLE OF FRIENDS.
WHERE YOU GENTS COMING FROM?
OH, HERE AND THERE.
YOU MAY ASK. CAN'T SAY AS WE HAVE.
MAY I ASK IF YOU'VE COME ACROSS A MAN AND WOMAN ON ONE HORSE ANYWHERE BETWEEN HERE AND THERE?
HOW ABOUT ANY... SICK-LOOKING FOLKS?
NO, JUST FOLKS RIDIN' ALONE NOW 'N' AGAIN.
YOU WORRY ABOUT TRAVELIN' ALONE?
I RELY ON MEETING STRANGERS AS FRIENDLY AS YOU FELLAS. BY THE WAY, MAY I COMPLIMENT YOU ON THAT FINE HAT YOU'RE WEARING?
YOU MAY. IT'S SOME FANCY HAT, HEY? HOW MUCH MONEY YOU GOT?
OH, I DON'T WANT TO BUY IT.
THAT AIN'T WHY I ASKED.

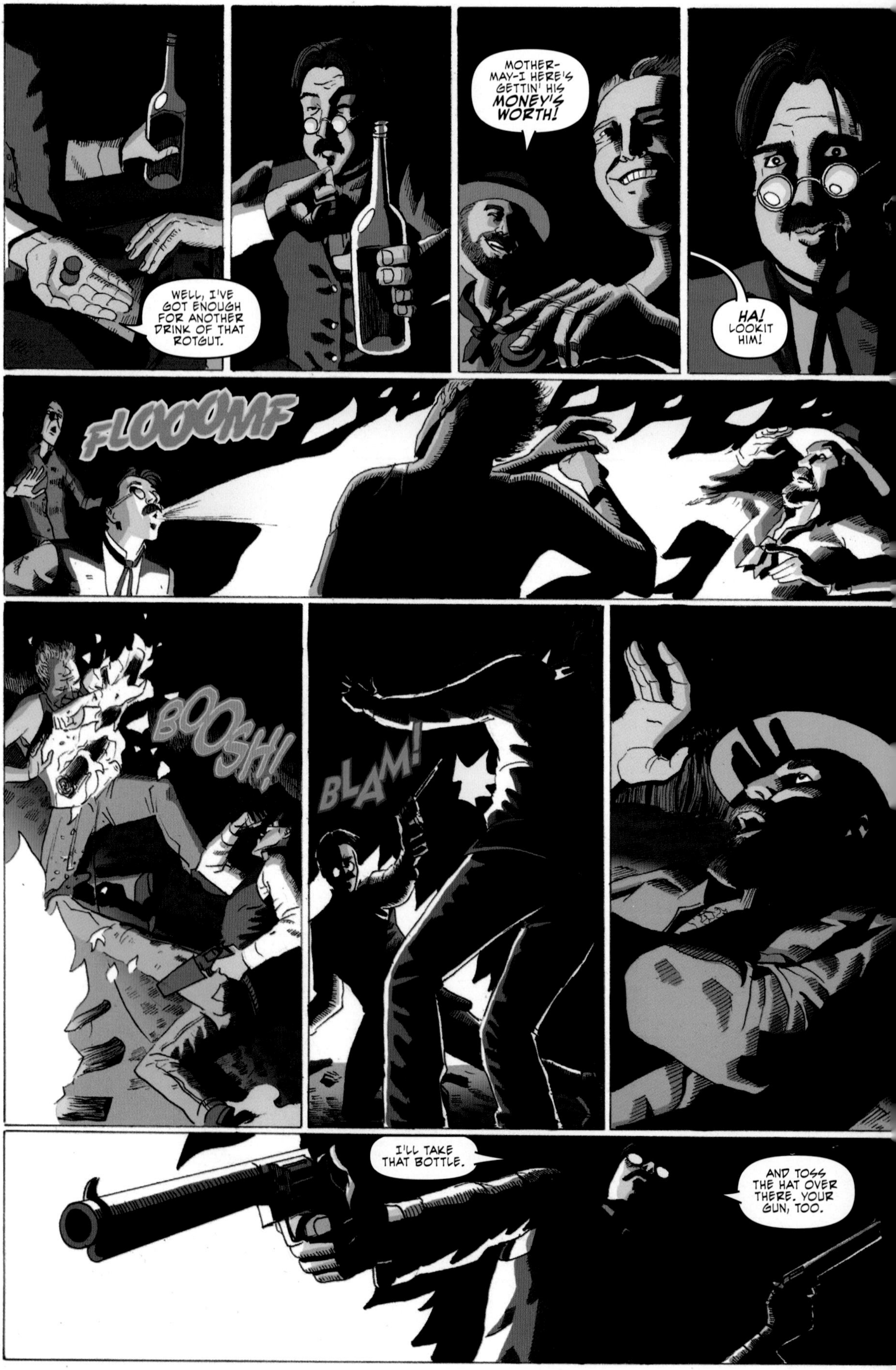
WELL, I'VE GOT ENOUGH FOR ANOTHER DRINK OF THAT ROTGUT.
MOTHER-MAY-I HERE'S GETTIN' HIS MONEY'S WORTH!
HA! LOOKIT HIM!
FLOOOMF
BOOSH!
BLAM!
I'LL TAKE THAT BOTTLE.
AND TOSS THE HAT OVER THERE. YOUR GUN, TOO.

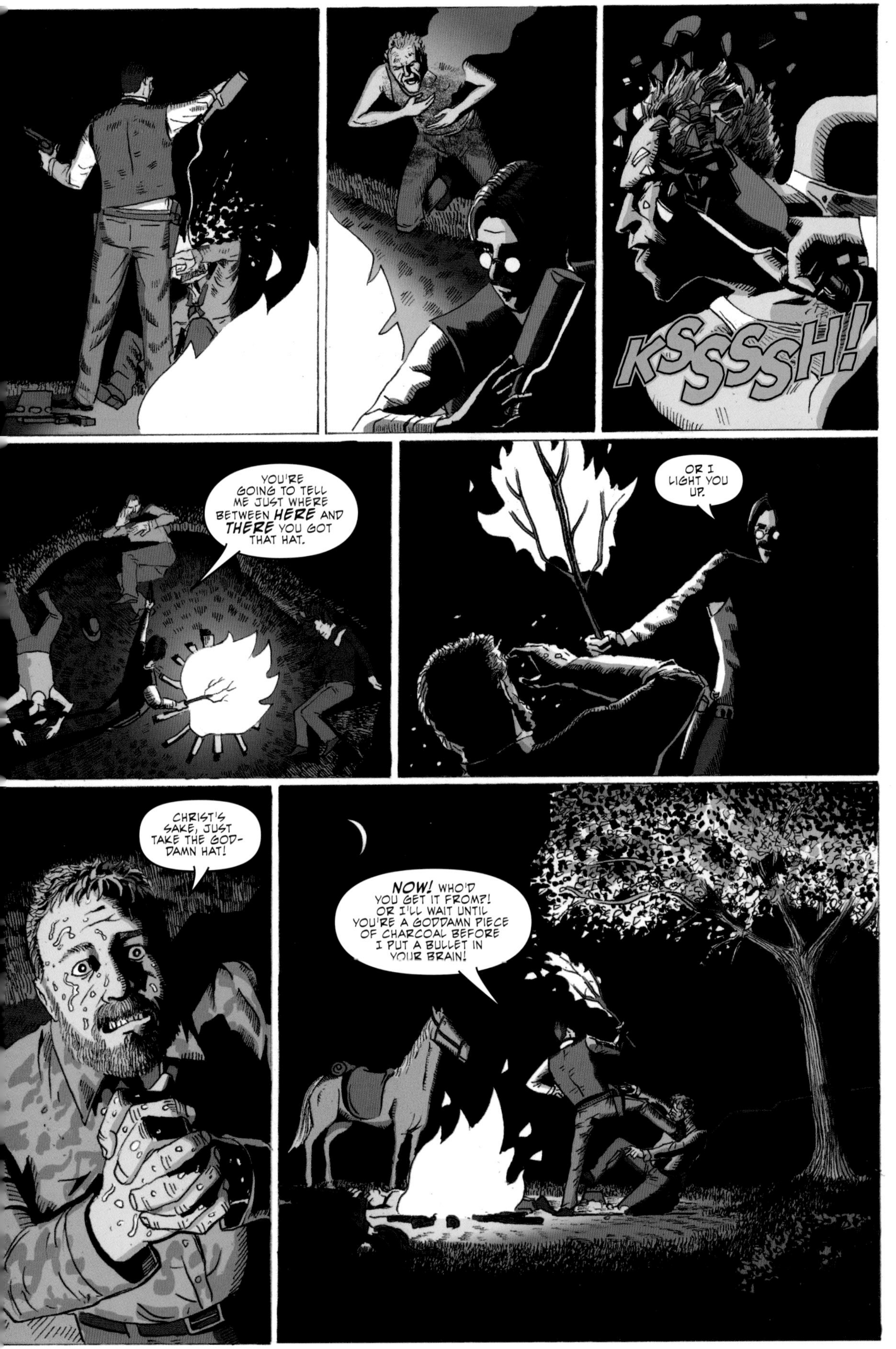
KSSSSH!
YOU'RE GOING TO TELL ME JUST WHERE BETWEEN HERE AND THERE YOU GOT THAT HAT.
OR I LIGHT YOU UP.
CHRIST'S SAKE, JUST TAKE THE GOD-DAMN HAT!
NOW! WHO'D YOU GET IT FROM?! OR I'LL WAIT UNTIL YOU'RE A GODDAMN PIECE OF CHARCOAL BEFORE I PUT A BULLET IN YOUR BRAIN!

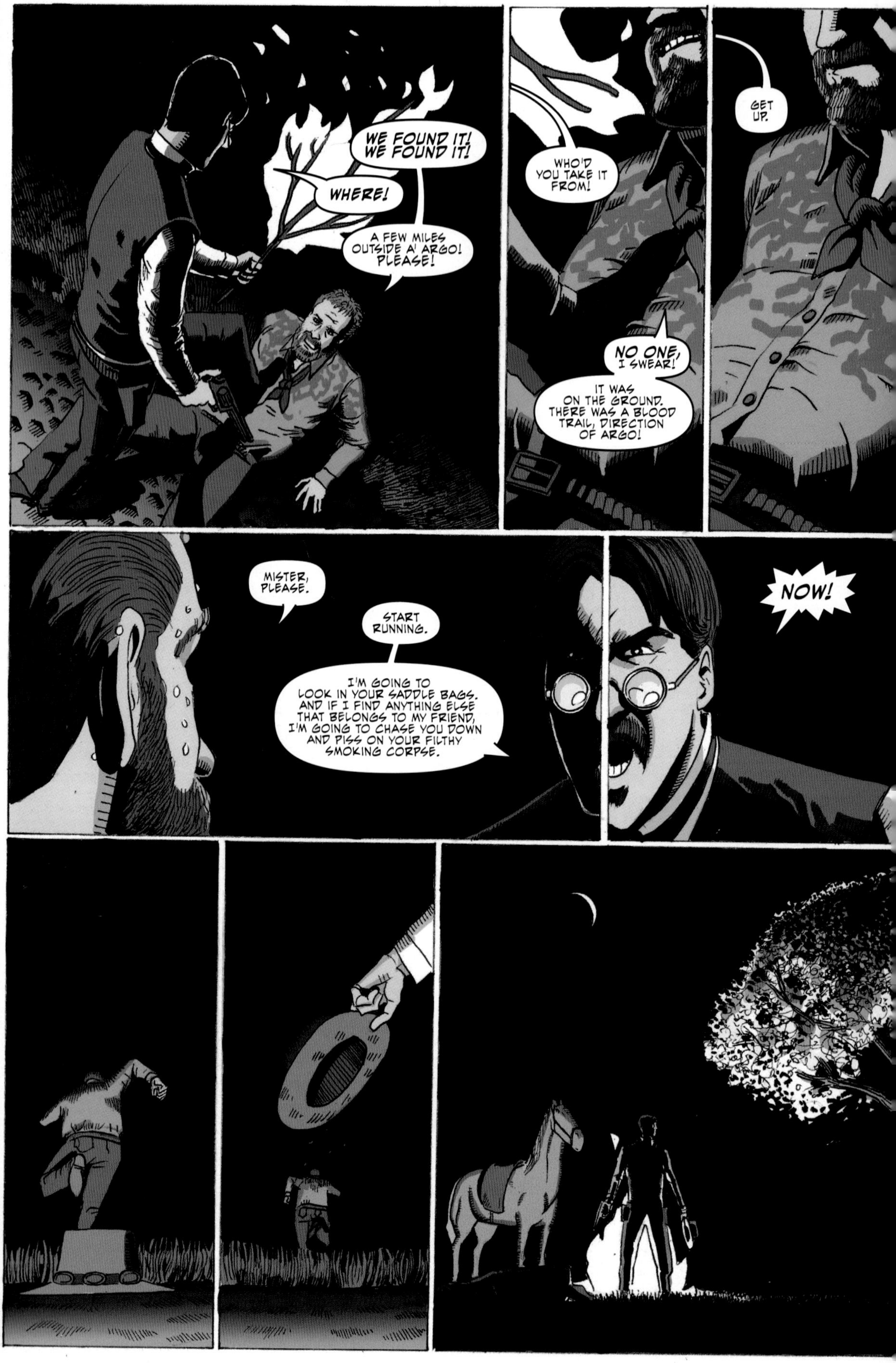
WE FOUND IT! WE FOUND IT!
WHERE!
A FEW MILES OUTSIDE A' ARGO! PLEASE!
WHO'D YOU TAKE IT FROM!
NO ONE, I SWEAR!
IT WAS ON THE GROUND. THERE WAS A BLOOD TRAIL, DIRECTION OF ARGO!
GET UP.
MISTER, PLEASE.
START RUNNING.
I'M GOING TO LOOK IN YOUR SADDLE BAGS. AND IF I FIND ANYTHING ELSE THAT BELONGS TO MY FRIEND, I'M GOING TO CHASE YOU DOWN AND PISS ON YOUR FILTHY SMOKING CORPSE.
NOW!

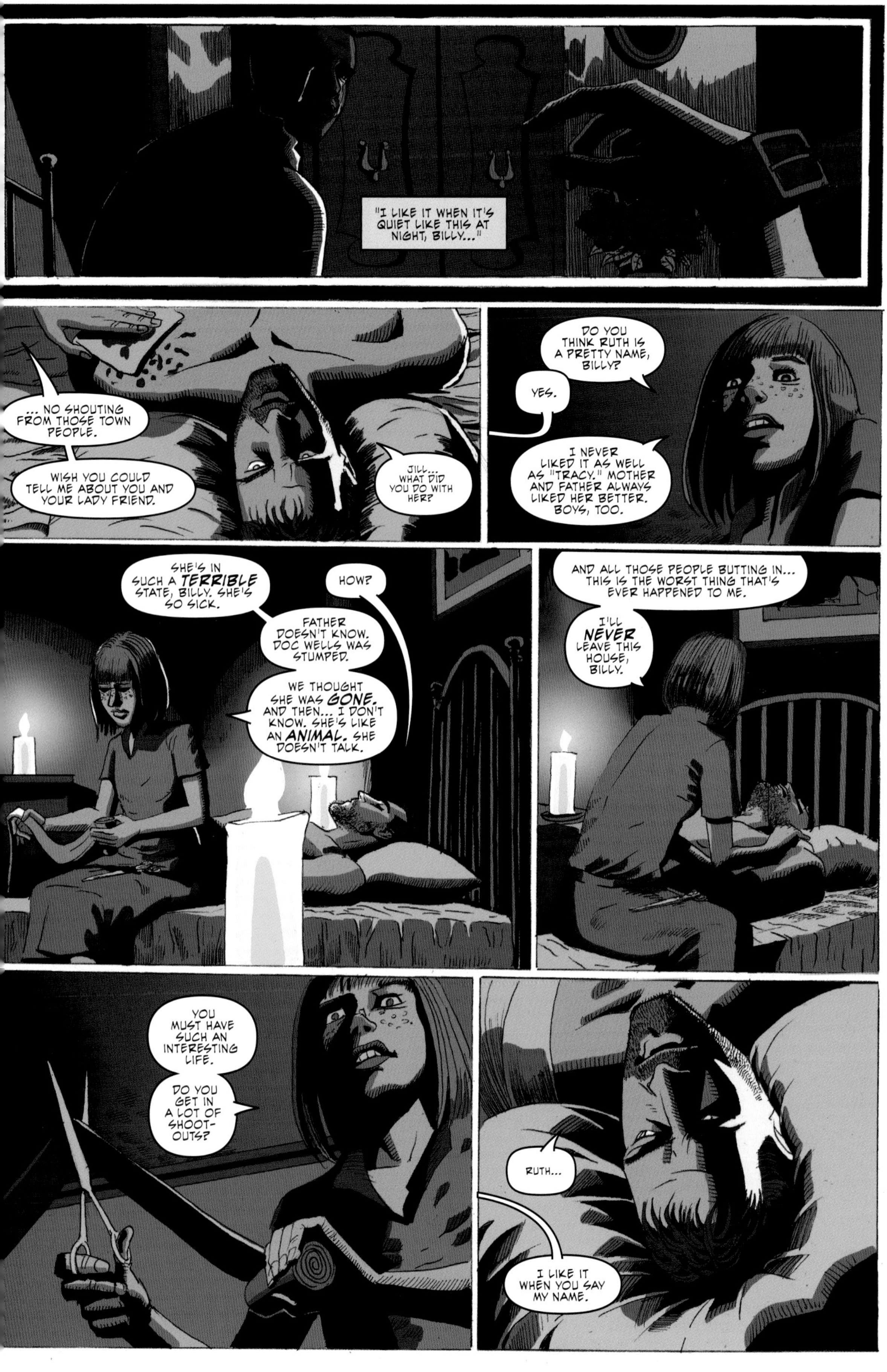
"I LIKE IT WHEN IT'S QUIET LIKE THIS AT NIGHT, BILLY..."
... NO SHOUTING FROM THOSE TOWN PEOPLE.
WISH YOU COULD TELL ME ABOUT YOU AND YOUR LADY FRIEND.
JILL... WHAT DID YOU DO WITH HER?
DO YOU THINK RUTH IS A PRETTY NAME, BILLY?
YES.
I NEVER LIKED IT AS WELL AS "TRACY." MOTHER AND FATHER ALWAYS LIKED HER BETTER. BOYS, TOO.
SHE'S IN SUCH A TERRIBLE STATE, BILLY. SHE'S SO SICK.
HOW?
FATHER DOESN'T KNOW. DOC WELLS WAS STUMPED.
WE THOUGHT SHE WAS GONE. AND THEN... I DON'T KNOW. SHE'S LIKE AN ANIMAL. SHE DOESN'T TALK.
AND ALL THOSE PEOPLE BUTTING IN... THIS IS THE WORST THING THAT'S EVER HAPPENED TO ME.
I'LL NEVER LEAVE THIS HOUSE, BILLY.
YOU MUST HAVE SUCH AN INTERESTING LIFE.
DO YOU GET IN A LOT OF SHOOT-OUTS?
RUTH...
I LIKE IT WHEN YOU SAY MY NAME.

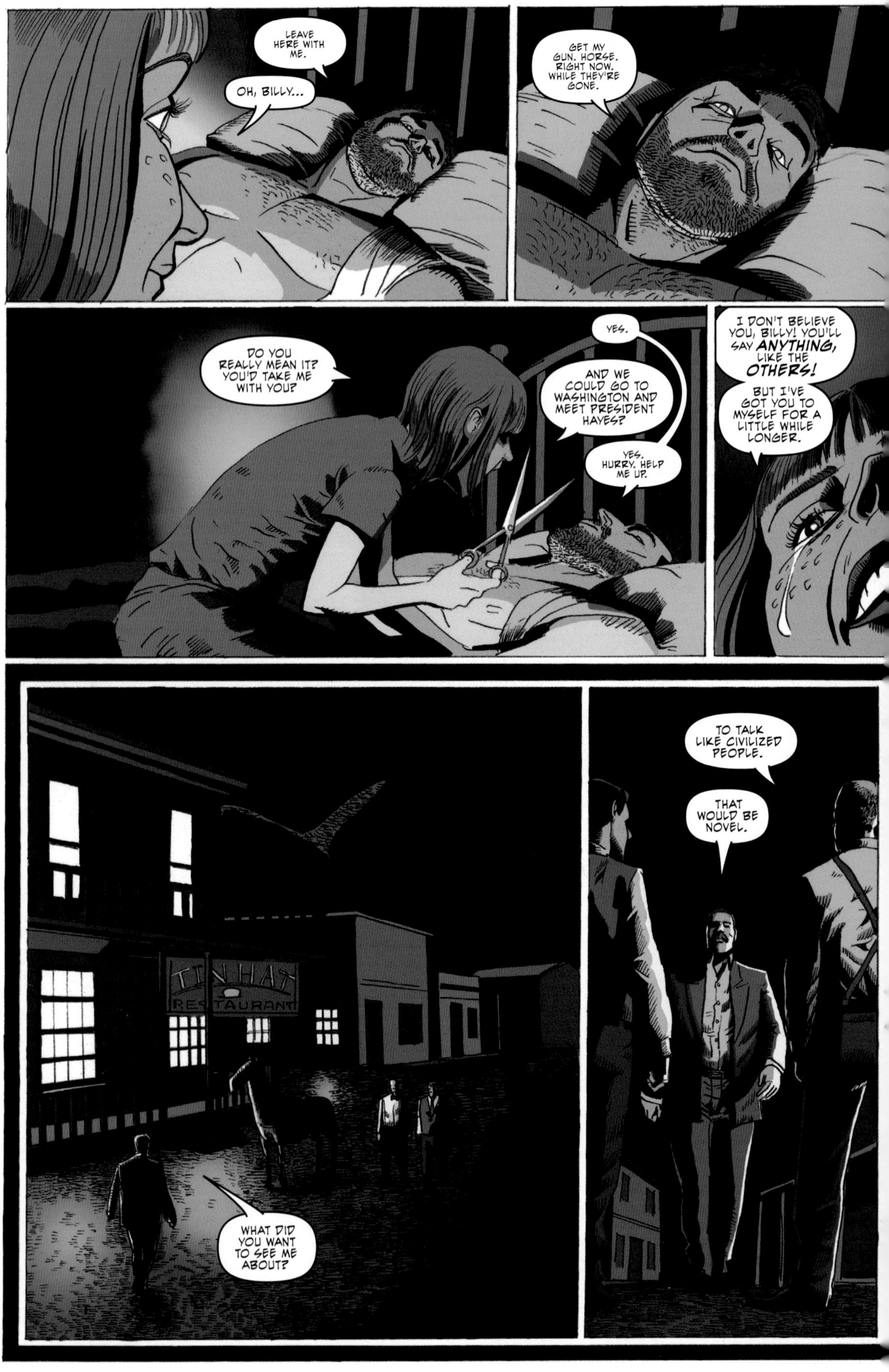
LEAVE HERE WITH ME.
OH, BILLY...
GET MY GUN. HORSE. RIGHT NOW. WHILE THEY'RE GONE.
DO YOU REALLY MEAN IT? YOU'D TAKE ME WITH YOU?
YES.
AND WE COULD GO TO WASHINGTON AND MEET PRESIDENT HAYES?
YES. HURRY. HELP ME UP.
I DON'T BELIEVE YOU, BILLY! YOU'LL SAY **ANYTHING,** LIKE THE **OTHERS!**
BUT I'VE GOT YOU TO MYSELF FOR A LITTLE WHILE LONGER.
TIN HAT RESTAURANT
WHAT DID YOU WANT TO SEE ME ABOUT?
TO TALK LIKE CIVILIZED PEOPLE.
THAT WOULD BE NOVEL.

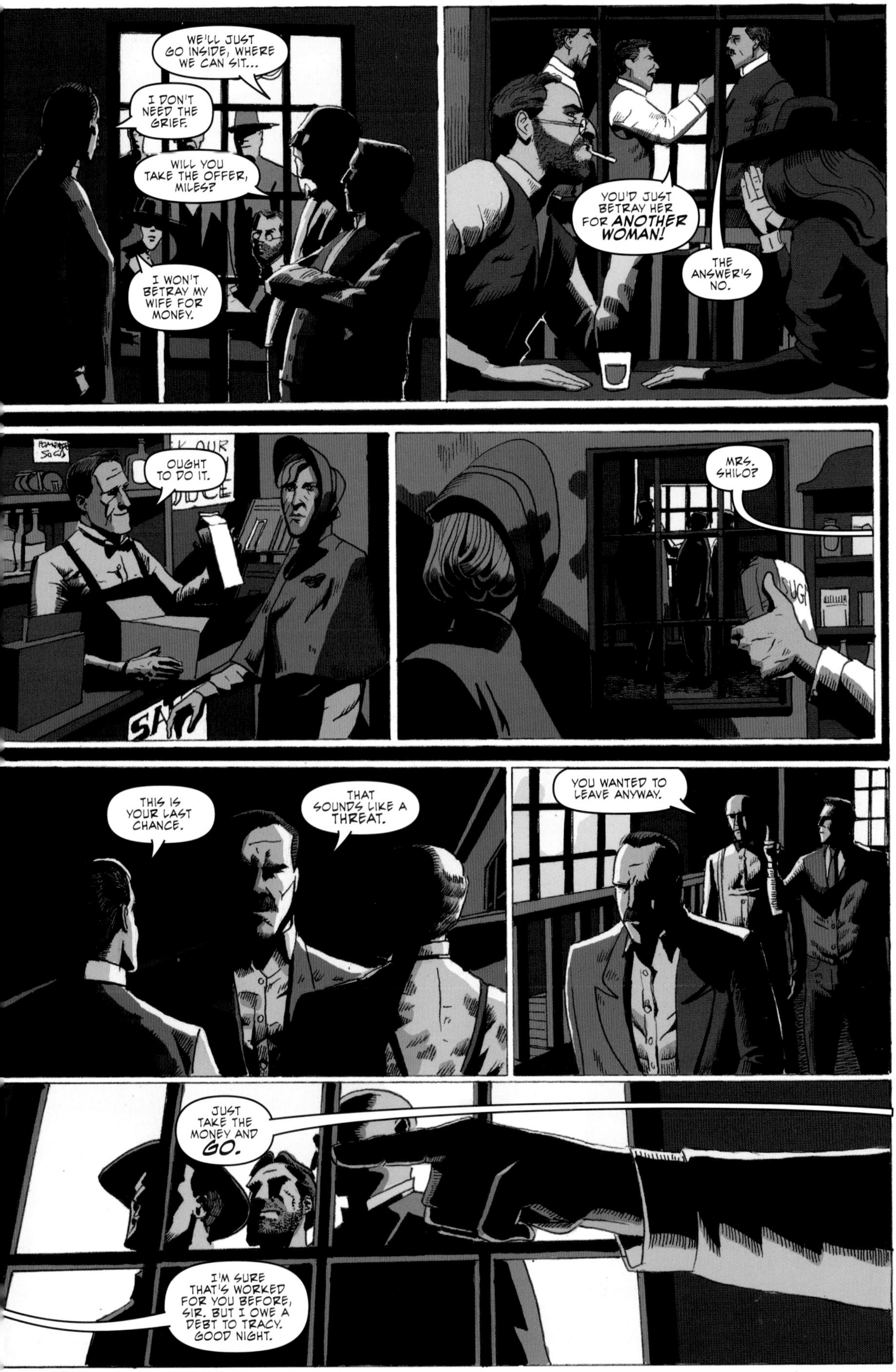
WE'LL JUST GO INSIDE, WHERE WE CAN SIT...
I DON'T NEED THE GRIEF.
WILL YOU TAKE THE OFFER, MILES?
I WON'T BETRAY MY WIFE FOR MONEY.
YOU'D JUST BETRAY HER FOR ANOTHER WOMAN!
THE ANSWER'S NO.
OUGHT TO DO IT.
MRS. SHILO?
THIS IS YOUR LAST CHANCE.
THAT SOUNDS LIKE A THREAT.
YOU WANTED TO LEAVE ANYWAY.
JUST TAKE THE MONEY AND GO.
I'M SURE THAT'S WORKED FOR YOU BEFORE, SIR. BUT I OWE A DEBT TO TRACY. GOOD NIGHT.

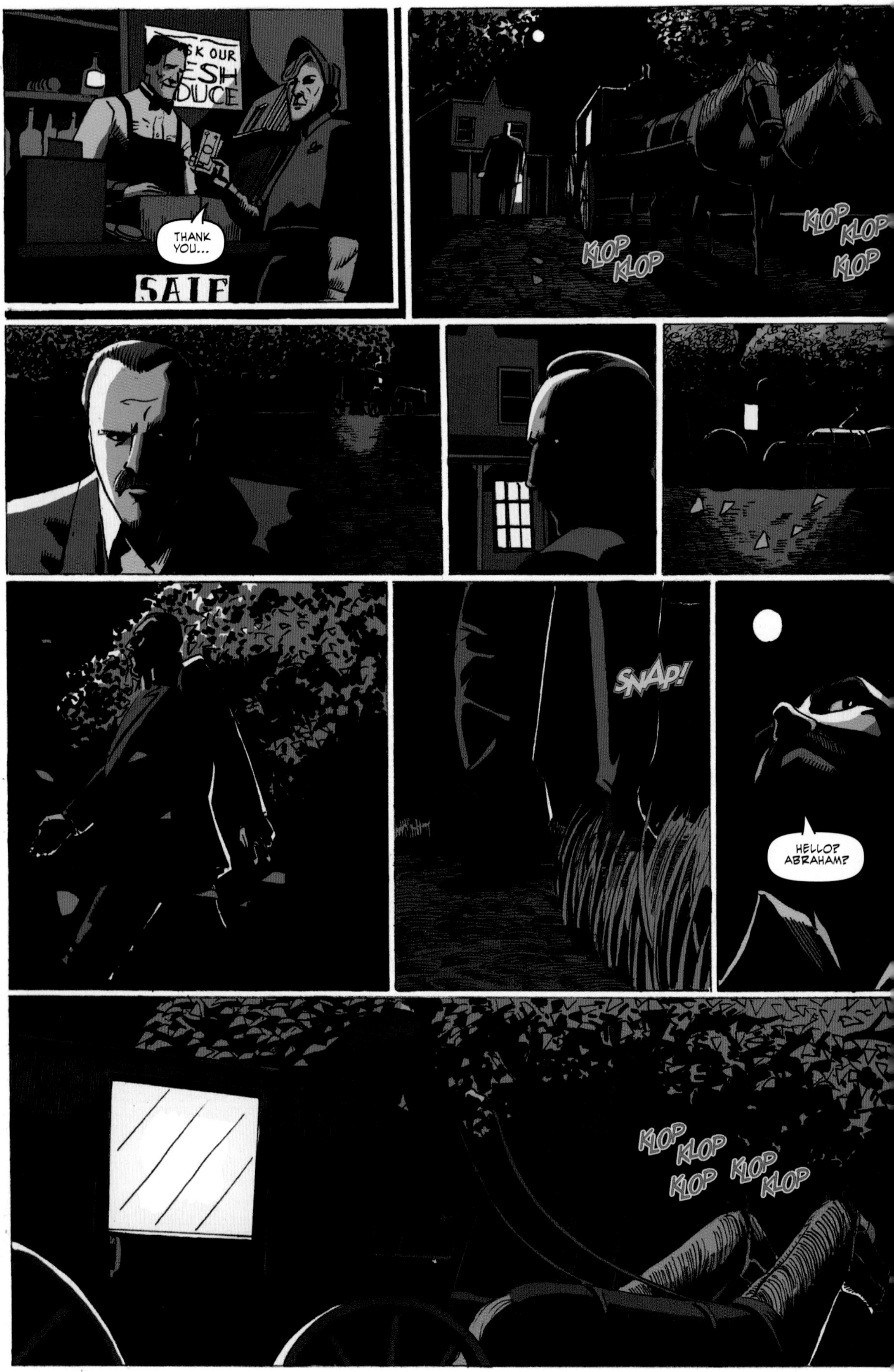
THANK YOU...
KLOP KLOP
KLOP KLOP KLOP
SNAP!
HELLO? ABRAHAM?
KLOP KLOP KLOP KLOP KLOP

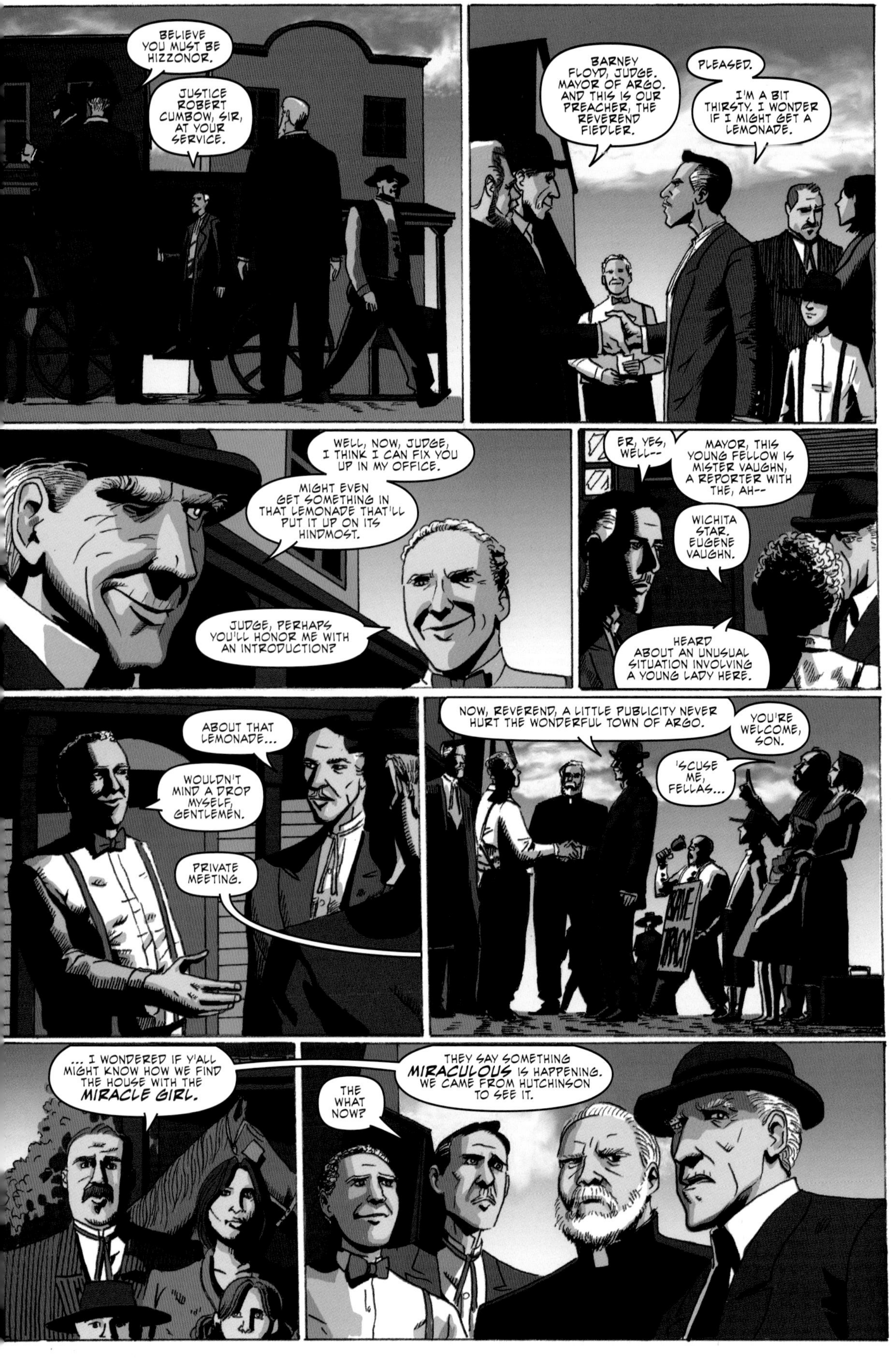
BELIEVE YOU MUST BE HIZZONOR.
JUSTICE ROBERT CUMBOW, SIR, AT YOUR SERVICE.
BARNEY FLOYD, JUDGE. MAYOR OF ARGO. AND THIS IS OUR PREACHER, THE REVEREND FIEDLER.
PLEASED.
I'M A BIT THIRSTY. I WONDER IF I MIGHT GET A LEMONADE.
WELL, NOW, JUDGE, I THINK I CAN FIX YOU UP IN MY OFFICE.
MIGHT EVEN GET SOMETHING IN THAT LEMONADE THAT'LL PUT IT UP ON ITS HINDMOST.
JUDGE, PERHAPS YOU'LL HONOR ME WITH AN INTRODUCTION?
ER, YES, WELL--
MAYOR, THIS YOUNG FELLOW IS MISTER VAUGHN, A REPORTER WITH THE, AH--
WICHITA STAR. EUGENE VAUGHN.
HEARD ABOUT AN UNUSUAL SITUATION INVOLVING A YOUNG LADY HERE.
ABOUT THAT LEMONADE...
WOULDN'T MIND A DROP MYSELF, GENTLEMEN.
PRIVATE MEETING.
NOW, REVEREND, A LITTLE PUBLICITY NEVER HURT THE WONDERFUL TOWN OF ARGO.
YOU'RE WELCOME, SON.
'SCUSE ME, FELLAS...
... I WONDERED IF Y'ALL MIGHT KNOW HOW WE FIND THE HOUSE WITH THE MIRACLE GIRL.
THEY SAY SOMETHING MIRACULOUS IS HAPPENING. WE CAME FROM HUTCHINSON TO SEE IT.
THE WHAT NOW?

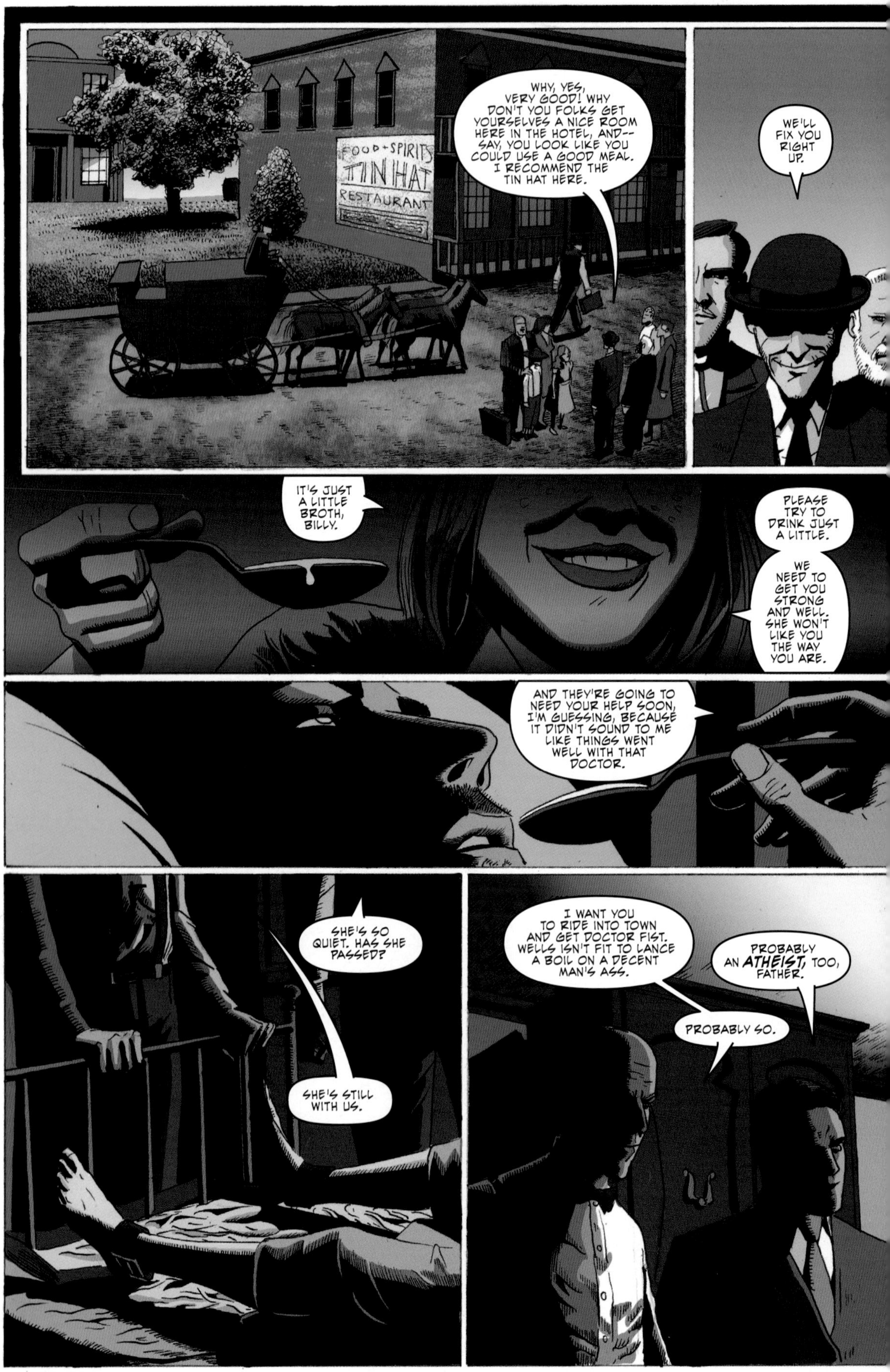

WHY, YES, VERY GOOD! WHY DON'T YOU FOLKS GET YOURSELVES A NICE ROOM HERE IN THE HOTEL, AND-- SAY, YOU LOOK LIKE YOU COULD USE A GOOD MEAL. I RECOMMEND THE TIN HAT HERE.
FOOD + SPIRITS
TIN HAT
RESTAURANT
WE'LL FIX YOU RIGHT UP.
IT'S JUST A LITTLE BROTH, BILLY.
PLEASE TRY TO DRINK JUST A LITTLE.
WE NEED TO GET YOU STRONG AND WELL. SHE WON'T LIKE YOU THE WAY YOU ARE.
AND THEY'RE GOING TO NEED YOUR HELP SOON, I'M GUESSING, BECAUSE IT DIDN'T SOUND TO ME LIKE THINGS WENT WELL WITH THAT DOCTOR.
SHE'S SO QUIET. HAS SHE PASSED?
SHE'S STILL WITH US.
I WANT YOU TO RIDE INTO TOWN AND GET DOCTOR FIST. WELLS ISN'T FIT TO LANCE A BOIL ON A DECENT MAN'S ASS.
PROBABLY AN ATHEIST, TOO, FATHER.
PROBABLY SO.

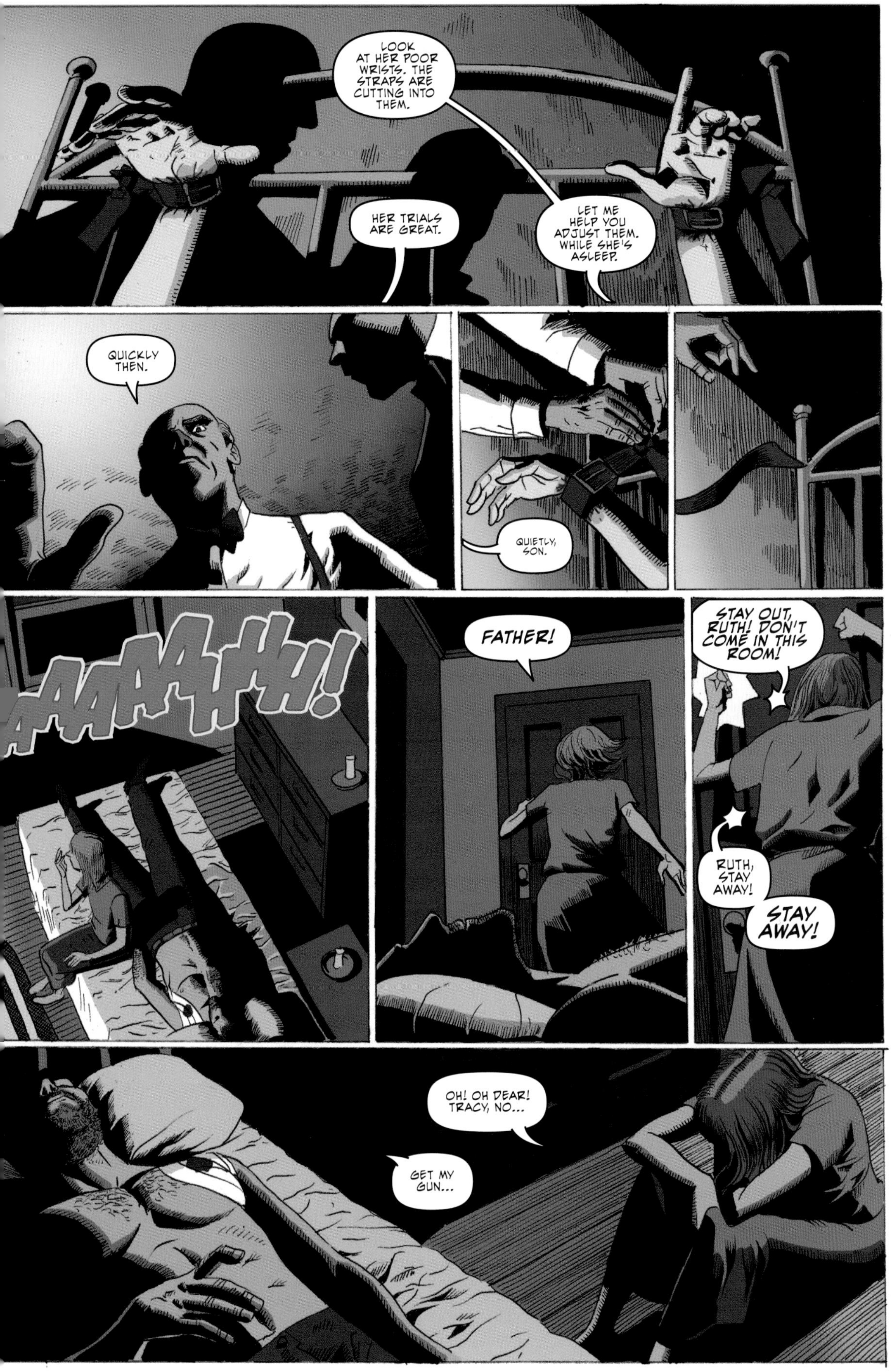
LOOK AT HER POOR WRISTS. THE STRAPS ARE CUTTING INTO THEM.
HER TRIALS ARE GREAT.
LET ME HELP YOU ADJUST THEM. WHILE SHE'S ASLEEP.
QUICKLY THEN.
QUIETLY, SON.
AAAAAAHHH!
FATHER!
STAY OUT, RUTH! DON'T COME IN THIS ROOM!
RUTH, STAY AWAY!
STAY AWAY!
OH! OH DEAR! TRACY, NO...
GET MY GUN...

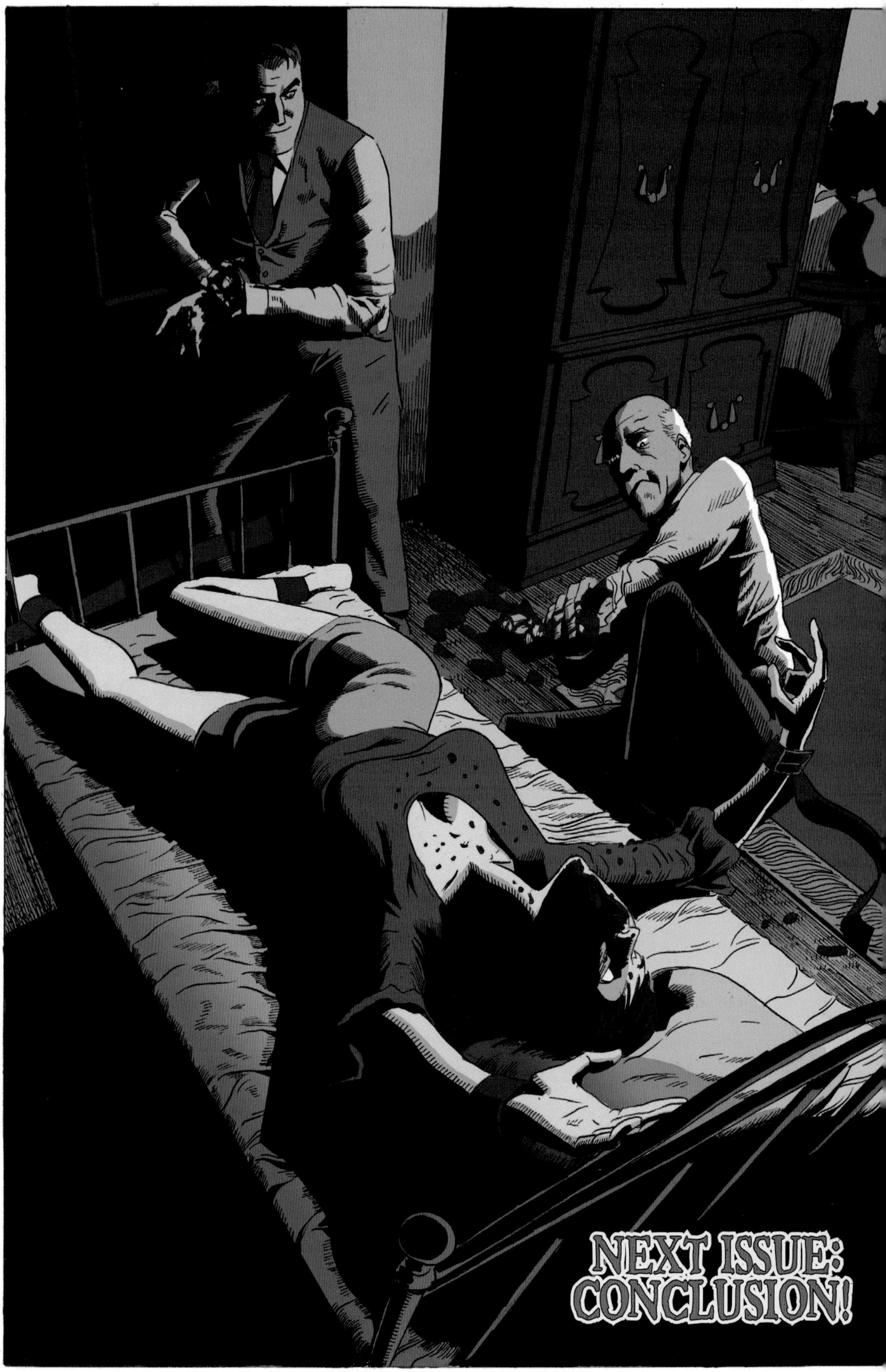
NEXT ISSUE:
CONCLUSION!

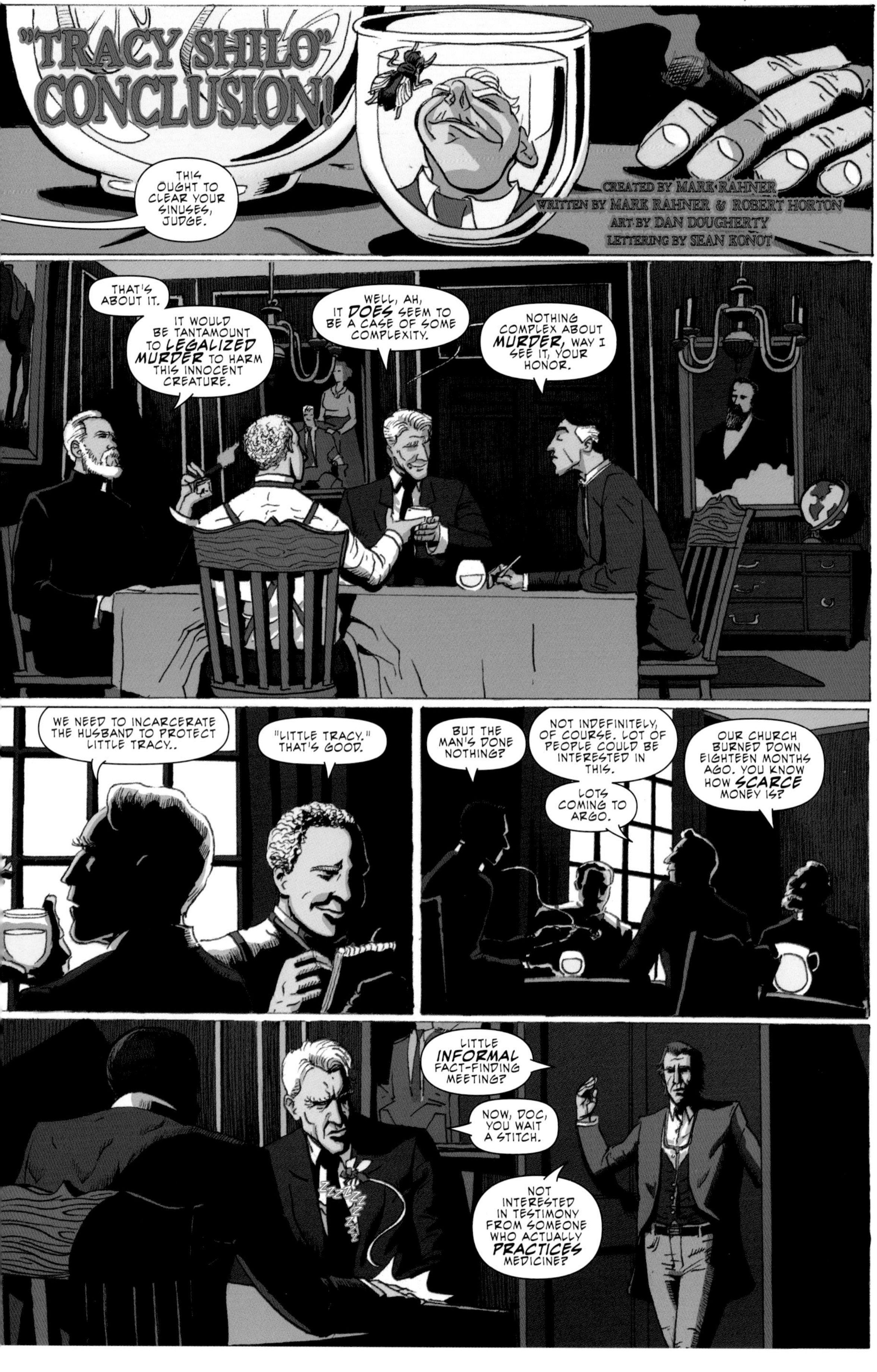
"TRACY SHILO" CONCLUSION!
THIS OUGHT TO CLEAR YOUR SINUSES, JUDGE.
CREATED BY MARK RAHNER
WRITTEN BY MARK RAHNER & ROBERT HORTON
ART BY DAN DOUGHERTY
LETTERING BY SEAN KONOT
THAT'S ABOUT IT.
IT WOULD BE TANTAMOUNT TO LEGALIZED MURDER TO HARM THIS INNOCENT CREATURE.
WELL, AH, IT DOES SEEM TO BE A CASE OF SOME COMPLEXITY.
NOTHING COMPLEX ABOUT MURDER, WAY I SEE IT, YOUR HONOR.
WE NEED TO INCARCERATE THE HUSBAND TO PROTECT LITTLE TRACY..
"LITTLE TRACY." THAT'S GOOD.
BUT THE MAN'S DONE NOTHING?
NOT INDEFINITELY, OF COURSE. LOT OF PEOPLE COULD BE INTERESTED IN THIS.
LOTS COMING TO ARGO.
OUR CHURCH BURNED DOWN EIGHTEEN MONTHS AGO. YOU KNOW HOW SCARCE MONEY IS?
LITTLE INFORMAL FACT-FINDING MEETING?
NOW, DOC, YOU WAIT A STITCH.
NOT INTERESTED IN TESTIMONY FROM SOMEONE WHO ACTUALLY PRACTICES MEDICINE?

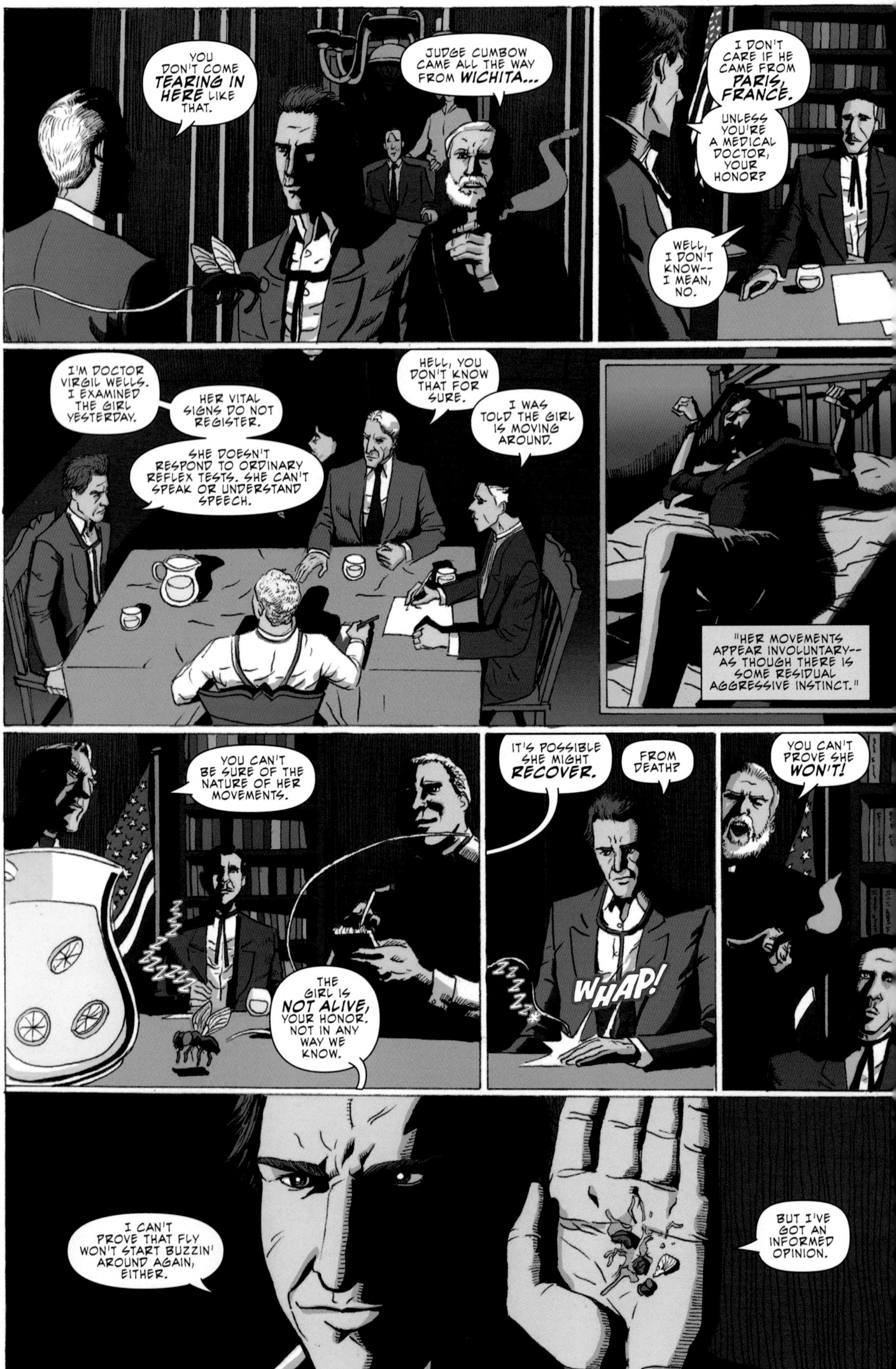
YOU DON'T COME TEARING IN HERE LIKE THAT.
JUDGE CUMBOW CAME ALL THE WAY FROM WICHITA...
I DON'T CARE IF HE CAME FROM PARIS, FRANCE.
UNLESS YOU'RE A MEDICAL DOCTOR, YOUR HONOR?
WELL, I DON'T KNOW-- I MEAN, NO.
I'M DOCTOR VIRGIL WELLS. I EXAMINED THE GIRL YESTERDAY.
HER VITAL SIGNS DO NOT REGISTER.
SHE DOESN'T RESPOND TO ORDINARY REFLEX TESTS. SHE CAN'T SPEAK OR UNDERSTAND SPEECH.
HELL, YOU DON'T KNOW THAT FOR SURE.
I WAS TOLD THE GIRL IS MOVING AROUND.
"HER MOVEMENTS APPEAR INVOLUNTARY-- AS THOUGH THERE IS SOME RESIDUAL AGGRESSIVE INSTINCT."
YOU CAN'T BE SURE OF THE NATURE OF HER MOVEMENTS.
THE GIRL IS NOT ALIVE, YOUR HONOR. NOT IN ANY WAY WE KNOW.
IT'S POSSIBLE SHE MIGHT RECOVER.
FROM DEATH?
WHAP!
YOU CAN'T PROVE SHE WON'T!
I CAN'T PROVE THAT FLY WON'T START BUZZIN' AROUND AGAIN, EITHER.
BUT I'VE GOT AN INFORMED OPINION.

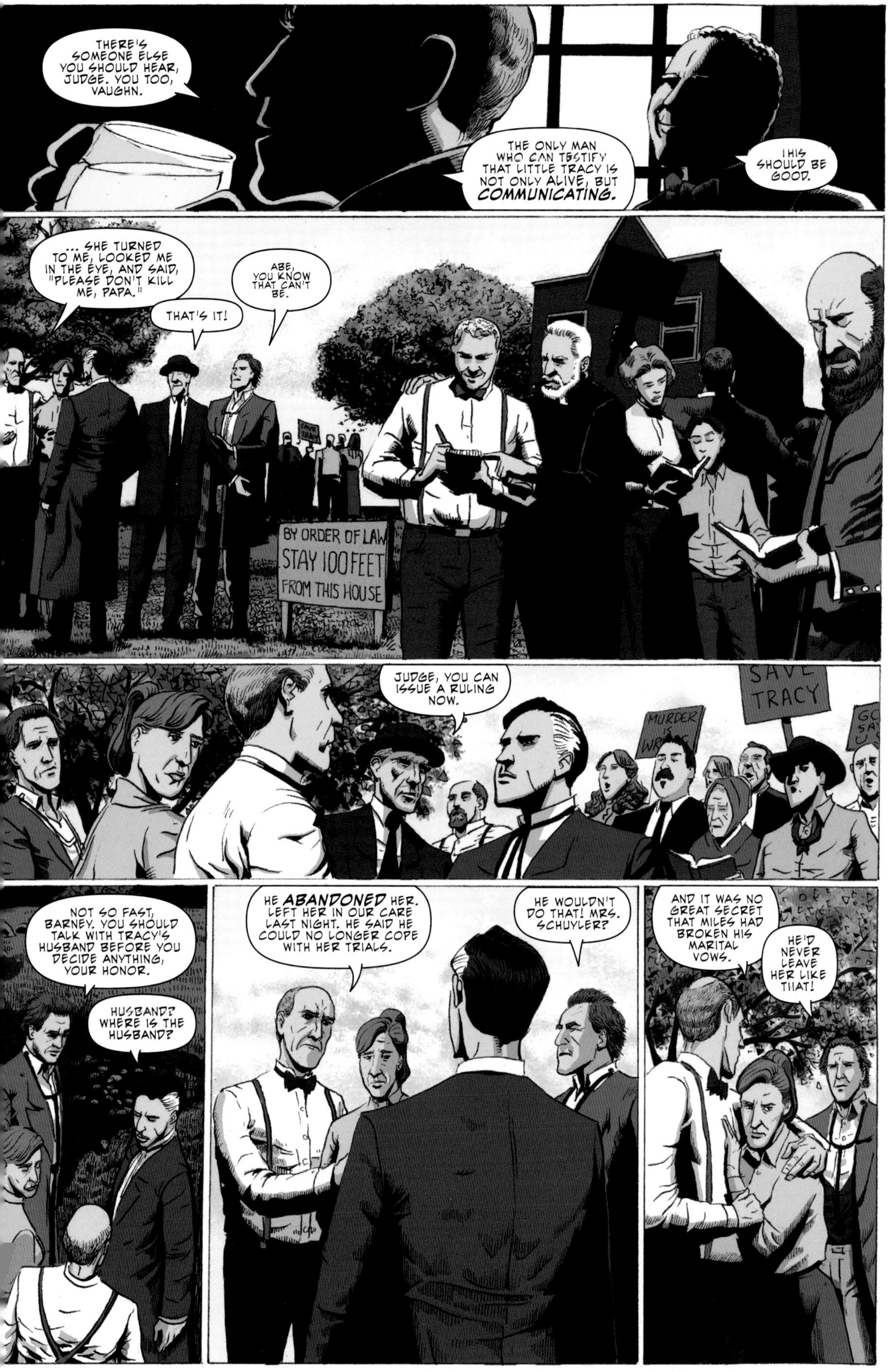
THERE'S SOMEONE ELSE YOU SHOULD HEAR, JUDGE. YOU TOO, VAUGHN.
THE ONLY MAN WHO CAN TESTIFY THAT LITTLE TRACY IS NOT ONLY ALIVE, BUT COMMUNICATING.
THIS SHOULD BE GOOD.
... SHE TURNED TO ME, LOOKED ME IN THE EYE, AND SAID, "PLEASE DON'T KILL ME, PAPA."
THAT'S IT!
ABE, YOU KNOW THAT CAN'T BE.
BY ORDER OF LAW
STAY 100 FEET
FROM THIS HOUSE
JUDGE, YOU CAN ISSUE A RULING NOW.
SAVE TRACY
NOT SO FAST, BARNEY. YOU SHOULD TALK WITH TRACY'S HUSBAND BEFORE YOU DECIDE ANYTHING, YOUR HONOR.
HUSBAND? WHERE IS THE HUSBAND?
HE ABANDONED HER. LEFT HER IN OUR CARE LAST NIGHT. HE SAID HE COULD NO LONGER COPE WITH HER TRIALS.
HE WOULDN'T DO THAT! MRS. SCHUYLER?
AND IT WAS NO GREAT SECRET THAT MILES HAD BROKEN HIS MARITAL VOWS.
HE'D NEVER LEAVE HER LIKE THAT!

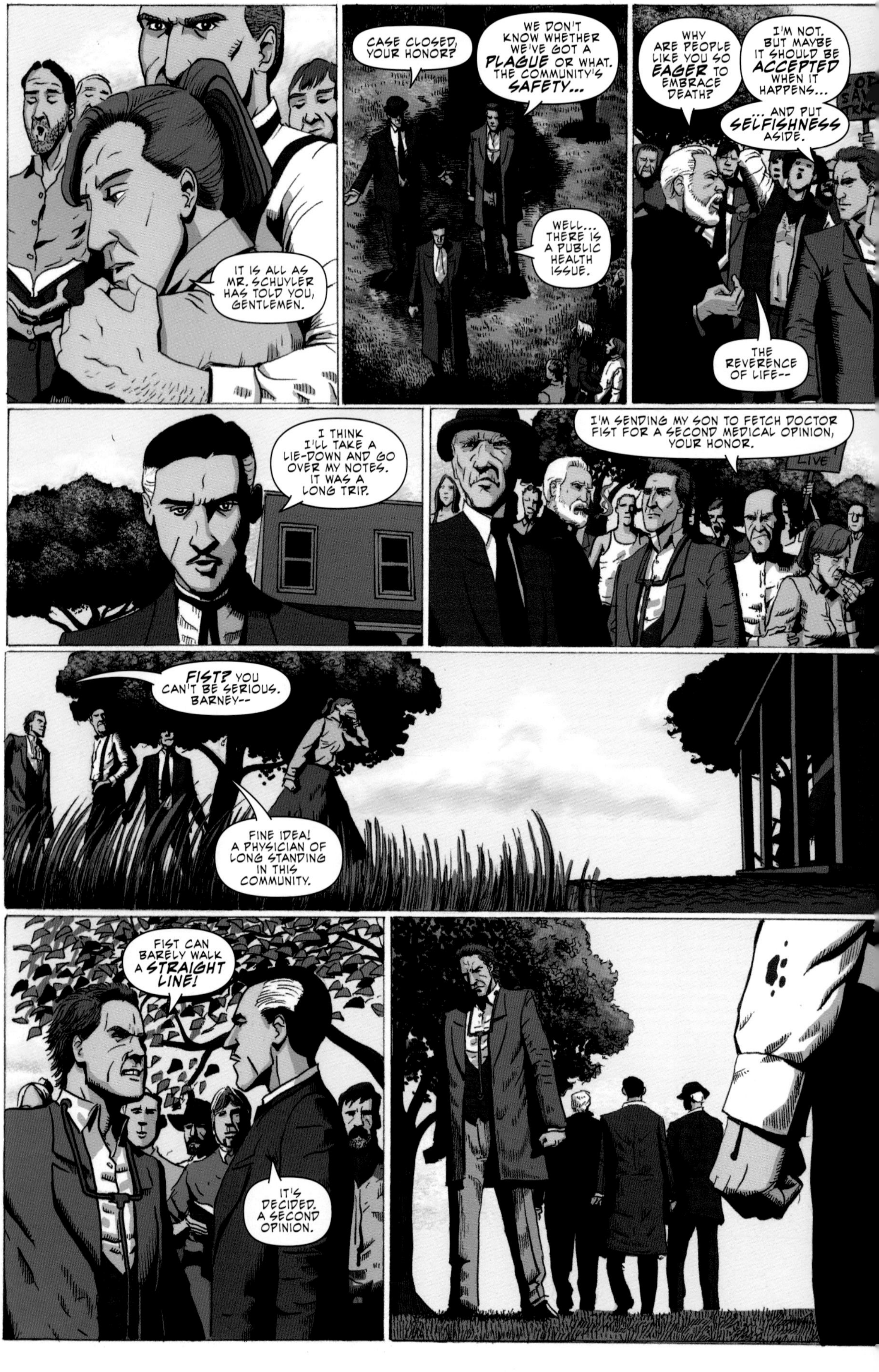
IT IS ALL AS MR. SCHUYLER HAS TOLD YOU, GENTLEMEN.
CASE CLOSED, YOUR HONOR?
WE DON'T KNOW WHETHER WE'VE GOT A PLAGUE OR WHAT. THE COMMUNITY'S SAFETY...
WELL... THERE IS A PUBLIC HEALTH ISSUE.
WHY ARE PEOPLE LIKE YOU SO EAGER TO EMBRACE DEATH?
I'M NOT. BUT MAYBE IT SHOULD BE ACCEPTED WHEN IT HAPPENS...
... AND PUT SELFISHNESS ASIDE.
THE REVERENCE OF LIFE--
I THINK I'LL TAKE A LIE-DOWN AND GO OVER MY NOTES. IT WAS A LONG TRIP.
I'M SENDING MY SON TO FETCH DOCTOR FIST FOR A SECOND MEDICAL OPINION, YOUR HONOR.
FIST? YOU CAN'T BE SERIOUS. BARNEY--
FINE IDEA! A PHYSICIAN OF LONG STANDING IN THIS COMMUNITY.
FIST CAN BARELY WALK A STRAIGHT LINE!
IT'S DECIDED. A SECOND OPINION.

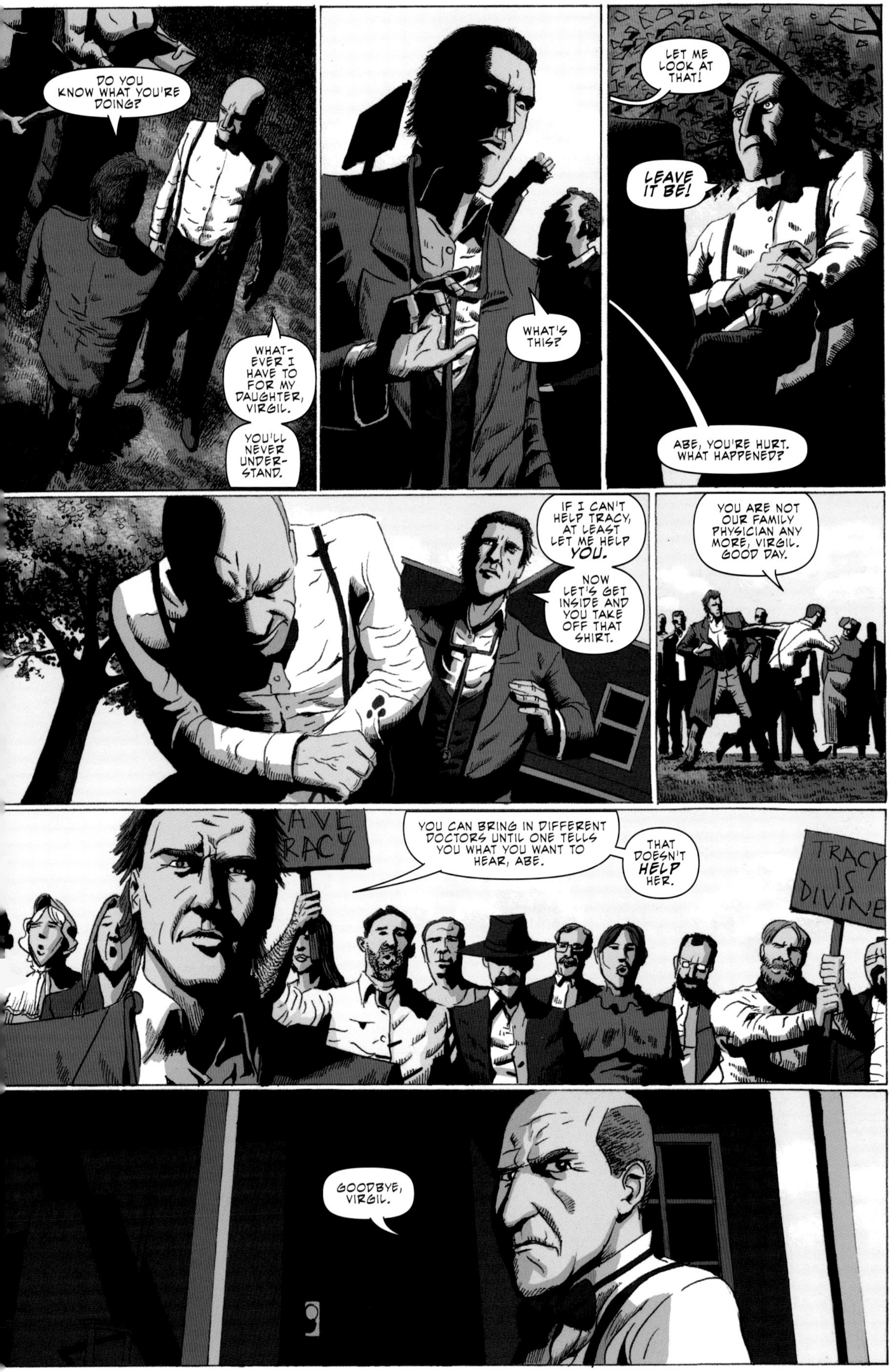
DO YOU KNOW WHAT YOU'RE DOING?
WHAT-EVER I HAVE TO FOR MY DAUGHTER, VIRGIL.
YOU'LL NEVER UNDER-STAND.
WHAT'S THIS?
LET ME LOOK AT THAT!
LEAVE IT BE!
ABE, YOU'RE HURT. WHAT HAPPENED?
IF I CAN'T HELP TRACY, AT LEAST LET ME HELP YOU.
NOW LET'S GET INSIDE AND YOU TAKE OFF THAT SHIRT.
YOU ARE NOT OUR FAMILY PHYSICIAN ANY MORE, VIRGIL. GOOD DAY.
YOU CAN BRING IN DIFFERENT DOCTORS UNTIL ONE TELLS YOU WHAT YOU WANT TO HEAR, ABE.
THAT DOESN'T HELP HER.
TRACY IS DIVINE
GOODBYE, VIRGIL.

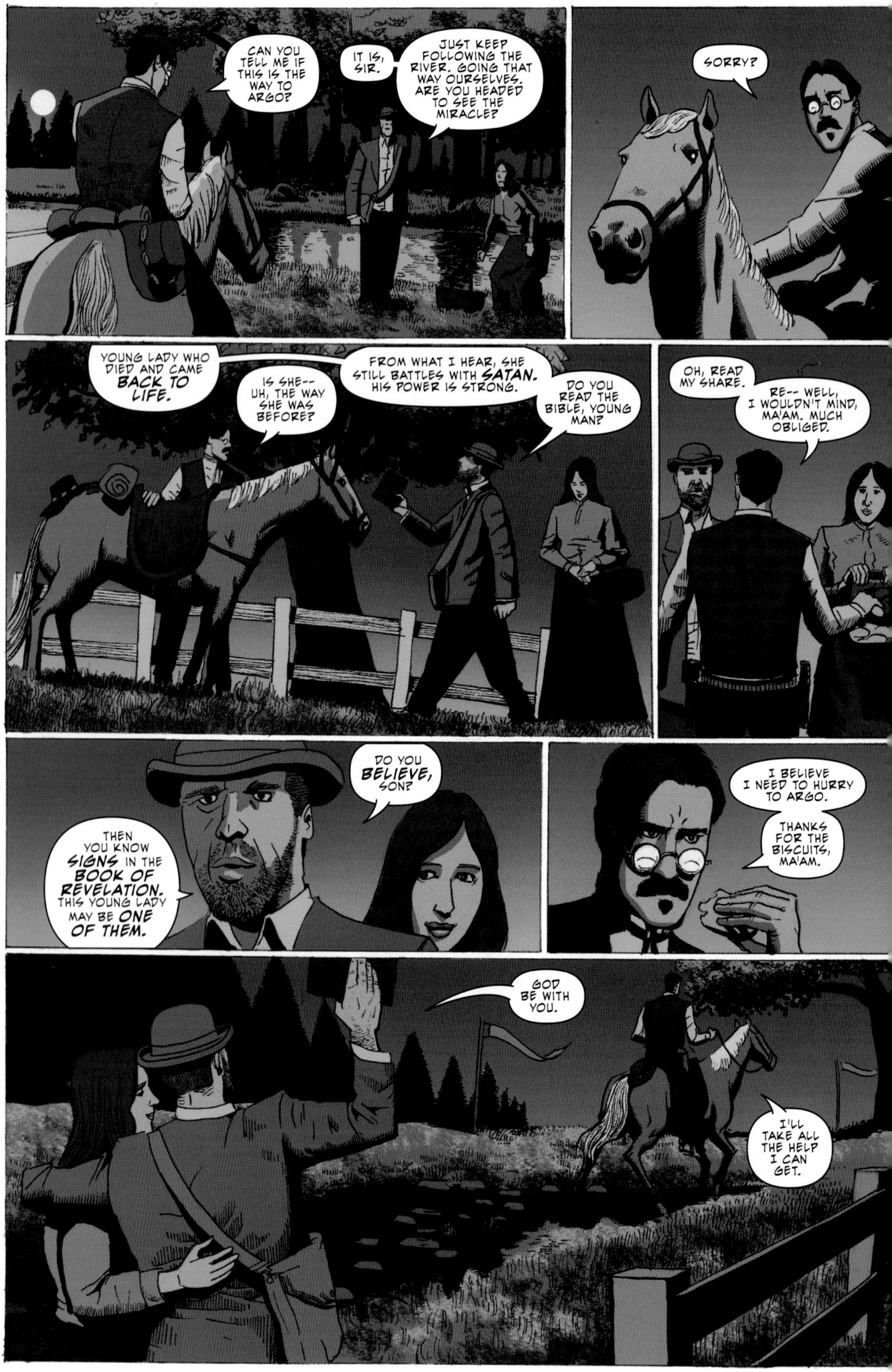
CAN YOU TELL ME IF THIS IS THE WAY TO ARGO?
IT IS, SIR.
JUST KEEP FOLLOWING THE RIVER. GOING THAT WAY OURSELVES. ARE YOU HEADED TO SEE THE MIRACLE?
SORRY?
YOUNG LADY WHO DIED AND CAME BACK TO LIFE.
FROM WHAT I HEAR, SHE STILL BATTLES WITH SATAN. HIS POWER IS STRONG.
IS SHE-- UH, THE WAY SHE WAS BEFORE?
DO YOU READ THE BIBLE, YOUNG MAN?
OH, READ MY SHARE.
RE-- WELL, I WOULDN'T MIND, MA'AM. MUCH OBLIGED.
DO YOU BELIEVE, SON?
THEN YOU KNOW SIGNS IN THE BOOK OF REVELATION. THIS YOUNG LADY MAY BE ONE OF THEM.
I BELIEVE I NEED TO HURRY TO ARGO.
THANKS FOR THE BISCUITS, MA'AM.
GOD BE WITH YOU.
I'LL TAKE ALL THE HELP I CAN GET.

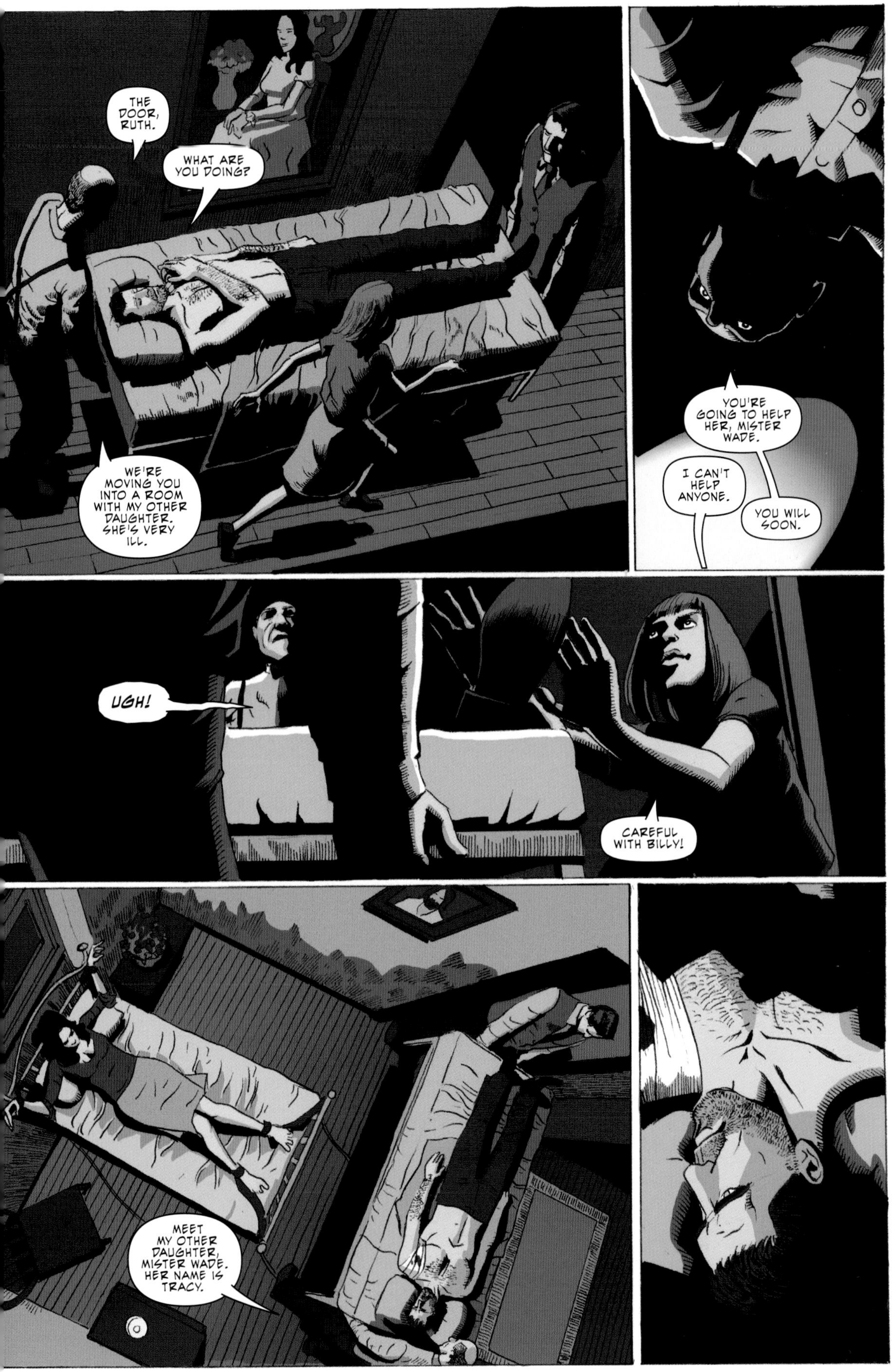
THE DOOR, RUTH.
WHAT ARE YOU DOING?
WE'RE MOVING YOU INTO A ROOM WITH MY OTHER DAUGHTER. SHE'S VERY ILL.
YOU'RE GOING TO HELP HER, MISTER WADE.
I CAN'T HELP ANYONE.
YOU WILL SOON.
UGH!
CAREFUL WITH BILLY!
MEET MY OTHER DAUGHTER, MISTER WADE. HER NAME IS TRACY.

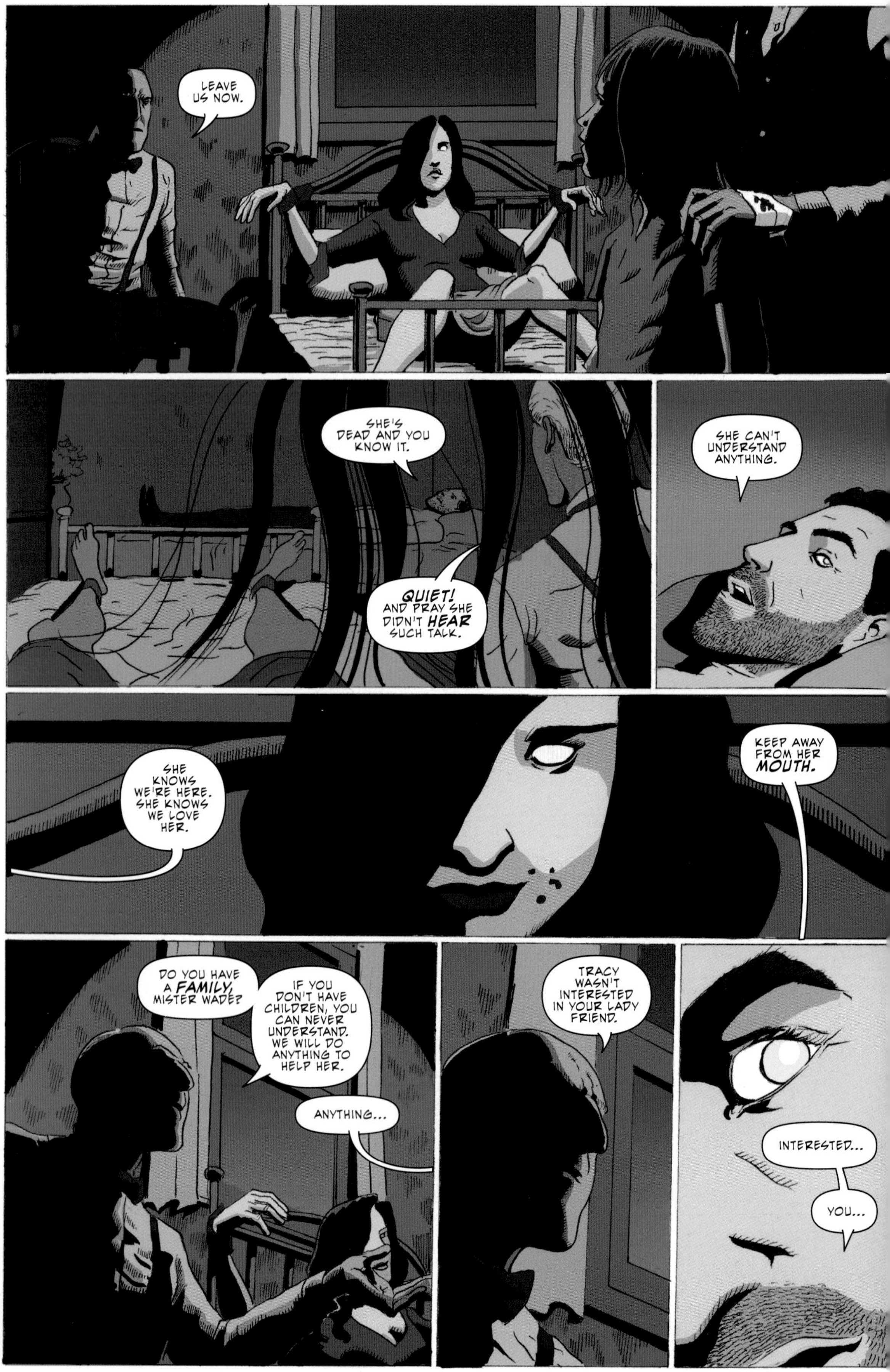
LEAVE US NOW.
SHE'S DEAD AND YOU KNOW IT.
QUIET! AND PRAY SHE DIDN'T HEAR SUCH TALK.
SHE CAN'T UNDERSTAND ANYTHING.
SHE KNOWS WE'RE HERE. SHE KNOWS WE LOVE HER.
KEEP AWAY FROM HER MOUTH.
DO YOU HAVE A FAMILY, MISTER WADE?
IF YOU DON'T HAVE CHILDREN, YOU CAN NEVER UNDERSTAND. WE WILL DO ANYTHING TO HELP HER.
ANYTHING...
TRACY WASN'T INTERESTED IN YOUR LADY FRIEND.
INTERESTED...
YOU...

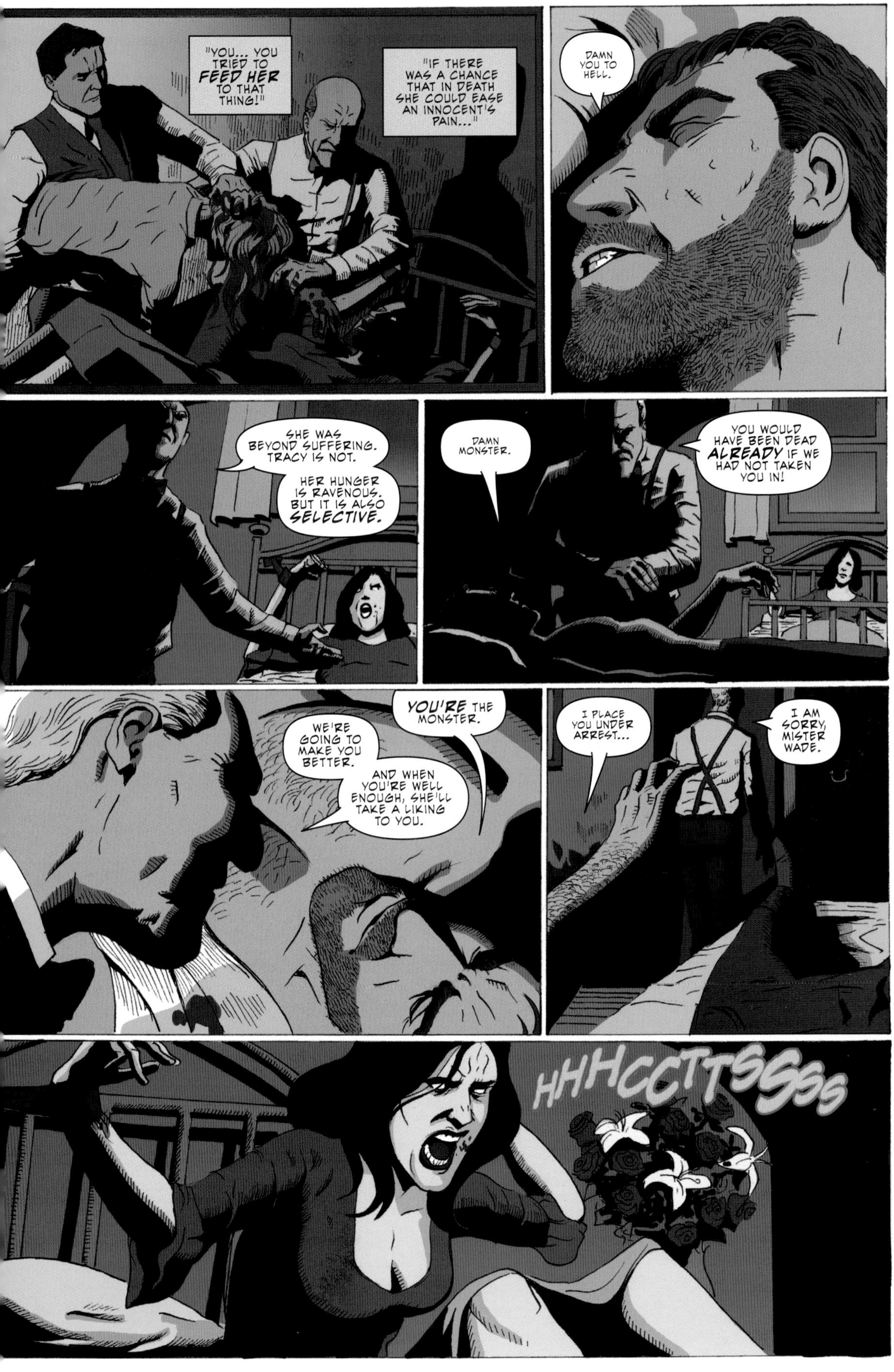
"YOU... YOU TRIED TO FEED HER TO THAT THING!"
"IF THERE WAS A CHANCE THAT IN DEATH SHE COULD EASE AN INNOCENT'S PAIN..."
DAMN YOU TO HELL.
SHE WAS BEYOND SUFFERING. TRACY IS NOT.
HER HUNGER IS RAVENOUS. BUT IT IS ALSO SELECTIVE.
DAMN MONSTER.
YOU WOULD HAVE BEEN DEAD ALREADY IF WE HAD NOT TAKEN YOU IN!
WE'RE GOING TO MAKE YOU BETTER.
AND WHEN YOU'RE WELL ENOUGH, SHE'LL TAKE A LIKING TO YOU.
YOU'RE THE MONSTER.
I PLACE YOU UNDER ARREST...
I AM SORRY, MISTER WADE.
HHHCCTTSSSS

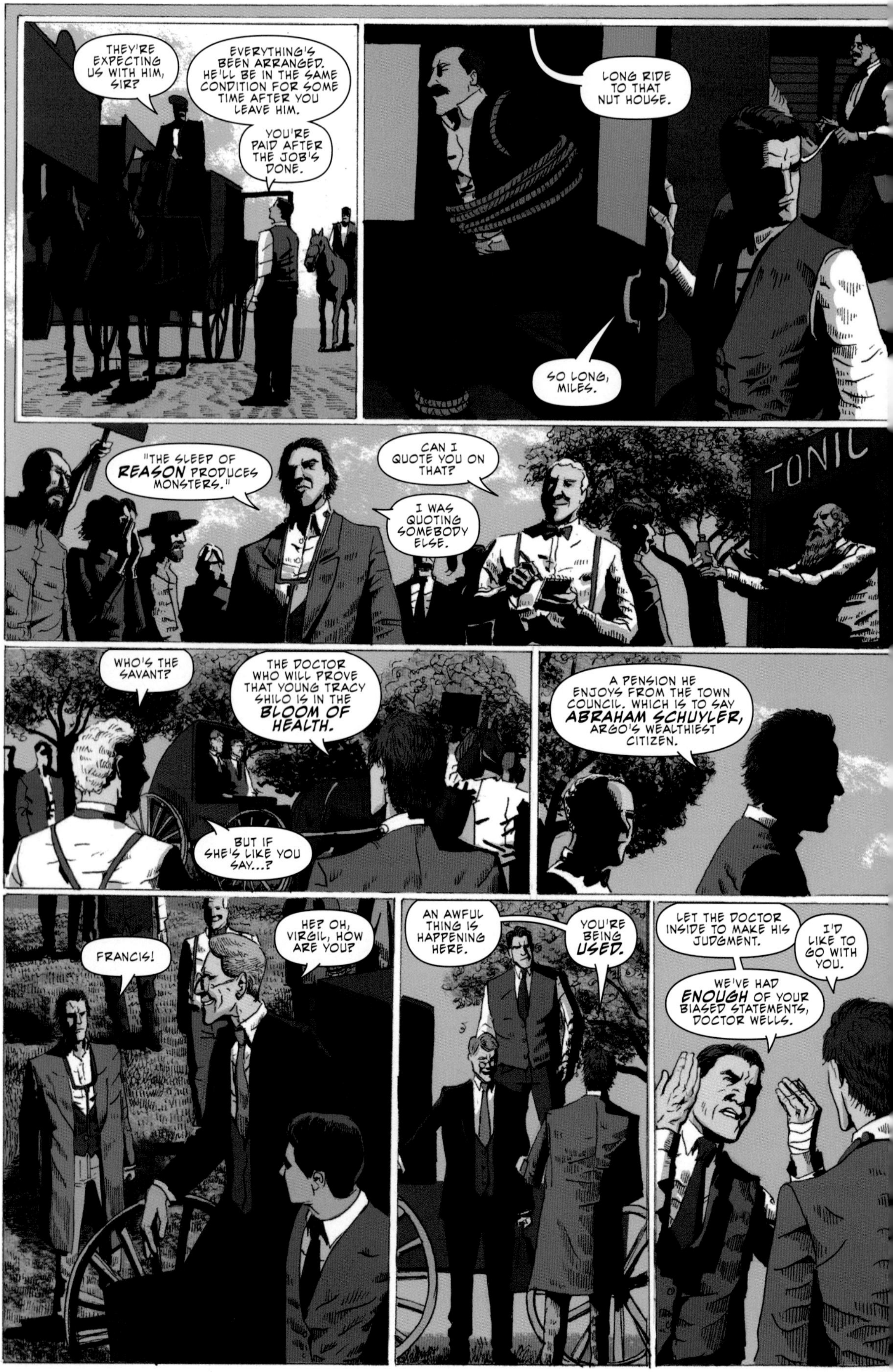
THEY'RE EXPECTING US WITH HIM, SIR?
EVERYTHING'S BEEN ARRANGED. HE'LL BE IN THE SAME CONDITION FOR SOME TIME AFTER YOU LEAVE HIM.
YOU'RE PAID AFTER THE JOB'S DONE.
LONG RIDE TO THAT NUT HOUSE.
SO LONG, MILES.
"THE SLEEP OF REASON PRODUCES MONSTERS."
CAN I QUOTE YOU ON THAT?
I WAS QUOTING SOMEBODY ELSE.
TONIC
WHO'S THE SAVANT?
THE DOCTOR WHO WILL PROVE THAT YOUNG TRACY SHILO IS IN THE BLOOM OF HEALTH.
BUT IF SHE'S LIKE YOU SAY...?
A PENSION HE ENJOYS FROM THE TOWN COUNCIL. WHICH IS TO SAY ABRAHAM SCHUYLER, ARGO'S WEALTHIEST CITIZEN.
FRANCIS!
HE? OH, VIRGIL, HOW ARE YOU?
AN AWFUL THING IS HAPPENING HERE.
YOU'RE BEING USED.
LET THE DOCTOR INSIDE TO MAKE HIS JUDGMENT.
I'D LIKE TO GO WITH YOU.
WE'VE HAD ENOUGH OF YOUR BIASED STATEMENTS, DOCTOR WELLS.

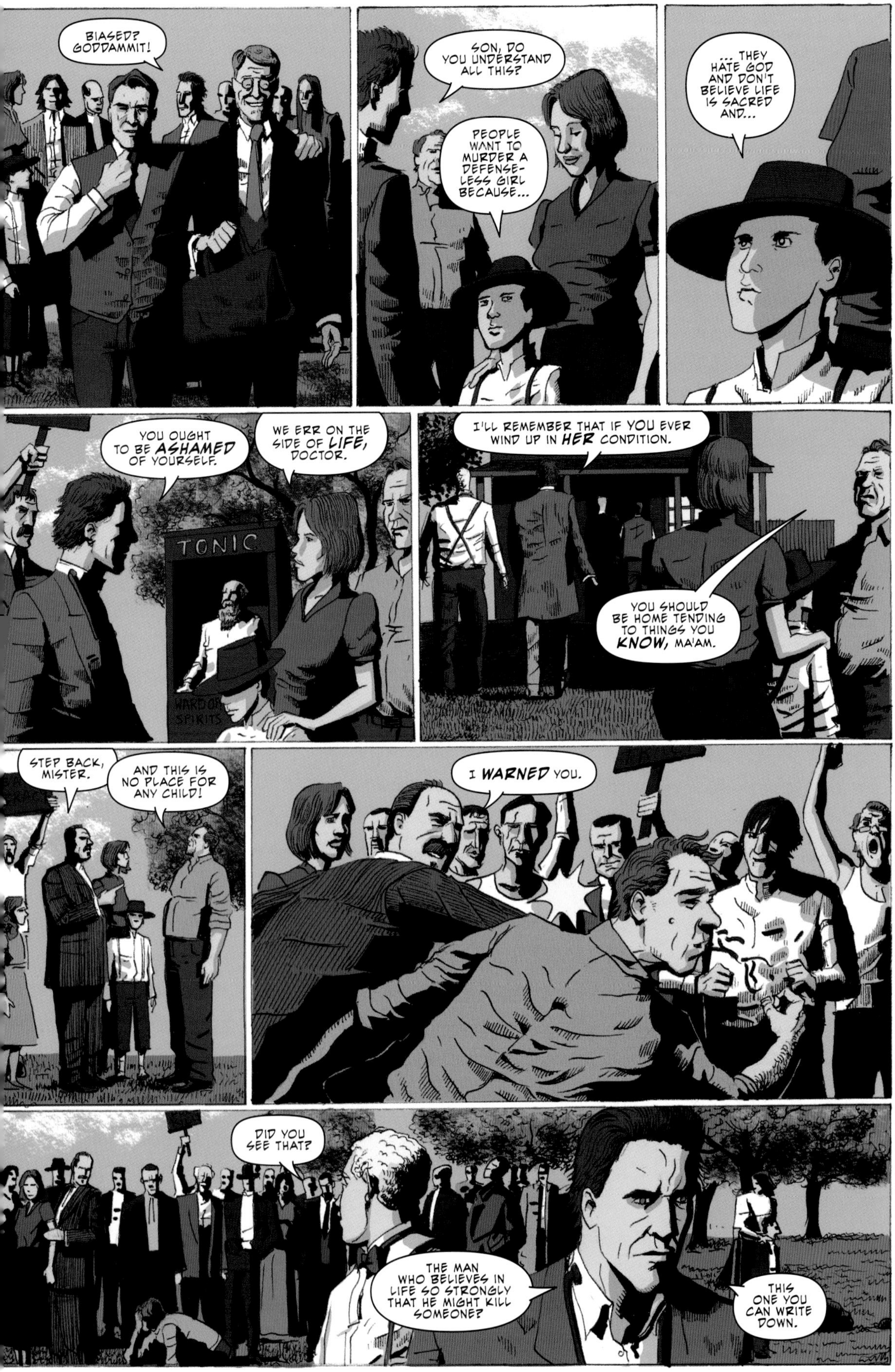
BIASED? GODDAMMIT!
SON, DO YOU UNDERSTAND ALL THIS?
PEOPLE WANT TO MURDER A DEFENSE-LESS GIRL BECAUSE...
... THEY HATE GOD AND DON'T BELIEVE LIFE IS SACRED AND...
YOU OUGHT TO BE ASHAMED OF YOURSELF.
WE ERR ON THE SIDE OF LIFE, DOCTOR.
TONIC
WARD OFF SPIRITS
I'LL REMEMBER THAT IF YOU EVER WIND UP IN HER CONDITION.
YOU SHOULD BE HOME TENDING TO THINGS YOU KNOW, MA'AM.
STEP BACK, MISTER.
AND THIS IS NO PLACE FOR ANY CHILD!
I WARNED YOU.
DID YOU SEE THAT?
THE MAN WHO BELIEVES IN LIFE SO STRONGLY THAT HE MIGHT KILL SOMEONE?
THIS ONE YOU CAN WRITE DOWN.

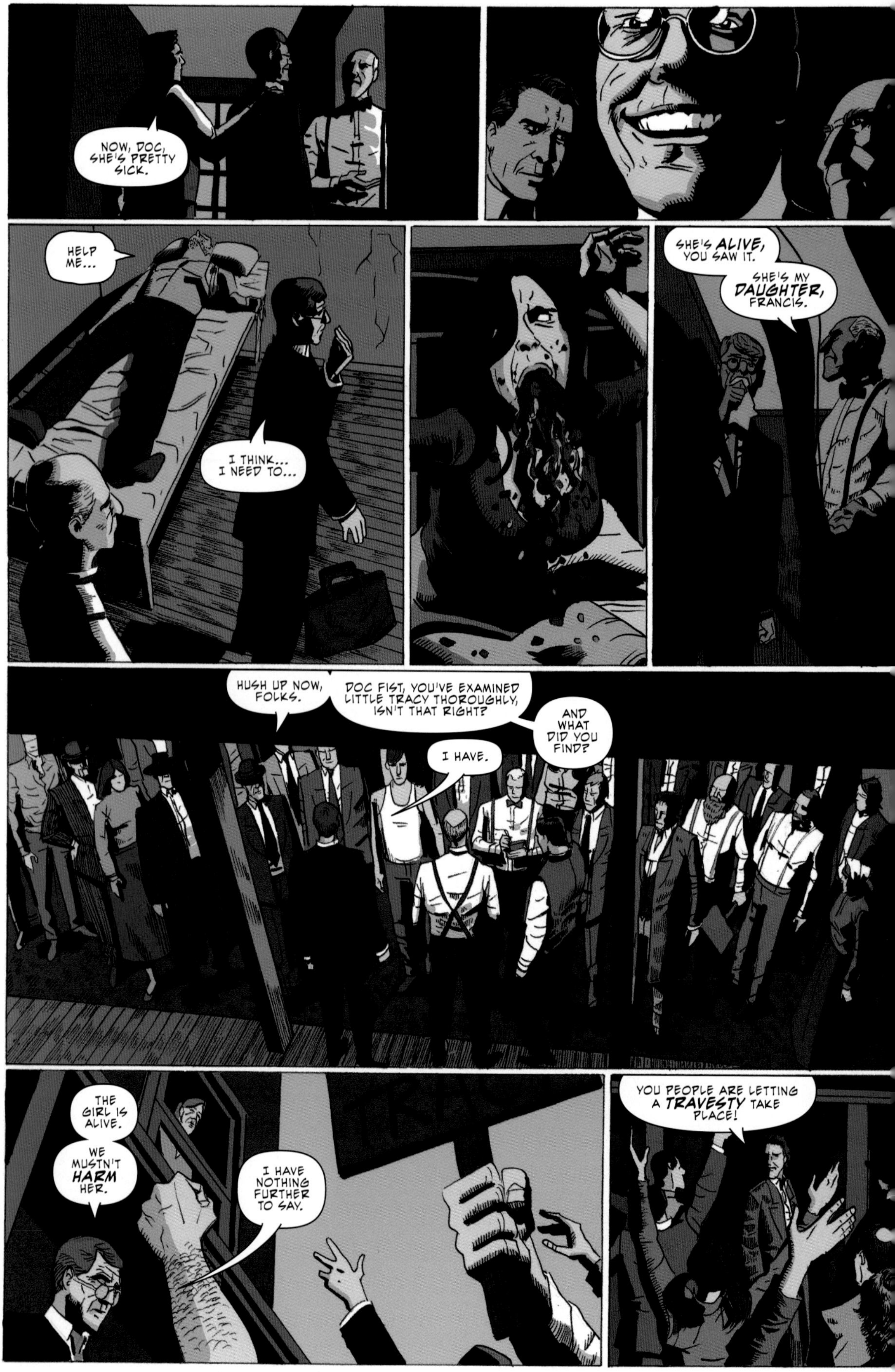
NOW, DOC, SHE'S PRETTY SICK.
HELP ME...
I THINK... I NEED TO...
SHE'S ALIVE, YOU SAW IT.
SHE'S MY DAUGHTER, FRANCIS.
HUSH UP NOW, FOLKS.
DOC FIST, YOU'VE EXAMINED LITTLE TRACY THOROUGHLY, ISN'T THAT RIGHT?
I HAVE.
AND WHAT DID YOU FIND?
THE GIRL IS ALIVE.
WE MUSTN'T HARM HER.
I HAVE NOTHING FURTHER TO SAY.
YOU PEOPLE ARE LETTING A TRAVESTY TAKE PLACE!

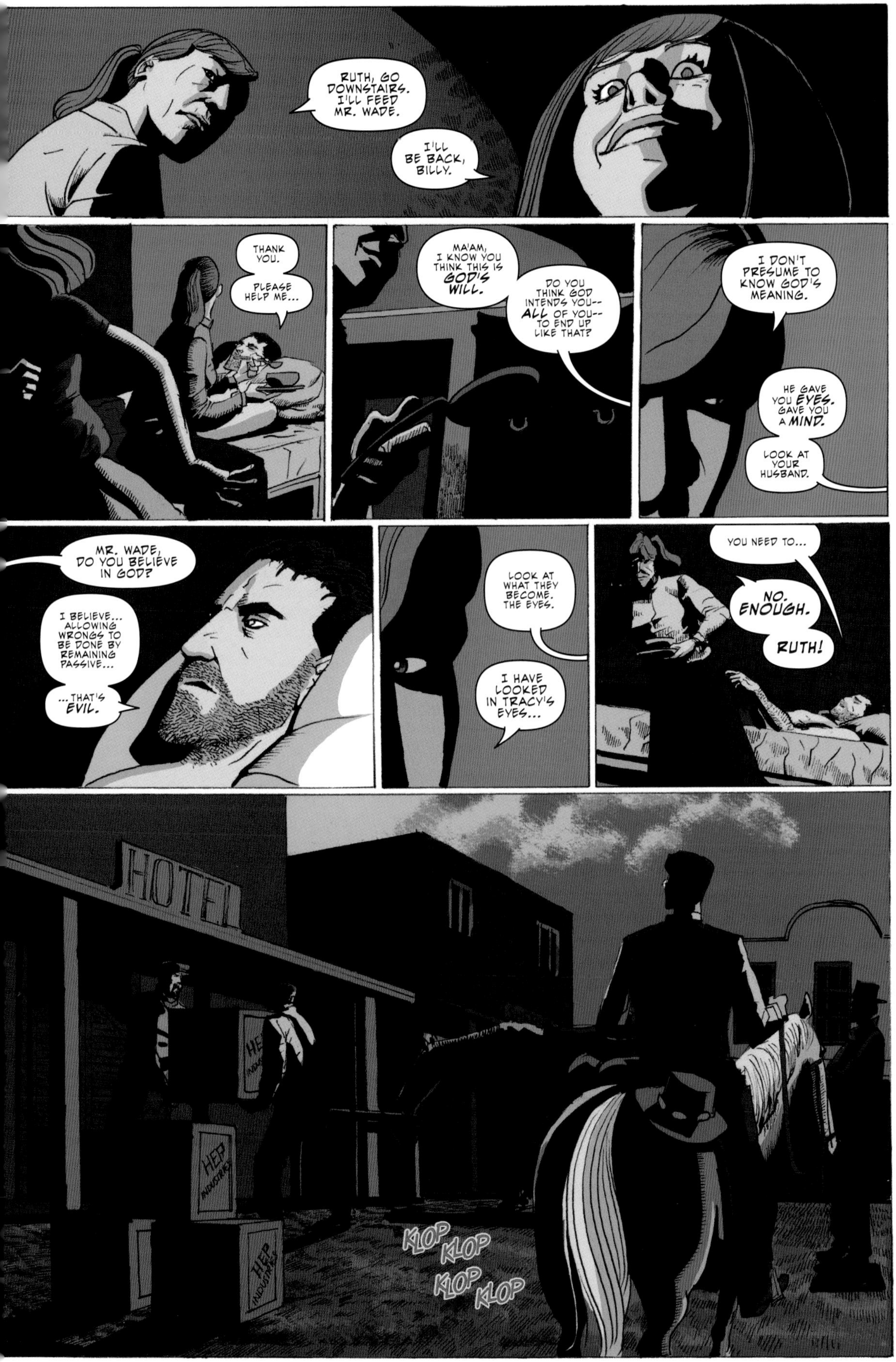
RUTH, GO DOWNSTAIRS. I'LL FEED MR. WADE.
I'LL BE BACK, BILLY.
THANK YOU.
PLEASE HELP ME...
MA'AM, I KNOW YOU THINK THIS IS GOD'S WILL.
DO YOU THINK GOD INTENDS YOU--ALL OF YOU--TO END UP LIKE THAT?
I DON'T PRESUME TO KNOW GOD'S MEANING.
HE GAVE YOU EYES. GAVE YOU A MIND.
LOOK AT YOUR HUSBAND.
MR. WADE, DO YOU BELIEVE IN GOD?
I BELIEVE... ALLOWING WRONGS TO BE DONE BY REMAINING PASSIVE...
...THAT'S EVIL.
LOOK AT WHAT THEY BECOME. THE EYES.
I HAVE LOOKED IN TRACY'S EYES...
YOU NEED TO...
NO. ENOUGH.
RUTH!
HOTEL
HEP INDUSTRIES
HEP INDUSTRIES
KLOP KLOP KLOP KLOP

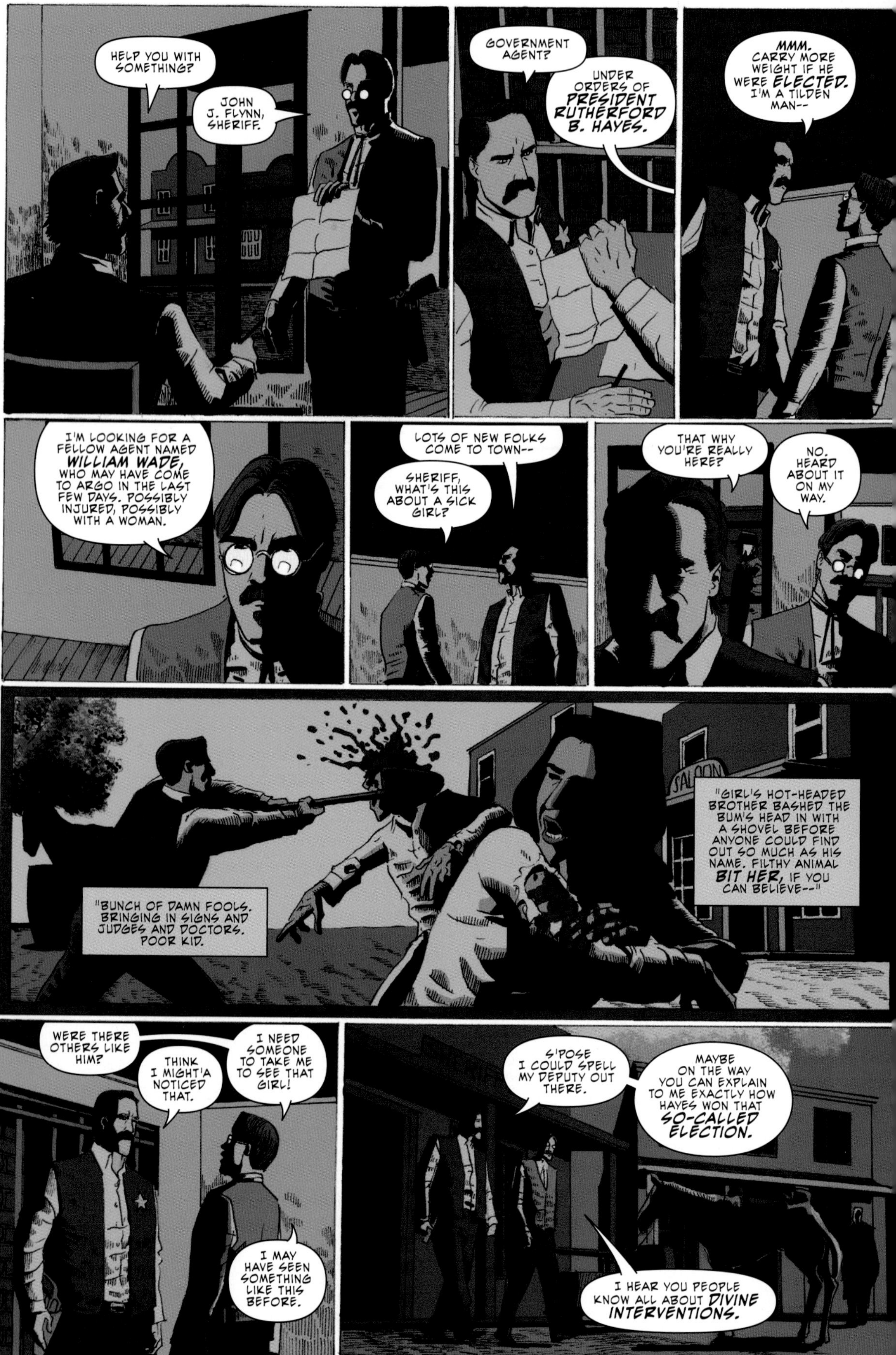

HELP YOU WITH SOMETHING?
JOHN J. FLYNN, SHERIFF.
GOVERNMENT AGENT?
UNDER ORDERS OF PRESIDENT RUTHERFORD B. HAYES.
MMM. CARRY MORE WEIGHT IF HE WERE ELECTED. I'M A TILDEN MAN--
I'M LOOKING FOR A FELLOW AGENT NAMED WILLIAM WADE, WHO MAY HAVE COME TO ARGO IN THE LAST FEW DAYS. POSSIBLY INJURED, POSSIBLY WITH A WOMAN.
LOTS OF NEW FOLKS COME TO TOWN--
SHERIFF, WHAT'S THIS ABOUT A SICK GIRL?
THAT WHY YOU'RE REALLY HERE?
NO. HEARD ABOUT IT ON MY WAY.
SALOON
"BUNCH OF DAMN FOOLS. BRINGING IN SIGNS AND JUDGES AND DOCTORS. POOR KID.
"GIRL'S HOT-HEADED BROTHER BASHED THE BUM'S HEAD IN WITH A SHOVEL BEFORE ANYONE COULD FIND OUT SO MUCH AS HIS NAME. FILTHY ANIMAL BIT HER, IF YOU CAN BELIEVE--"
WERE THERE OTHERS LIKE HIM?
THINK I MIGHT'A NOTICED THAT.
I NEED SOMEONE TO TAKE ME TO SEE THAT GIRL!
I MAY HAVE SEEN SOMETHING LIKE THIS BEFORE.
S'POSE I COULD SPELL MY DEPUTY OUT THERE.
MAYBE ON THE WAY YOU CAN EXPLAIN TO ME EXACTLY HOW HAYES WON THAT SO-CALLED ELECTION.
I HEAR YOU PEOPLE KNOW ALL ABOUT DIVINE INTERVENTIONS.

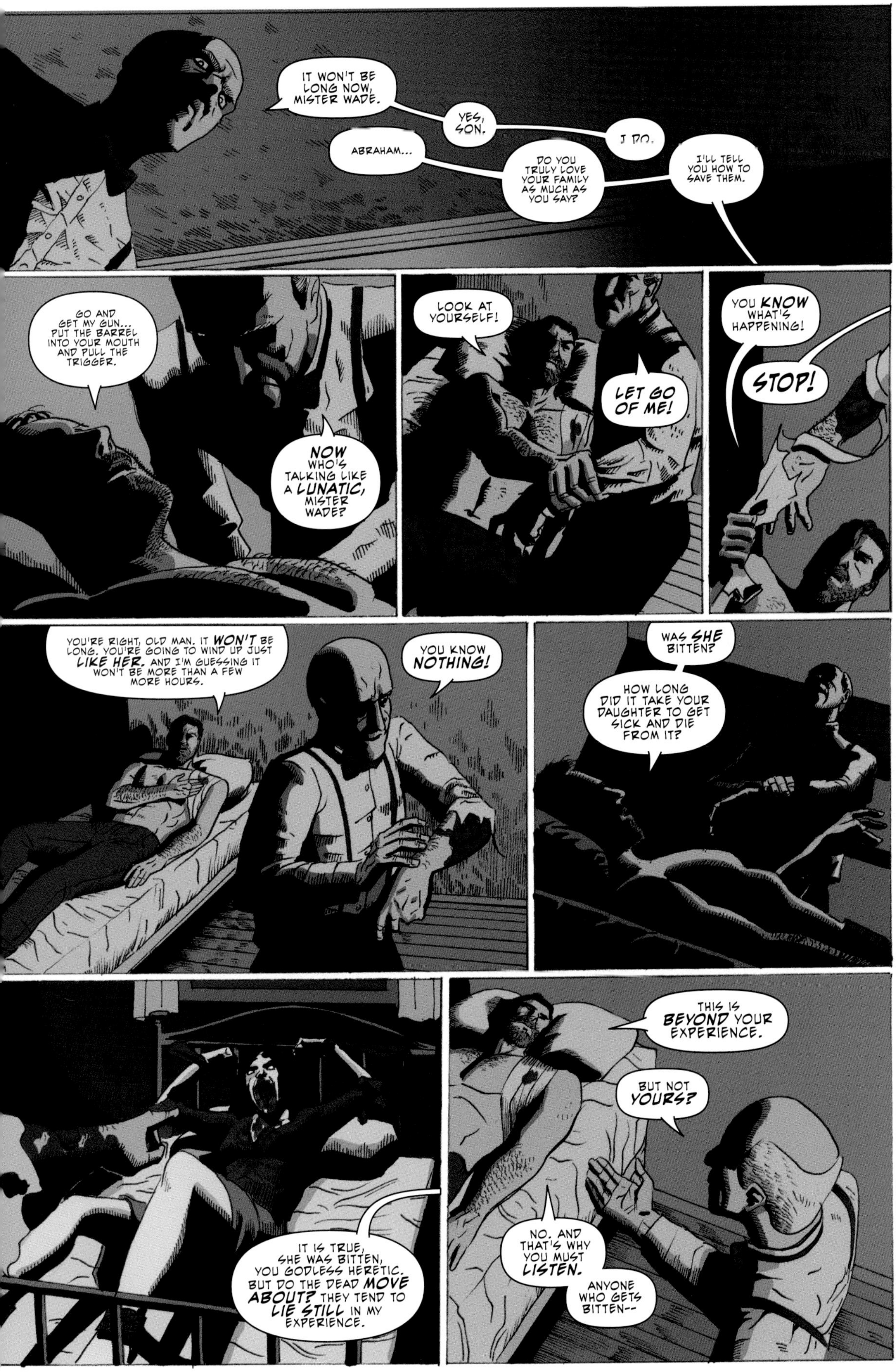
IT WON'T BE LONG NOW, MISTER WADE.
YES, SON.
I DO.
ABRAHAM...
DO YOU TRULY LOVE YOUR FAMILY AS MUCH AS YOU SAY?
I'LL TELL YOU HOW TO SAVE THEM.
GO AND GET MY GUN... PUT THE BARREL INTO YOUR MOUTH AND PULL THE TRIGGER.
NOW WHO'S TALKING LIKE A LUNATIC, MISTER WADE?
LOOK AT YOURSELF!
LET GO OF ME!
YOU KNOW WHAT'S HAPPENING!
STOP!
YOU'RE RIGHT, OLD MAN. IT WON'T BE LONG. YOU'RE GOING TO WIND UP JUST LIKE HER. AND I'M GUESSING IT WON'T BE MORE THAN A FEW MORE HOURS.
YOU KNOW NOTHING!
WAS SHE BITTEN?
HOW LONG DID IT TAKE YOUR DAUGHTER TO GET SICK AND DIE FROM IT?
IT IS TRUE, SHE WAS BITTEN, YOU GODLESS HERETIC. BUT DO THE DEAD MOVE ABOUT? THEY TEND TO LIE STILL IN MY EXPERIENCE.
THIS IS BEYOND YOUR EXPERIENCE.
BUT NOT YOURS?
NO. AND THAT'S WHY YOU MUST LISTEN.
ANYONE WHO GETS BITTEN--

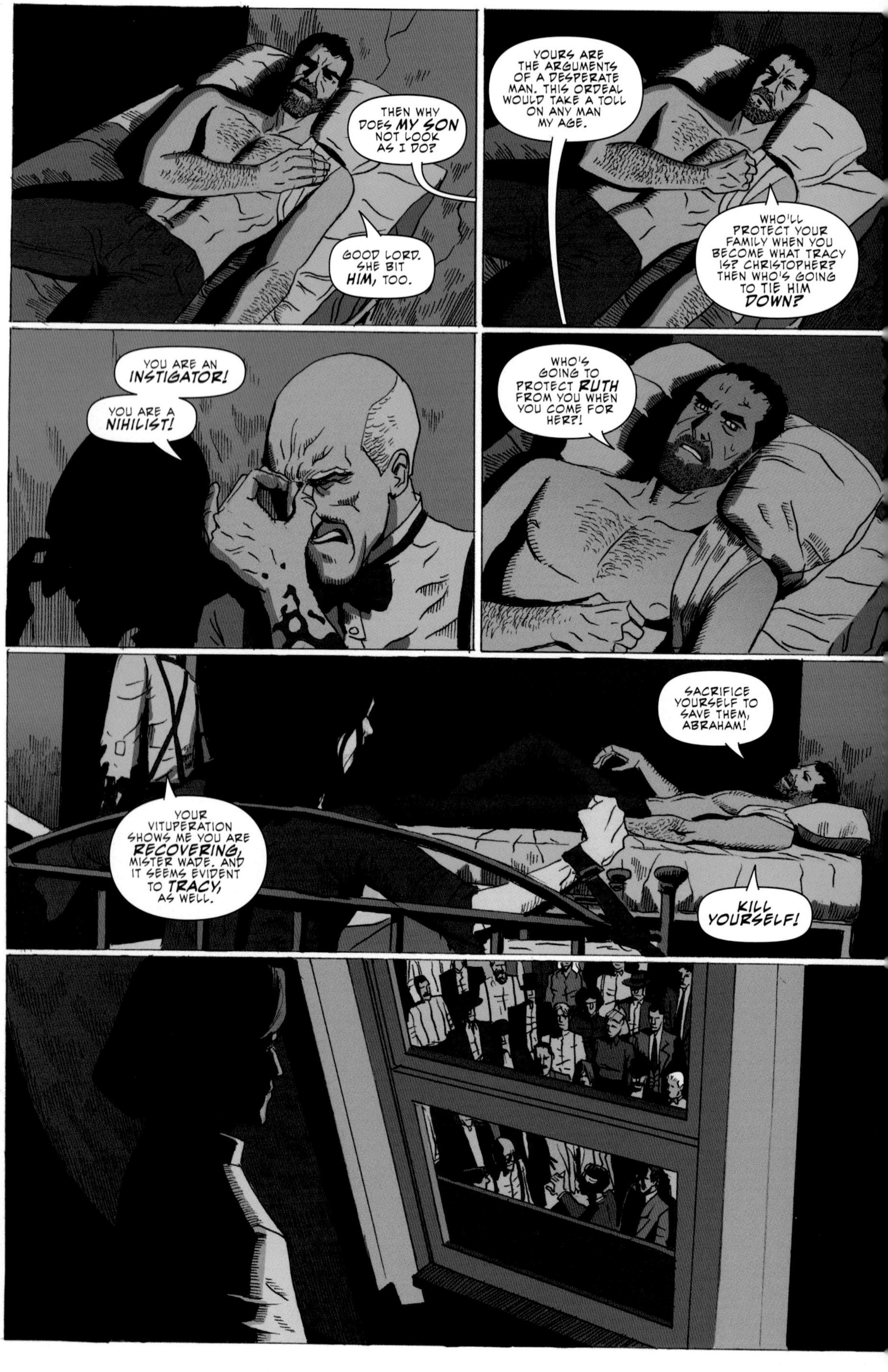
THEN WHY DOES MY SON NOT LOOK AS I DO?
GOOD LORD. SHE BIT HIM, TOO.
YOURS ARE THE ARGUMENTS OF A DESPERATE MAN. THIS ORDEAL WOULD TAKE A TOLL ON ANY MAN MY AGE.
WHO'LL PROTECT YOUR FAMILY WHEN YOU BECOME WHAT TRACY IS? CHRISTOPHER? THEN WHO'S GOING TO TIE HIM DOWN?
YOU ARE AN INSTIGATOR!
YOU ARE A NIHILIST!
WHO'S GOING TO PROTECT RUTH FROM YOU WHEN YOU COME FOR HER?!
SACRIFICE YOURSELF TO SAVE THEM, ABRAHAM!
YOUR VITUPERATION SHOWS ME YOU ARE RECOVERING, MISTER WADE. AND IT SEEMS EVIDENT TO TRACY, AS WELL.
KILL YOURSELF!

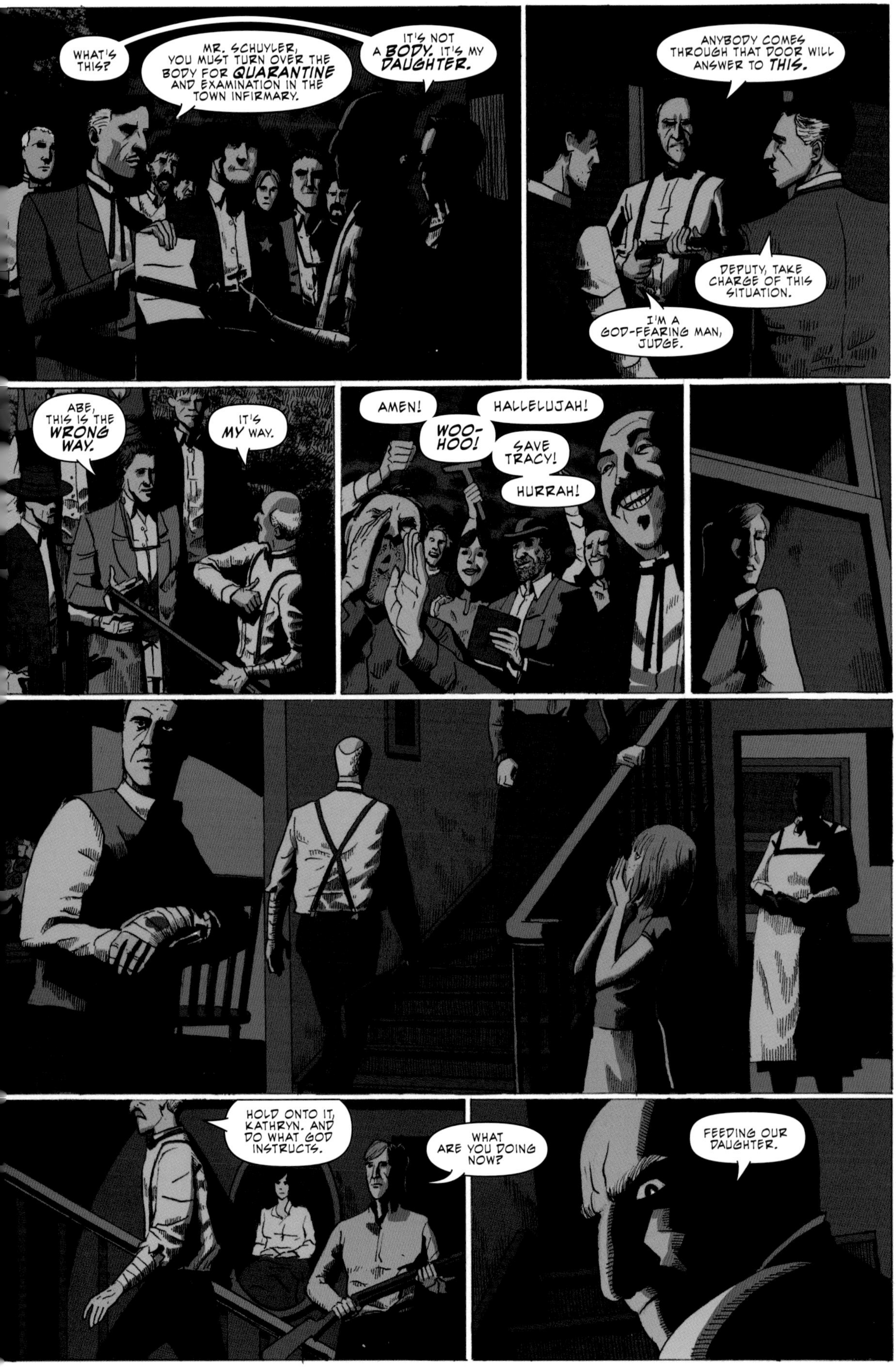
WHAT'S THIS?
MR. SCHUYLER, YOU MUST TURN OVER THE BODY FOR QUARANTINE AND EXAMINATION IN THE TOWN INFIRMARY.
IT'S NOT A BODY. IT'S MY DAUGHTER.
ANYBODY COMES THROUGH THAT DOOR WILL ANSWER TO THIS.
DEPUTY, TAKE CHARGE OF THIS SITUATION.
I'M A GOD-FEARING MAN, JUDGE.
ABE, THIS IS THE WRONG WAY.
IT'S MY WAY.
AMEN!
HALLELUJAH!
WOO-HOO!
SAVE TRACY!
HURRAH!
HOLD ONTO IT, KATHRYN. AND DO WHAT GOD INSTRUCTS.
WHAT ARE YOU DOING NOW?
FEEDING OUR DAUGHTER.

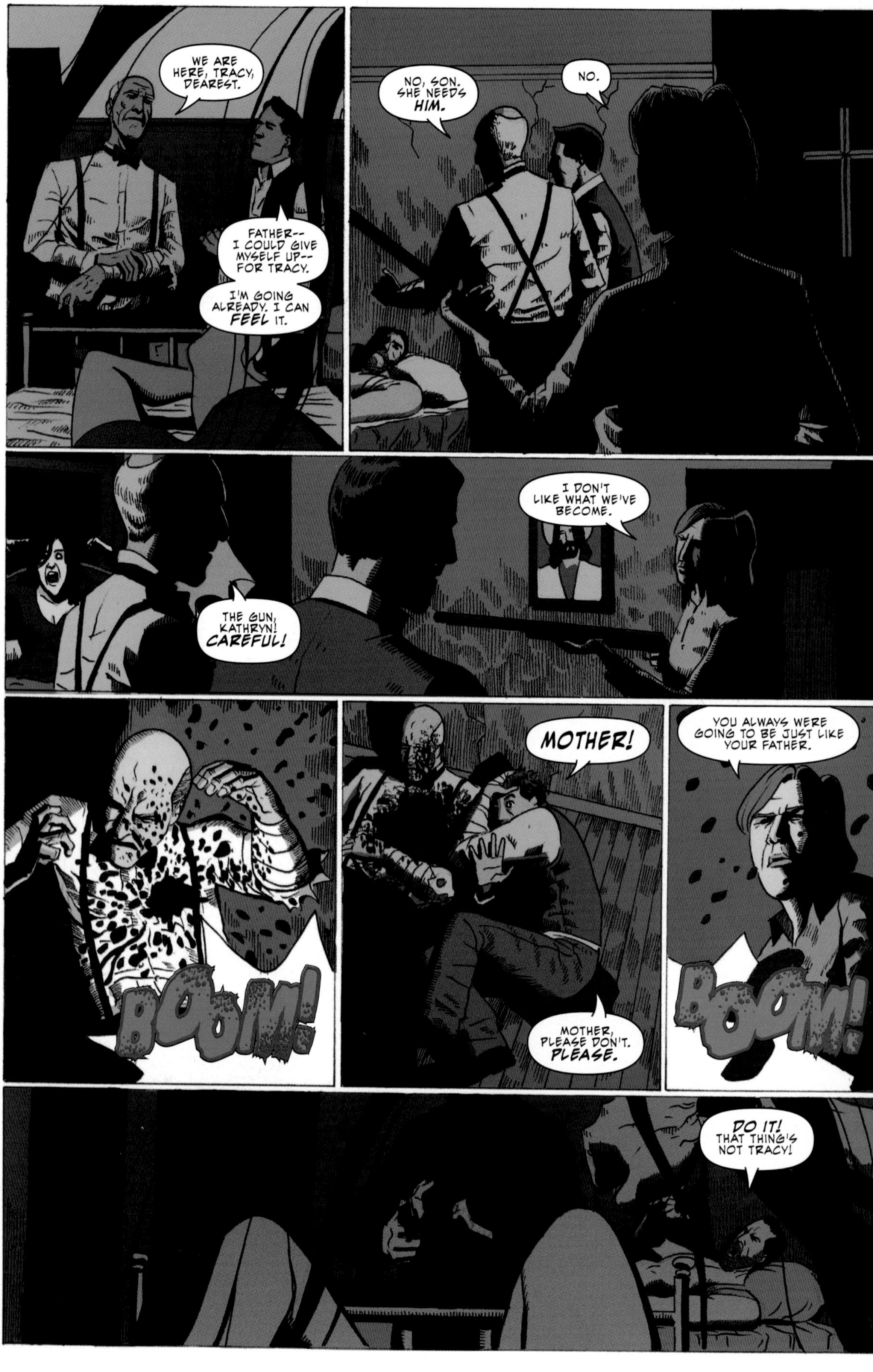
WE ARE HERE, TRACY, DEAREST.
FATHER-- I COULD GIVE MYSELF UP-- FOR TRACY.
I'M GOING ALREADY. I CAN FEEL IT.
NO, SON. SHE NEEDS HIM.
NO.
I DON'T LIKE WHAT WE'VE BECOME.
THE GUN, KATHRYN! CAREFUL!
BOOM!
MOTHER!
MOTHER, PLEASE DON'T. PLEASE.
YOU ALWAYS WERE GOING TO BE JUST LIKE YOUR FATHER.
BOOM!
DO IT! THAT THING'S NOT TRACY!

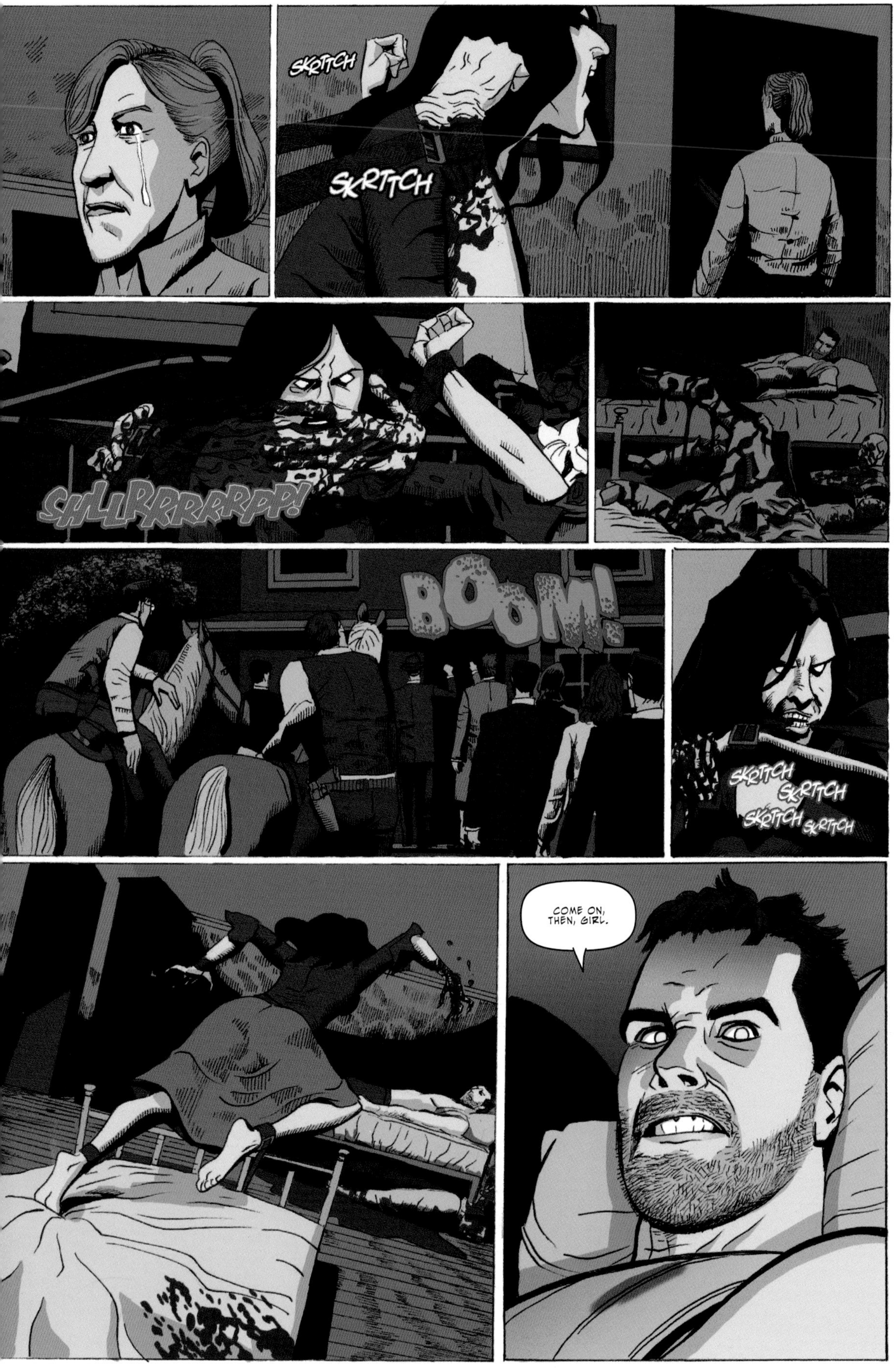
SKRITCH
SKRITCH
SHLLRRRRRRPP!
BOOM!
SKRITCH SKRITCH SKRITCH SKRITCH
COME ON, THEN, GIRL.

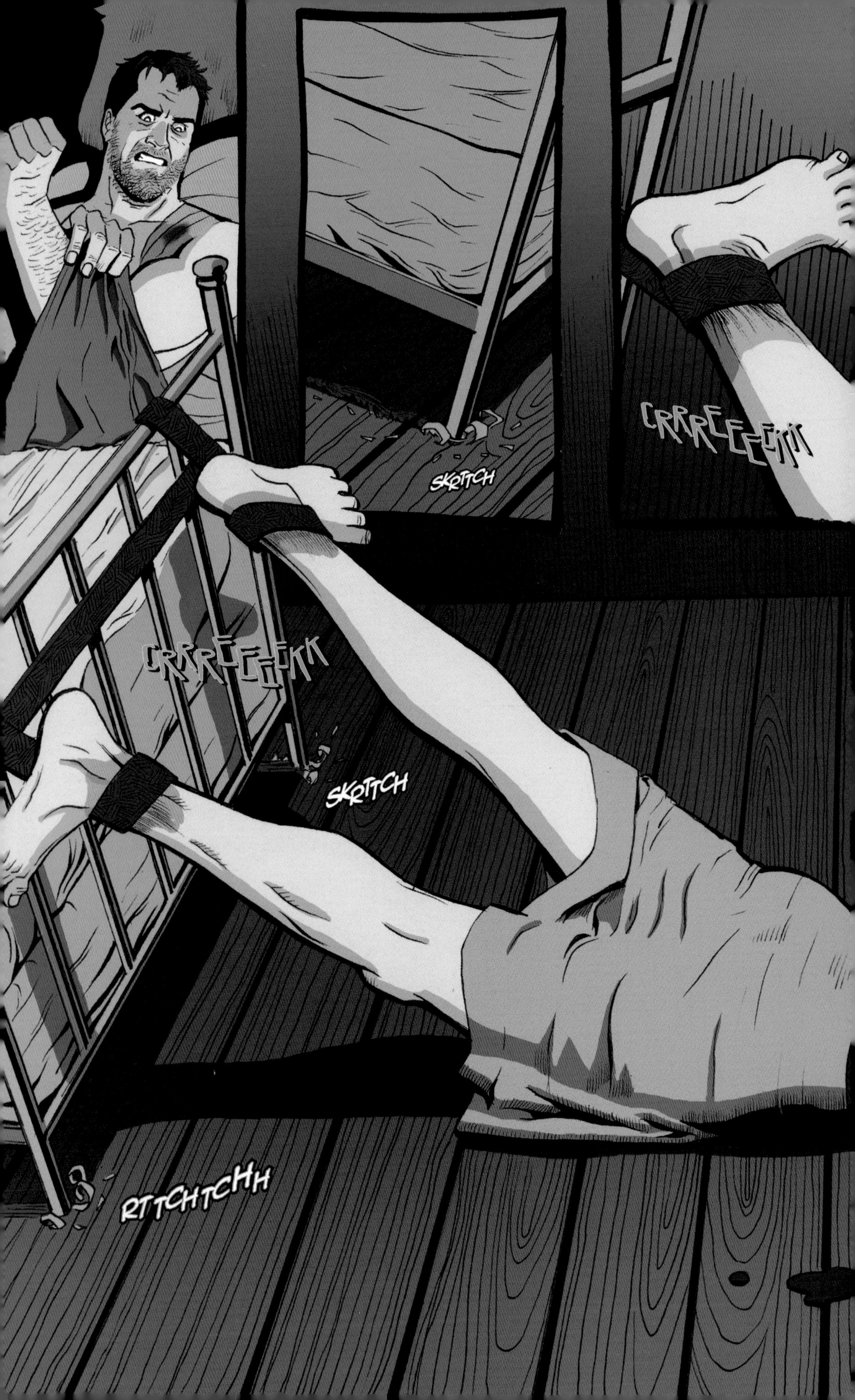
SKRTTCH
CRRRREEEEKK
CRRRREEEEKK
SKRTTCH
RTTCHTCHH

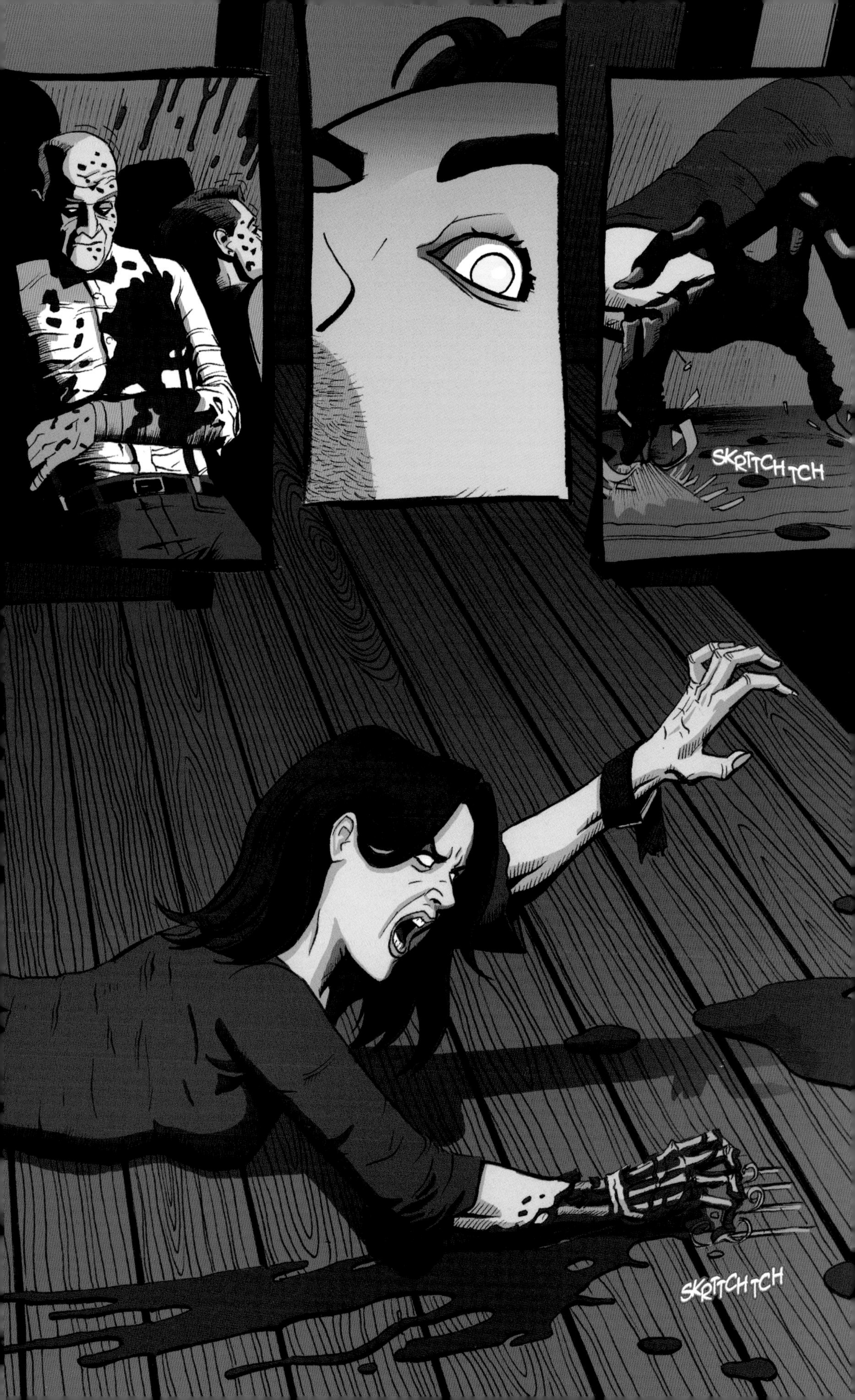
SKRITCH TCH
SKRITCH TCH

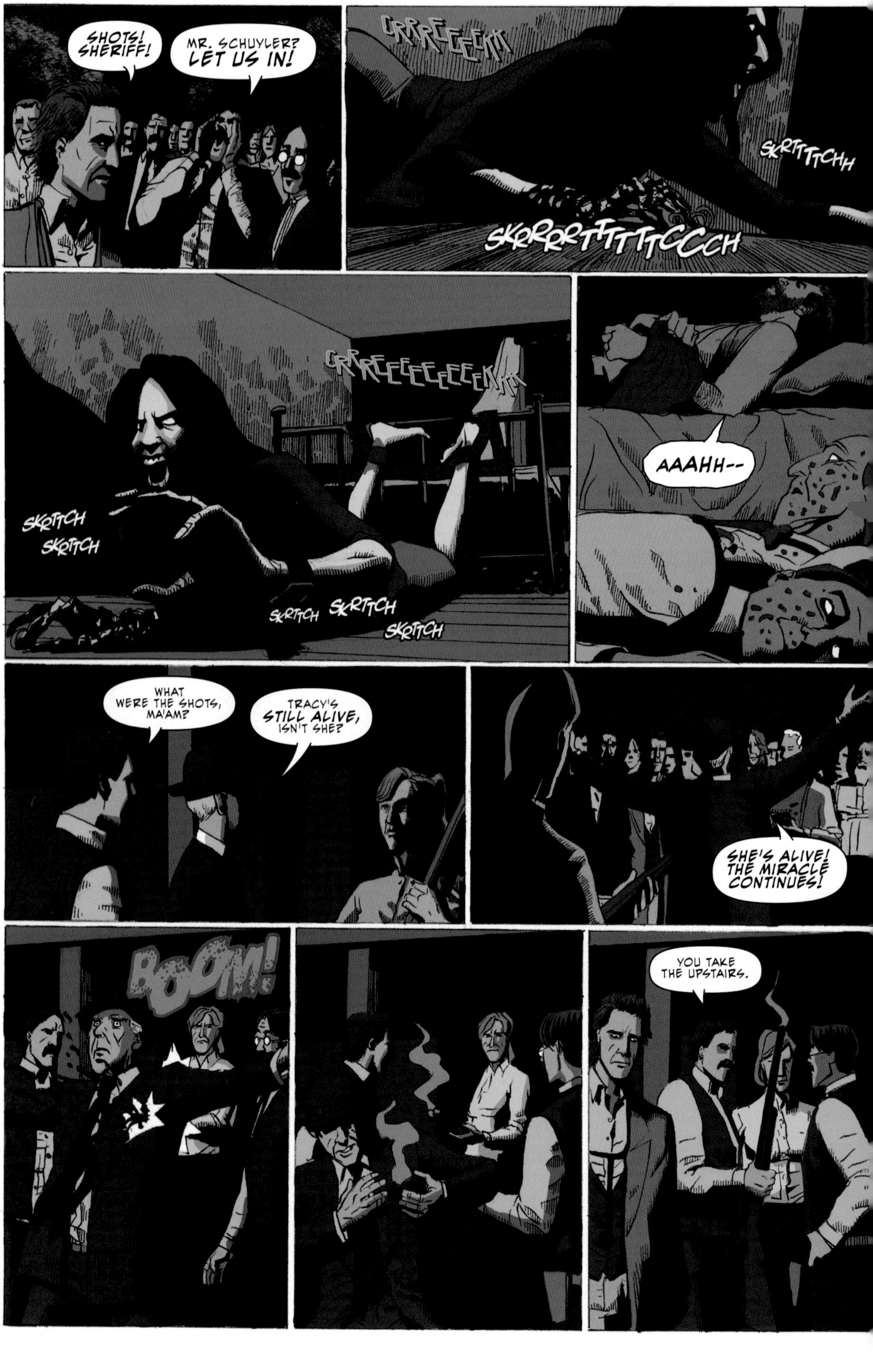
SHOTS! SHERIFF!
MR. SCHUYLER? LET US IN!
CRRRREEEEKK
SKRTTTTCHH
SKRRRRTTTTTTCCCH
CRRRREEEEEEEEEEKKK
SKRTTCH
SKRTTCH
SKRTTCH
SKRTTCH
SKRTTCH
AAAHH--
WHAT WERE THE SHOTS, MA'AM?
TRACY'S STILL ALIVE, ISN'T SHE?
SHE'S ALIVE! THE MIRACLE CONTINUES!
BOOM!
YOU TAKE THE UPSTAIRS.

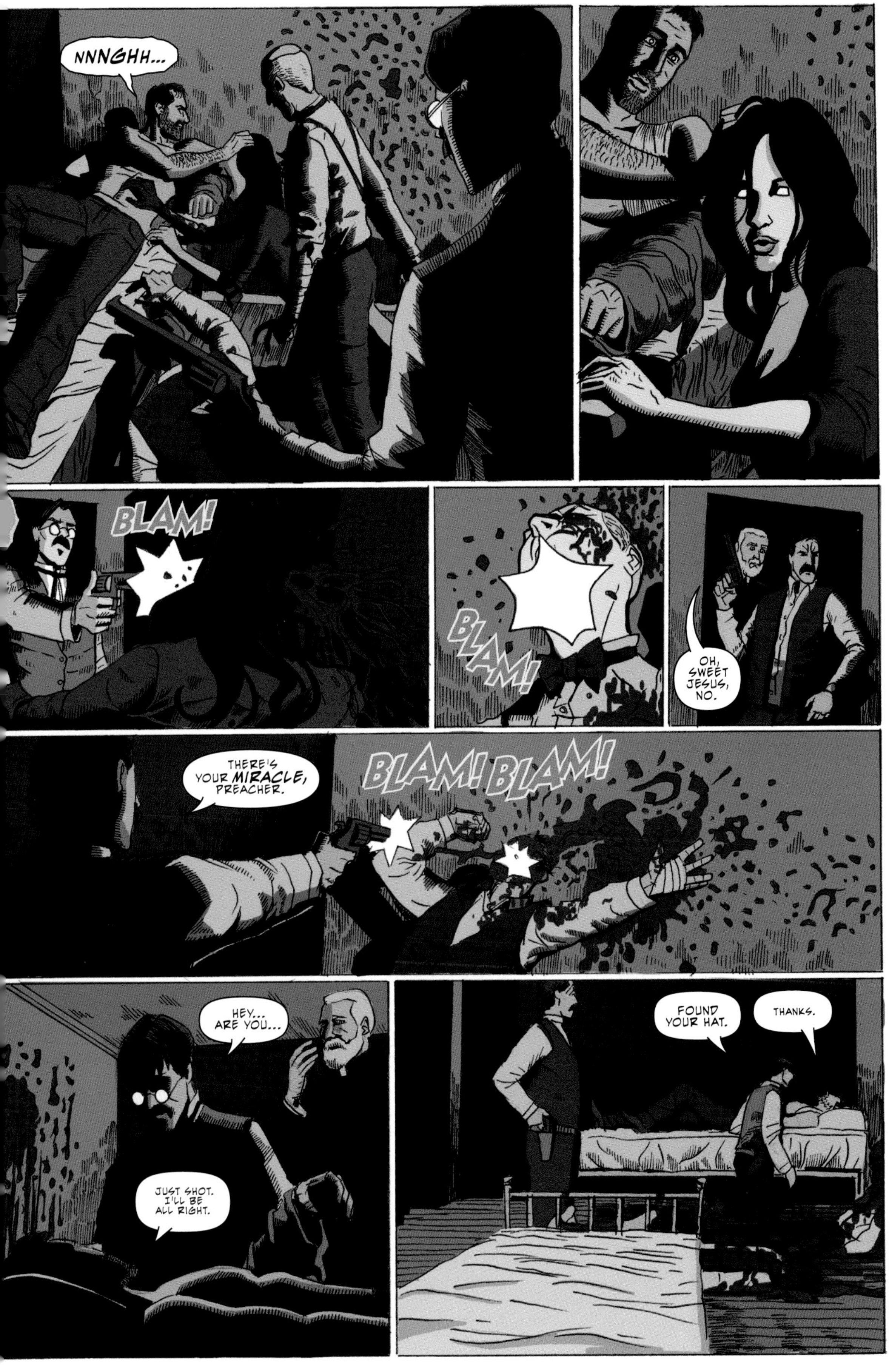

NNNGHH...
BLAM!
BLAM!
OH, SWEET JESUS, NO.
THERE'S YOUR MIRACLE, PREACHER.
BLAM! BLAM!
HEY... ARE YOU...
JUST SHOT. I'LL BE ALL RIGHT.
FOUND YOUR HAT.
THANKS.

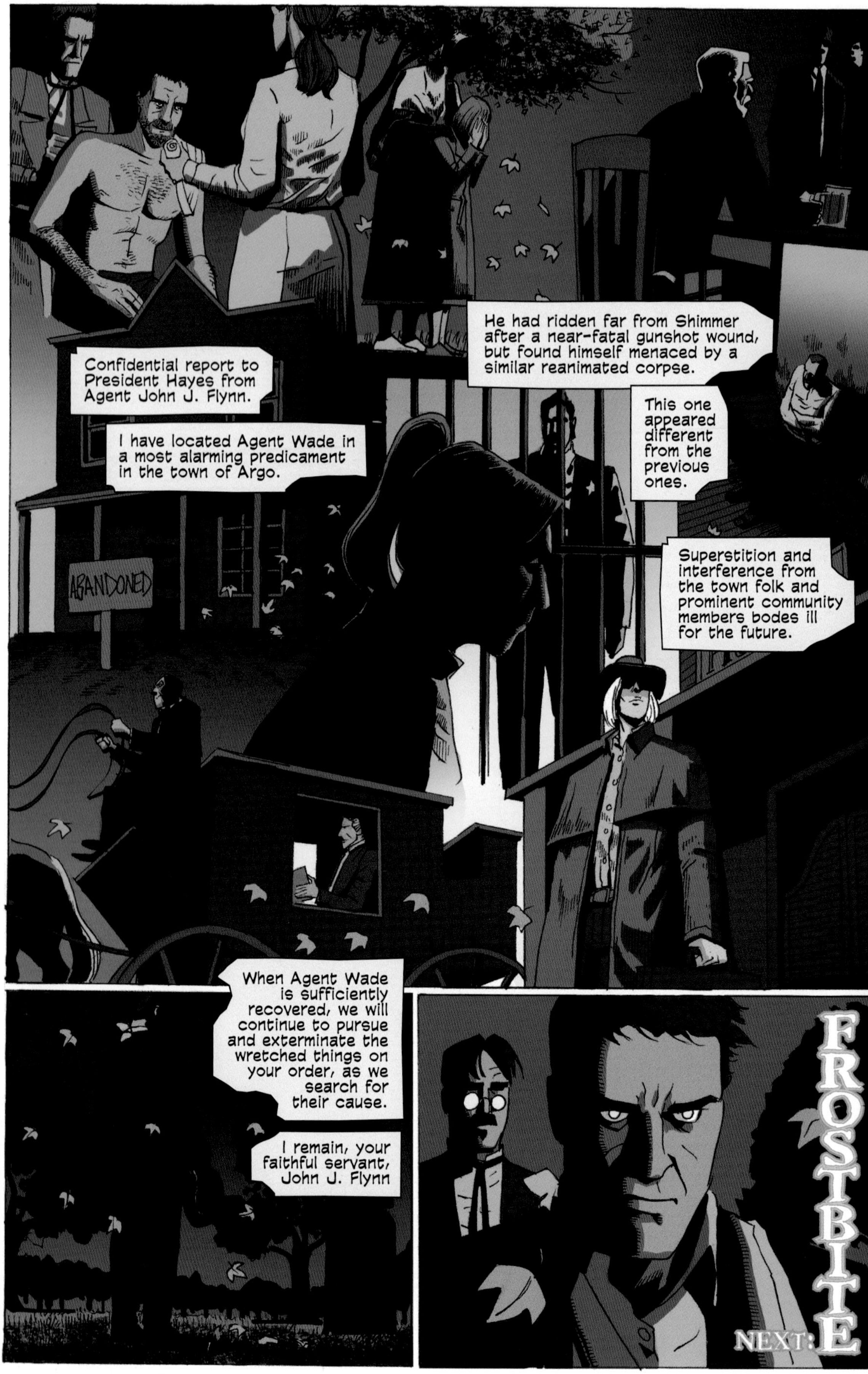
Confidential report to President Hayes from Agent John J. Flynn.
I have located Agent Wade in a most alarming predicament in the town of Argo.
ABANDONED
He had ridden far from Shimmer after a near-fatal gunshot wound, but found himself menaced by a similar reanimated corpse.
This one appeared different from the previous ones.
Superstition and interference from the town folk and prominent community members bodes ill for the future.
When Agent Wade is sufficiently recovered, we will continue to pursue and exterminate the wretched things on your order, as we search for their cause.
I remain, your faithful servant, John J. Flynn
NEXT: FROSTBITE

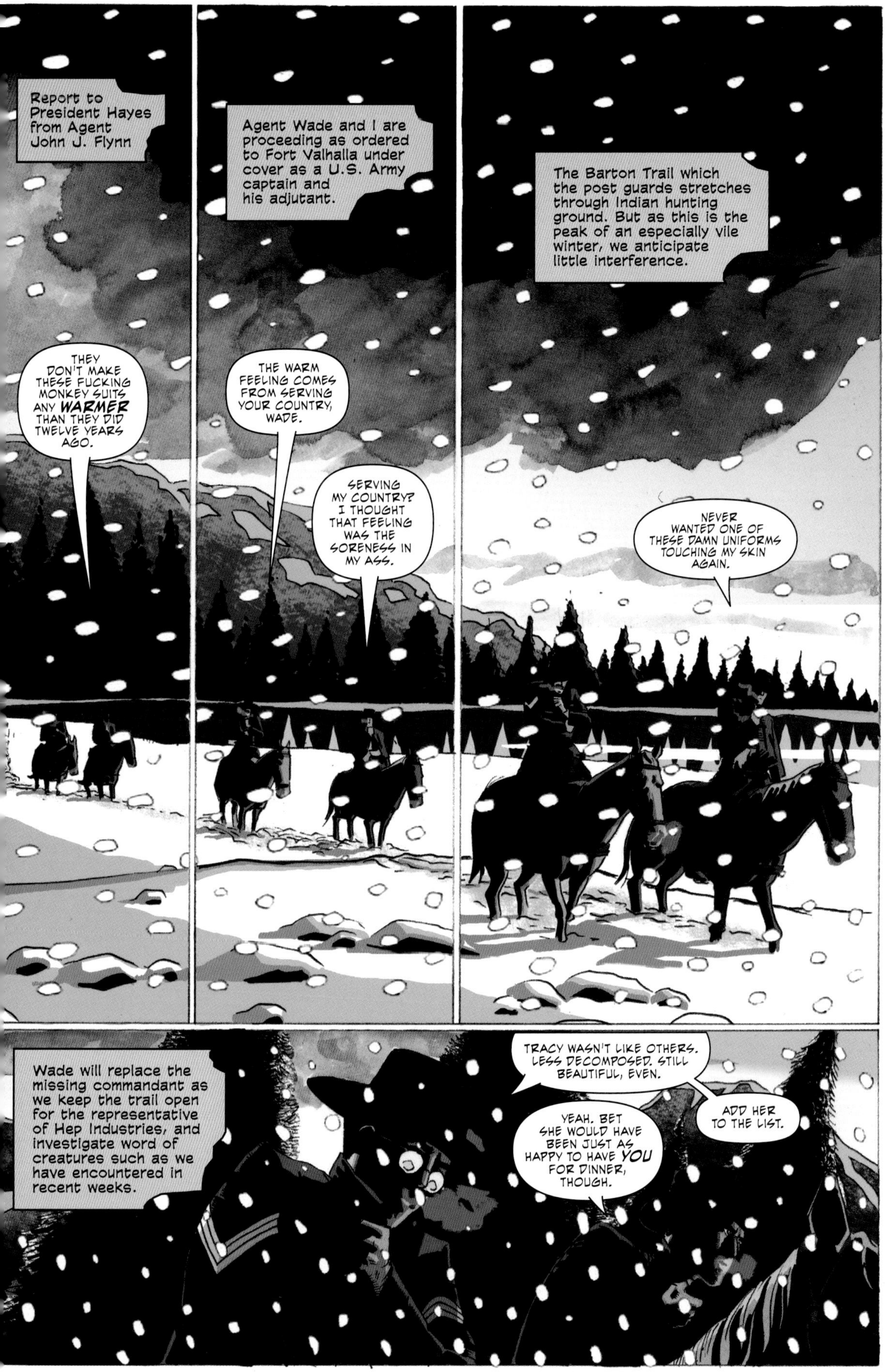

Report to President Hayes from Agent John J. Flynn
THEY DON'T MAKE THESE FUCKING MONKEY SUITS ANY **WARMER** THAN THEY DID TWELVE YEARS AGO.
Agent Wade and I are proceeding as ordered to Fort Valhalla under cover as a U.S. Army captain and his adjutant.
THE WARM FEELING COMES FROM SERVING YOUR COUNTRY, WADE.
SERVING MY COUNTRY? I THOUGHT THAT FEELING WAS THE SORENESS IN MY ASS.
The Barton Trail which the post guards stretches through Indian hunting ground. But as this is the peak of an especially vile winter, we anticipate little interference.
NEVER WANTED ONE OF THESE DAMN UNIFORMS TOUCHING MY SKIN AGAIN.
Wade will replace the missing commandant as we keep the trail open for the representative of Hep Industries, and investigate word of creatures such as we have encountered in recent weeks.
TRACY WASN'T LIKE OTHERS. LESS DECOMPOSED. STILL BEAUTIFUL, EVEN.
YEAH. BET SHE WOULD HAVE BEEN JUST AS HAPPY TO HAVE **YOU** FOR DINNER, THOUGH.
ADD HER TO THE LIST.

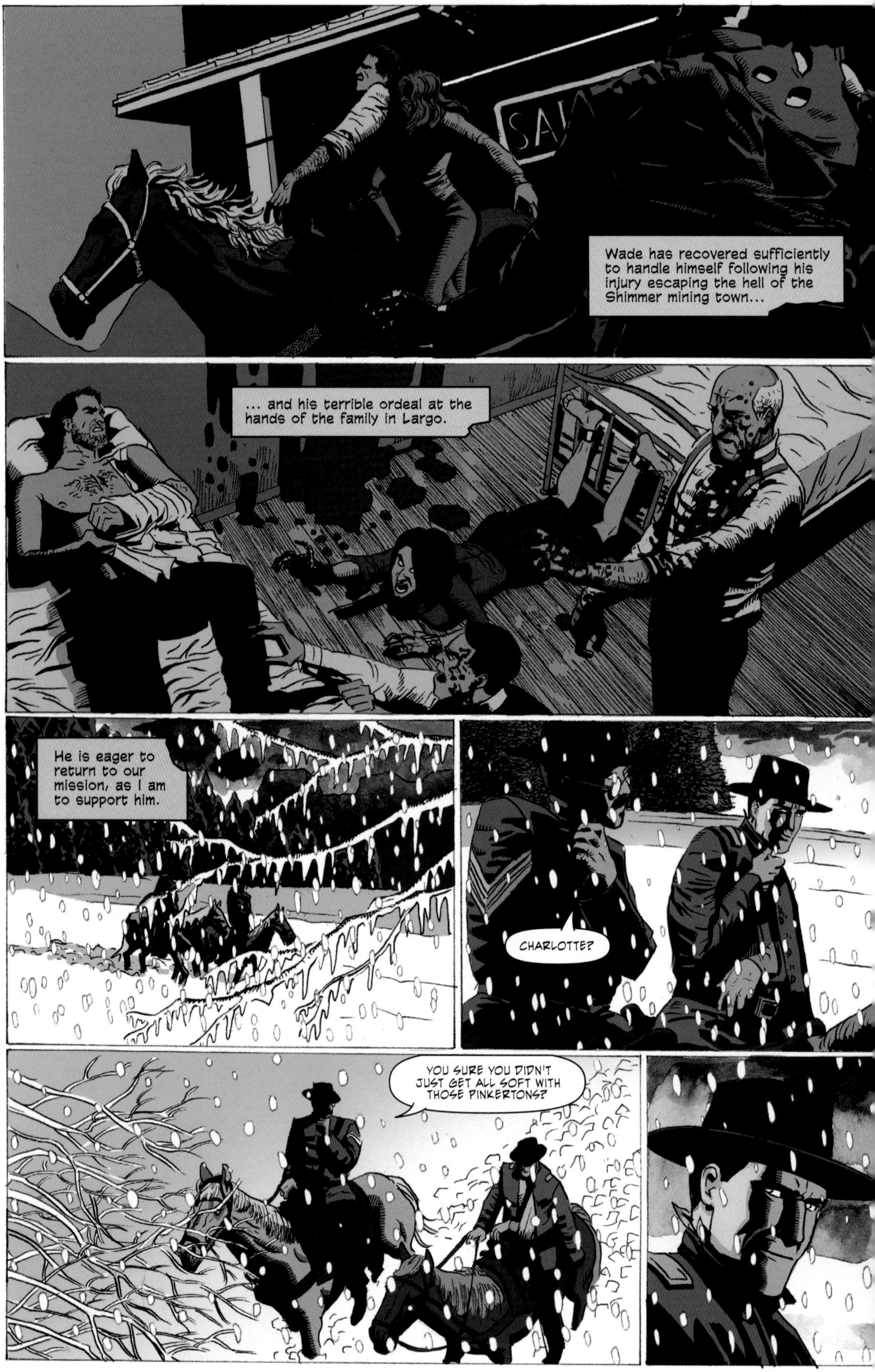
Wade has recovered sufficiently to handle himself following his injury escaping the hell of the Shimmer mining town...
... and his terrible ordeal at the hands of the family in Largo.
He is eager to return to our mission, as I am to support him.
CHARLOTTE?
YOU SURE YOU DIDN'T JUST GET ALL SOFT WITH THOSE PINKERTONS?

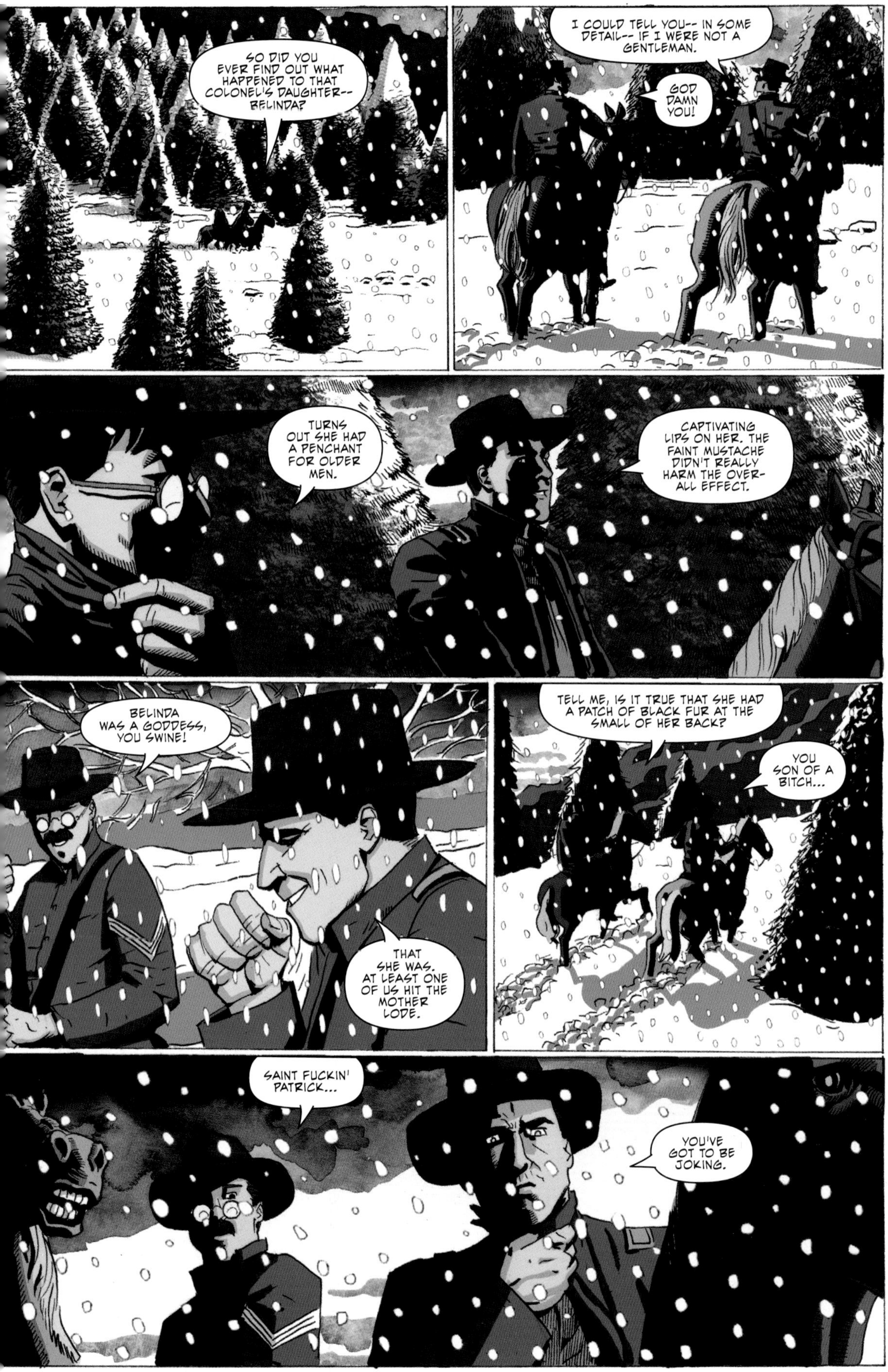
SO DID YOU EVER FIND OUT WHAT HAPPENED TO THAT COLONEL'S DAUGHTER-- BELINDA?
I COULD TELL YOU-- IN SOME DETAIL-- IF I WERE NOT A GENTLEMAN.
GOD DAMN YOU!
TURNS OUT SHE HAD A PENCHANT FOR OLDER MEN.
CAPTIVATING LIPS ON HER. THE FAINT MUSTACHE DIDN'T REALLY HARM THE OVER-ALL EFFECT.
BELINDA WAS A GODDESS, YOU SWINE!
THAT SHE WAS. AT LEAST ONE OF US HIT THE MOTHER LODE.
TELL ME, IS IT TRUE THAT SHE HAD A PATCH OF BLACK FUR AT THE SMALL OF HER BACK?
YOU SON OF A BITCH...
SAINT FUCKIN' PATRICK...
YOU'VE GOT TO BE JOKING.

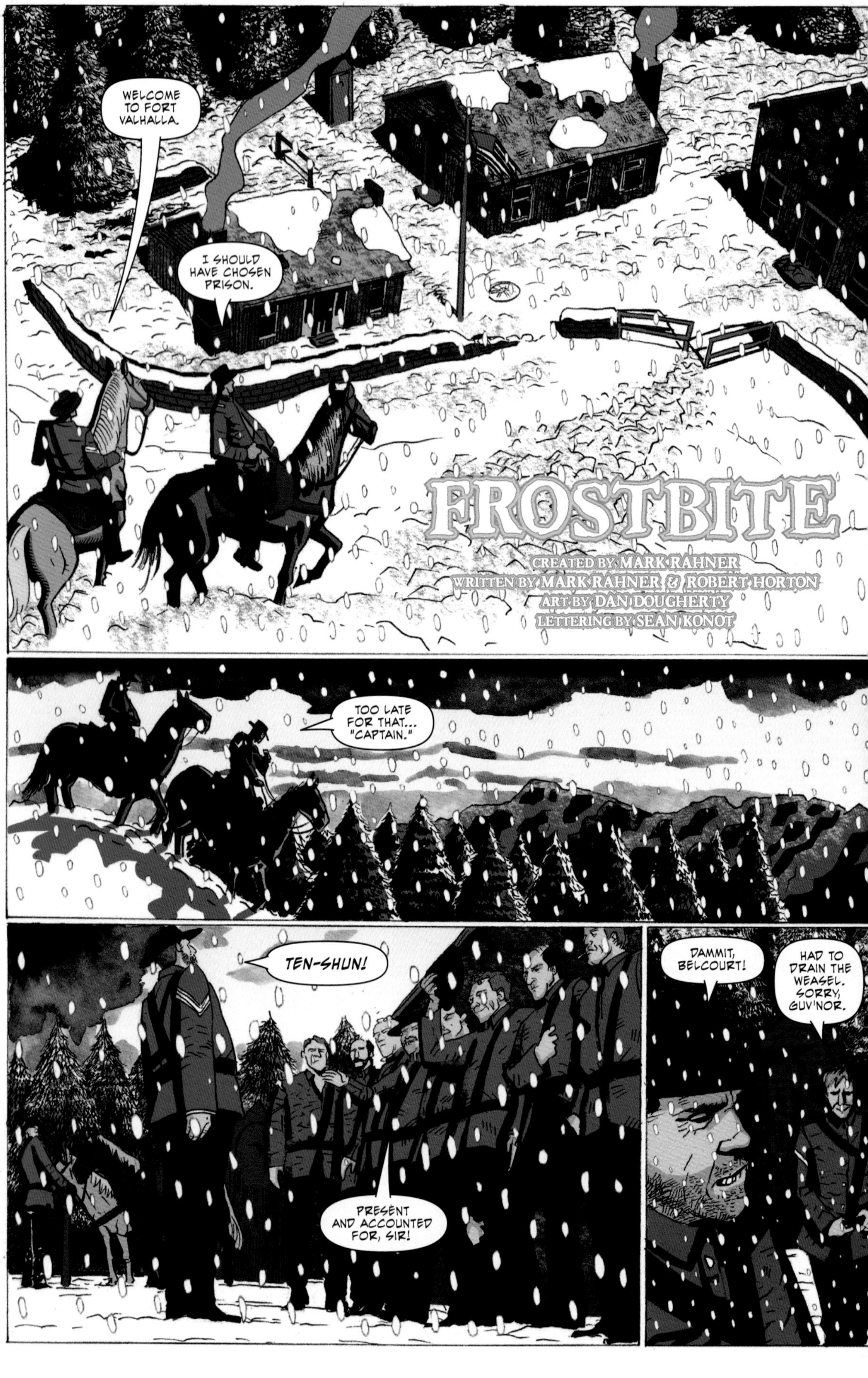
WELCOME TO FORT VALHALLA.
I SHOULD HAVE CHOSEN PRISON.
FROSTBITE
CREATED BY MARK RAHNER
WRITTEN BY MARK RAHNER & ROBERT HORTON
ART BY DAN DOUGHERTY
LETTERING BY SEAN KONOT
TOO LATE FOR THAT... "CAPTAIN."
TEN-SHUN!
PRESENT AND ACCOUNTED FOR, SIR!
DAMMIT, BELCOURT!
HAD TO DRAIN THE WEASEL. SORRY, GUV'NOR.

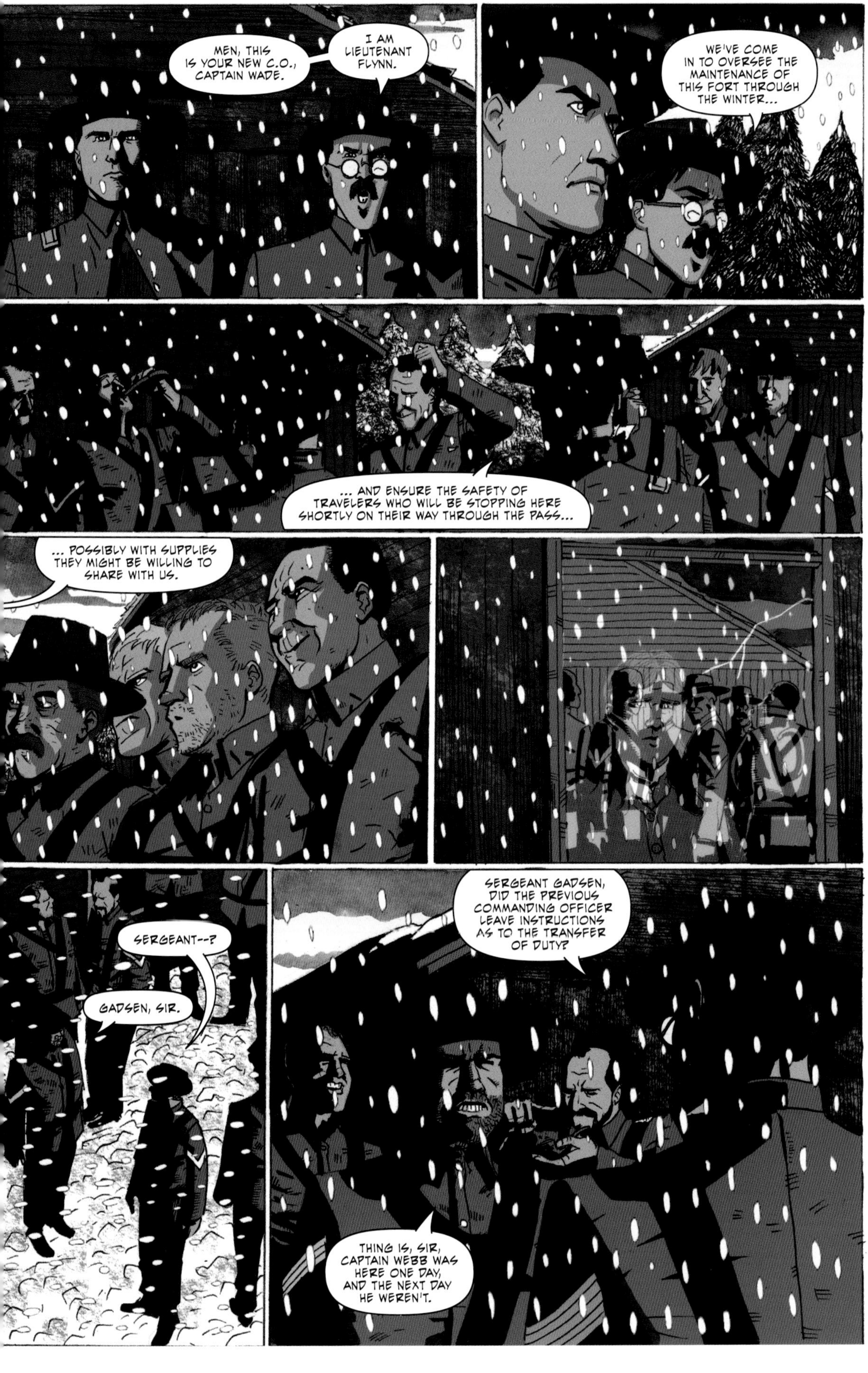
MEN, THIS IS YOUR NEW C.O., CAPTAIN WADE.
I AM LIEUTENANT FLYNN.
WE'VE COME IN TO OVERSEE THE MAINTENANCE OF THIS FORT THROUGH THE WINTER...
... AND ENSURE THE SAFETY OF TRAVELERS WHO WILL BE STOPPING HERE SHORTLY ON THEIR WAY THROUGH THE PASS...
... POSSIBLY WITH SUPPLIES THEY MIGHT BE WILLING TO SHARE WITH US.
SERGEANT--?
GADSEN, SIR.
SERGEANT GADSEN, DID THE PREVIOUS COMMANDING OFFICER LEAVE INSTRUCTIONS AS TO THE TRANSFER OF DUTY?
THING IS, SIR, CAPTAIN WEBB WAS HERE ONE DAY, AND THE NEXT DAY HE WEREN'T.

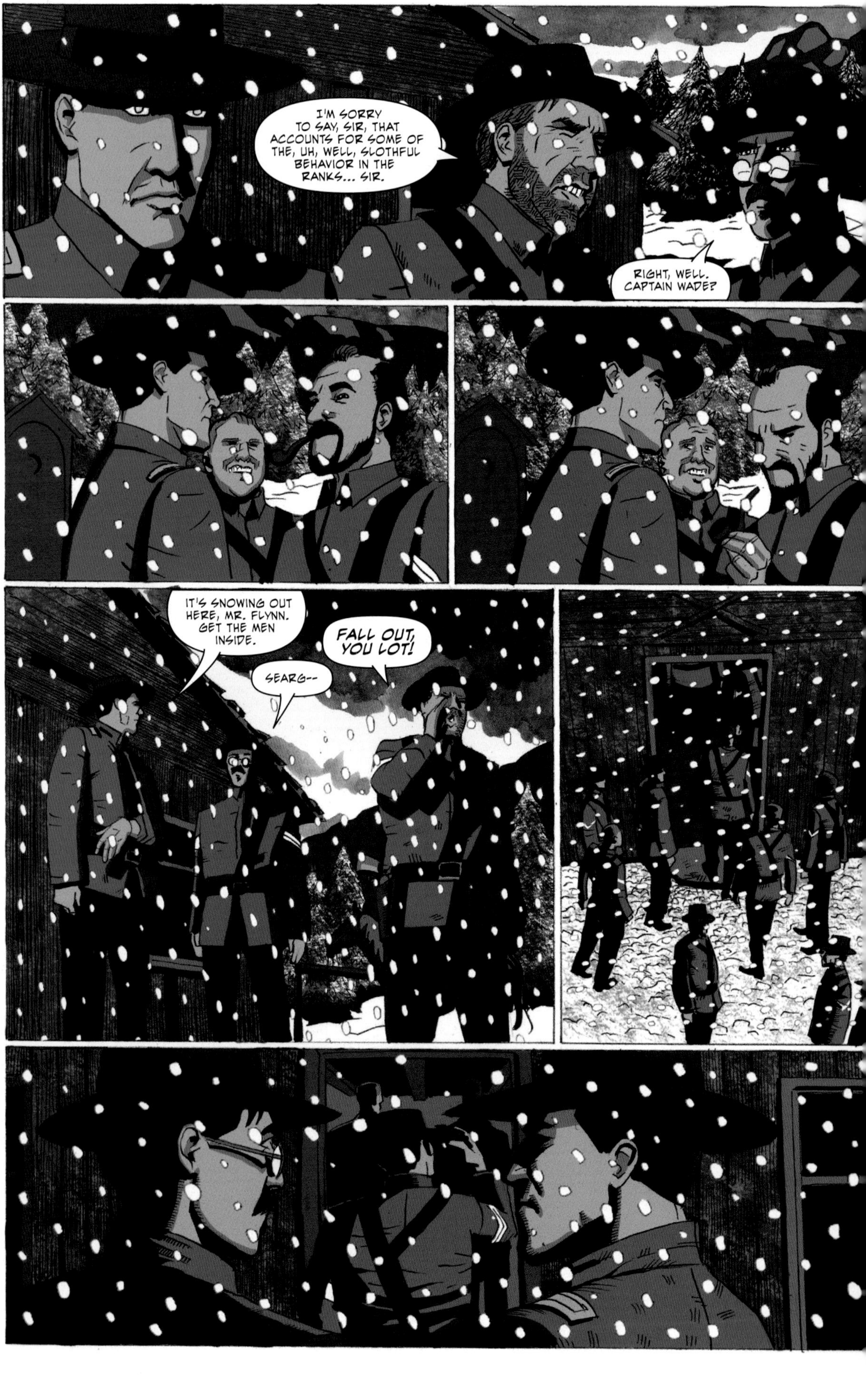
I'M SORRY TO SAY, SIR, THAT ACCOUNTS FOR SOME OF THE, UH, WELL, SLOTHFUL BEHAVIOR IN THE RANKS... SIR.
RIGHT, WELL. CAPTAIN WADE?
IT'S SNOWING OUT HERE, MR. FLYNN. GET THE MEN INSIDE.
SEARG--
FALL OUT, YOU LOT!

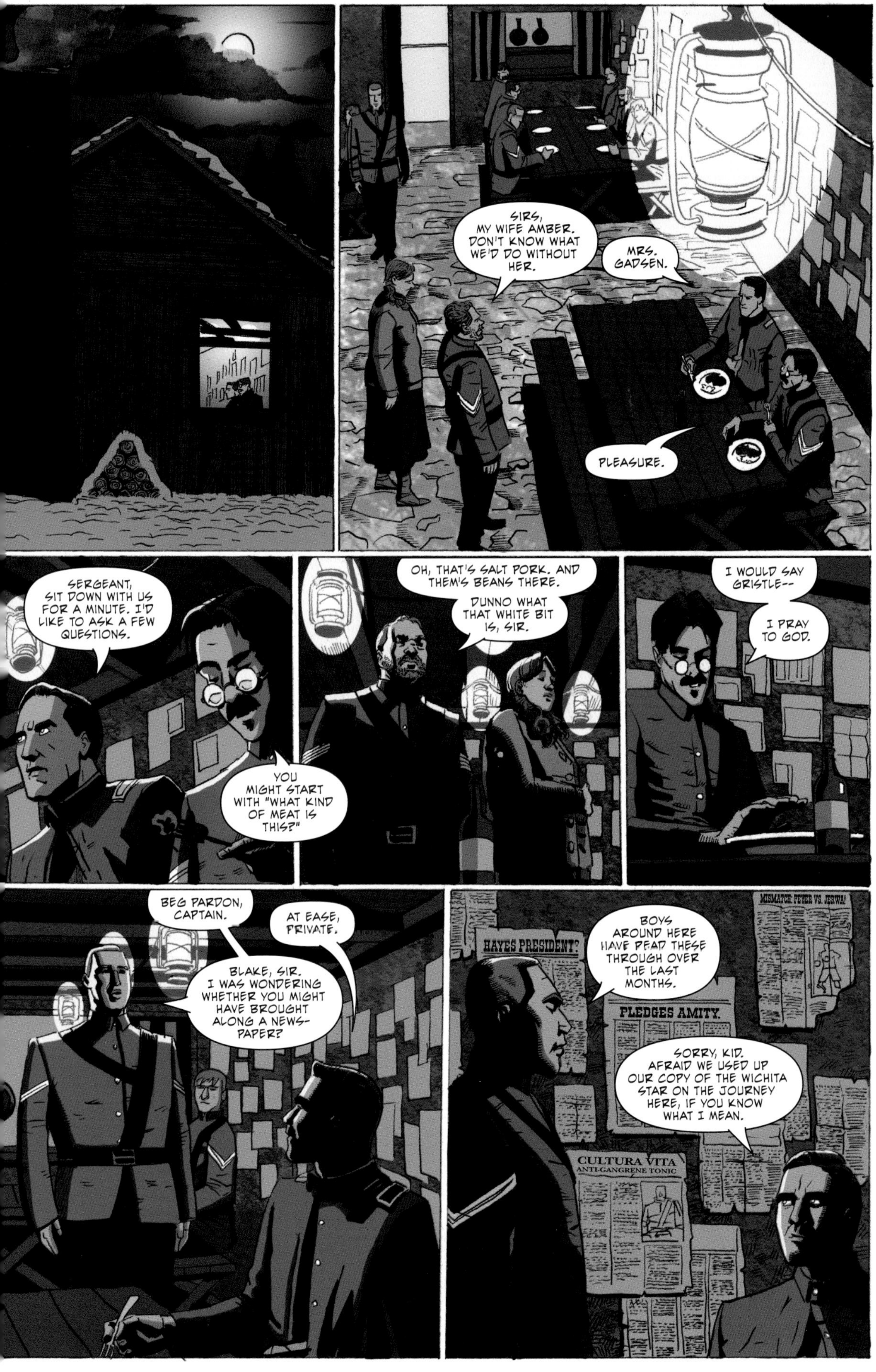
SIRS, MY WIFE AMBER. DON'T KNOW WHAT WE'D DO WITHOUT HER.
MRS. GADSEN.
PLEASURE.
SERGEANT, SIT DOWN WITH US FOR A MINUTE. I'D LIKE TO ASK A FEW QUESTIONS.
YOU MIGHT START WITH "WHAT KIND OF MEAT IS THIS?"
OH, THAT'S SALT PORK. AND THEM'S BEANS THERE.
DUNNO WHAT THAT WHITE BIT IS, SIR.
I WOULD SAY GRISTLE--
I PRAY TO GOD.
BEG PARDON, CAPTAIN.
AT EASE, PRIVATE.
BLAKE, SIR. I WAS WONDERING WHETHER YOU MIGHT HAVE BROUGHT ALONG A NEWS-PAPER?
HAYES PRESIDENT?
BOYS AROUND HERE HAVE READ THESE THROUGH OVER THE LAST MONTHS.
PLEDGES AMITY.
SORRY, KID. AFRAID WE USED UP OUR COPY OF THE WICHITA STAR ON THE JOURNEY HERE, IF YOU KNOW WHAT I MEAN.
CULTURA VITA
ANTI-GANGRENE TONIC

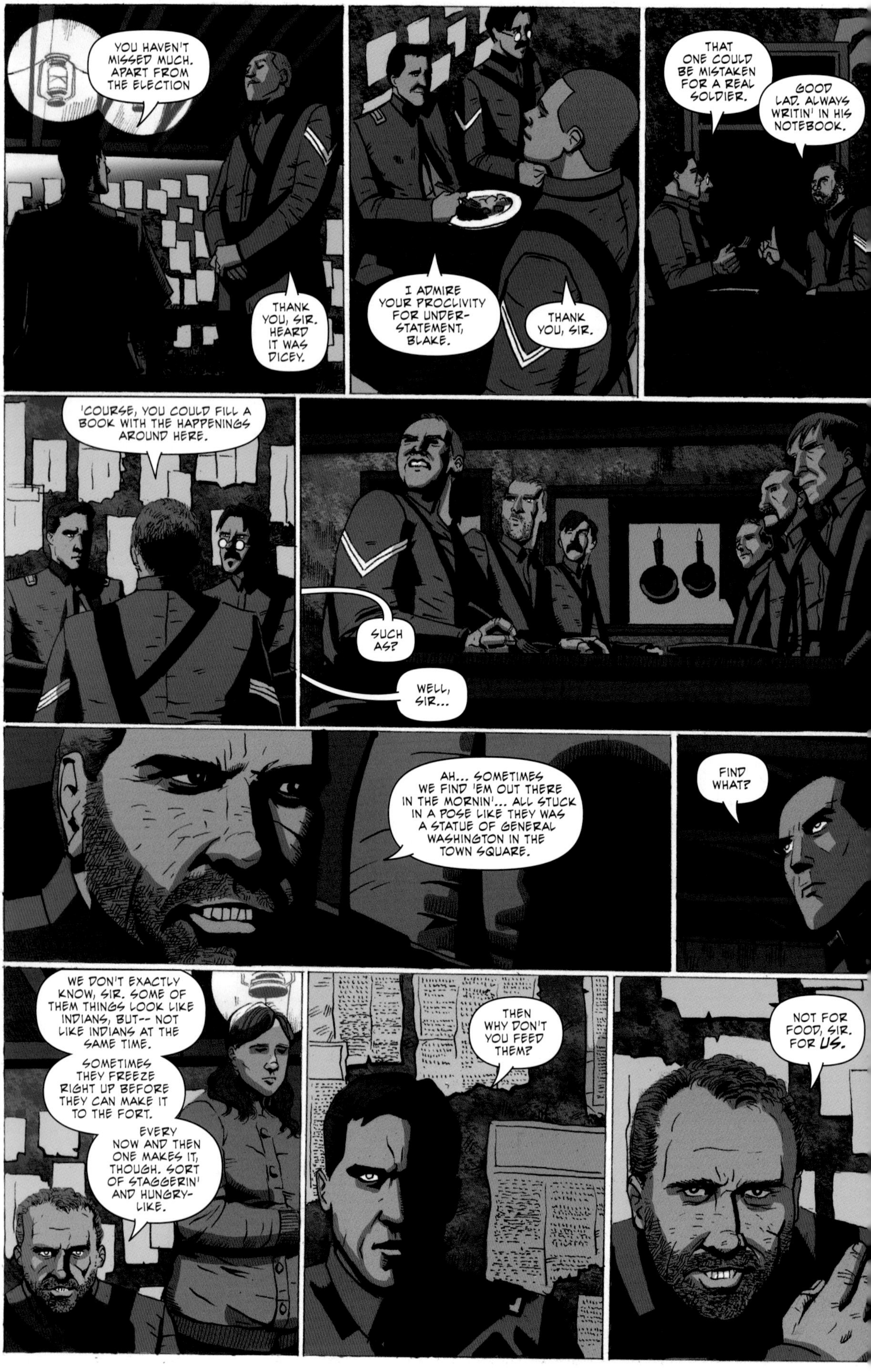
YOU HAVEN'T MISSED MUCH. APART FROM THE ELECTION
THANK YOU, SIR. HEARD IT WAS DICEY.
I ADMIRE YOUR PROCLIVITY FOR UNDER-STATEMENT, BLAKE.
THANK YOU, SIR.
THAT ONE COULD BE MISTAKEN FOR A REAL SOLDIER.
GOOD LAD. ALWAYS WRITIN' IN HIS NOTEBOOK.
'COURSE, YOU COULD FILL A BOOK WITH THE HAPPENINGS AROUND HERE.
SUCH AS?
WELL, SIR...
AH... SOMETIMES WE FIND 'EM OUT THERE IN THE MORNIN'... ALL STUCK IN A POSE LIKE THEY WAS A STATUE OF GENERAL WASHINGTON IN THE TOWN SQUARE.
FIND WHAT?
WE DON'T EXACTLY KNOW, SIR. SOME OF THEM THINGS LOOK LIKE INDIANS, BUT-- NOT LIKE INDIANS AT THE SAME TIME.
SOMETIMES THEY FREEZE RIGHT UP BEFORE THEY CAN MAKE IT TO THE FORT.
EVERY NOW AND THEN ONE MAKES IT, THOUGH. SORT OF STAGGERIN' AND HUNGRY-LIKE.
THEN WHY DON'T YOU FEED THEM?
NOT FOR FOOD, SIR. FOR US.

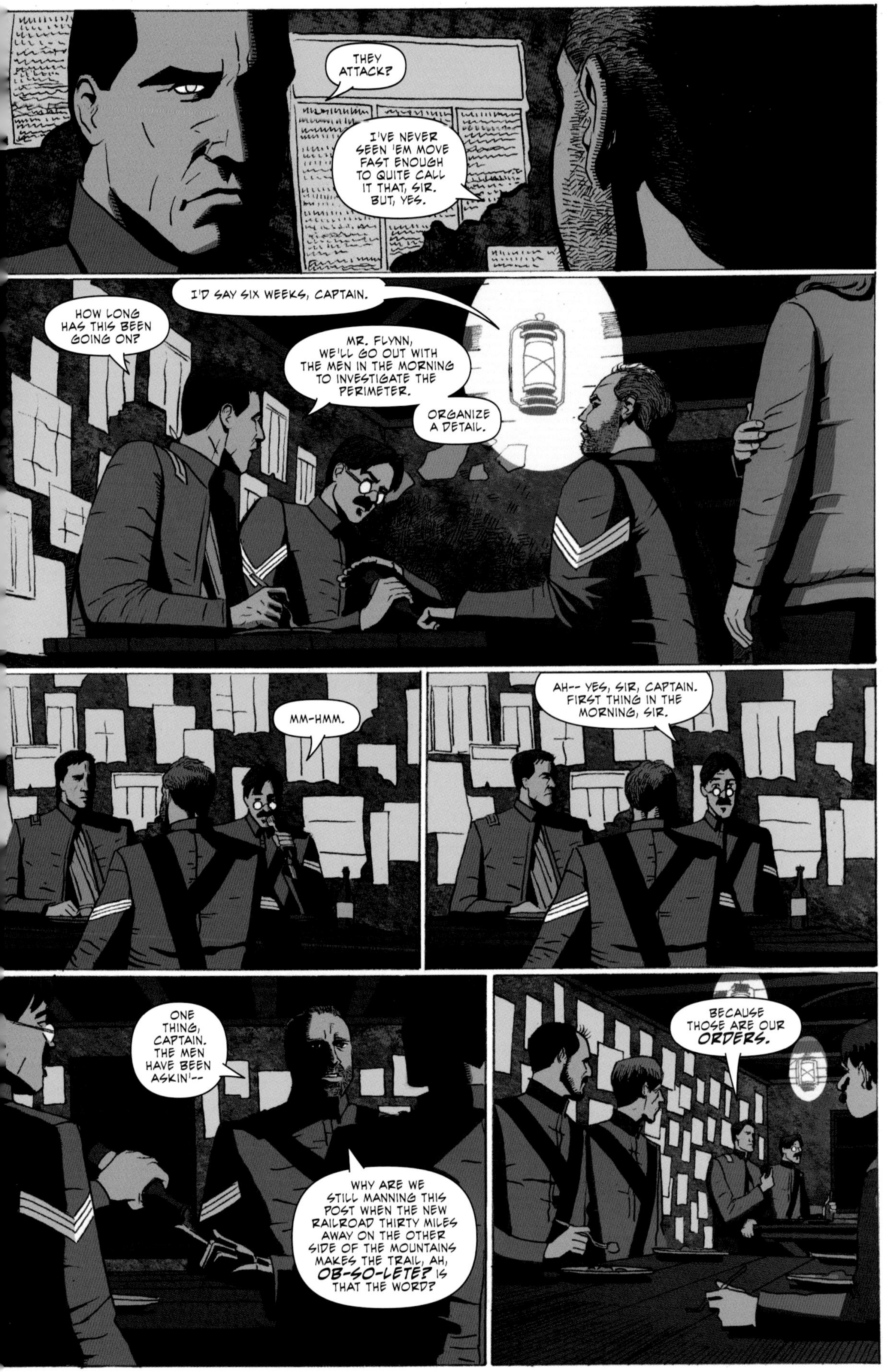
THEY ATTACK?
I'VE NEVER SEEN 'EM MOVE FAST ENOUGH TO QUITE CALL IT THAT, SIR. BUT, YES.
HOW LONG HAS THIS BEEN GOING ON?
I'D SAY SIX WEEKS, CAPTAIN.
MR. FLYNN, WE'LL GO OUT WITH THE MEN IN THE MORNING TO INVESTIGATE THE PERIMETER.
ORGANIZE A DETAIL.
MM-HMM.
AH-- YES, SIR, CAPTAIN. FIRST THING IN THE MORNING, SIR.
ONE THING, CAPTAIN. THE MEN HAVE BEEN ASKIN'--
WHY ARE WE STILL MANNING THIS POST WHEN THE NEW RAILROAD THIRTY MILES AWAY ON THE OTHER SIDE OF THE MOUNTAINS MAKES THE TRAIL, AH, OB-SO-LETE? IS THAT THE WORD?
BECAUSE THOSE ARE OUR ORDERS.

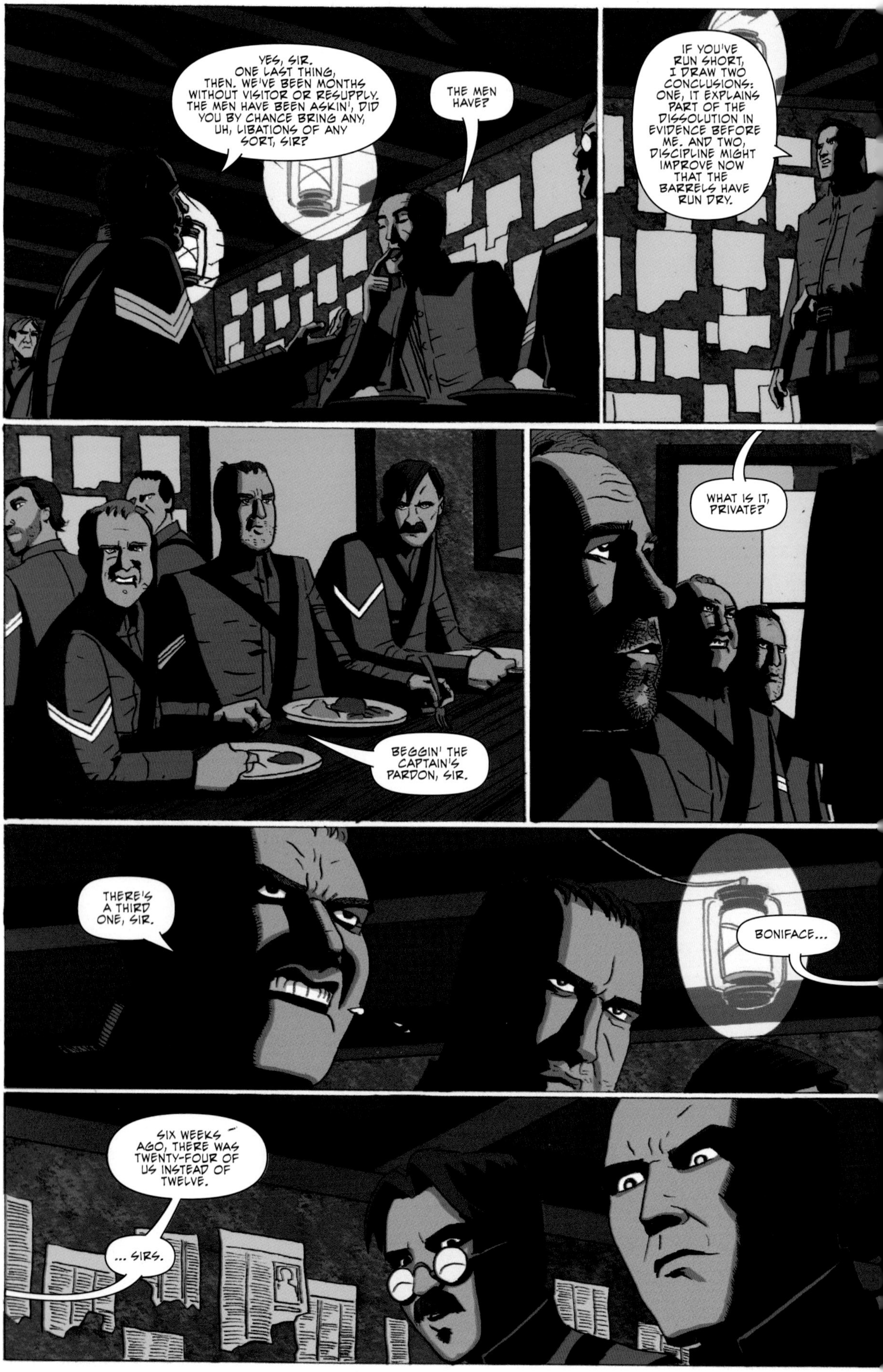
YES, SIR. ONE LAST THING, THEN. WE'VE BEEN MONTHS WITHOUT VISITOR OR RESUPPLY. THE MEN HAVE BEEN ASKIN', DID YOU BY CHANCE BRING ANY, UH, LIBATIONS OF ANY SORT, SIR?
THE MEN HAVE?
IF YOU'VE RUN SHORT, I DRAW TWO CONCLUSIONS: ONE, IT EXPLAINS PART OF THE DISSOLUTION IN EVIDENCE BEFORE ME. AND TWO, DISCIPLINE MIGHT IMPROVE NOW THAT THE BARRELS HAVE RUN DRY.
BEGGIN' THE CAPTAIN'S PARDON, SIR.
WHAT IS IT, PRIVATE?
THERE'S A THIRD ONE, SIR.
BONIFACE...
SIX WEEKS AGO, THERE WAS TWENTY-FOUR OF US INSTEAD OF TWELVE.
... SIRS.

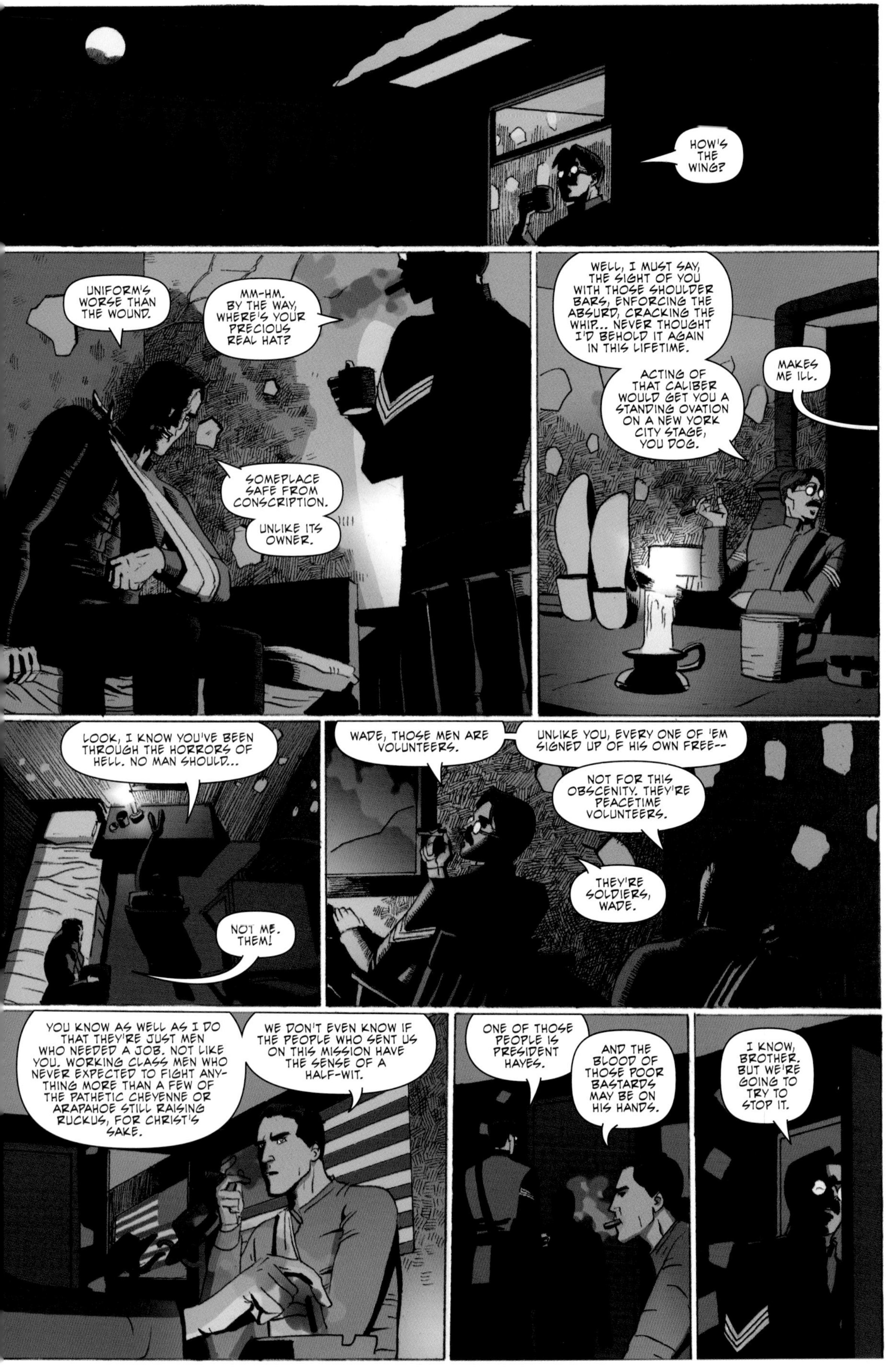
HOW'S THE WING?
UNIFORM'S WORSE THAN THE WOUND.
MM-HM. BY THE WAY, WHERE'S YOUR PRECIOUS REAL HAT?
SOMEPLACE SAFE FROM CONSCRIPTION.
UNLIKE ITS OWNER.
WELL, I MUST SAY, THE SIGHT OF YOU WITH THOSE SHOULDER BARS, ENFORCING THE ABSURD, CRACKING THE WHIP... NEVER THOUGHT I'D BEHOLD IT AGAIN IN THIS LIFETIME.
ACTING OF THAT CALIBER WOULD GET YOU A STANDING OVATION ON A NEW YORK CITY STAGE, YOU DOG.
MAKES ME ILL.
LOOK, I KNOW YOU'VE BEEN THROUGH THE HORRORS OF HELL. NO MAN SHOULD...
NOT ME. THEM!
WADE, THOSE MEN ARE VOLUNTEERS.
UNLIKE YOU, EVERY ONE OF 'EM SIGNED UP OF HIS OWN FREE--
NOT FOR THIS OBSCENITY. THEY'RE PEACETIME VOLUNTEERS.
THEY'RE SOLDIERS, WADE.
YOU KNOW AS WELL AS I DO THAT THEY'RE JUST MEN WHO NEEDED A JOB. NOT LIKE YOU. WORKING CLASS MEN WHO NEVER EXPECTED TO FIGHT ANYTHING MORE THAN A FEW OF THE PATHETIC CHEYENNE OR ARAPAHOE STILL RAISING RUCKUS, FOR CHRIST'S SAKE.
WE DON'T EVEN KNOW IF THE PEOPLE WHO SENT US ON THIS MISSION HAVE THE SENSE OF A HALF-WIT.
ONE OF THOSE PEOPLE IS PRESIDENT HAYES.
AND THE BLOOD OF THOSE POOR BASTARDS MAY BE ON HIS HANDS.
I KNOW, BROTHER. BUT WE'RE GOING TO TRY TO STOP IT.

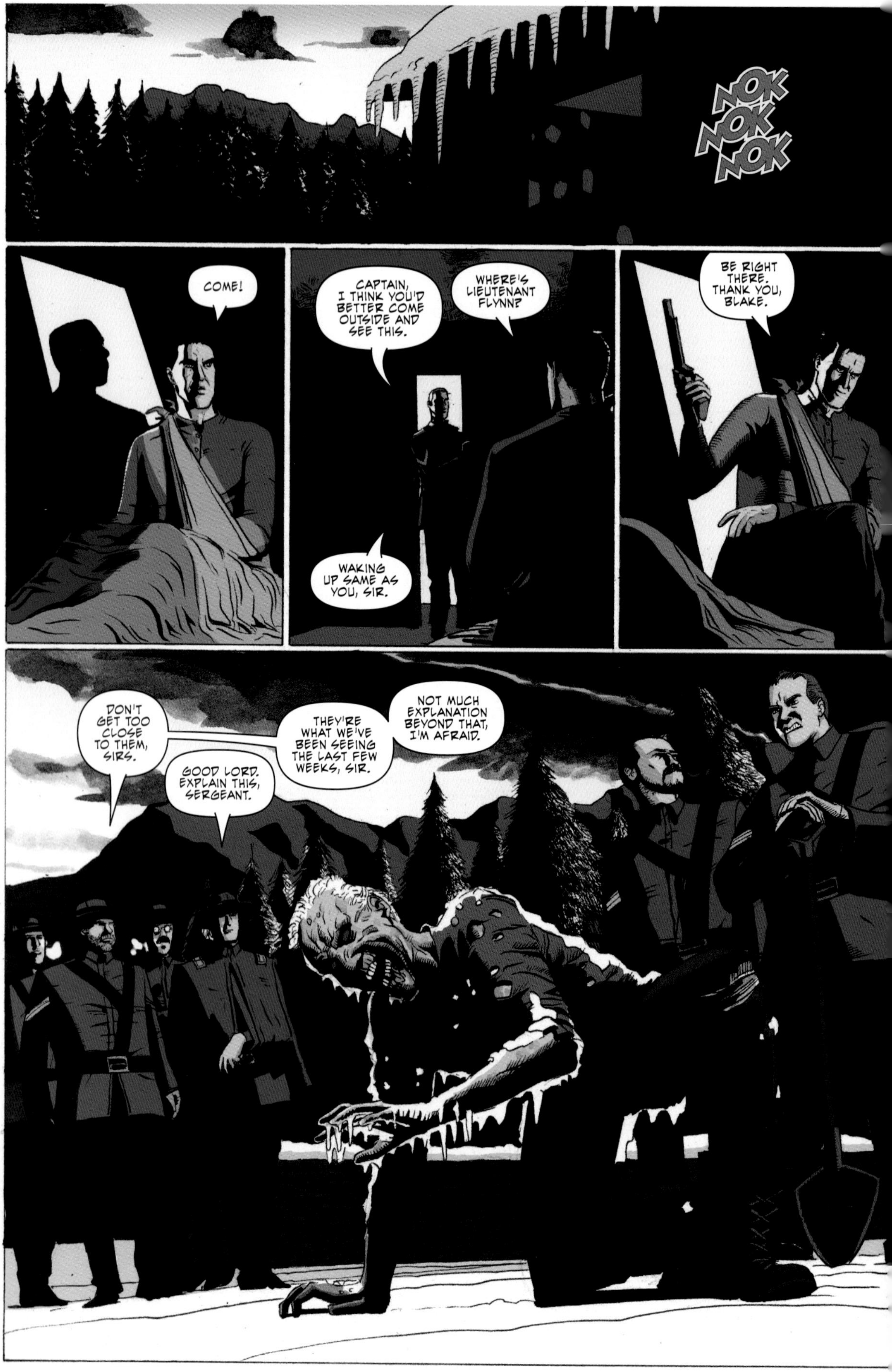
NOK NOK NOK
COME!
CAPTAIN, I THINK YOU'D BETTER COME OUTSIDE AND SEE THIS.
WHERE'S LIEUTENANT FLYNN?
WAKING UP SAME AS YOU, SIR.
BE RIGHT THERE. THANK YOU, BLAKE.
DON'T GET TOO CLOSE TO THEM, SIRS.
GOOD LORD. EXPLAIN THIS, SERGEANT.
THEY'RE WHAT WE'VE BEEN SEEING THE LAST FEW WEEKS, SIR.
NOT MUCH EXPLANATION BEYOND THAT, I'M AFRAID.

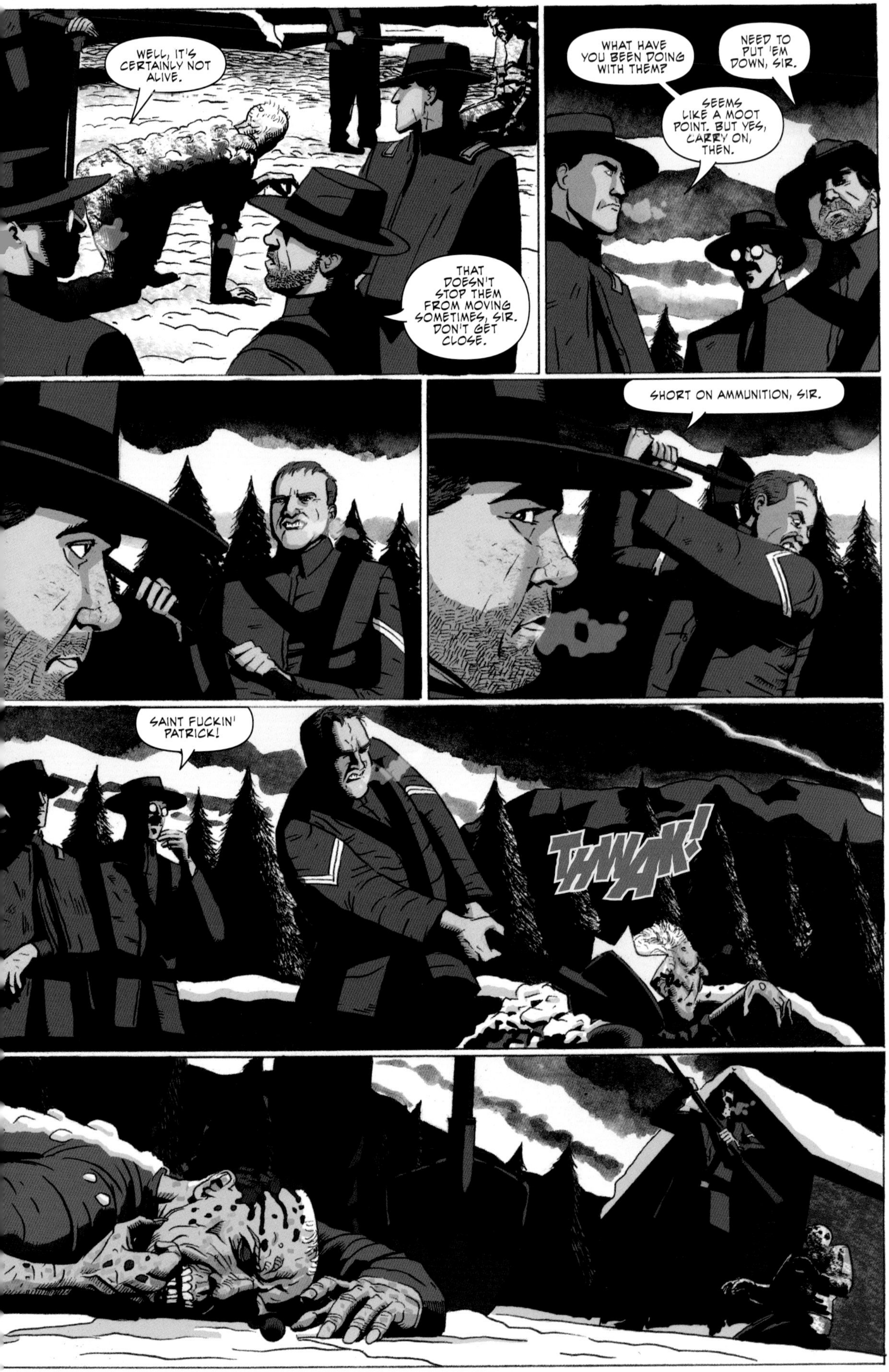
WELL, IT'S CERTAINLY NOT ALIVE.
THAT DOESN'T STOP THEM FROM MOVING SOMETIMES, SIR. DON'T GET CLOSE.
WHAT HAVE YOU BEEN DOING WITH THEM?
NEED TO PUT 'EM DOWN, SIR.
SEEMS LIKE A MOOT POINT. BUT YES, CARRY ON, THEN.
SHORT ON AMMUNITION, SIR.
SAINT FUCKIN' PATRICK!
THWAK!

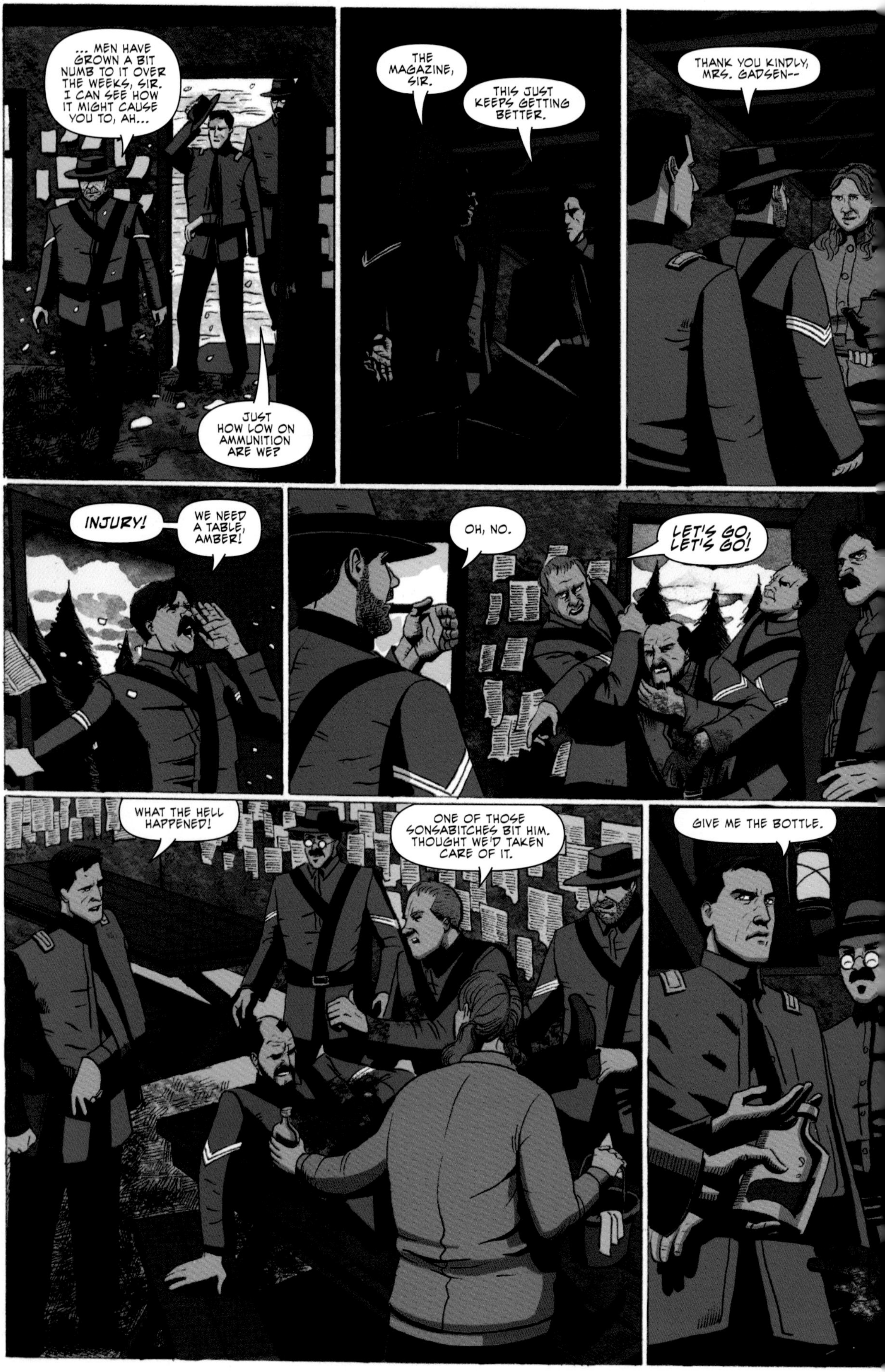
... MEN HAVE GROWN A BIT NUMB TO IT OVER THE WEEKS, SIR. I CAN SEE HOW IT MIGHT CAUSE YOU TO, AH...
JUST HOW LOW ON AMMUNITION ARE WE?
THE MAGAZINE, SIR.
THIS JUST KEEPS GETTING BETTER.
THANK YOU KINDLY, MRS. GADSEN--
INJURY!
WE NEED A TABLE, AMBER!
OH, NO.
LET'S GO, LET'S GO!
WHAT THE HELL HAPPENED!
ONE OF THOSE SONSABITCHES BIT HIM. THOUGHT WE'D TAKEN CARE OF IT.
GIVE ME THE BOTTLE.

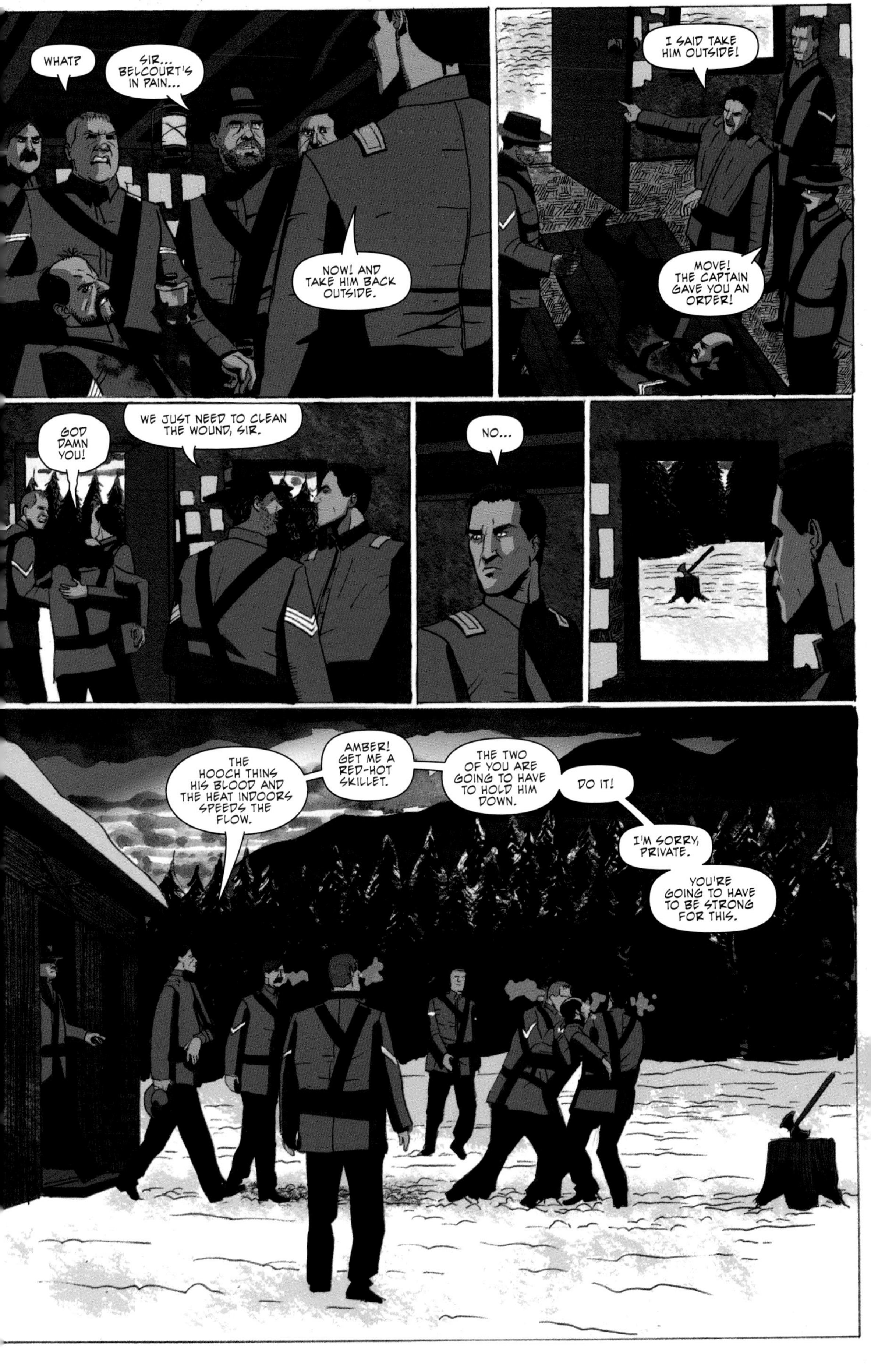
WHAT?
SIR... BELCOURT'S IN PAIN...
NOW! AND TAKE HIM BACK OUTSIDE.
I SAID TAKE HIM OUTSIDE!
MOVE! THE CAPTAIN GAVE YOU AN ORDER!
GOD DAMN YOU!
WE JUST NEED TO CLEAN THE WOUND, SIR.
NO...
THE HOOCH THINS HIS BLOOD AND THE HEAT INDOORS SPEEDS THE FLOW.
AMBER! GET ME A RED-HOT SKILLET.
THE TWO OF YOU ARE GOING TO HAVE TO HOLD HIM DOWN.
DO IT!
I'M SORRY, PRIVATE.
YOU'RE GOING TO HAVE TO BE STRONG FOR THIS.

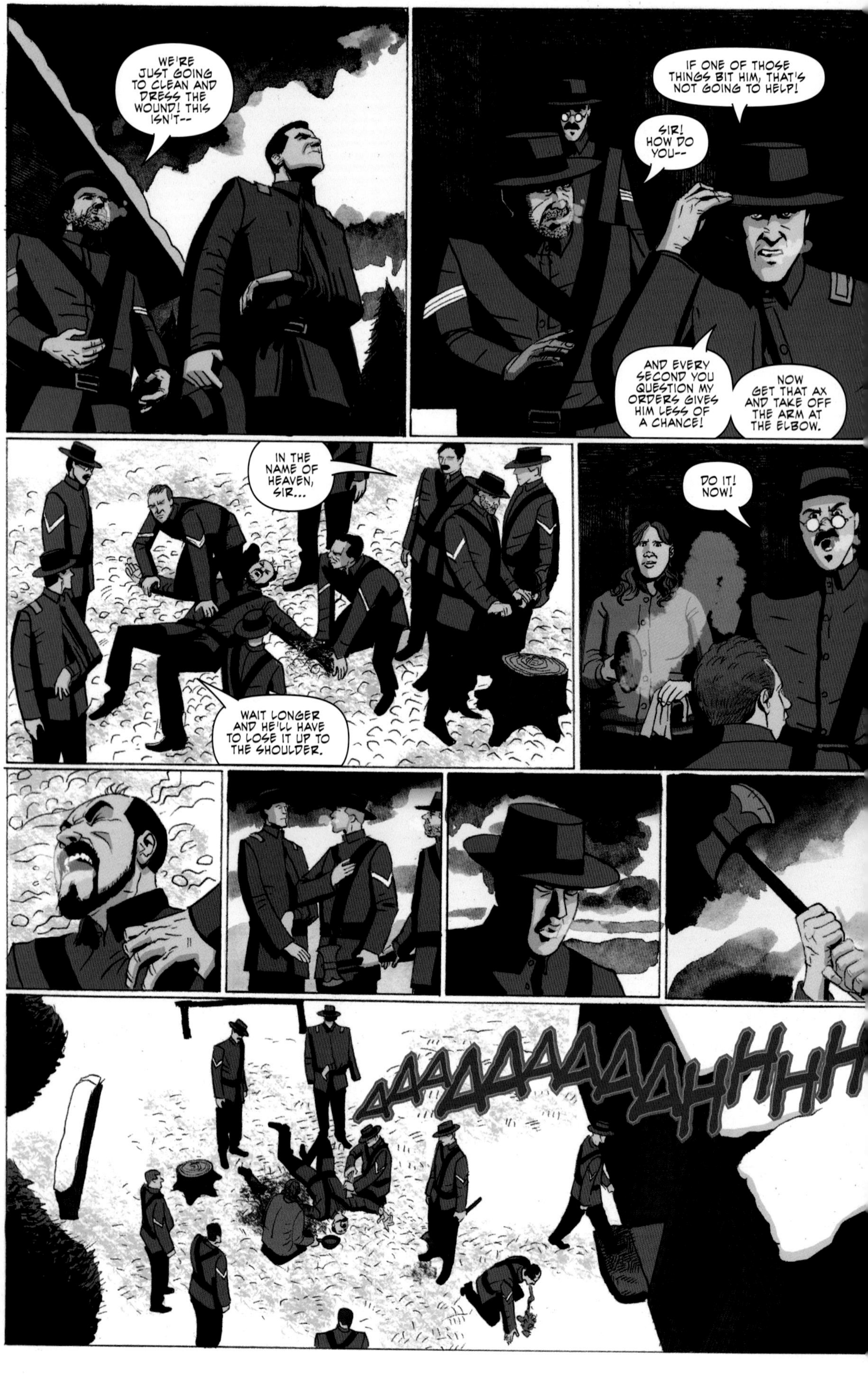
WE'RE JUST GOING TO CLEAN AND DRESS THE WOUND! THIS ISN'T--
IF ONE OF THOSE THINGS BIT HIM, THAT'S NOT GOING TO HELP!
SIR! HOW DO YOU--
AND EVERY SECOND YOU QUESTION MY ORDERS GIVES HIM LESS OF A CHANCE!
NOW GET THAT AX AND TAKE OFF THE ARM AT THE ELBOW.
IN THE NAME OF HEAVEN, SIR...
WAIT LONGER AND HE'LL HAVE TO LOSE IT UP TO THE SHOULDER.
DO IT! NOW!
AAAAAAAAAHHHH

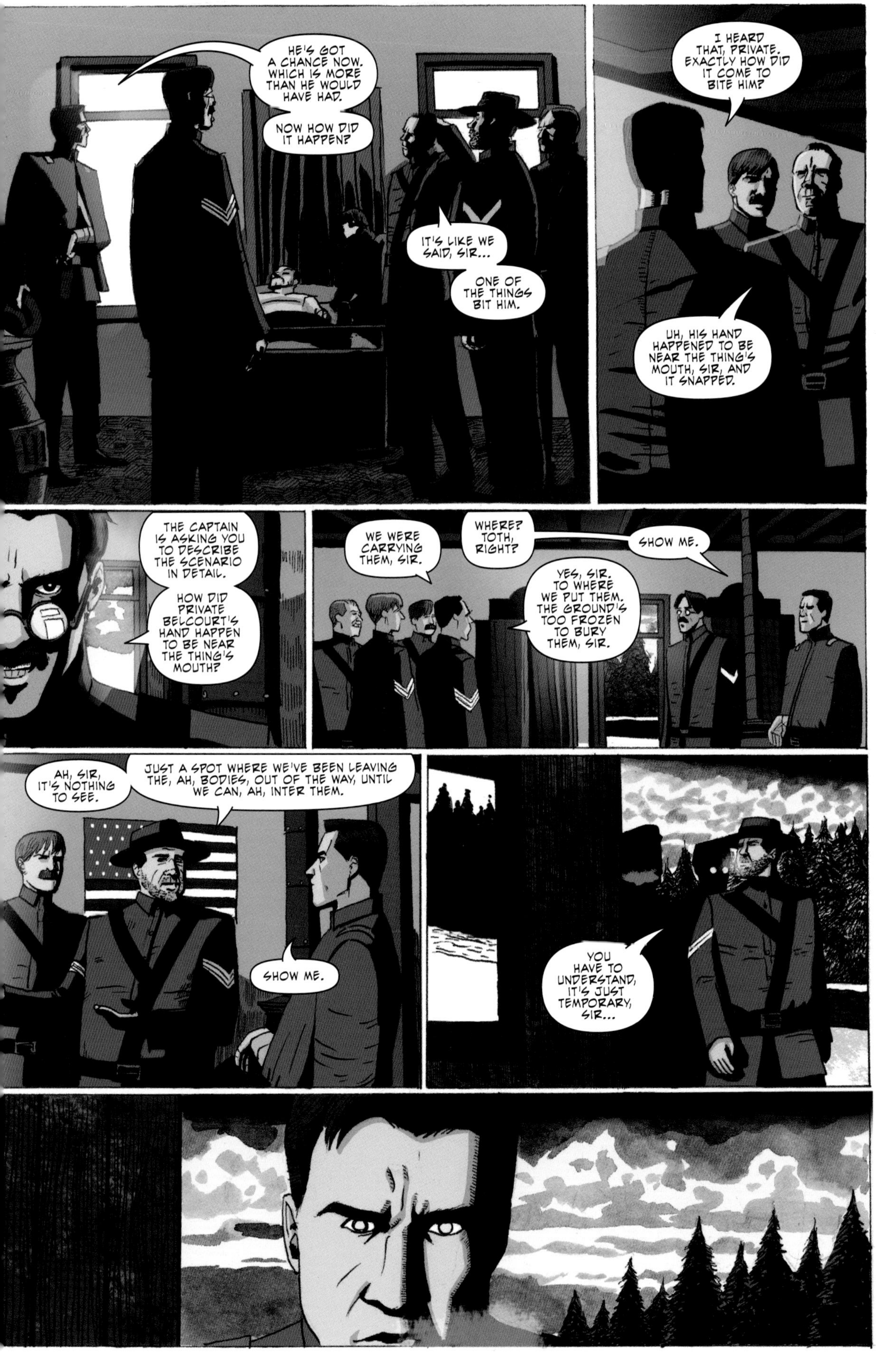
HE'S GOT A CHANCE NOW. WHICH IS MORE THAN HE WOULD HAVE HAD.
NOW HOW DID IT HAPPEN?
IT'S LIKE WE SAID, SIR...
ONE OF THE THINGS BIT HIM.
I HEARD THAT, PRIVATE. EXACTLY HOW DID IT COME TO BITE HIM?
UH, HIS HAND HAPPENED TO BE NEAR THE THING'S MOUTH, SIR, AND IT SNAPPED.
THE CAPTAIN IS ASKING YOU TO DESCRIBE THE SCENARIO IN DETAIL.
HOW DID PRIVATE BELCOURT'S HAND HAPPEN TO BE NEAR THE THING'S MOUTH?
WE WERE CARRYING THEM, SIR.
WHERE? TOTH, RIGHT?
SHOW ME.
YES, SIR. TO WHERE WE PUT THEM. THE GROUND'S TOO FROZEN TO BURY THEM, SIR.
AH, SIR, IT'S NOTHING TO SEE.
JUST A SPOT WHERE WE'VE BEEN LEAVING THE, AH, BODIES, OUT OF THE WAY, UNTIL WE CAN, AH, INTER THEM.
SHOW ME.
YOU HAVE TO UNDERSTAND, IT'S JUST TEMPORARY, SIR...

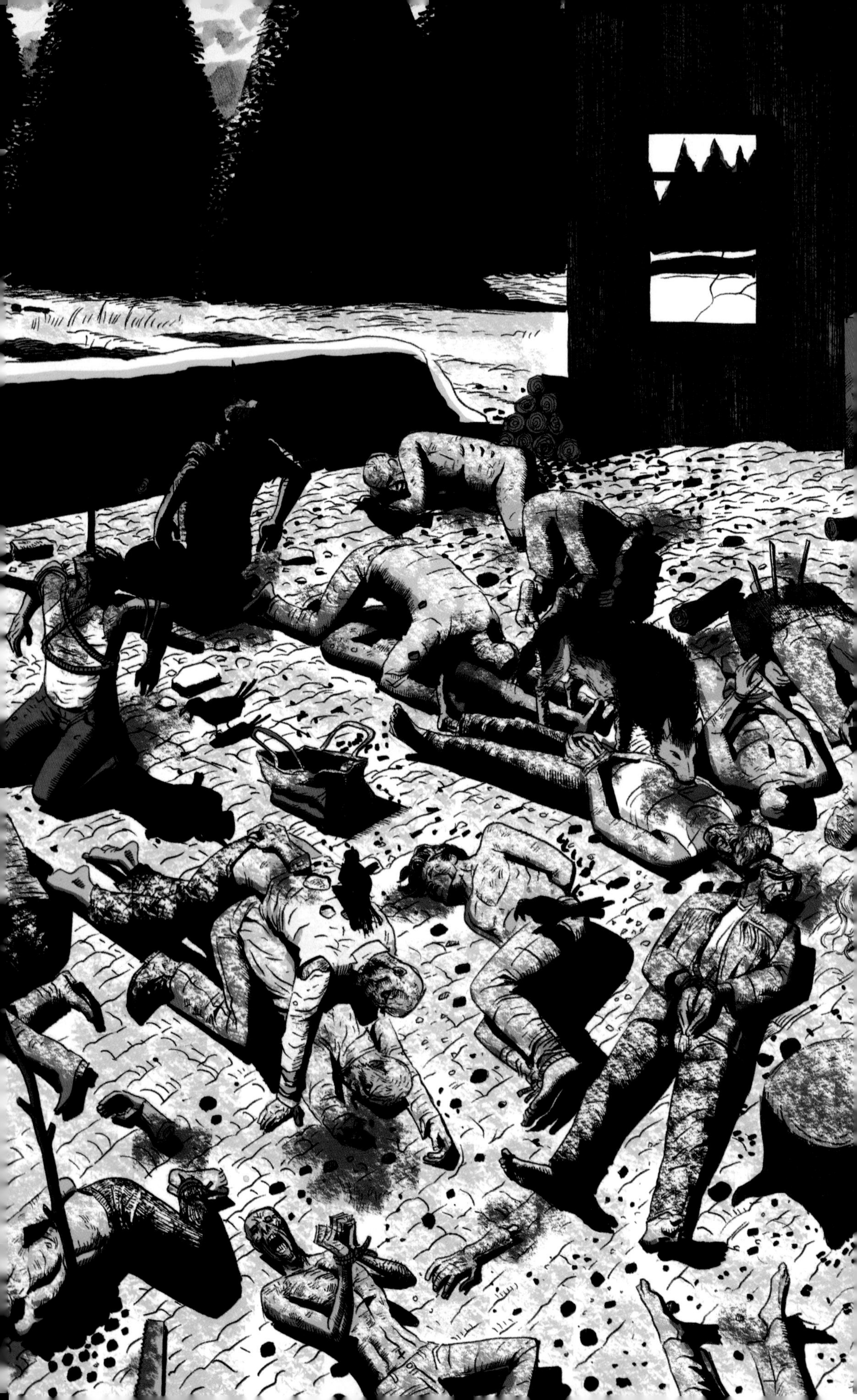

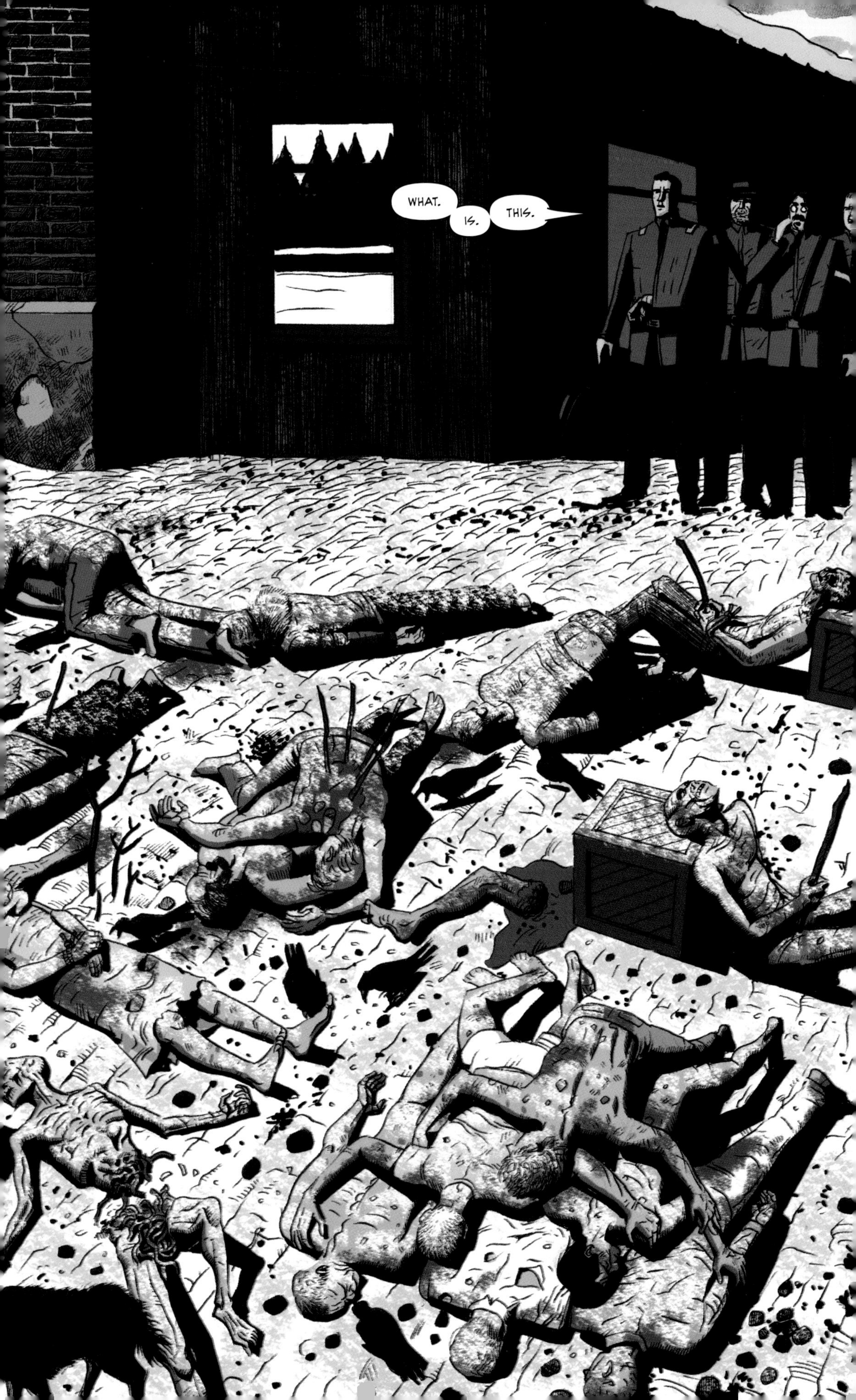
WHAT.
IS.
THIS.

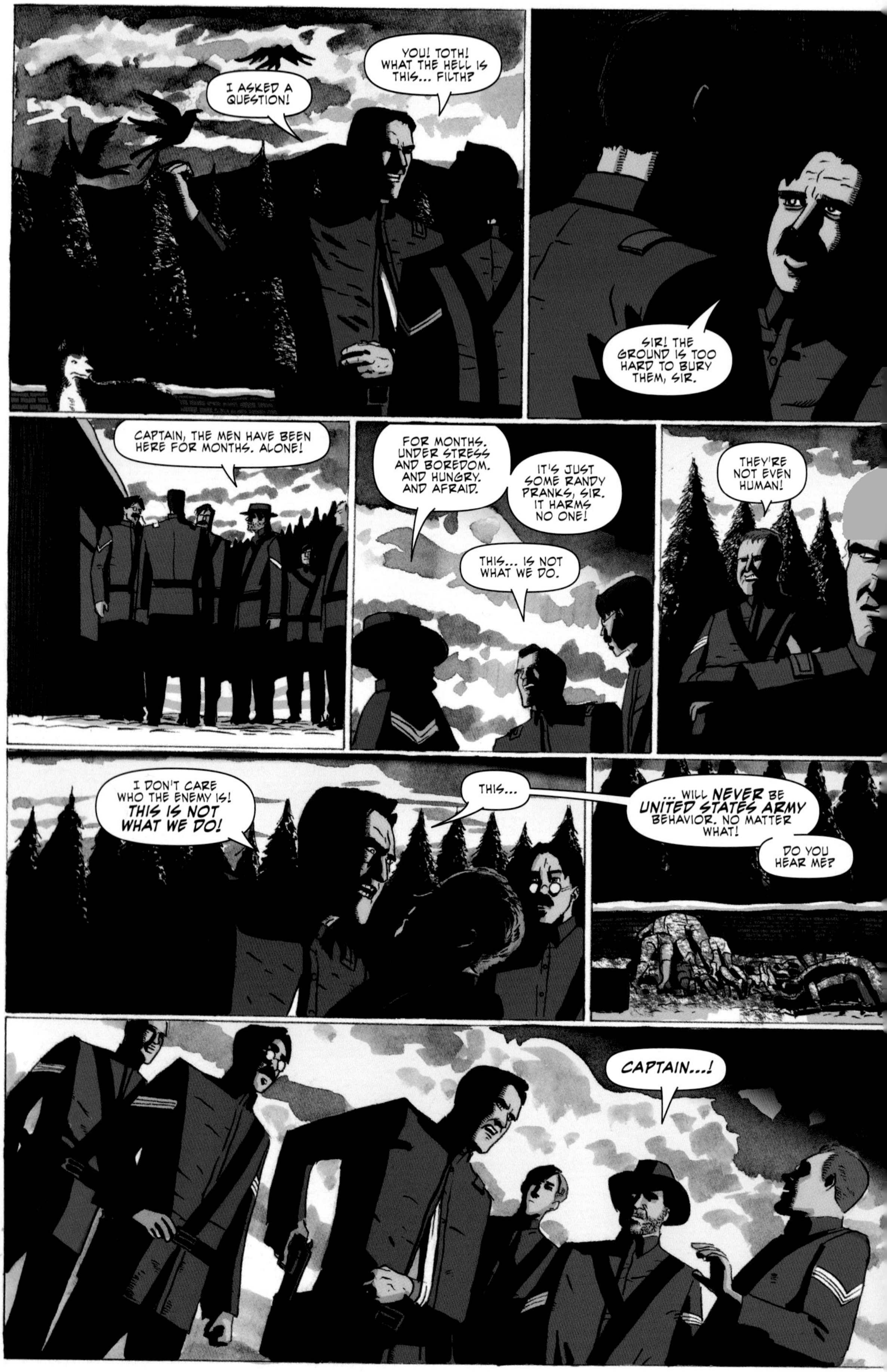
YOU! TOTH! WHAT THE HELL IS THIS... FILTH?
I ASKED A QUESTION!
SIR! THE GROUND IS TOO HARD TO BURY THEM, SIR.
CAPTAIN, THE MEN HAVE BEEN HERE FOR MONTHS. ALONE!
FOR MONTHS. UNDER STRESS AND BOREDOM. AND HUNGRY. AND AFRAID.
IT'S JUST SOME RANDY PRANKS, SIR. IT HARMS NO ONE!
THIS... IS NOT WHAT WE DO.
THEY'RE NOT EVEN HUMAN!
I DON'T CARE WHO THE ENEMY IS! THIS IS NOT WHAT WE DO!
THIS...
... WILL NEVER BE UNITED STATES ARMY BEHAVIOR. NO MATTER WHAT!
DO YOU HEAR ME?
CAPTAIN...!

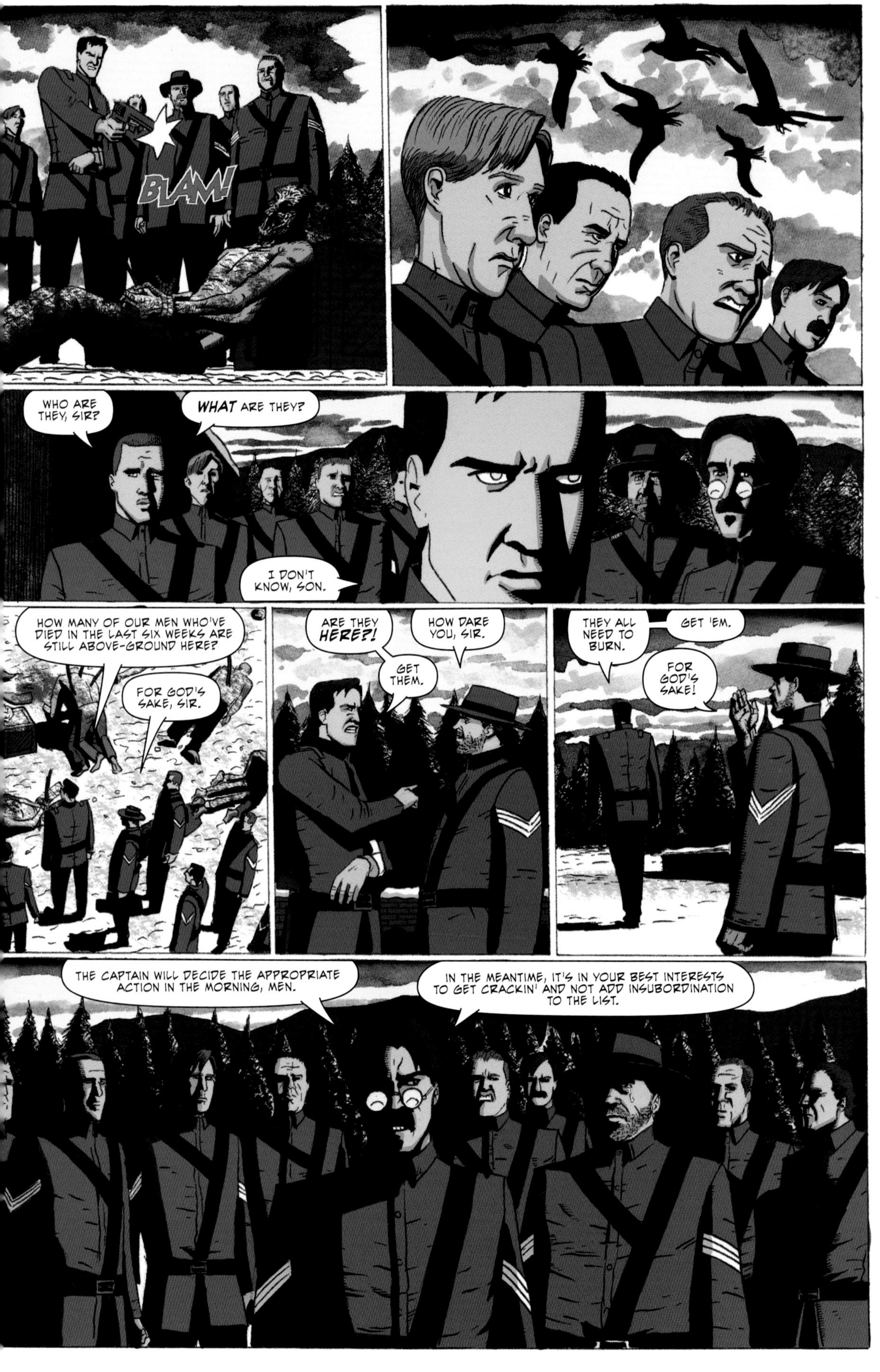
BLAM!
WHO ARE THEY, SIR?
WHAT ARE THEY?
I DON'T KNOW, SON.
HOW MANY OF OUR MEN WHO'VE DIED IN THE LAST SIX WEEKS ARE STILL ABOVE-GROUND HERE?
FOR GOD'S SAKE, SIR.
ARE THEY HERE?!
HOW DARE YOU, SIR.
GET THEM.
THEY ALL NEED TO BURN.
GET 'EM.
FOR GOD'S SAKE!
THE CAPTAIN WILL DECIDE THE APPROPRIATE ACTION IN THE MORNING, MEN.
IN THE MEANTIME, IT'S IN YOUR BEST INTERESTS TO GET CRACKIN' AND NOT ADD INSUBORDINATION TO THE LIST.

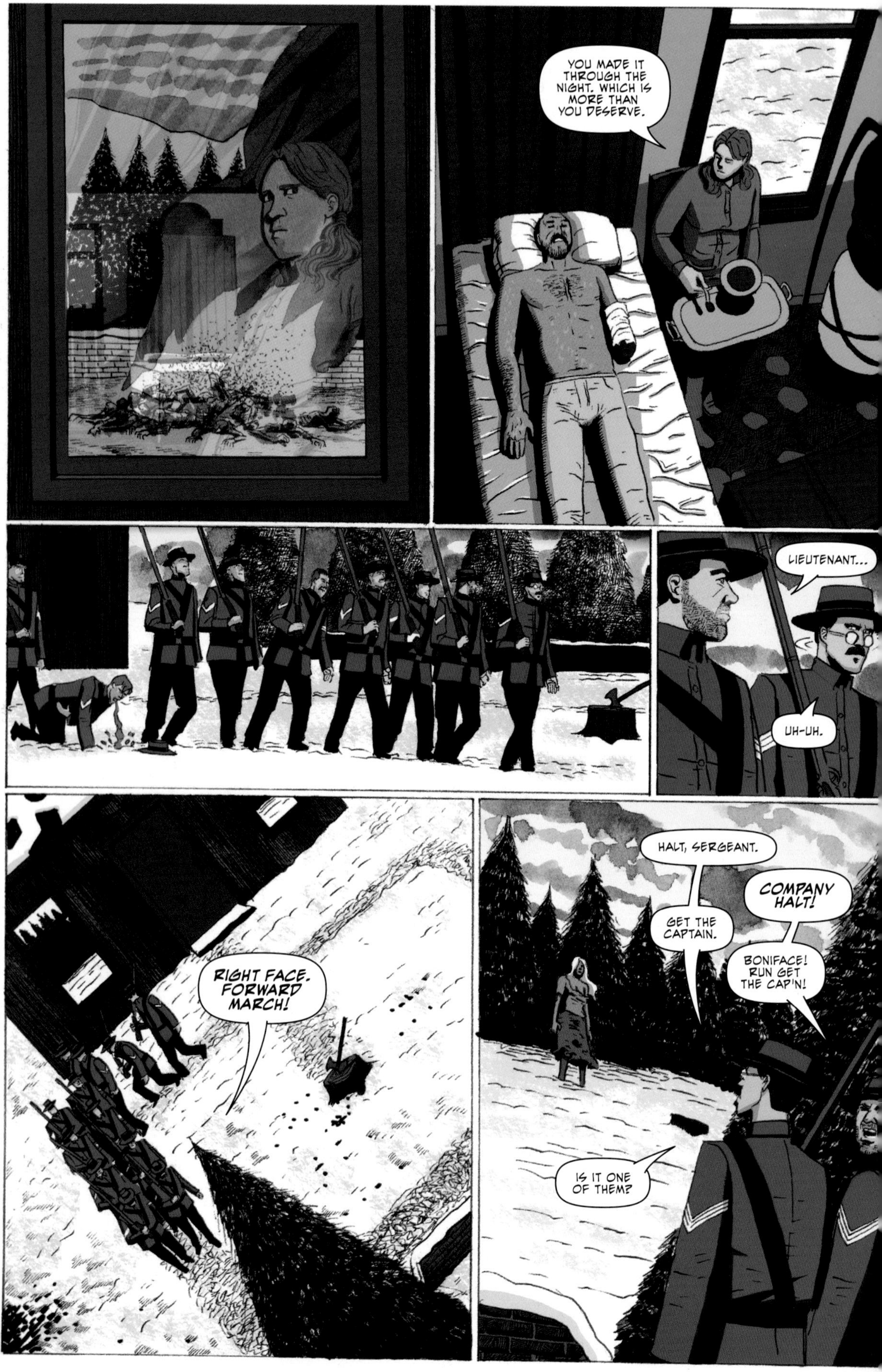
YOU MADE IT THROUGH THE NIGHT. WHICH IS MORE THAN YOU DESERVE.
LIEUTENANT...
UH-UH.
RIGHT FACE. FORWARD MARCH!
HALT, SERGEANT.
GET THE CAPTAIN.
COMPANY HALT!
BONIFACE! RUN GET THE CAP'N!
IS IT ONE OF THEM?

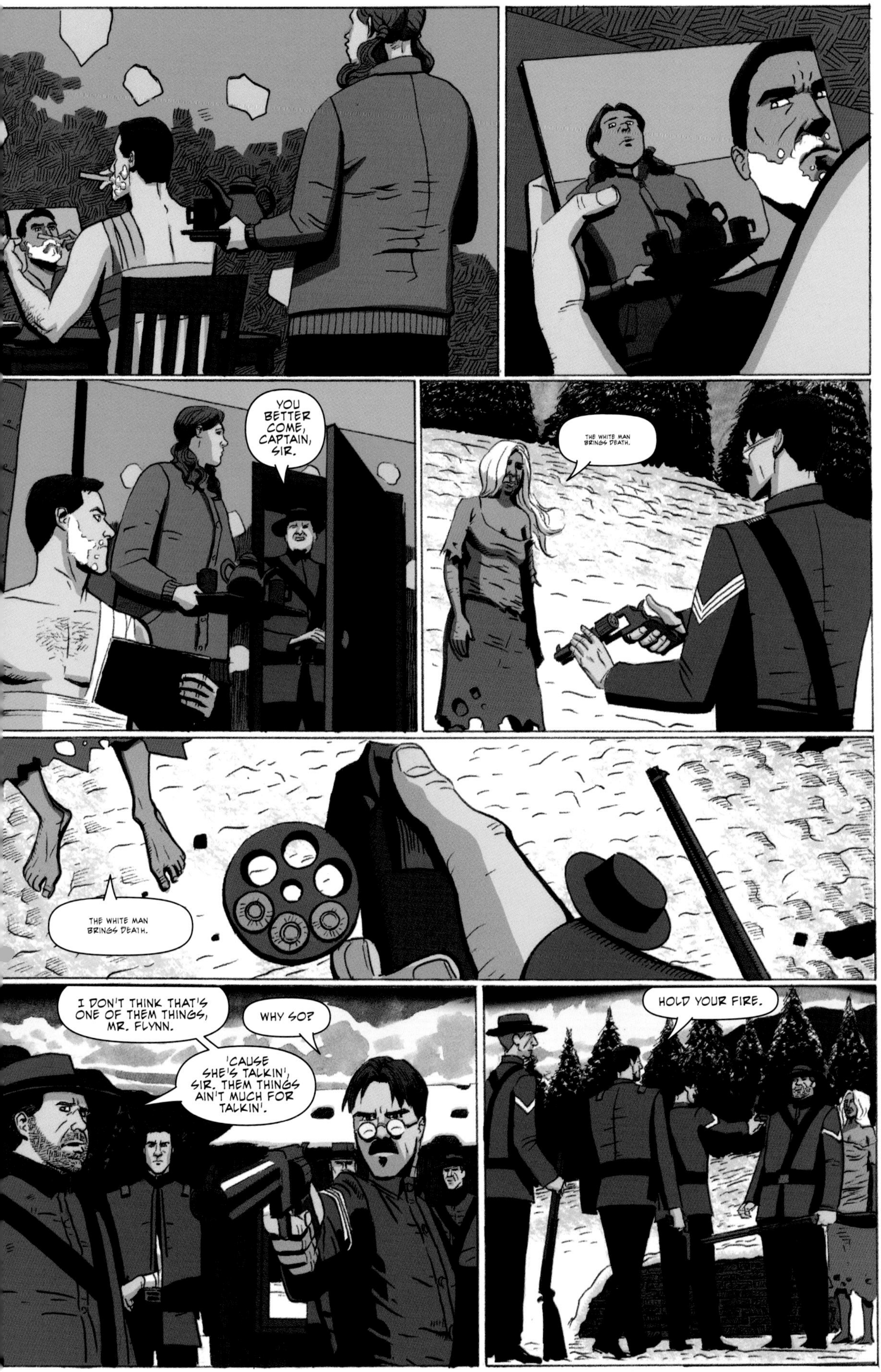
YOU BETTER COME, CAPTAIN, SIR.
THE WHITE MAN BRINGS DEATH.
THE WHITE MAN BRINGS DEATH.
I DON'T THINK THAT'S ONE OF THEM THINGS, MR. FLYNN.
WHY SO?
'CAUSE SHE'S TALKIN', SIR. THEM THINGS AIN'T MUCH FOR TALKIN'.
HOLD YOUR FIRE.

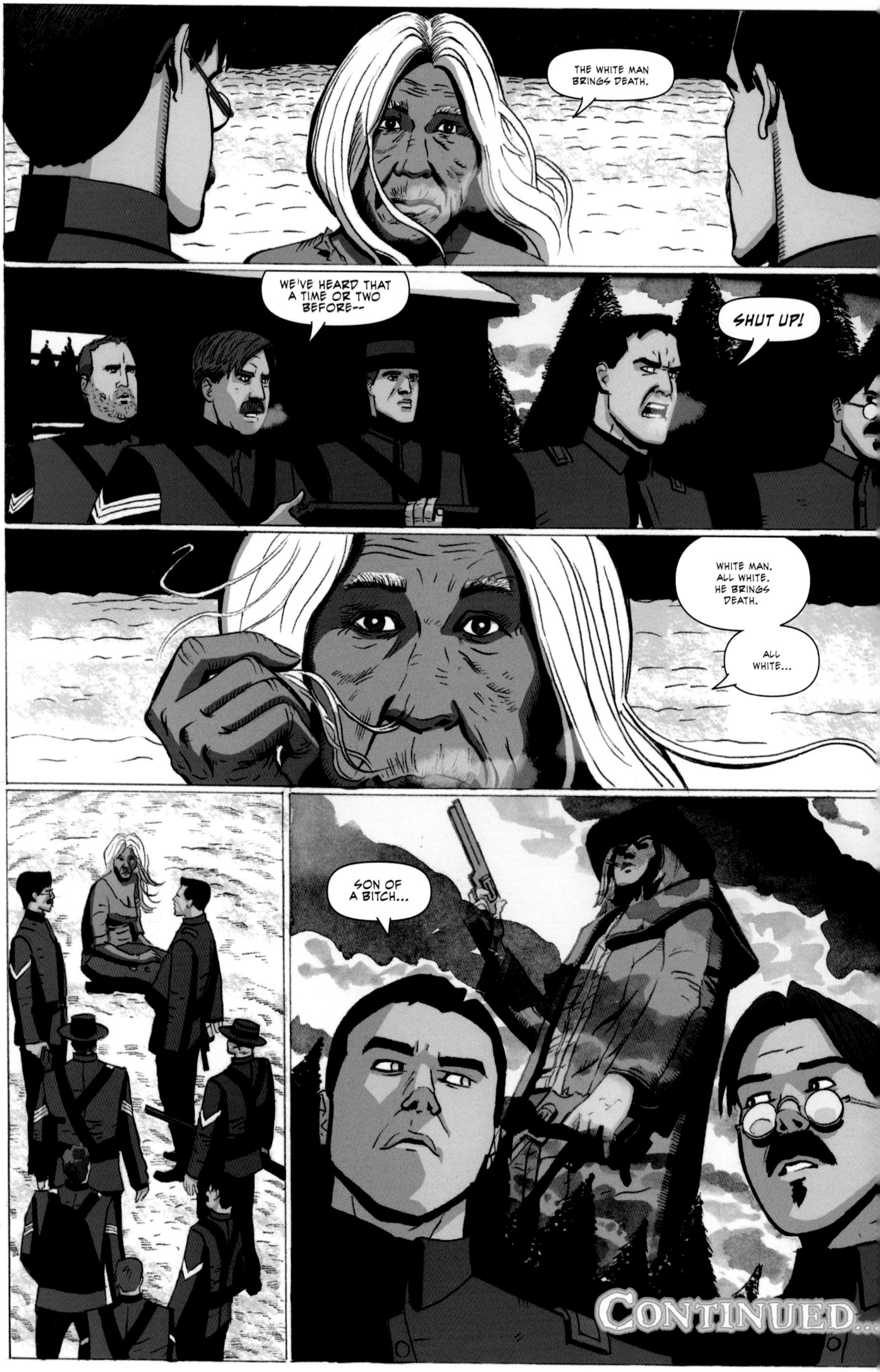
THE WHITE MAN BRINGS DEATH.
WE'VE HEARD THAT A TIME OR TWO BEFORE--
SHUT UP!
WHITE MAN. ALL WHITE. HE BRINGS DEATH.
ALL WHITE...
SON OF A BITCH...
CONTINUED...

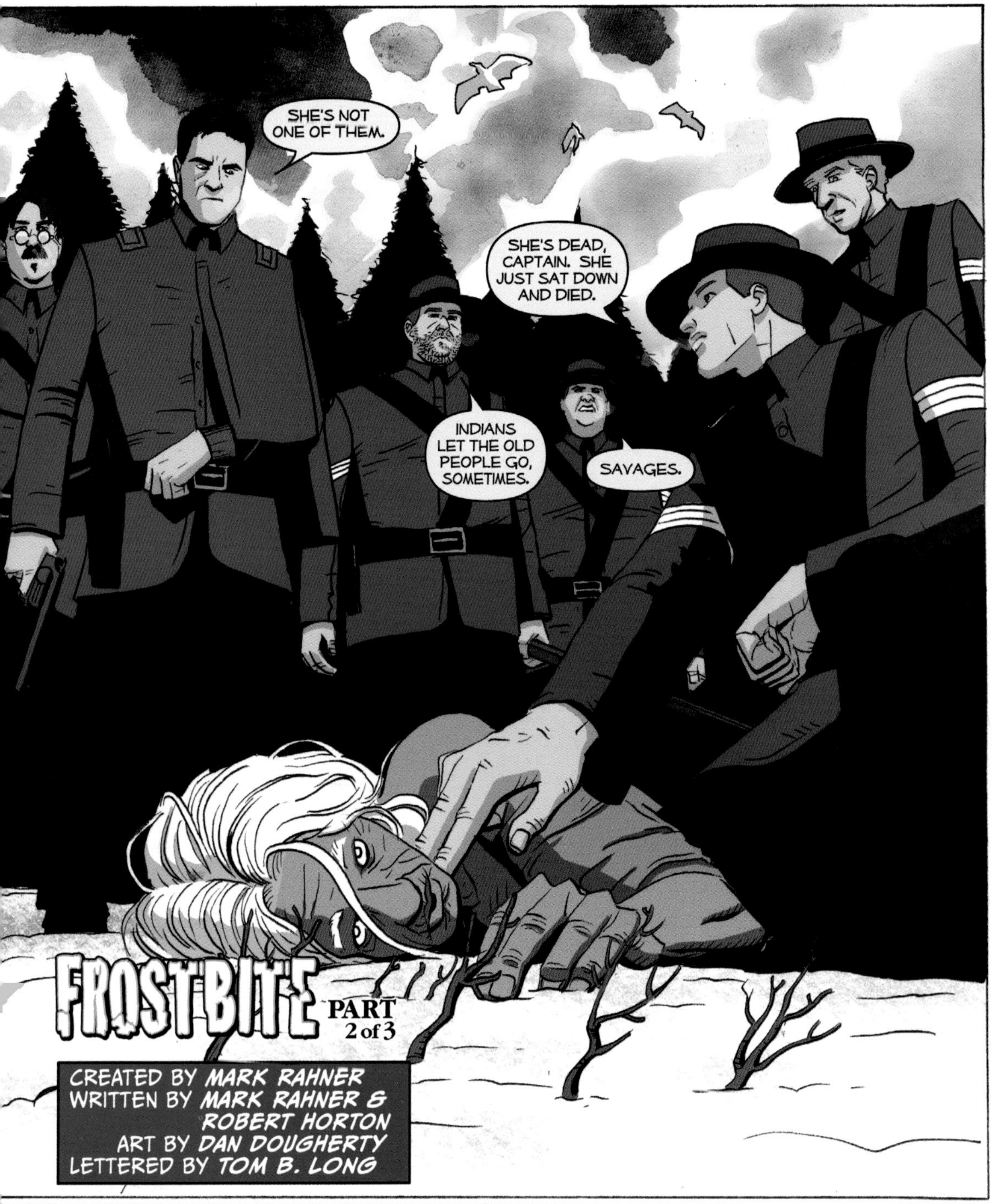
SHE'S NOT ONE OF THEM.
SHE'S DEAD, CAPTAIN. SHE JUST SAT DOWN AND DIED.
INDIANS LET THE OLD PEOPLE GO, SOMETIMES.
SAVAGES.
FROSTBITE PART 2 of 3
CREATED BY MARK RAHNER
WRITTEN BY MARK RAHNER & ROBERT HORTON
ART BY DAN DOUGHERTY
LETTERED BY TOM B. LONG

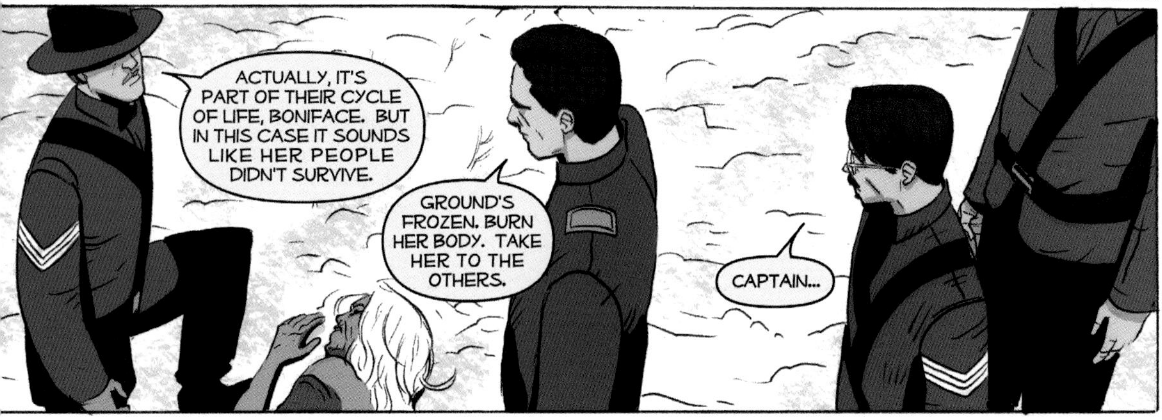
ACTUALLY, IT'S PART OF THEIR CYCLE OF LIFE, BONIFACE. BUT IN THIS CASE IT SOUNDS LIKE HER PEOPLE DIDN'T SURVIVE.
GROUND'S FROZEN. BURN HER BODY. TAKE HER TO THE OTHERS.
CAPTAIN...

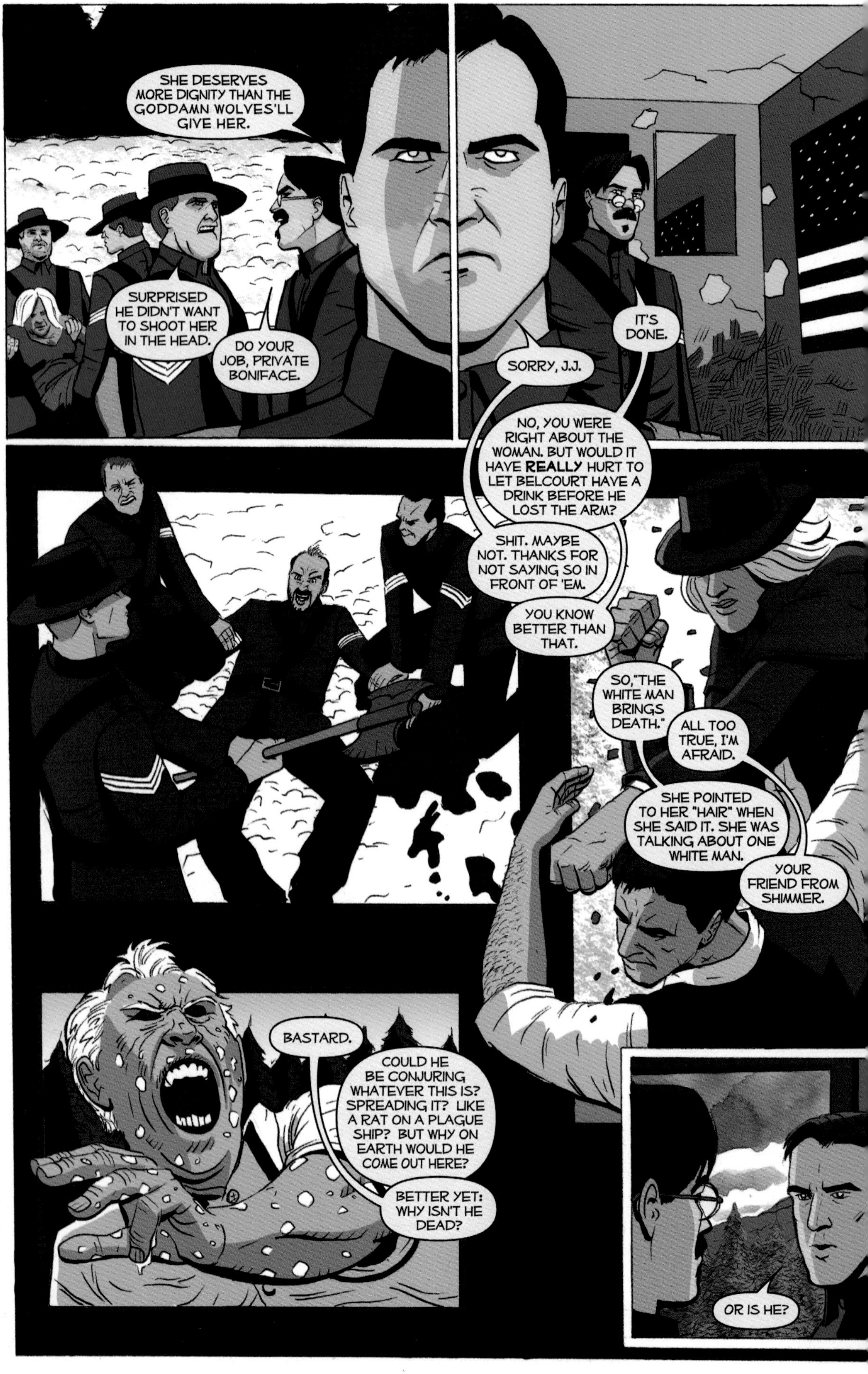
SHE DESERVES MORE DIGNITY THAN THE GODDAMN WOLVES'LL GIVE HER.
SURPRISED HE DIDN'T WANT TO SHOOT HER IN THE HEAD.
DO YOUR JOB, PRIVATE BONIFACE.
IT'S DONE.
SORRY, J.J.
NO, YOU WERE RIGHT ABOUT THE WOMAN. BUT WOULD IT HAVE REALLY HURT TO LET BELCOURT HAVE A DRINK BEFORE HE LOST THE ARM?
SHIT. MAYBE NOT. THANKS FOR NOT SAYING SO IN FRONT OF 'EM.
YOU KNOW BETTER THAN THAT.
SO,"THE WHITE MAN BRINGS DEATH."
ALL TOO TRUE, I'M AFRAID.
SHE POINTED TO HER "HAIR" WHEN SHE SAID IT. SHE WAS TALKING ABOUT ONE WHITE MAN.
YOUR FRIEND FROM SHIMMER.
BASTARD.
COULD HE BE CONJURING WHATEVER THIS IS? SPREADING IT? LIKE A RAT ON A PLAGUE SHIP? BUT WHY ON EARTH WOULD HE COME OUT HERE?
BETTER YET: WHY ISN'T HE DEAD?
OR IS HE?

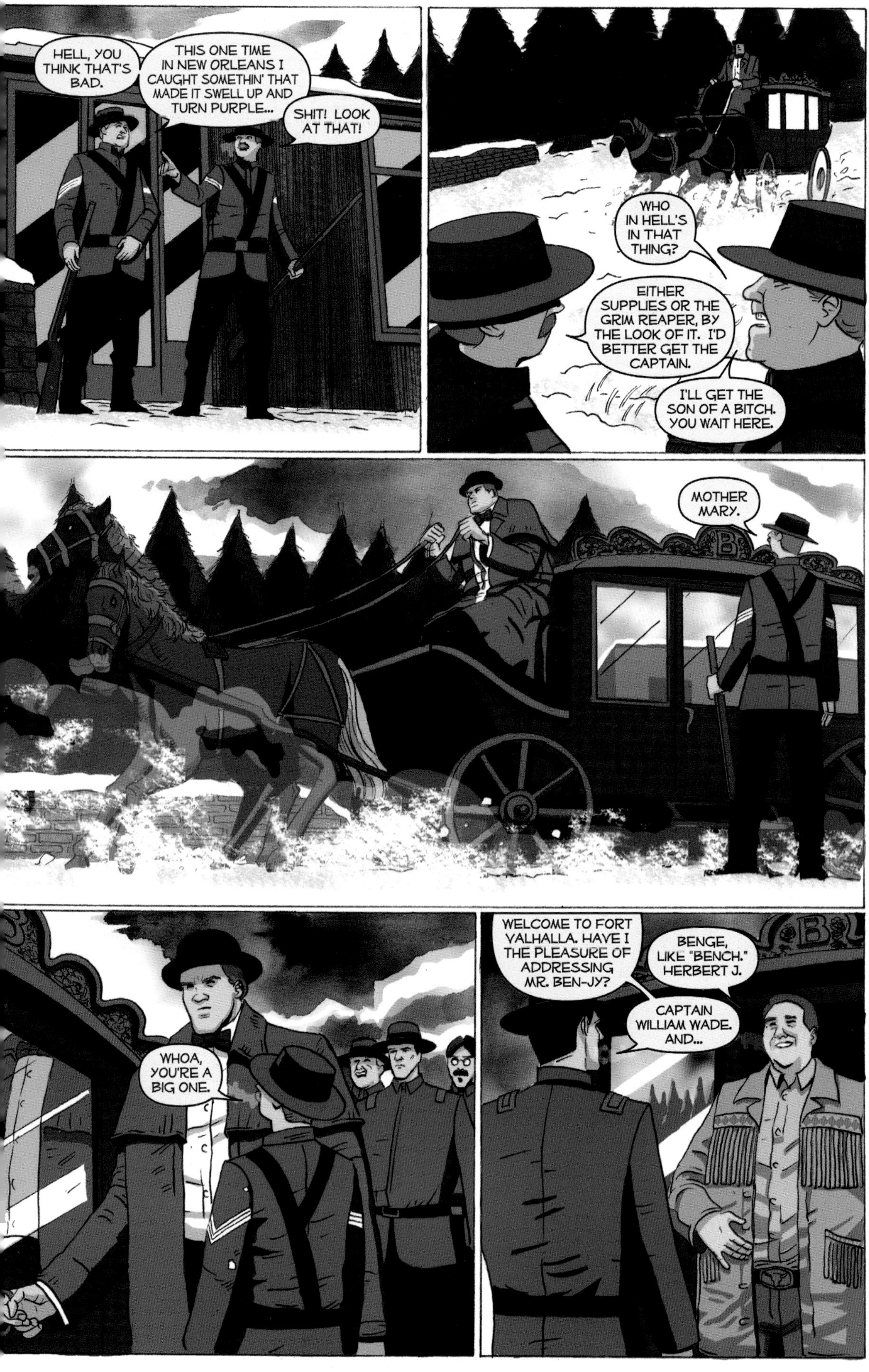
HELL, YOU THINK THAT'S BAD.
THIS ONE TIME IN NEW ORLEANS I CAUGHT SOMETHIN' THAT MADE IT SWELL UP AND TURN PURPLE...
SHIT! LOOK AT THAT!
WHO IN HELL'S IN THAT THING?
EITHER SUPPLIES OR THE GRIM REAPER, BY THE LOOK OF IT. I'D BETTER GET THE CAPTAIN.
I'LL GET THE SON OF A BITCH. YOU WAIT HERE.
MOTHER MARY.
WHOA, YOU'RE A BIG ONE.
WELCOME TO FORT VALHALLA. HAVE I THE PLEASURE OF ADDRESSING MR. BEN-JY?
BENGE, LIKE "BENCH." HERBERT J.
CAPTAIN WILLIAM WADE. AND...

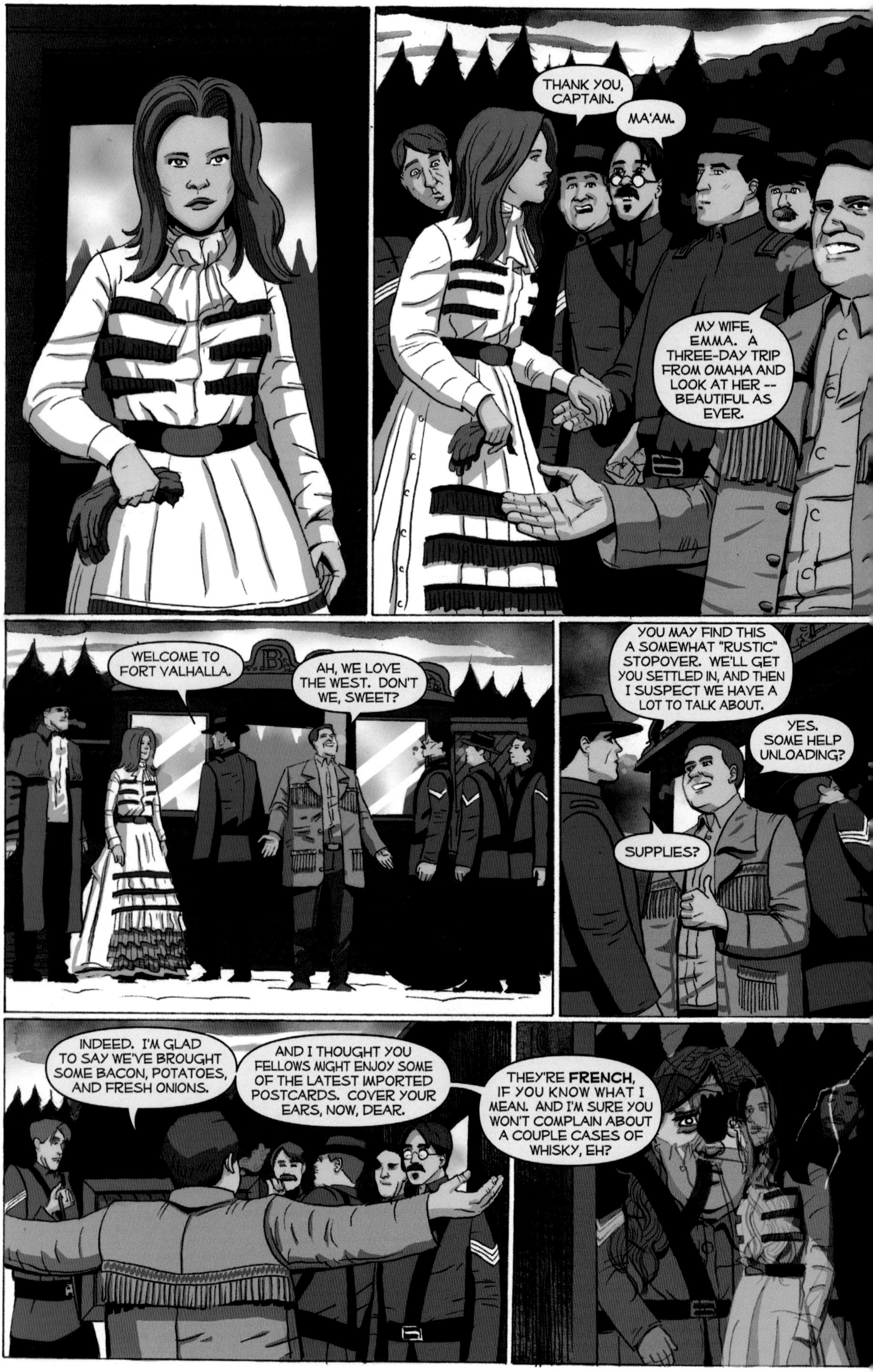
THANK YOU, CAPTAIN.
MA'AM.
MY WIFE, EMMA. A THREE-DAY TRIP FROM OMAHA AND LOOK AT HER -- BEAUTIFUL AS EVER.
WELCOME TO FORT VALHALLA.
AH, WE LOVE THE WEST. DON'T WE, SWEET?
YOU MAY FIND THIS A SOMEWHAT "RUSTIC" STOPOVER. WE'LL GET YOU SETTLED IN, AND THEN I SUSPECT WE HAVE A LOT TO TALK ABOUT.
YES. SOME HELP UNLOADING?
SUPPLIES?
INDEED. I'M GLAD TO SAY WE'VE BROUGHT SOME BACON, POTATOES, AND FRESH ONIONS.
AND I THOUGHT YOU FELLOWS MIGHT ENJOY SOME OF THE LATEST IMPORTED POSTCARDS. COVER YOUR EARS, NOW, DEAR.
THEY'RE **FRENCH**, IF YOU KNOW WHAT I MEAN. AND I'M SURE YOU WON'T COMPLAIN ABOUT A COUPLE CASES OF WHISKY, EH?

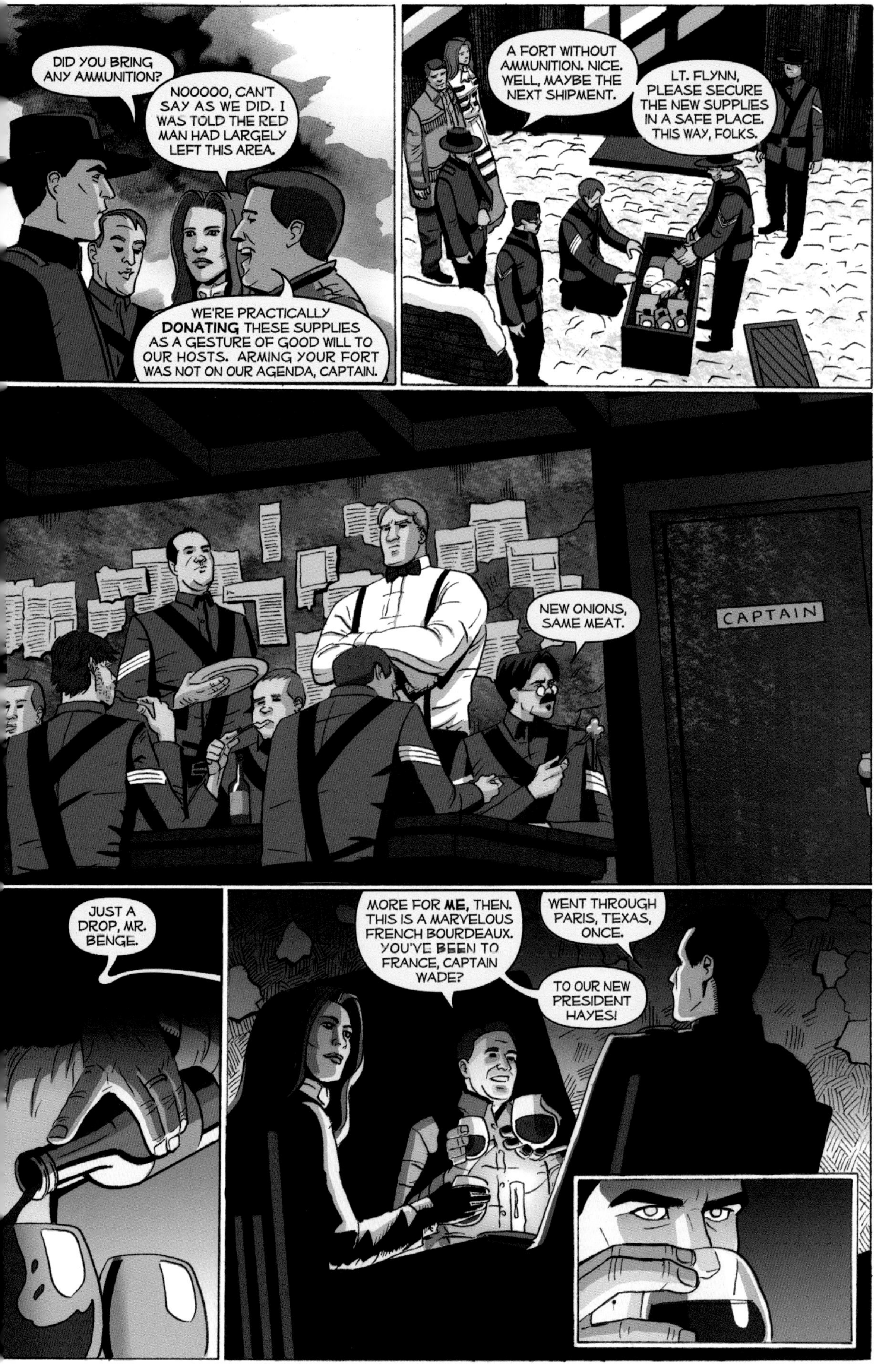
DID YOU BRING ANY AMMUNITION?
NOOOOO, CAN'T SAY AS WE DID. I WAS TOLD THE RED MAN HAD LARGELY LEFT THIS AREA.
WE'RE PRACTICALLY **DONATING** THESE SUPPLIES AS A GESTURE OF GOOD WILL TO OUR HOSTS. ARMING YOUR FORT WAS NOT ON OUR AGENDA, CAPTAIN.
A FORT WITHOUT AMMUNITION. NICE. WELL, MAYBE THE NEXT SHIPMENT.
LT. FLYNN, PLEASE SECURE THE NEW SUPPLIES IN A SAFE PLACE. THIS WAY, FOLKS.
NEW ONIONS, SAME MEAT.
CAPTAIN
JUST A DROP, MR. BENGE.
MORE FOR **ME,** THEN. THIS IS A MARVELOUS FRENCH BOURDEAUX. YOU'VE BEEN TO FRANCE, CAPTAIN WADE?
WENT THROUGH PARIS, TEXAS, ONCE.
TO OUR NEW PRESIDENT HAYES!

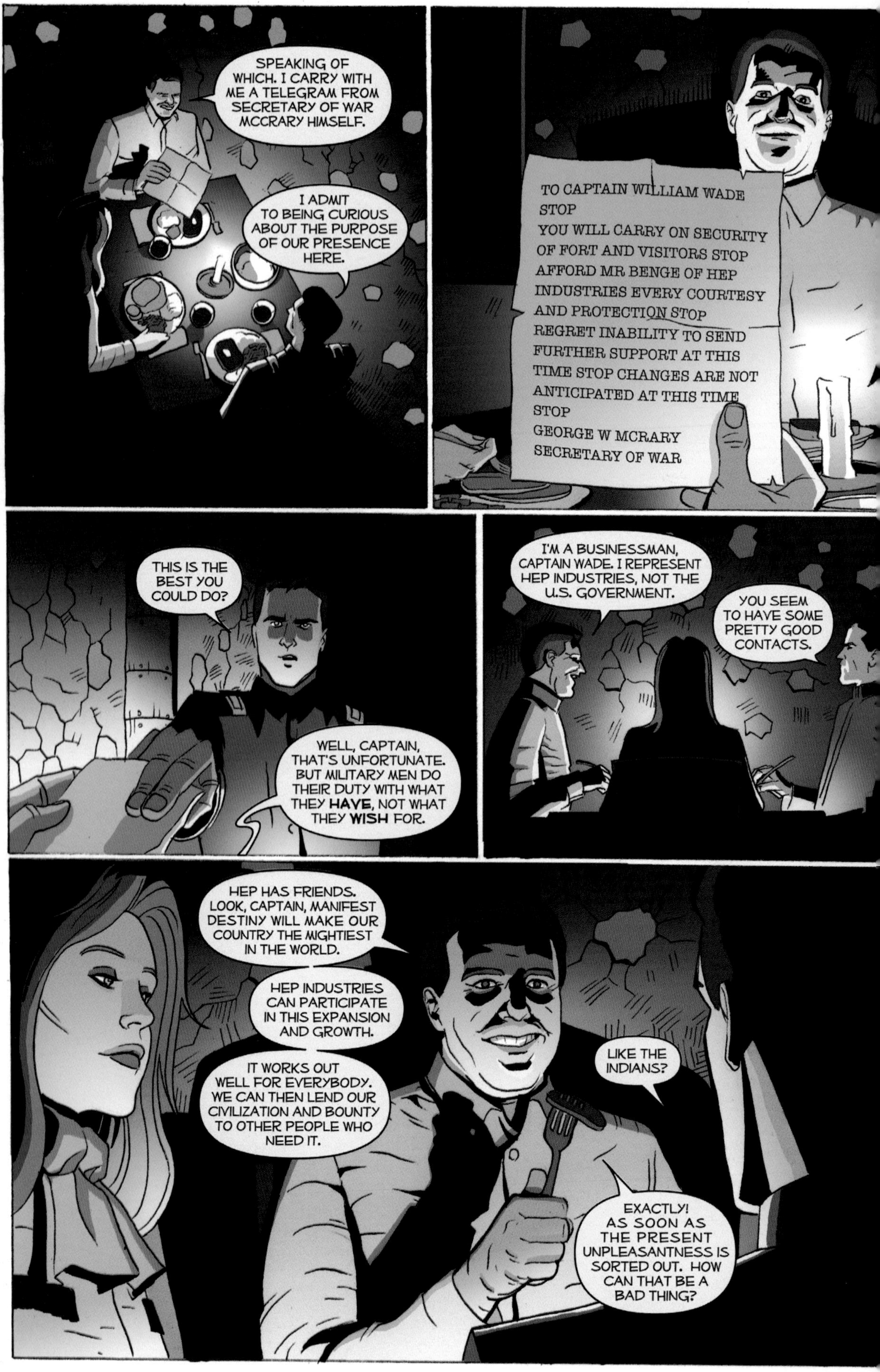
SPEAKING OF WHICH. I CARRY WITH ME A TELEGRAM FROM SECRETARY OF WAR MCCRARY HIMSELF.
I ADMIT TO BEING CURIOUS ABOUT THE PURPOSE OF OUR PRESENCE HERE.
TO CAPTAIN WILLIAM WADE STOP
YOU WILL CARRY ON SECURITY OF FORT AND VISITORS STOP
AFFORD MR BENGE OF HEP INDUSTRIES EVERY COURTESY AND PROTECTION STOP
REGRET INABILITY TO SEND FURTHER SUPPORT AT THIS TIME STOP CHANGES ARE NOT ANTICIPATED AT THIS TIME STOP
GEORGE W MCRARY
SECRETARY OF WAR
THIS IS THE BEST YOU COULD DO?
WELL, CAPTAIN, THAT'S UNFORTUNATE. BUT MILITARY MEN DO THEIR DUTY WITH WHAT THEY **HAVE**, NOT WHAT THEY **WISH** FOR.
I'M A BUSINESSMAN, CAPTAIN WADE. I REPRESENT HEP INDUSTRIES, NOT THE U.S. GOVERNMENT.
YOU SEEM TO HAVE SOME PRETTY GOOD CONTACTS.
HEP HAS FRIENDS. LOOK, CAPTAIN, MANIFEST DESTINY WILL MAKE OUR COUNTRY THE MIGHTIEST IN THE WORLD.
HEP INDUSTRIES CAN PARTICIPATE IN THIS EXPANSION AND GROWTH.
IT WORKS OUT WELL FOR EVERYBODY. WE CAN THEN LEND OUR CIVILIZATION AND BOUNTY TO OTHER PEOPLE WHO NEED IT.
LIKE THE INDIANS?
EXACTLY! AS SOON AS THE PRESENT UNPLEASANTNESS IS SORTED OUT. HOW CAN THAT BE A BAD THING?

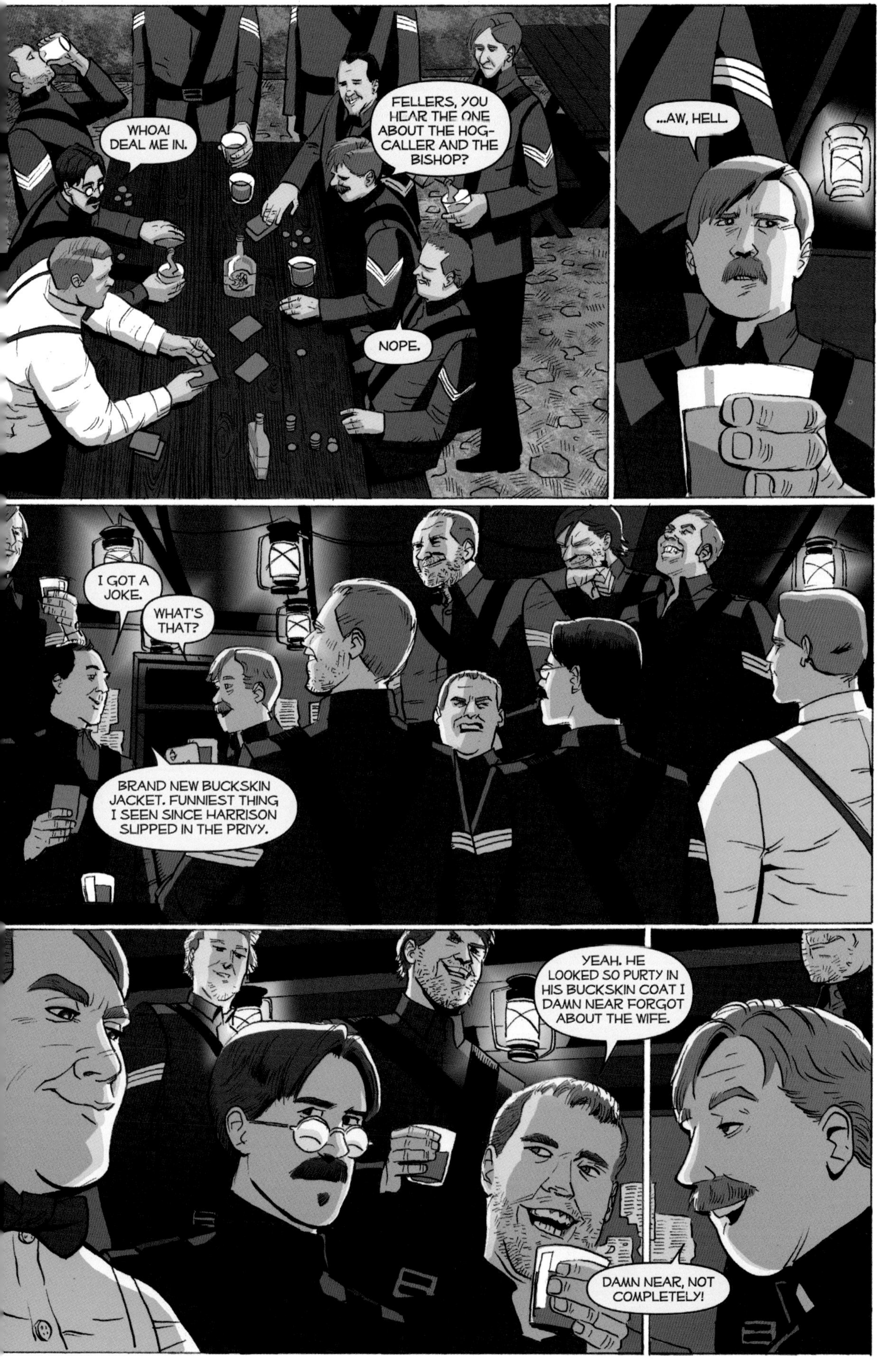
WHOA! DEAL ME IN.
FELLERS, YOU HEAR THE ONE ABOUT THE HOG-CALLER AND THE BISHOP?
NOPE.
...AW, HELL.
I GOT A JOKE.
WHAT'S THAT?
BRAND NEW BUCKSKIN JACKET. FUNNIEST THING I SEEN SINCE HARRISON SLIPPED IN THE PRIVY.
YEAH. HE LOOKED SO PURTY IN HIS BUCKSKIN COAT I DAMN NEAR FORGOT ABOUT THE WIFE.
DAMN NEAR, NOT COMPLETELY!

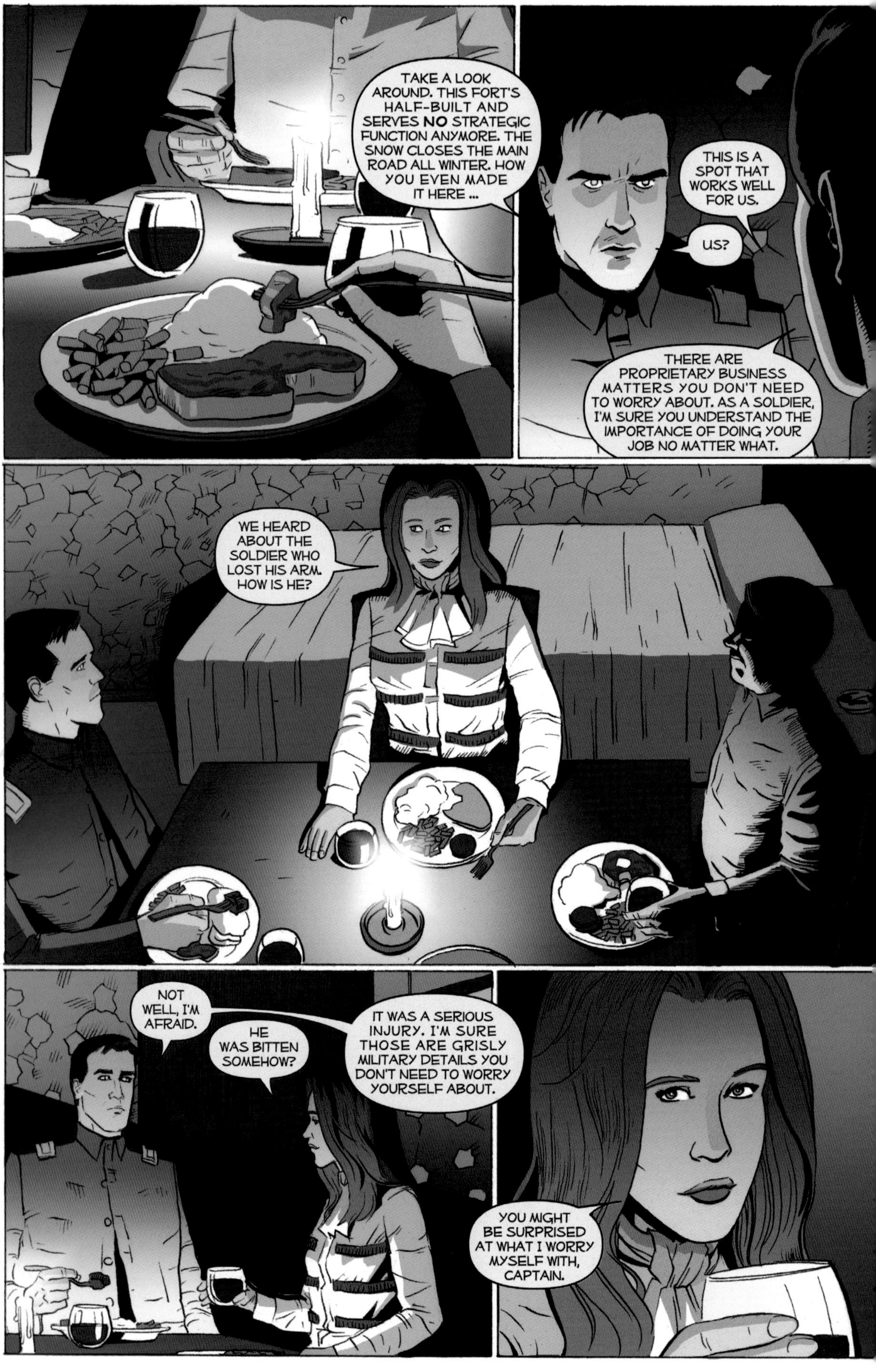
TAKE A LOOK AROUND. THIS FORT'S HALF-BUILT AND SERVES **NO** STRATEGIC FUNCTION ANYMORE. THE SNOW CLOSES THE MAIN ROAD ALL WINTER. HOW YOU EVEN MADE IT HERE ...
THIS IS A SPOT THAT WORKS WELL FOR US.
US?
THERE ARE PROPRIETARY BUSINESS MATTERS YOU DON'T NEED TO WORRY ABOUT. AS A SOLDIER, I'M SURE YOU UNDERSTAND THE IMPORTANCE OF DOING YOUR JOB NO MATTER WHAT.
WE HEARD ABOUT THE SOLDIER WHO LOST HIS ARM. HOW IS HE?
NOT WELL, I'M AFRAID.
HE WAS BITTEN SOMEHOW?
IT WAS A SERIOUS INJURY. I'M SURE THOSE ARE GRISLY MILITARY DETAILS YOU DON'T NEED TO WORRY YOURSELF ABOUT.
YOU MIGHT BE SURPRISED AT WHAT I WORRY MYSELF WITH, CAPTAIN.

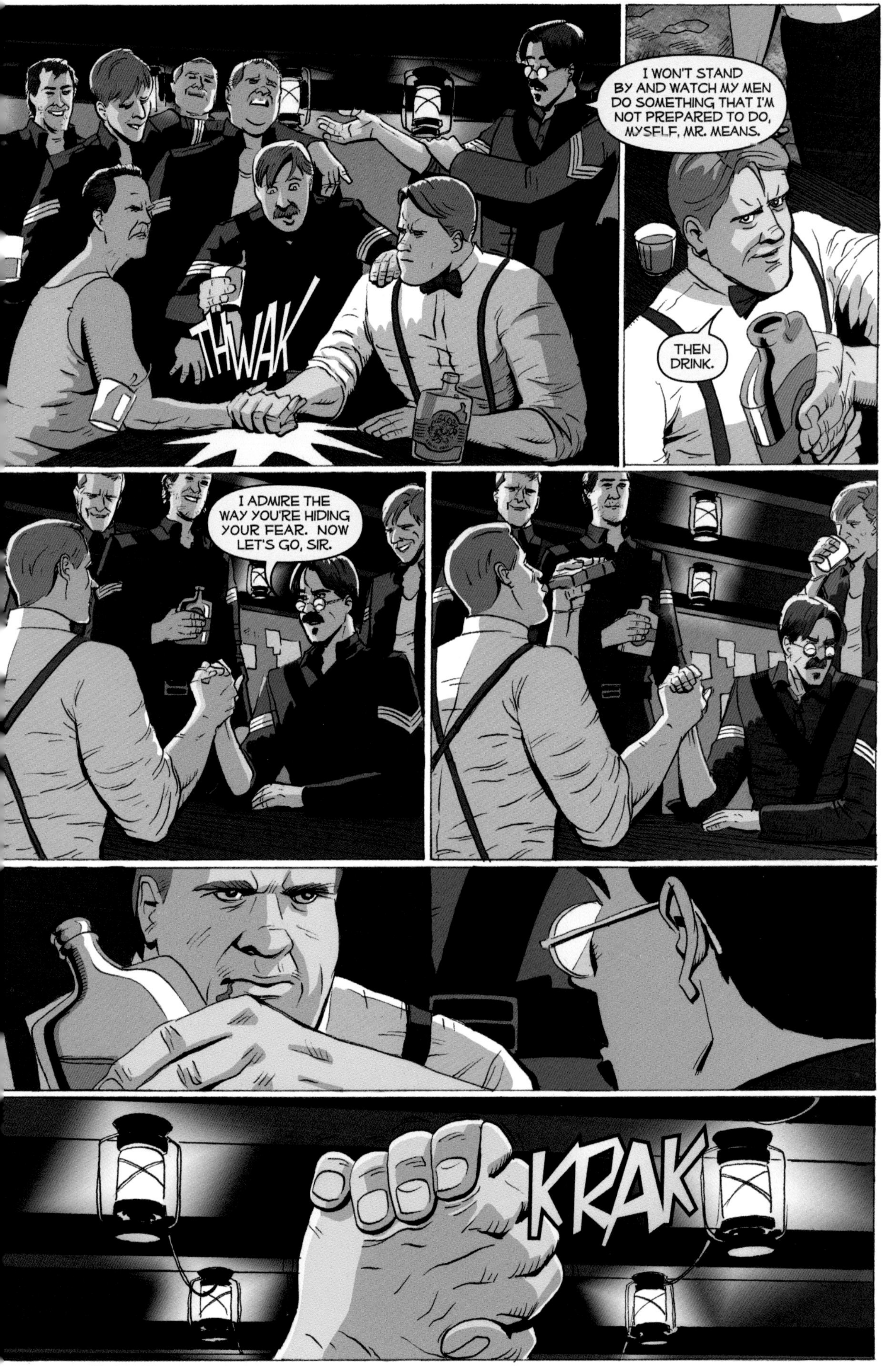
THWAK
I WON'T STAND BY AND WATCH MY MEN DO SOMETHING THAT I'M NOT PREPARED TO DO, MYSELF, MR. MEANS.
THEN DRINK.
I ADMIRE THE WAY YOU'RE HIDING YOUR FEAR. NOW LET'S GO, SIR.
KRAK

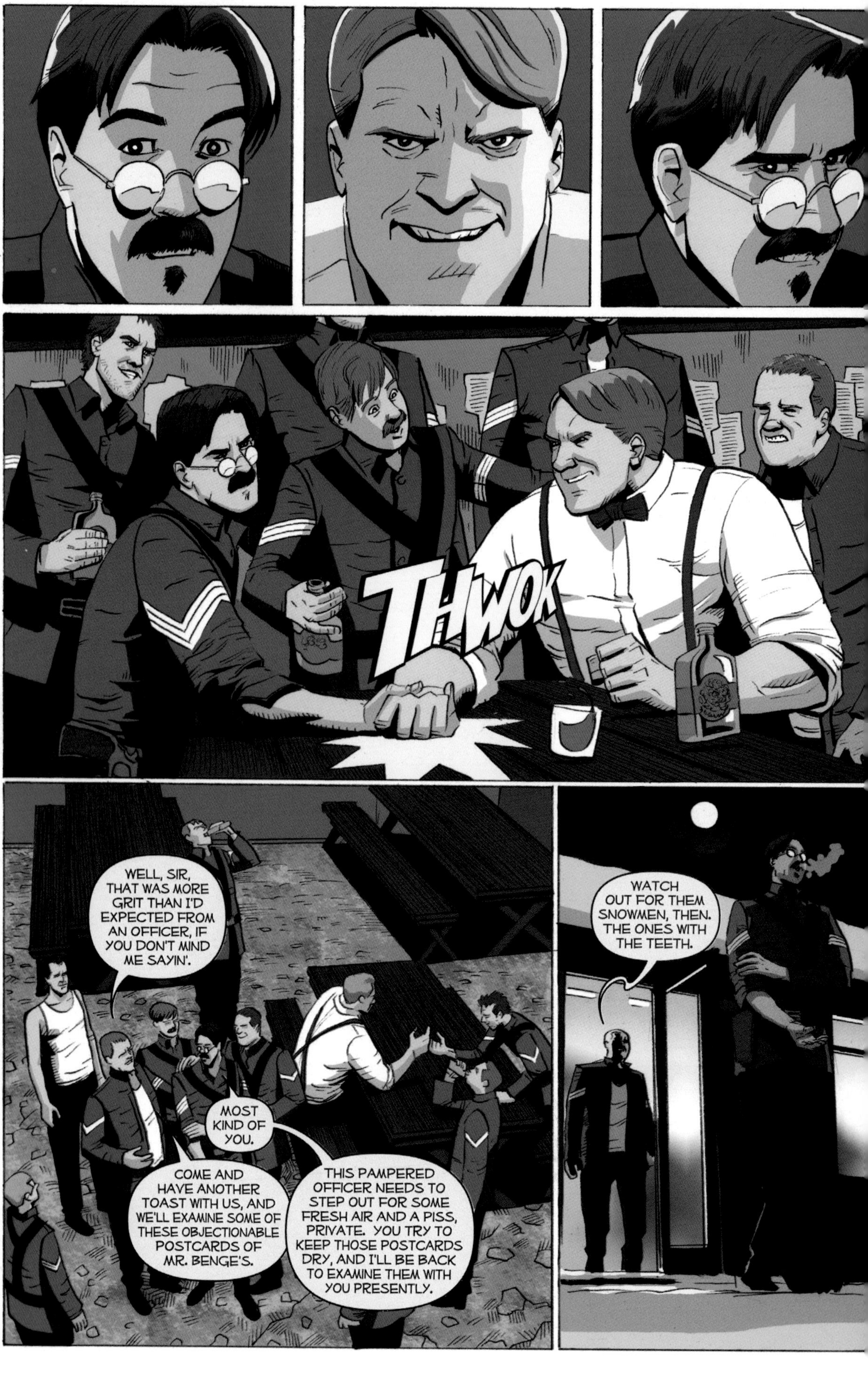
THWOK
WELL, SIR, THAT WAS MORE GRIT THAN I'D EXPECTED FROM AN OFFICER, IF YOU DON'T MIND ME SAYIN'.
MOST KIND OF YOU.
COME AND HAVE ANOTHER TOAST WITH US, AND WE'LL EXAMINE SOME OF THESE OBJECTIONABLE POSTCARDS OF MR. BENGE'S.
THIS PAMPERED OFFICER NEEDS TO STEP OUT FOR SOME FRESH AIR AND A PISS, PRIVATE. YOU TRY TO KEEP THOSE POSTCARDS DRY, AND I'LL BE BACK TO EXAMINE THEM WITH YOU PRESENTLY.
WATCH OUT FOR THEM SNOWMEN, THEN. THE ONES WITH THE TEETH.

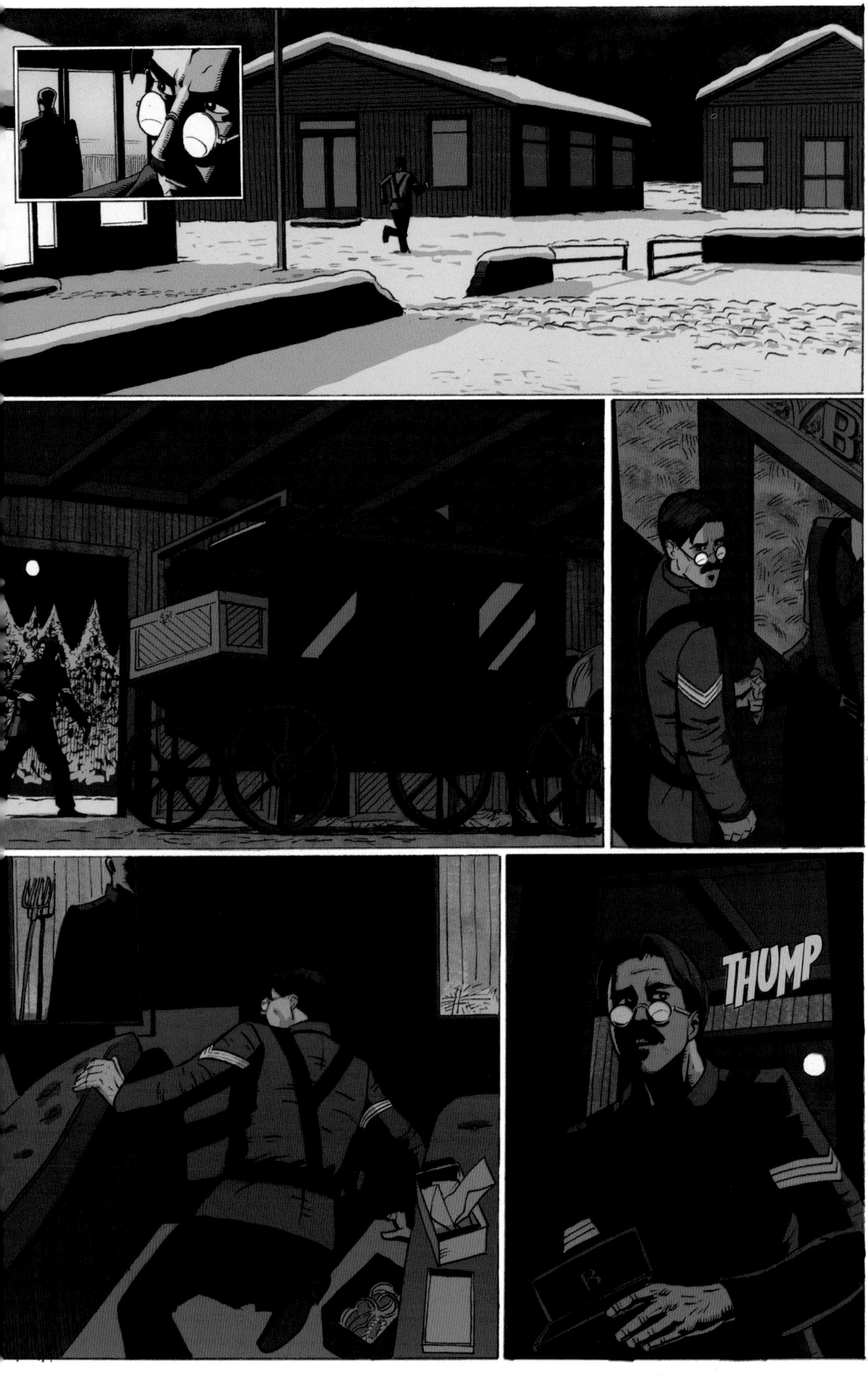
THUMP

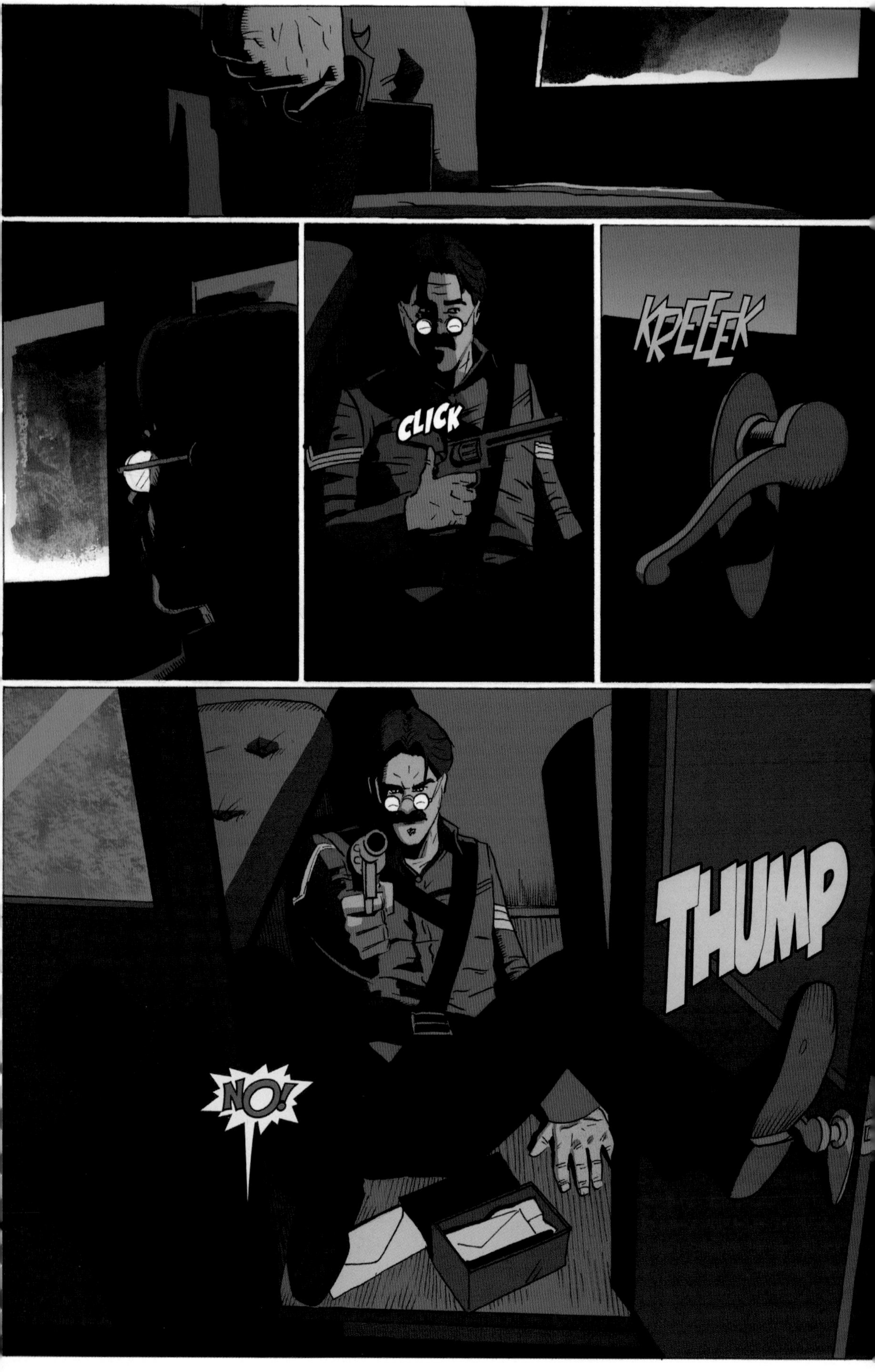
CLICK
KREEEK
THUMP
NO!

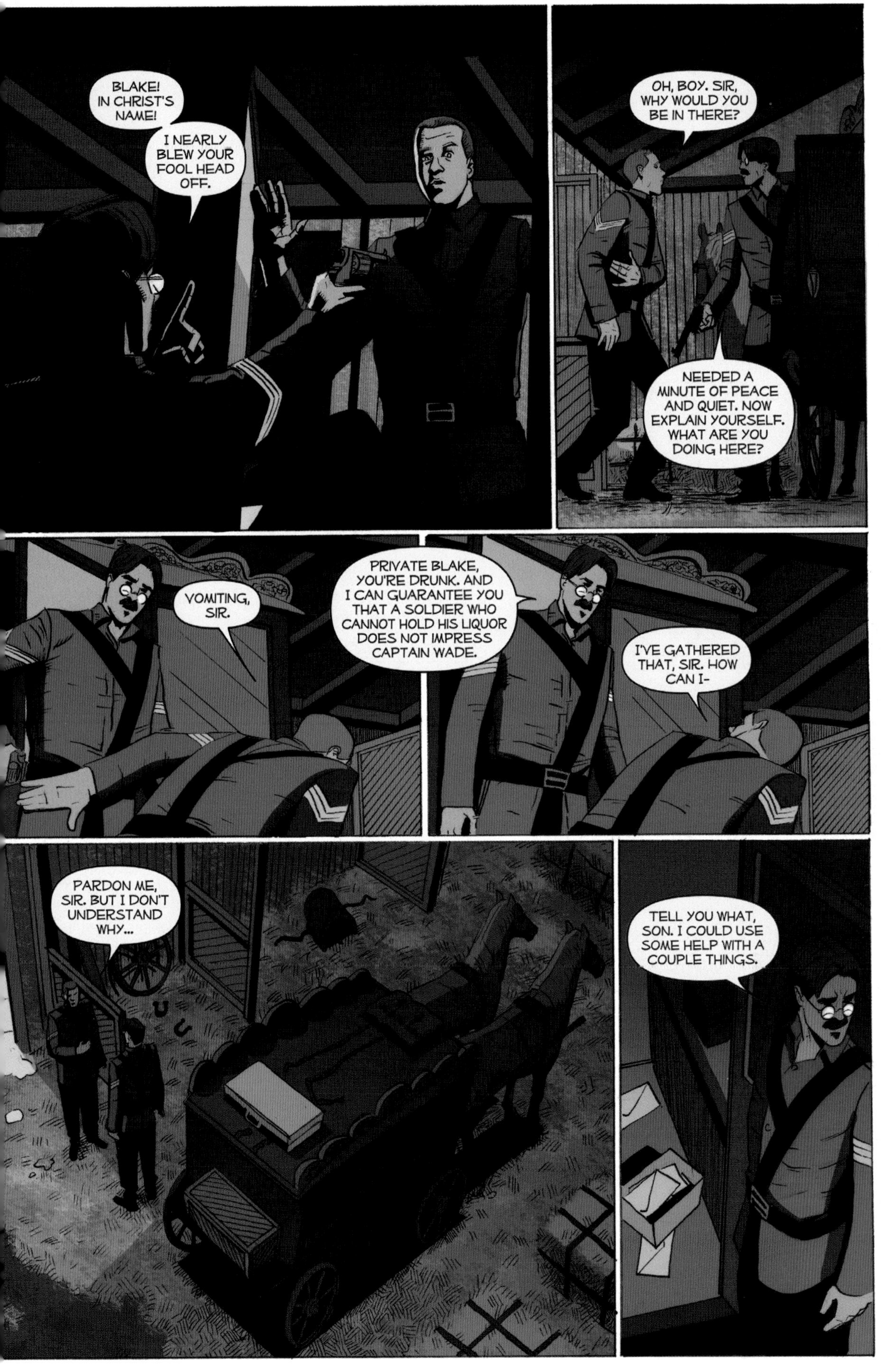
BLAKE! IN CHRIST'S NAME!
I NEARLY BLEW YOUR FOOL HEAD OFF.
OH, BOY. SIR, WHY WOULD YOU BE IN THERE?
NEEDED A MINUTE OF PEACE AND QUIET. NOW EXPLAIN YOURSELF. WHAT ARE YOU DOING HERE?
VOMITING, SIR.
PRIVATE BLAKE, YOU'RE DRUNK. AND I CAN GUARANTEE YOU THAT A SOLDIER WHO CANNOT HOLD HIS LIQUOR DOES NOT IMPRESS CAPTAIN WADE.
I'VE GATHERED THAT, SIR. HOW CAN I-
PARDON ME, SIR. BUT I DON'T UNDERSTAND WHY...
TELL YOU WHAT, SON. I COULD USE SOME HELP WITH A COUPLE THINGS.

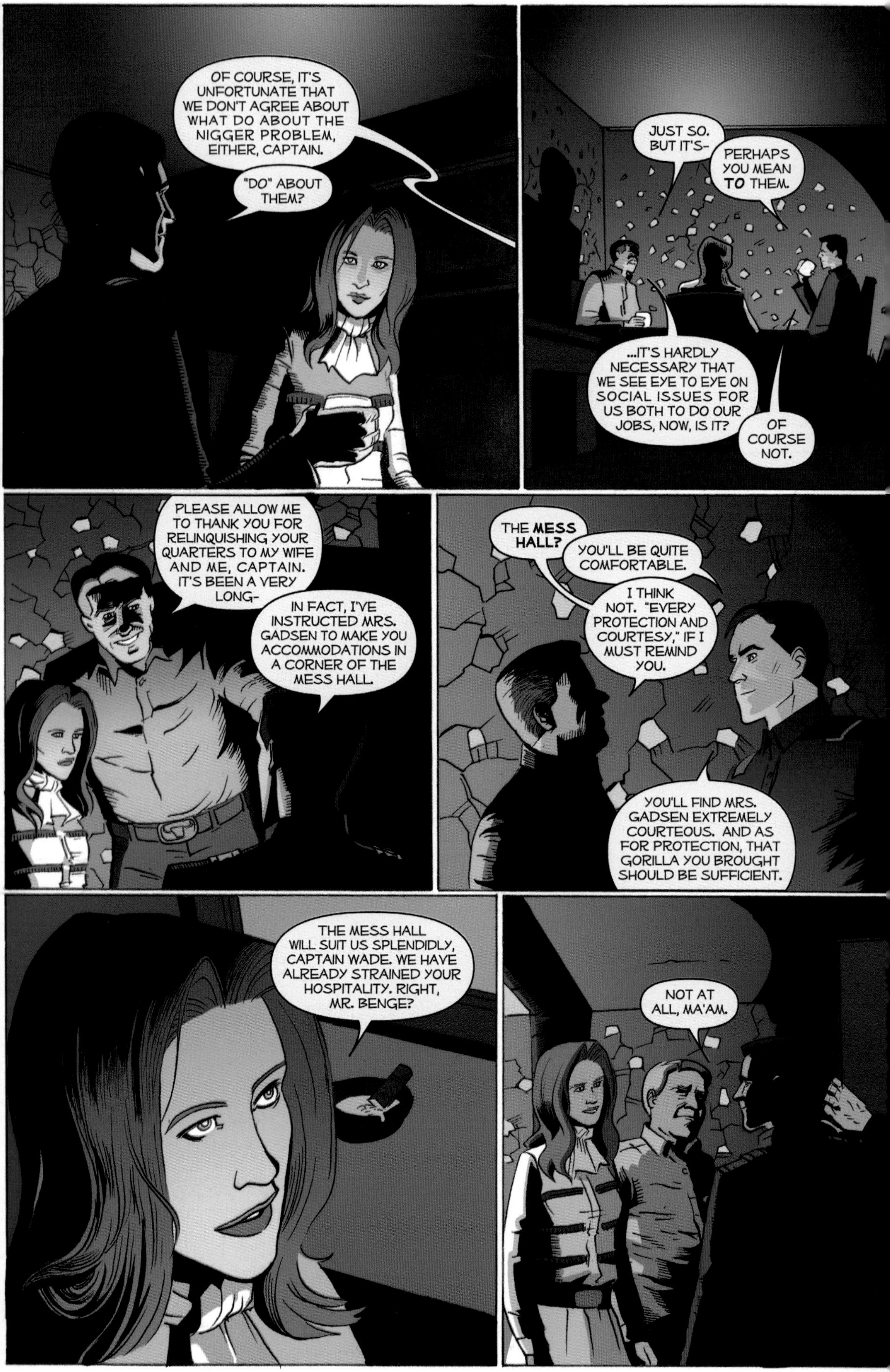
OF COURSE, IT'S UNFORTUNATE THAT WE DON'T AGREE ABOUT WHAT DO ABOUT THE NIGGER PROBLEM, EITHER, CAPTAIN.
"DO" ABOUT THEM?
JUST SO. BUT IT'S-
PERHAPS YOU MEAN **TO** THEM.
...IT'S HARDLY NECESSARY THAT WE SEE EYE TO EYE ON SOCIAL ISSUES FOR US BOTH TO DO OUR JOBS, NOW, IS IT?
OF COURSE NOT.
PLEASE ALLOW ME TO THANK YOU FOR RELINQUISHING YOUR QUARTERS TO MY WIFE AND ME, CAPTAIN. IT'S BEEN A VERY LONG-
IN FACT, I'VE INSTRUCTED MRS. GADSEN TO MAKE YOU ACCOMMODATIONS IN A CORNER OF THE MESS HALL.
THE **MESS HALL?**
YOU'LL BE QUITE COMFORTABLE.
I THINK NOT. "EVERY PROTECTION AND COURTESY," IF I MUST REMIND YOU.
YOU'LL FIND MRS. GADSEN EXTREMELY COURTEOUS. AND AS FOR PROTECTION, THAT GORILLA YOU BROUGHT SHOULD BE SUFFICIENT.
THE MESS HALL WILL SUIT US SPLENDIDLY, CAPTAIN WADE. WE HAVE ALREADY STRAINED YOUR HOSPITALITY. RIGHT, MR. BENGE?
NOT AT ALL, MA'AM.

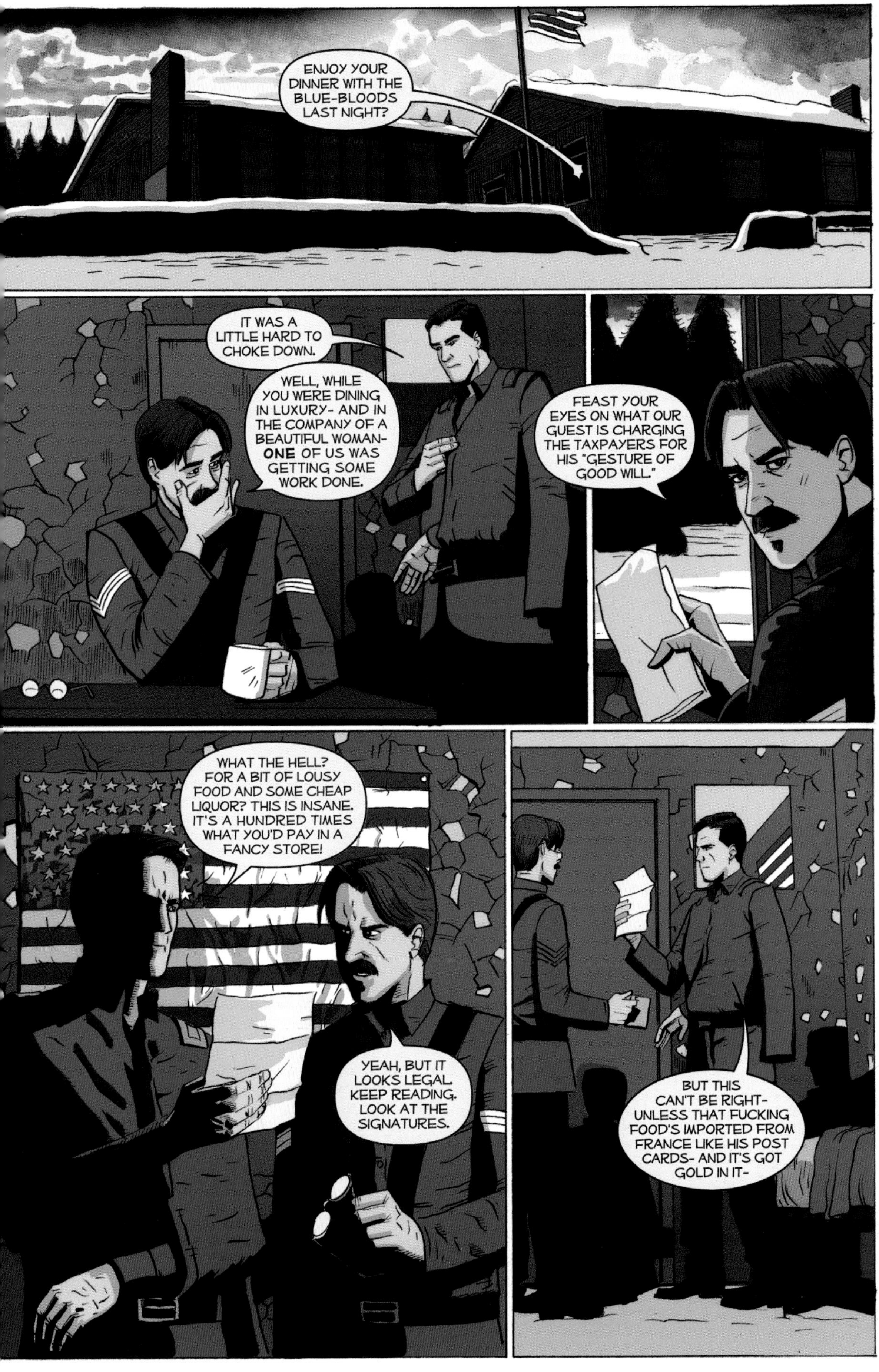
ENJOY YOUR DINNER WITH THE BLUE-BLOODS LAST NIGHT?
IT WAS A LITTLE HARD TO CHOKE DOWN.
WELL, WHILE YOU WERE DINING IN LUXURY- AND IN THE COMPANY OF A BEAUTIFUL WOMAN- **ONE** OF US WAS GETTING SOME WORK DONE.
FEAST YOUR EYES ON WHAT OUR GUEST IS CHARGING THE TAXPAYERS FOR HIS "GESTURE OF GOOD WILL."
WHAT THE HELL? FOR A BIT OF LOUSY FOOD AND SOME CHEAP LIQUOR? THIS IS INSANE. IT'S A HUNDRED TIMES WHAT YOU'D PAY IN A FANCY STORE!
YEAH, BUT IT LOOKS LEGAL. KEEP READING. LOOK AT THE SIGNATURES.
BUT THIS CAN'T BE RIGHT- UNLESS THAT FUCKING FOOD'S IMPORTED FROM FRANCE LIKE HIS POST CARDS- AND IT'S GOT GOLD IN IT-

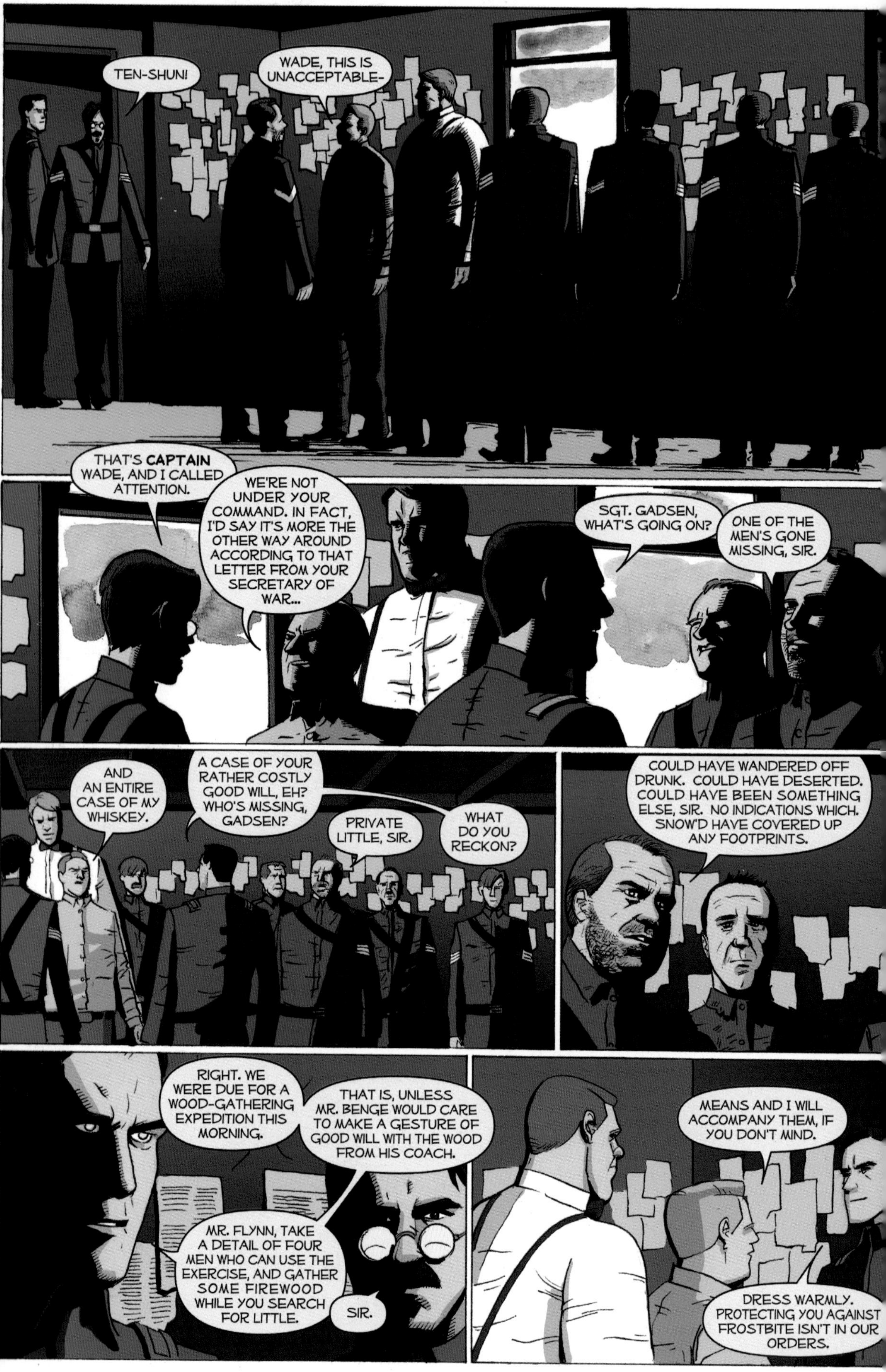
TEN-SHUN!
WADE, THIS IS UNACCEPTABLE-
THAT'S **CAPTAIN** WADE, AND I CALLED ATTENTION.
WE'RE NOT UNDER YOUR COMMAND. IN FACT, I'D SAY IT'S MORE THE OTHER WAY AROUND ACCORDING TO THAT LETTER FROM YOUR SECRETARY OF WAR...
SGT. GADSEN, WHAT'S GOING ON?
ONE OF THE MEN'S GONE MISSING, SIR.
AND AN ENTIRE CASE OF MY WHISKEY.
A CASE OF YOUR RATHER COSTLY GOOD WILL, EH? WHO'S MISSING, GADSEN?
PRIVATE LITTLE, SIR.
WHAT DO YOU RECKON?
COULD HAVE WANDERED OFF DRUNK. COULD HAVE DESERTED. COULD HAVE BEEN SOMETHING ELSE, SIR. NO INDICATIONS WHICH. SNOW'D HAVE COVERED UP ANY FOOTPRINTS.
RIGHT. WE WERE DUE FOR A WOOD-GATHERING EXPEDITION THIS MORNING.
THAT IS, UNLESS MR. BENGE WOULD CARE TO MAKE A GESTURE OF GOOD WILL WITH THE WOOD FROM HIS COACH.
MR. FLYNN, TAKE A DETAIL OF FOUR MEN WHO CAN USE THE EXERCISE, AND GATHER SOME FIREWOOD WHILE YOU SEARCH FOR LITTLE.
SIR.
MEANS AND I WILL ACCOMPANY THEM, IF YOU DON'T MIND.
DRESS WARMLY. PROTECTING YOU AGAINST FROSTBITE ISN'T IN OUR ORDERS.

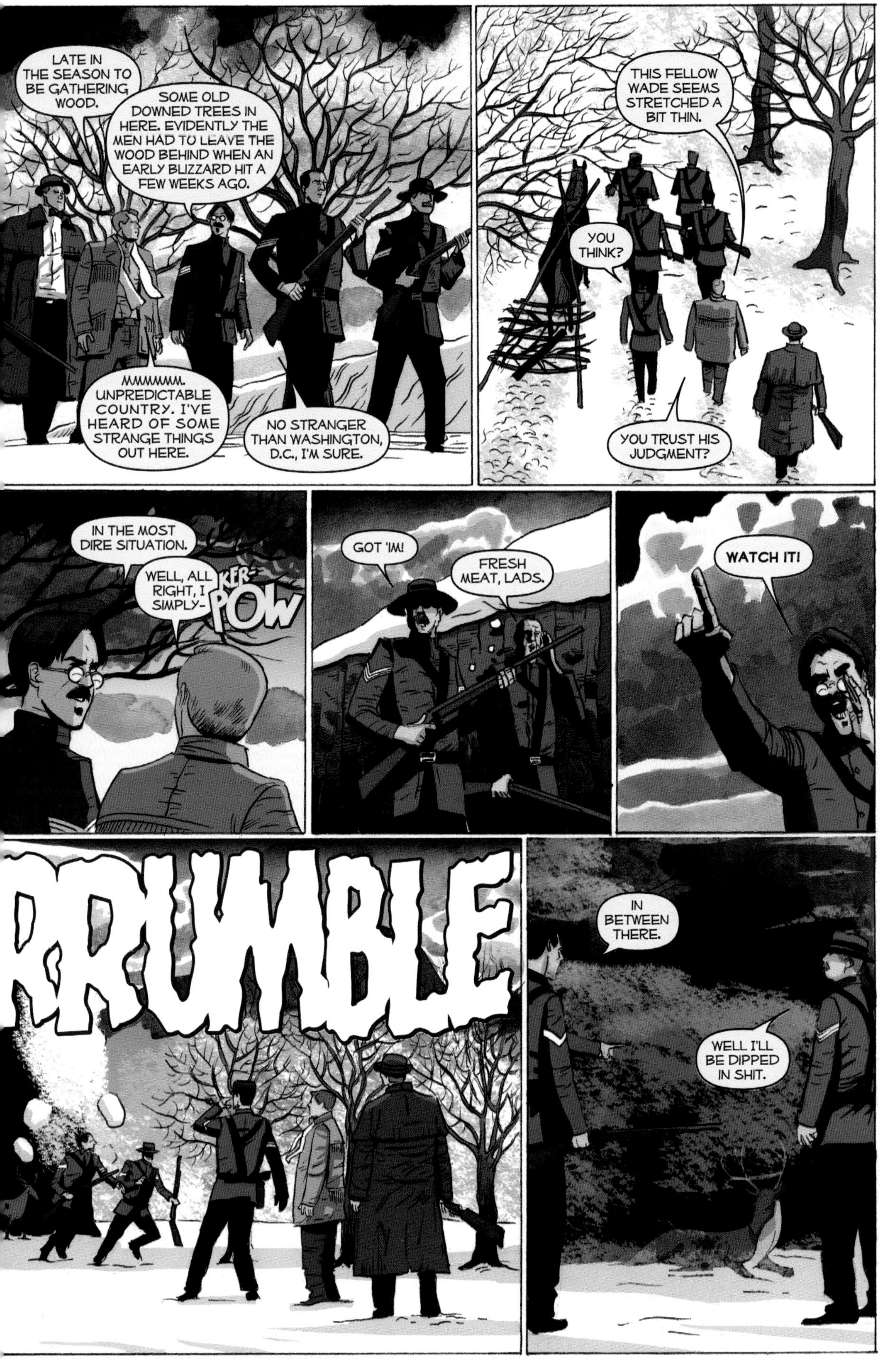
LATE IN THE SEASON TO BE GATHERING WOOD.
SOME OLD DOWNED TREES IN HERE. EVIDENTLY THE MEN HAD TO LEAVE THE WOOD BEHIND WHEN AN EARLY BLIZZARD HIT A FEW WEEKS AGO.
MMMMMM. UNPREDICTABLE COUNTRY. I'VE HEARD OF SOME STRANGE THINGS OUT HERE.
NO STRANGER THAN WASHINGTON, D.C., I'M SURE.
THIS FELLOW WADE SEEMS STRETCHED A BIT THIN.
YOU THINK?
YOU TRUST HIS JUDGMENT?
IN THE MOST DIRE SITUATION.
WELL, ALL RIGHT, I SIMPLY-
KER-POW
GOT 'IM!
FRESH MEAT, LADS.
WATCH IT!
RRUMBLE
IN BETWEEN THERE.
WELL I'LL BE DIPPED IN SHIT.

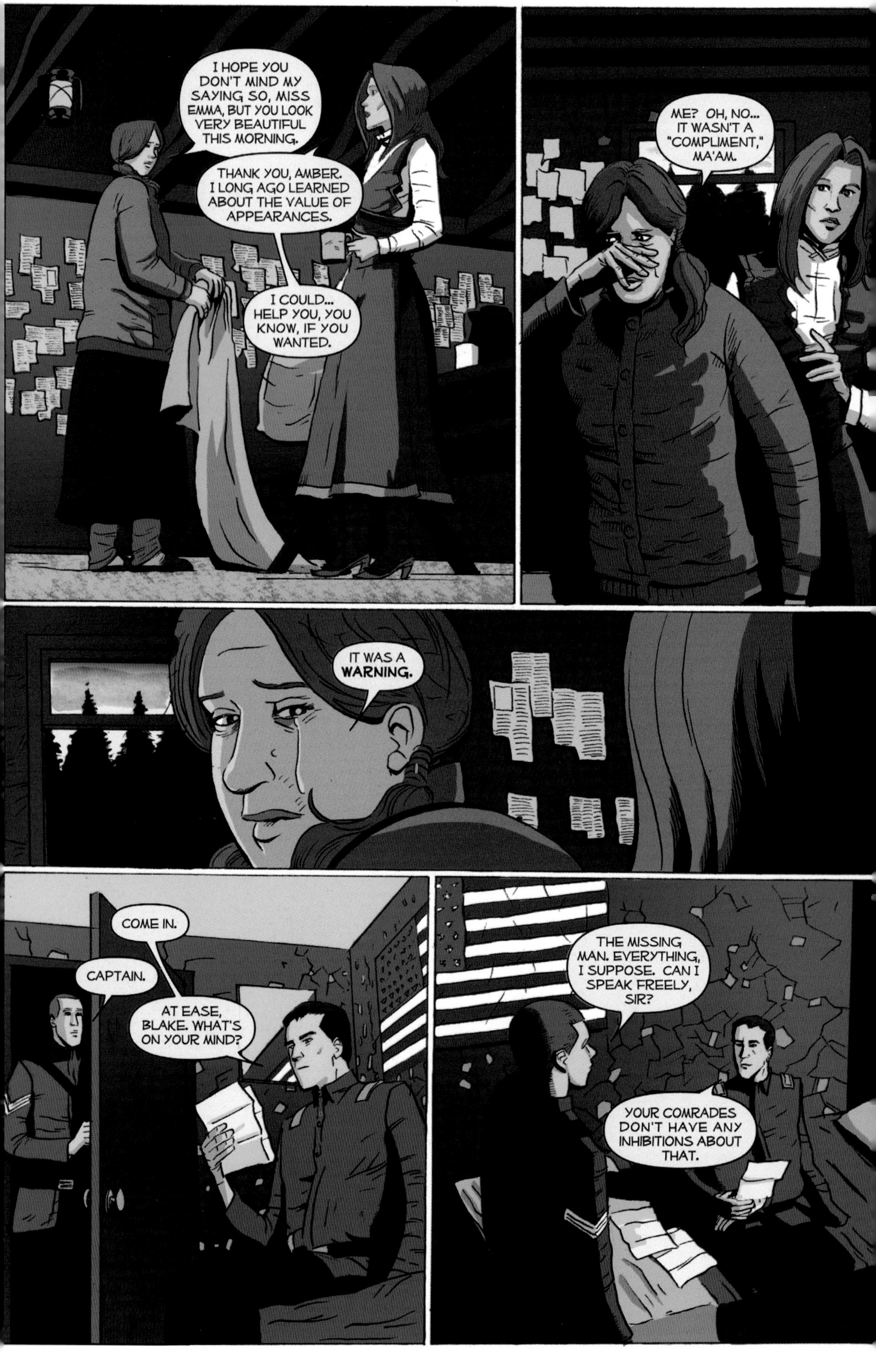
I HOPE YOU DON'T MIND MY SAYING SO, MISS EMMA, BUT YOU LOOK VERY BEAUTIFUL THIS MORNING.
THANK YOU, AMBER. I LONG AGO LEARNED ABOUT THE VALUE OF APPEARANCES.
I COULD... HELP YOU, YOU KNOW, IF YOU WANTED.
ME? OH, NO... IT WASN'T A "COMPLIMENT," MA'AM.
IT WAS A **WARNING.**
COME IN.
CAPTAIN.
AT EASE, BLAKE. WHAT'S ON YOUR MIND?
THE MISSING MAN. EVERYTHING, I SUPPOSE. CAN I SPEAK FREELY, SIR?
YOUR COMRADES DON'T HAVE ANY INHIBITIONS ABOUT THAT.

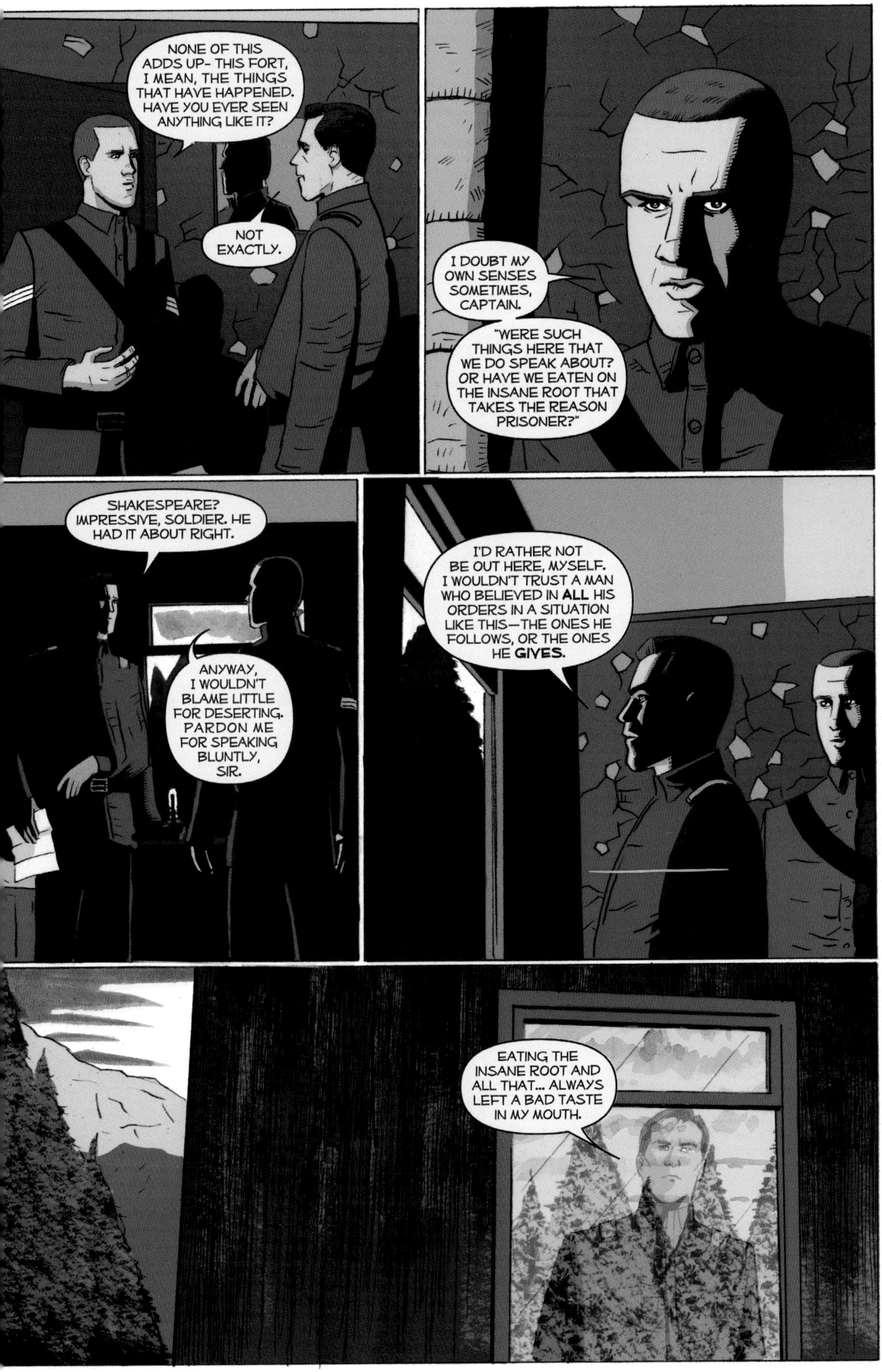
NONE OF THIS ADDS UP- THIS FORT, I MEAN, THE THINGS THAT HAVE HAPPENED. HAVE YOU EVER SEEN ANYTHING LIKE IT?
NOT EXACTLY.
I DOUBT MY OWN SENSES SOMETIMES, CAPTAIN.
"WERE SUCH THINGS HERE THAT WE DO SPEAK ABOUT? OR HAVE WE EATEN ON THE INSANE ROOT THAT TAKES THE REASON PRISONER?"
SHAKESPEARE? IMPRESSIVE, SOLDIER. HE HAD IT ABOUT RIGHT.
ANYWAY, I WOULDN'T BLAME LITTLE FOR DESERTING. PARDON ME FOR SPEAKING BLUNTLY, SIR.
I'D RATHER NOT BE OUT HERE, MYSELF. I WOULDN'T TRUST A MAN WHO BELIEVED IN **ALL** HIS ORDERS IN A SITUATION LIKE THIS—THE ONES HE FOLLOWS, OR THE ONES HE **GIVES**.
EATING THE INSANE ROOT AND ALL THAT... ALWAYS LEFT A BAD TASTE IN MY MOUTH.

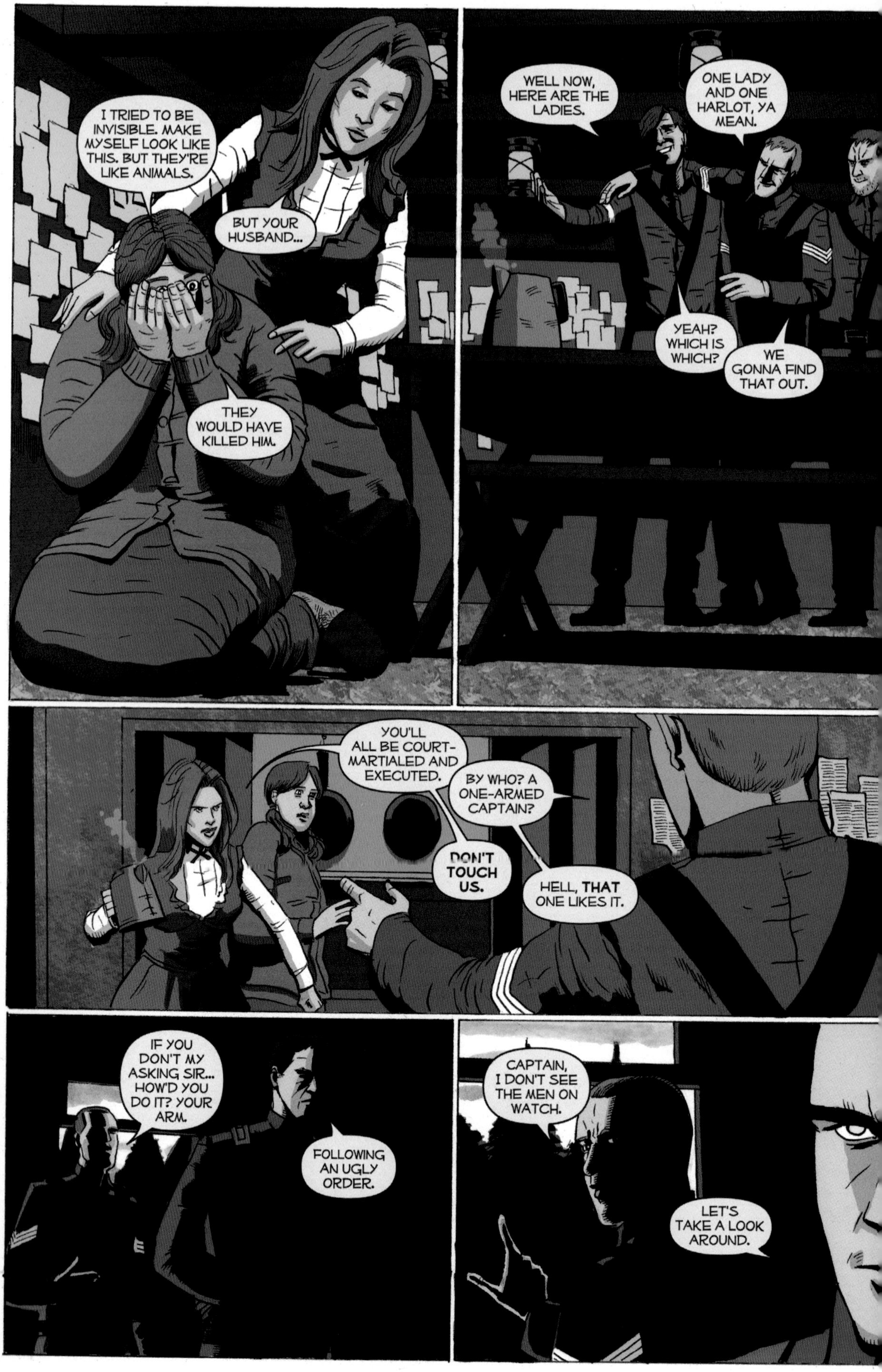
I TRIED TO BE INVISIBLE. MAKE MYSELF LOOK LIKE THIS. BUT THEY'RE LIKE ANIMALS.
BUT YOUR HUSBAND...
THEY WOULD HAVE KILLED HIM.
WELL NOW, HERE ARE THE LADIES.
ONE LADY AND ONE HARLOT, YA MEAN.
YEAH? WHICH IS WHICH?
WE GONNA FIND THAT OUT.
YOU'LL ALL BE COURT-MARTIALED AND EXECUTED.
BY WHO? A ONE-ARMED CAPTAIN?
DON'T TOUCH US.
HELL, THAT ONE LIKES IT.
IF YOU DON'T MY ASKING SIR... HOW'D YOU DO IT? YOUR ARM.
FOLLOWING AN UGLY ORDER.
CAPTAIN, I DON'T SEE THE MEN ON WATCH.
LET'S TAKE A LOOK AROUND.

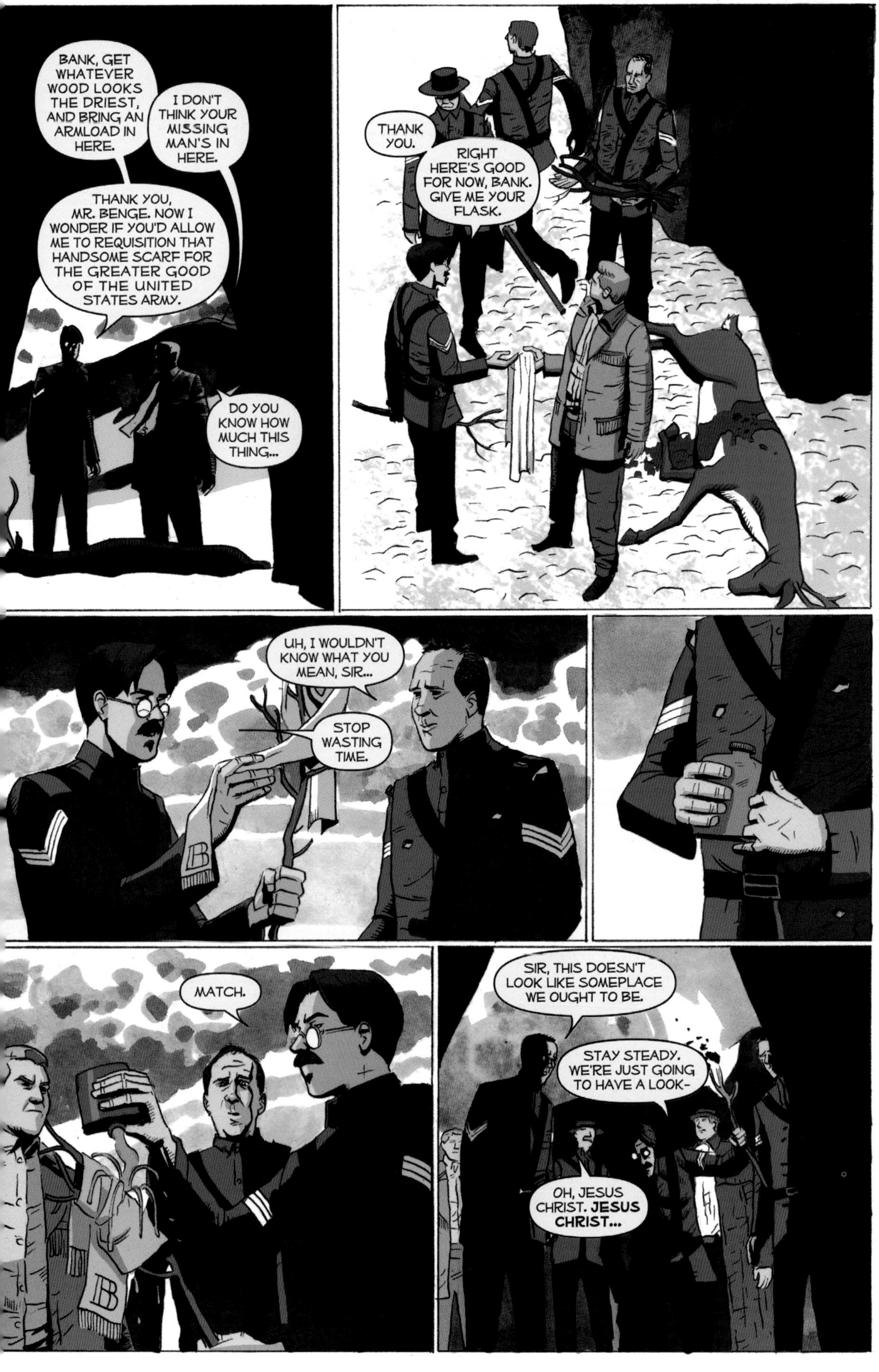
BANK, GET WHATEVER WOOD LOOKS THE DRIEST, AND BRING AN ARMLOAD IN HERE.
I DON'T THINK YOUR MISSING MAN'S IN HERE.
THANK YOU, MR. BENGE. NOW I WONDER IF YOU'D ALLOW ME TO REQUISITION THAT HANDSOME SCARF FOR THE GREATER GOOD OF THE UNITED STATES ARMY.
DO YOU KNOW HOW MUCH THIS THING...
THANK YOU.
RIGHT HERE'S GOOD FOR NOW, BANK. GIVE ME YOUR FLASK.
UH, I WOULDN'T KNOW WHAT YOU MEAN, SIR...
STOP WASTING TIME.
MATCH.
SIR, THIS DOESN'T LOOK LIKE SOMEPLACE WE OUGHT TO BE.
STAY STEADY. WE'RE JUST GOING TO HAVE A LOOK-
OH, JESUS CHRIST. **JESUS CHRIST...**

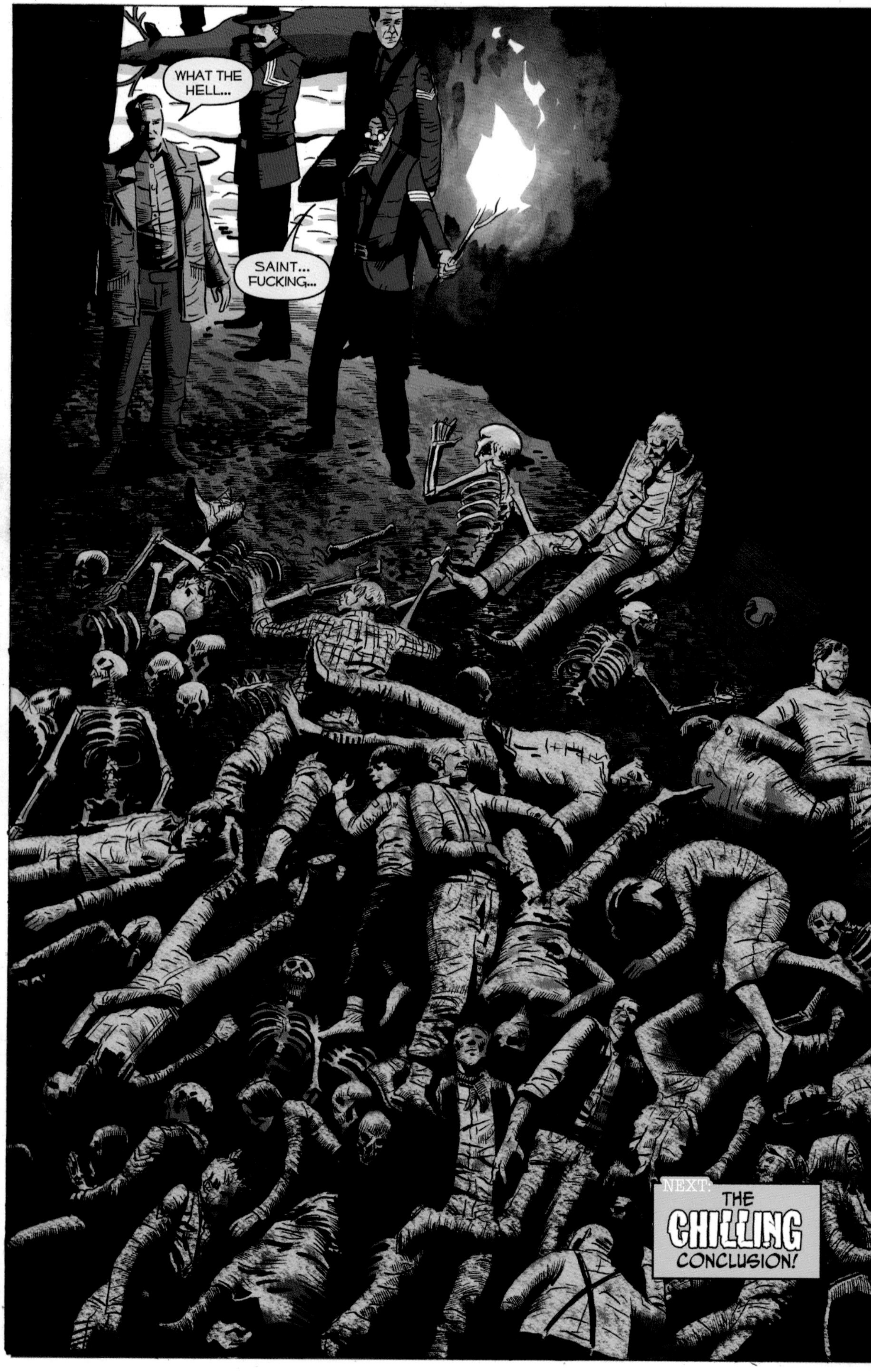
WHAT THE HELL...
SAINT... FUCKING...
NEXT: THE CHILLING CONCLUSION!

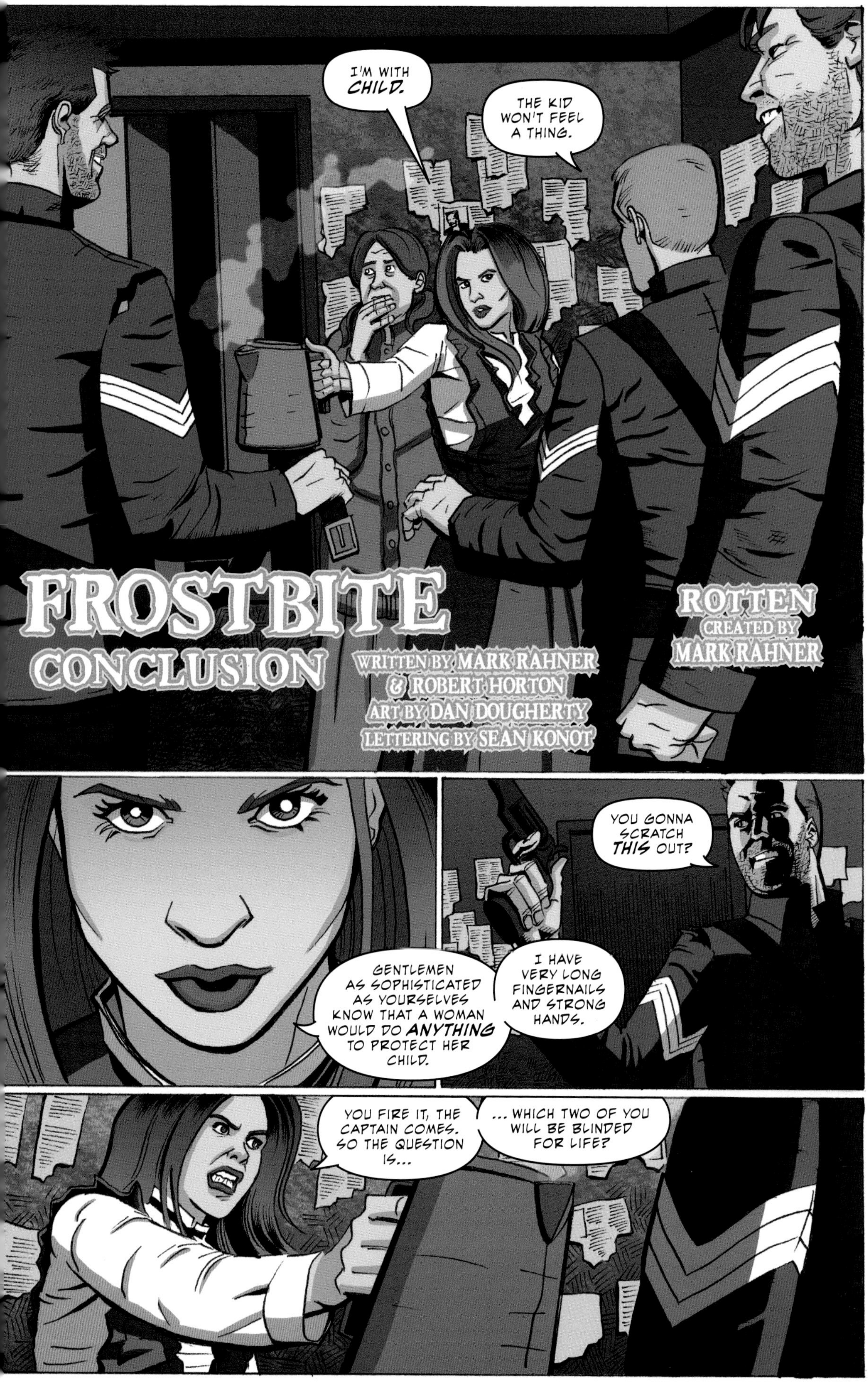
I'M WITH CHILD.
THE KID WON'T FEEL A THING.
FROSTBITE CONCLUSION
WRITTEN BY MARK RAHNER & ROBERT HORTON
ART BY DAN DOUGHERTY
LETTERING BY SEAN KONOT
ROTTEN CREATED BY MARK RAHNER
YOU GONNA SCRATCH THIS OUT?
GENTLEMEN AS SOPHISTICATED AS YOURSELVES KNOW THAT A WOMAN WOULD DO ANYTHING TO PROTECT HER CHILD.
I HAVE VERY LONG FINGERNAILS AND STRONG HANDS.
YOU FIRE IT, THE CAPTAIN COMES. SO THE QUESTION IS...
... WHICH TWO OF YOU WILL BE BLINDED FOR LIFE?

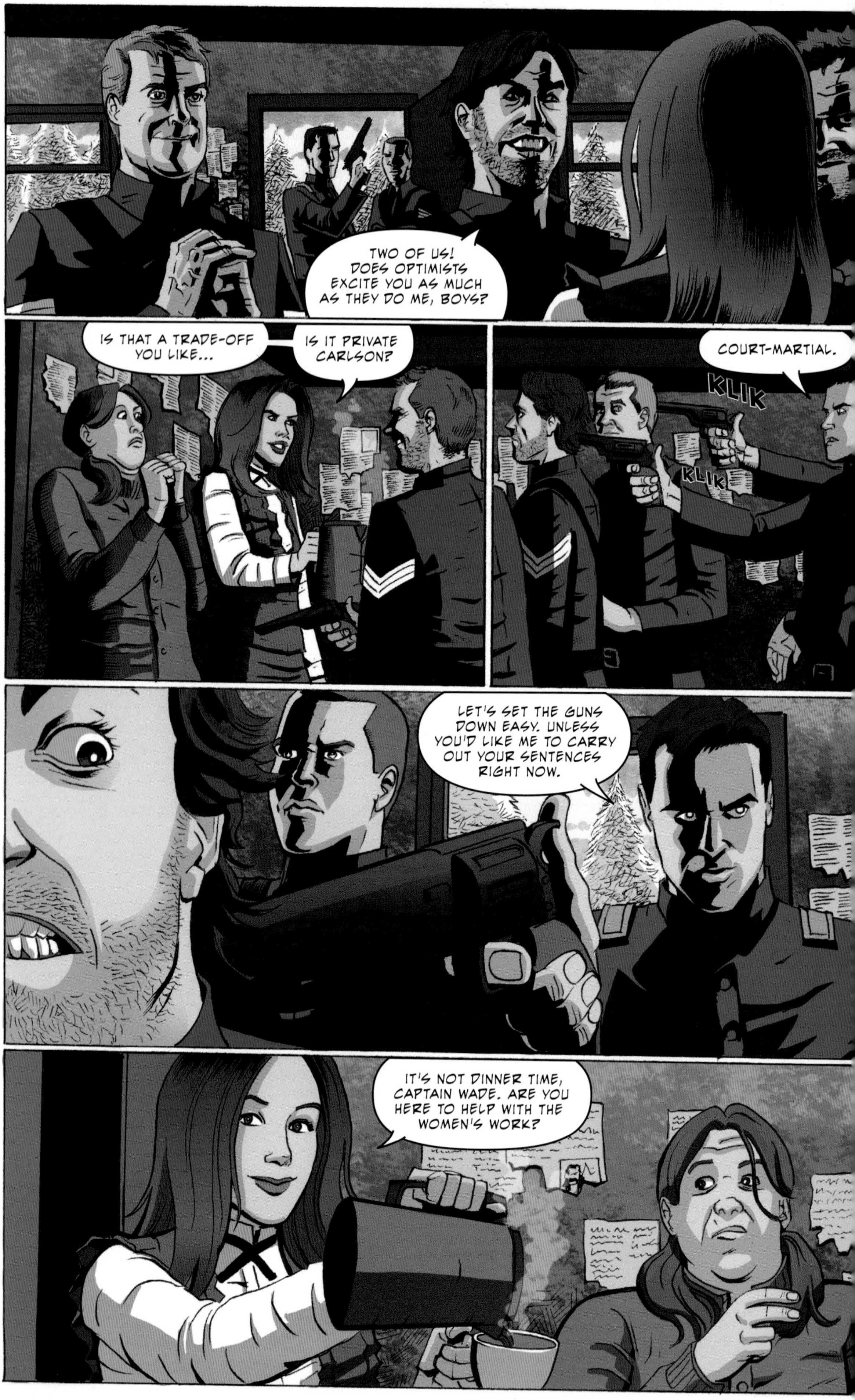
TWO OF US! DOES OPTIMISTS EXCITE YOU AS MUCH AS THEY DO ME, BOYS?
IS THAT A TRADE-OFF YOU LIKE...
IS IT PRIVATE CARLSON?
COURT-MARTIAL.
KLIK
KLIK
LET'S SET THE GUNS DOWN EASY. UNLESS YOU'D LIKE ME TO CARRY OUT YOUR SENTENCES RIGHT NOW.
IT'S NOT DINNER TIME, CAPTAIN WADE. ARE YOU HERE TO HELP WITH THE WOMEN'S WORK?

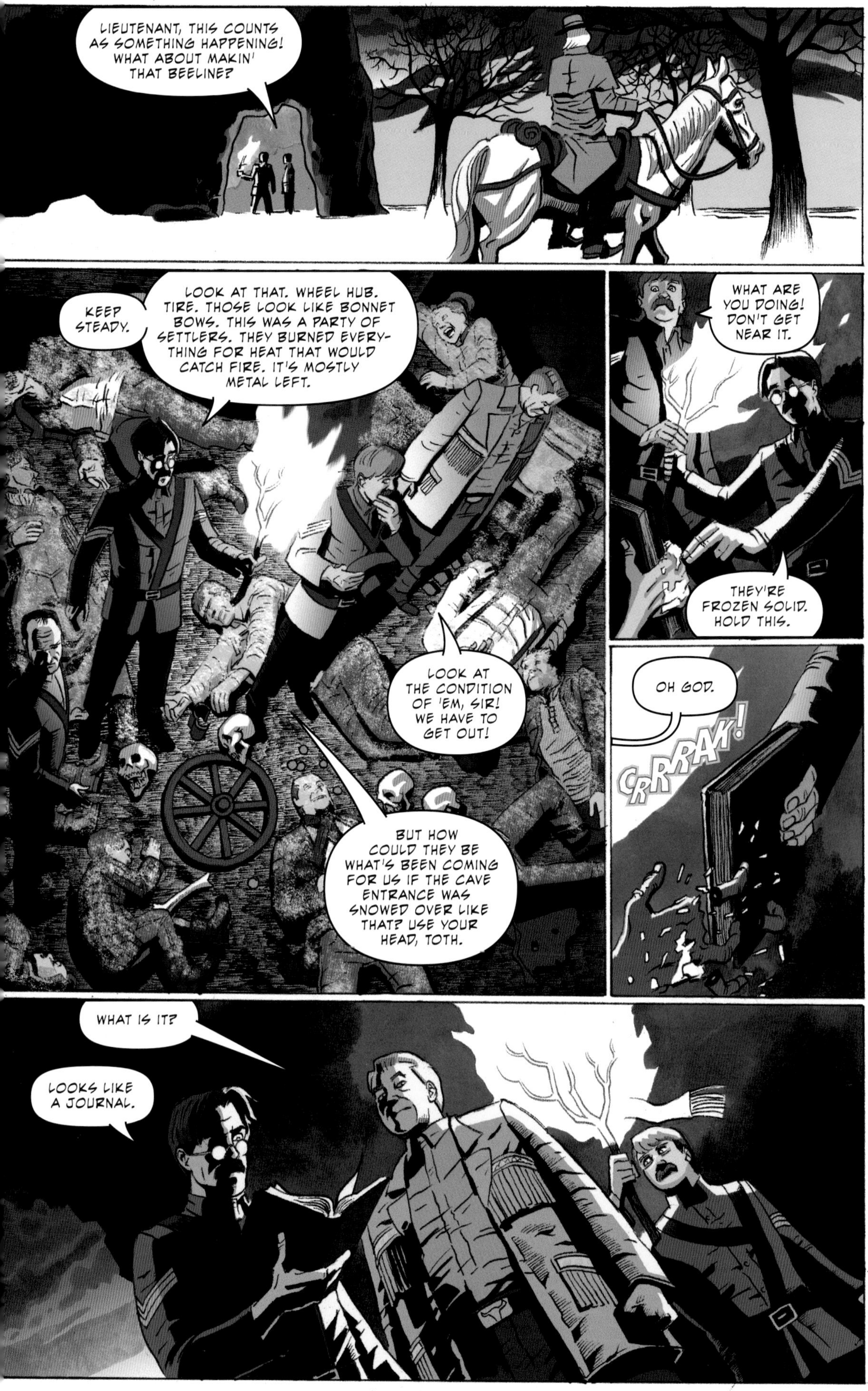
LIEUTENANT, THIS COUNTS AS SOMETHING HAPPENING! WHAT ABOUT MAKIN' THAT BEELINE?
KEEP STEADY.
LOOK AT THAT. WHEEL HUB. TIRE. THOSE LOOK LIKE BONNET BOWS. THIS WAS A PARTY OF SETTLERS. THEY BURNED EVERYTHING FOR HEAT THAT WOULD CATCH FIRE. IT'S MOSTLY METAL LEFT.
LOOK AT THE CONDITION OF 'EM, SIR! WE HAVE TO GET OUT!
BUT HOW COULD THEY BE WHAT'S BEEN COMING FOR US IF THE CAVE ENTRANCE WAS SNOWED OVER LIKE THAT? USE YOUR HEAD, TOTH.
WHAT ARE YOU DOING! DON'T GET NEAR IT.
THEY'RE FROZEN SOLID. HOLD THIS.
OH GOD.
CRRRAK!
WHAT IS IT?
LOOKS LIKE A JOURNAL.

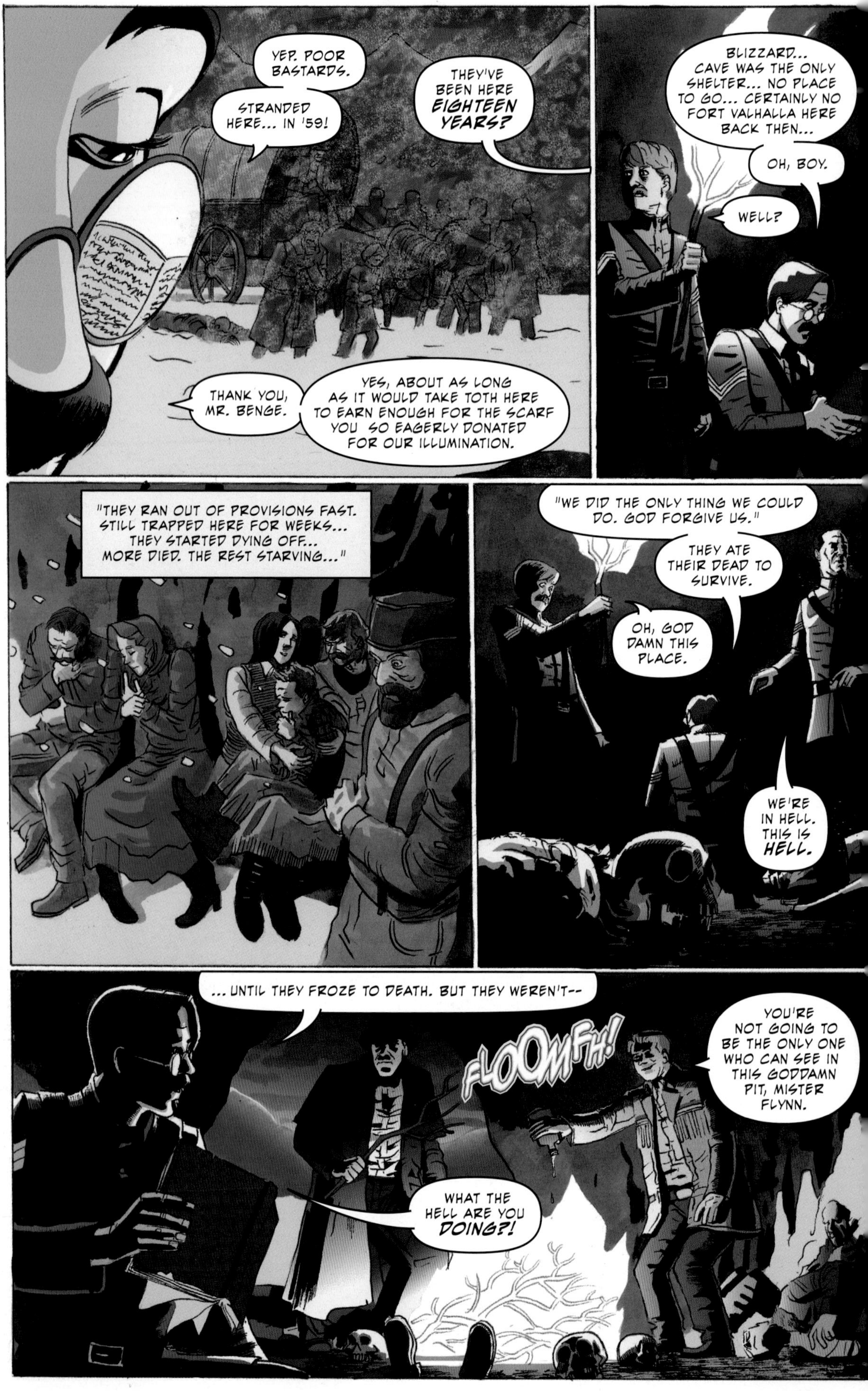
YEP. POOR BASTARDS.
STRANDED HERE... IN '59!
THEY'VE BEEN HERE *EIGHTEEN YEARS?*
THANK YOU, MR. BENGE.
YES, ABOUT AS LONG AS IT WOULD TAKE TOTH HERE TO EARN ENOUGH FOR THE SCARF YOU SO EAGERLY DONATED FOR OUR ILLUMINATION.
BLIZZARD... CAVE WAS THE ONLY SHELTER... NO PLACE TO GO... CERTAINLY NO FORT VALHALLA HERE BACK THEN...
OH, BOY.
WELL?
"THEY RAN OUT OF PROVISIONS FAST. STILL TRAPPED HERE FOR WEEKS... THEY STARTED DYING OFF... MORE DIED. THE REST STARVING..."
"WE DID THE ONLY THING WE COULD DO. GOD FORGIVE US."
THEY ATE THEIR DEAD TO SURVIVE.
OH, GOD DAMN THIS PLACE.
WE'RE IN HELL. THIS IS *HELL.*
... UNTIL THEY FROZE TO DEATH. BUT THEY WEREN'T--
FLOOMFH!
YOU'RE NOT GOING TO BE THE ONLY ONE WHO CAN SEE IN THIS GODDAMN PIT, MISTER FLYNN.
WHAT THE HELL ARE YOU *DOING?!*

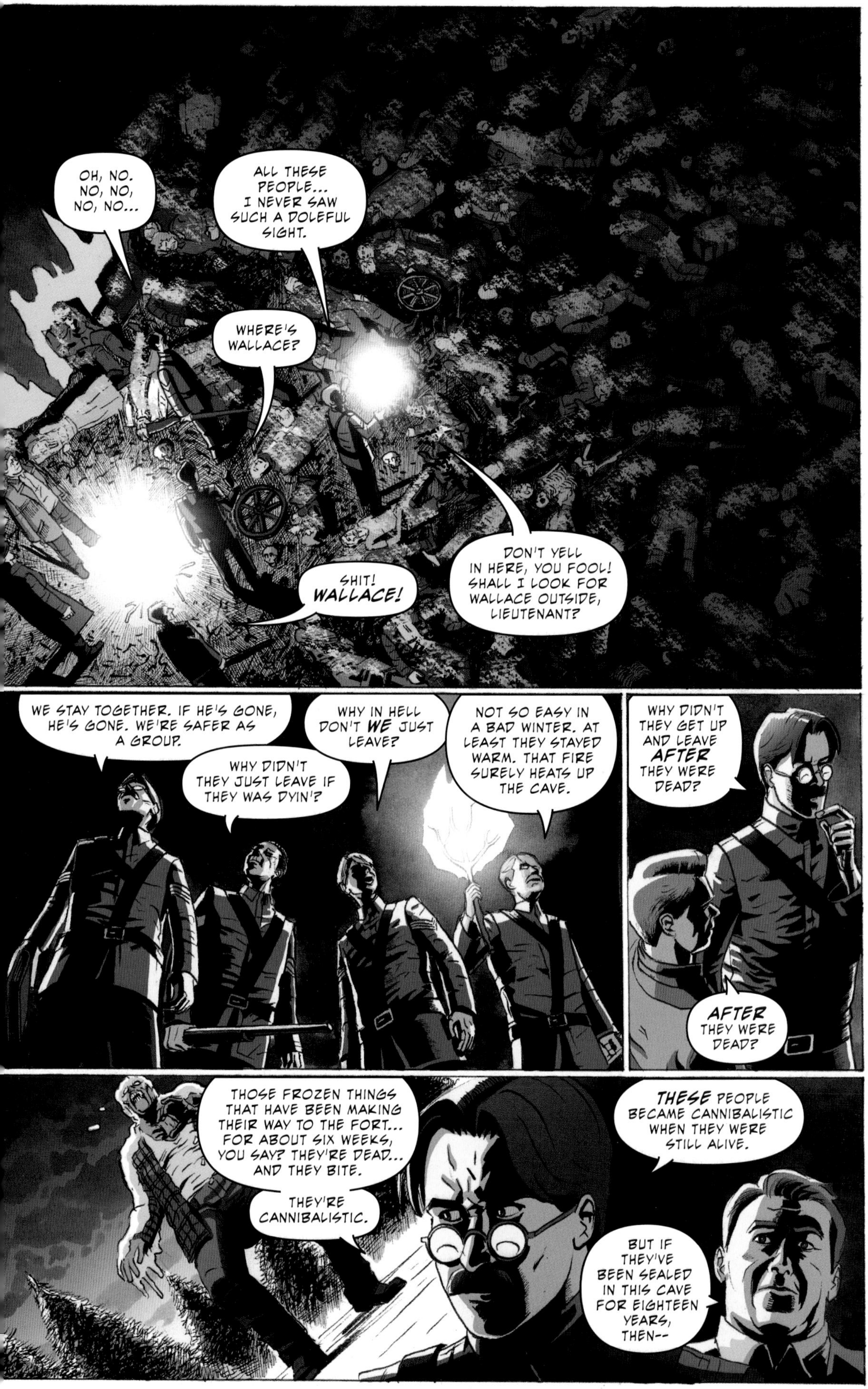
OH, NO. NO, NO, NO, NO...
ALL THESE PEOPLE... I NEVER SAW SUCH A DOLEFUL SIGHT.
WHERE'S WALLACE?
SHIT! WALLACE!
DON'T YELL IN HERE, YOU FOOL! SHALL I LOOK FOR WALLACE OUTSIDE, LIEUTENANT?
WE STAY TOGETHER. IF HE'S GONE, HE'S GONE. WE'RE SAFER AS A GROUP.
WHY DIDN'T THEY JUST LEAVE IF THEY WAS DYIN'?
WHY IN HELL DON'T WE JUST LEAVE?
NOT SO EASY IN A BAD WINTER. AT LEAST THEY STAYED WARM. THAT FIRE SURELY HEATS UP THE CAVE.
WHY DIDN'T THEY GET UP AND LEAVE AFTER THEY WERE DEAD?
AFTER THEY WERE DEAD?
THOSE FROZEN THINGS THAT HAVE BEEN MAKING THEIR WAY TO THE FORT... FOR ABOUT SIX WEEKS, YOU SAY? THEY'RE DEAD... AND THEY BITE.
THEY'RE CANNIBALISTIC.
THESE PEOPLE BECAME CANNIBALISTIC WHEN THEY WERE STILL ALIVE.
BUT IF THEY'VE BEEN SEALED IN THIS CAVE FOR EIGHTEEN YEARS, THEN--

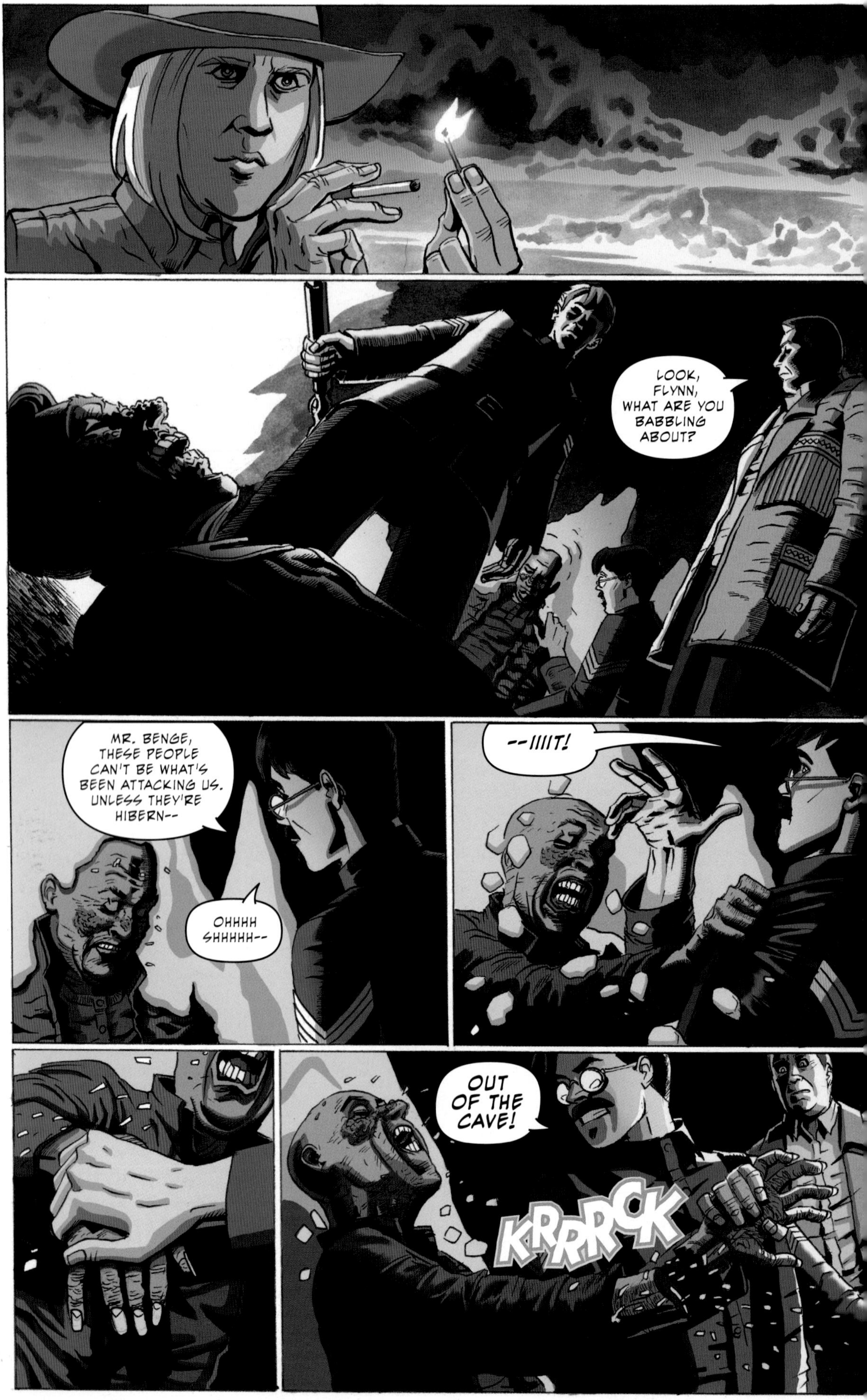

LOOK, FLYNN, WHAT ARE YOU BABBLING ABOUT?
MR. BENGE, THESE PEOPLE CAN'T BE WHAT'S BEEN ATTACKING US. UNLESS THEY'RE HIBERN--
OHHHH SHHHHH--
--IIIIT!
OUT OF THE CAVE!
KRRRCK

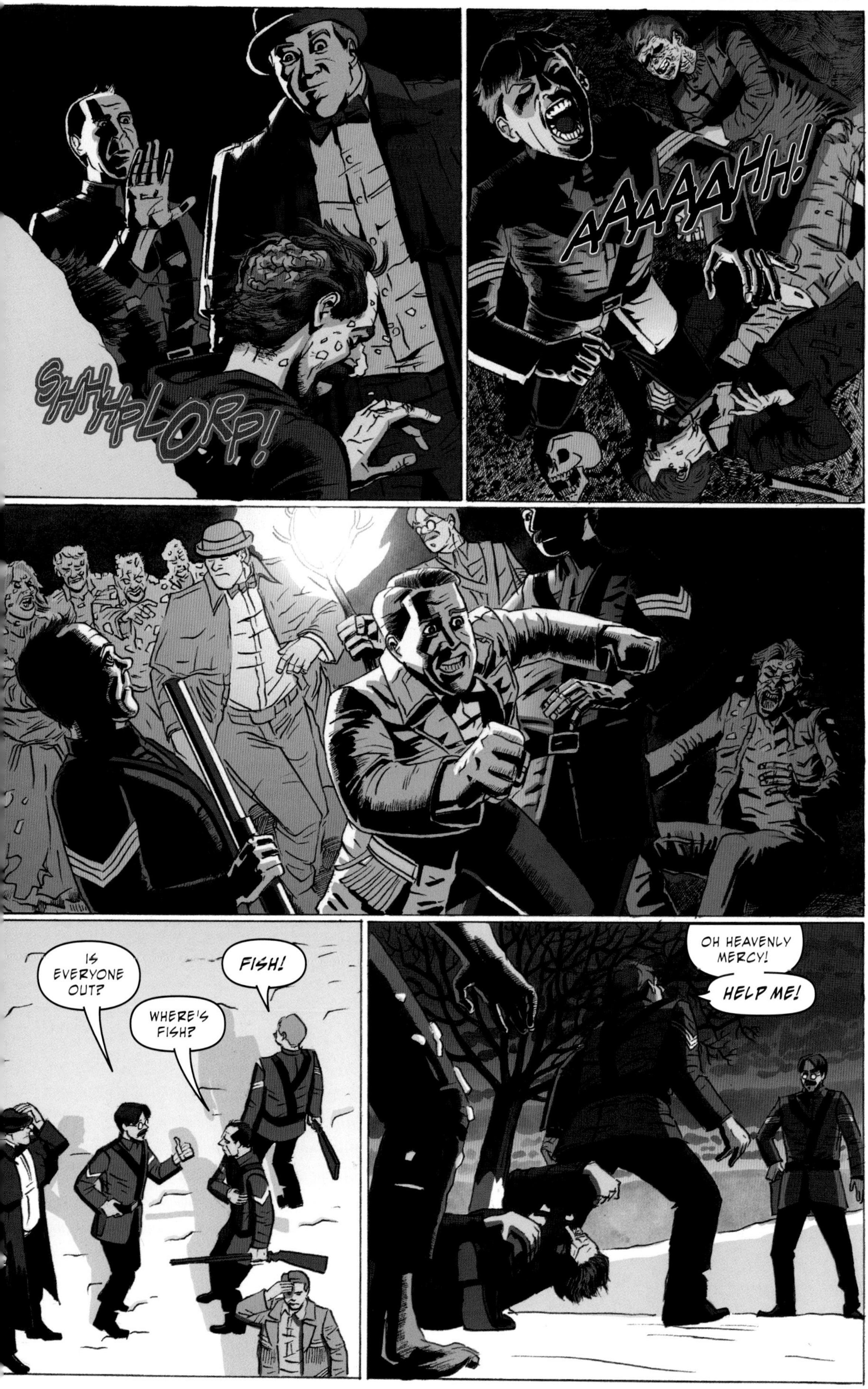
SHHHPLORP!
AAAAAHH!
IS EVERYONE OUT?
WHERE'S FISH?
FISH!
OH HEAVENLY MERCY!
HELP ME!

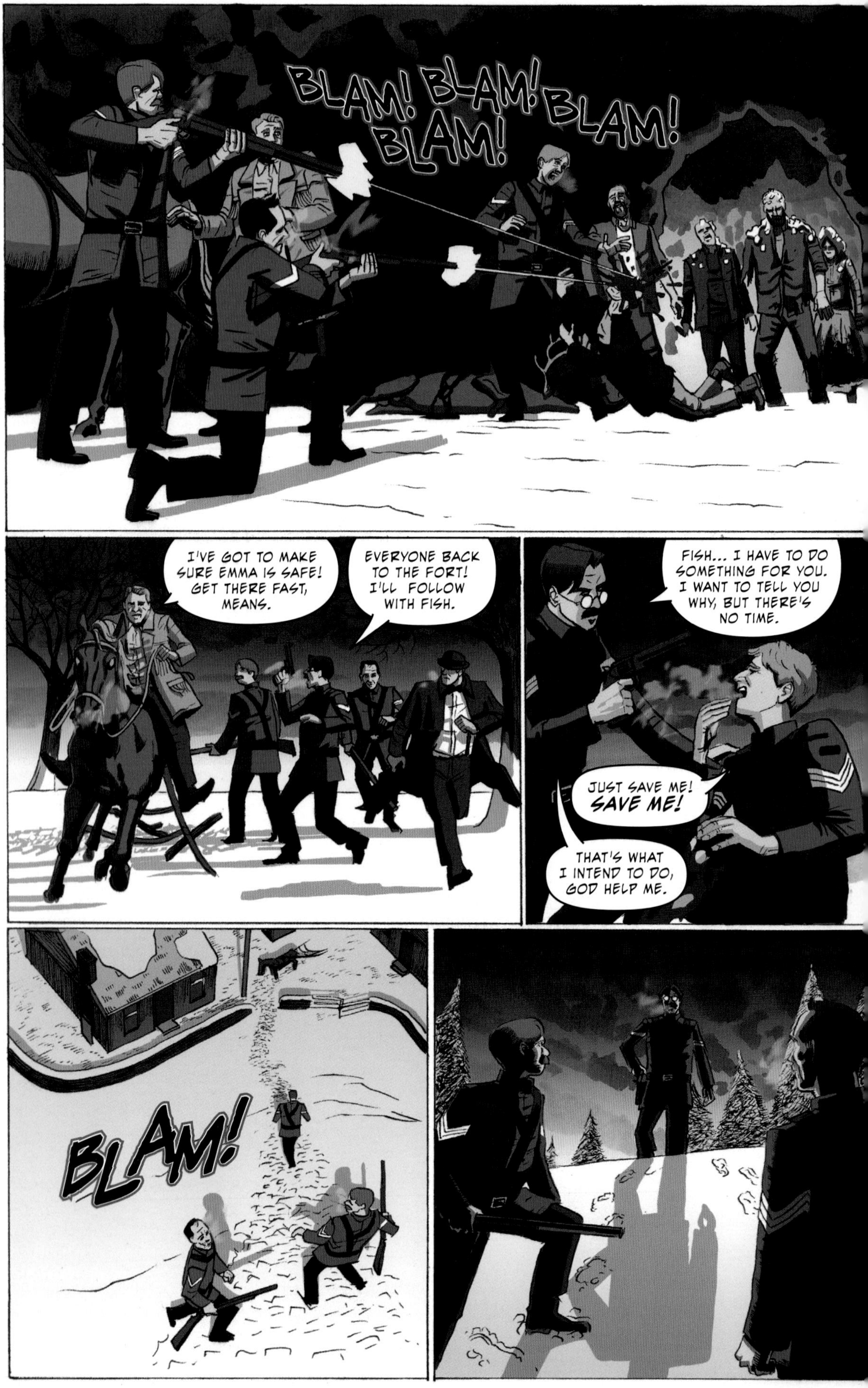
BLAM! BLAM! BLAM! BLAM!
I'VE GOT TO MAKE SURE EMMA IS SAFE! GET THERE FAST, MEANS.
EVERYONE BACK TO THE FORT! I'LL FOLLOW WITH FISH.
FISH... I HAVE TO DO SOMETHING FOR YOU. I WANT TO TELL YOU WHY, BUT THERE'S NO TIME.
JUST SAVE ME! SAVE ME!
THAT'S WHAT I INTEND TO DO, GOD HELP ME.
BLAM!

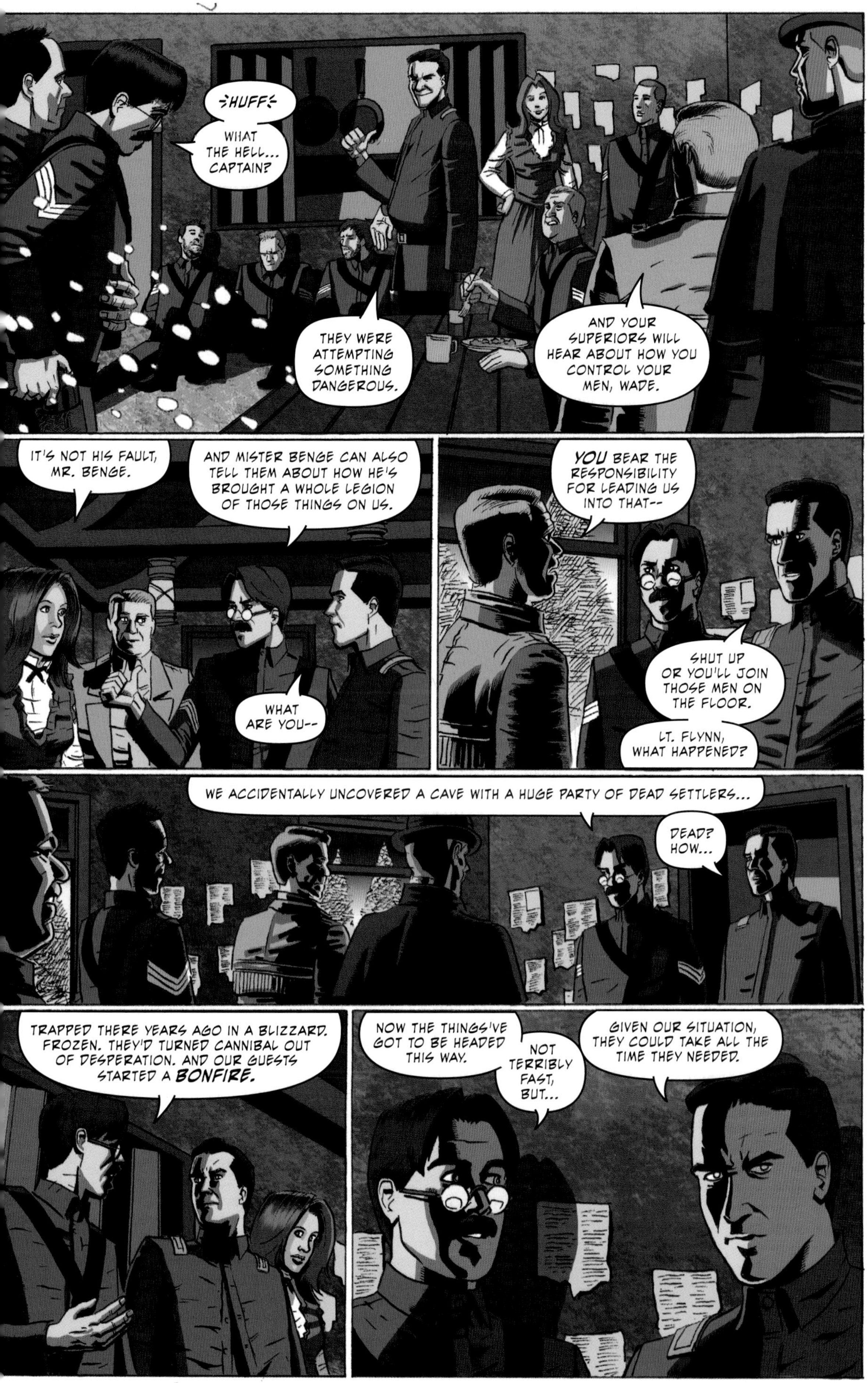

⊰HUFF⊱
WHAT THE HELL... CAPTAIN?
THEY WERE ATTEMPTING SOMETHING DANGEROUS.
AND YOUR SUPERIORS WILL HEAR ABOUT HOW YOU CONTROL YOUR MEN, WADE.
IT'S NOT HIS FAULT, MR. BENGE.
AND MISTER BENGE CAN ALSO TELL THEM ABOUT HOW HE'S BROUGHT A WHOLE LEGION OF THOSE THINGS ON US.
WHAT ARE YOU--
YOU BEAR THE RESPONSIBILITY FOR LEADING US INTO THAT--
SHUT UP OR YOU'LL JOIN THOSE MEN ON THE FLOOR.
LT. FLYNN, WHAT HAPPENED?
WE ACCIDENTALLY UNCOVERED A CAVE WITH A HUGE PARTY OF DEAD SETTLERS...
DEAD? HOW...
TRAPPED THERE YEARS AGO IN A BLIZZARD. FROZEN. THEY'D TURNED CANNIBAL OUT OF DESPERATION. AND OUR GUESTS STARTED A BONFIRE.
NOW THE THINGS'VE GOT TO BE HEADED THIS WAY.
NOT TERRIBLY FAST, BUT...
GIVEN OUR SITUATION, THEY COULD TAKE ALL THE TIME THEY NEEDED.

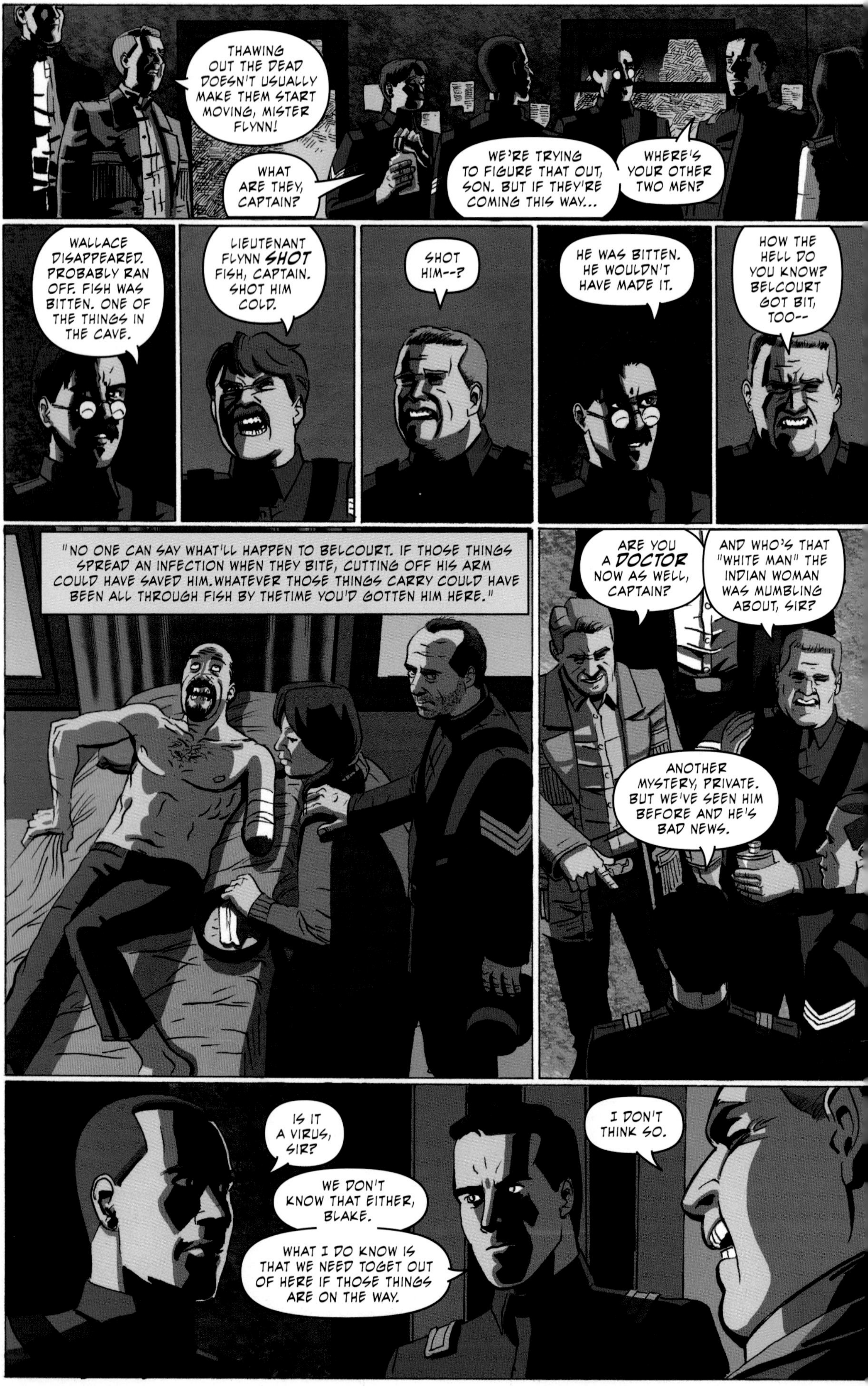
THAWING OUT THE DEAD DOESN'T USUALLY MAKE THEM START MOVING, MISTER FLYNN!
WHAT ARE THEY, CAPTAIN?
WE'RE TRYING TO FIGURE THAT OUT, SON. BUT IF THEY'RE COMING THIS WAY...
WHERE'S YOUR OTHER TWO MEN?
WALLACE DISAPPEARED. PROBABLY RAN OFF. FISH WAS BITTEN. ONE OF THE THINGS IN THE CAVE.
LIEUTENANT FLYNN SHOT FISH, CAPTAIN. SHOT HIM COLD.
SHOT HIM--?
HE WAS BITTEN. HE WOULDN'T HAVE MADE IT.
HOW THE HELL DO YOU KNOW? BELCOURT GOT BIT, TOO--
"NO ONE CAN SAY WHAT'LL HAPPEN TO BELCOURT. IF THOSE THINGS SPREAD AN INFECTION WHEN THEY BITE, CUTTING OFF HIS ARM COULD HAVE SAVED HIM.WHATEVER THOSE THINGS CARRY COULD HAVE BEEN ALL THROUGH FISH BY THETIME YOU'D GOTTEN HIM HERE."
ARE YOU A DOCTOR NOW AS WELL, CAPTAIN?
AND WHO'S THAT "WHITE MAN" THE INDIAN WOMAN WAS MUMBLING ABOUT, SIR?
ANOTHER MYSTERY, PRIVATE. BUT WE'VE SEEN HIM BEFORE AND HE'S BAD NEWS.
IS IT A VIRUS, SIR?
WE DON'T KNOW THAT EITHER, BLAKE.
WHAT I DO KNOW IS THAT WE NEED TOGET OUT OF HERE IF THOSE THINGS ARE ON THE WAY.
I DON'T THINK SO.

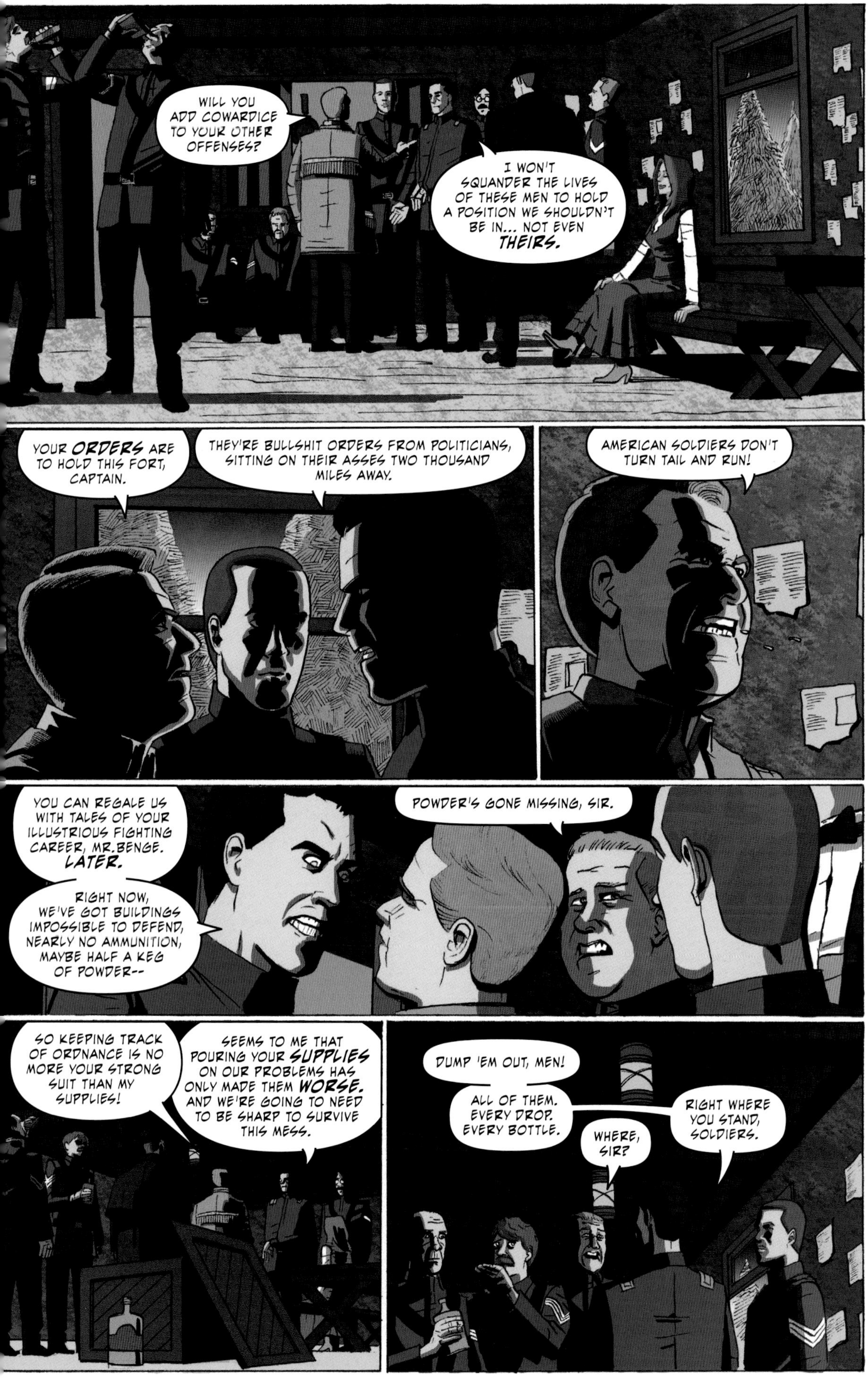
WILL YOU ADD COWARDICE TO YOUR OTHER OFFENSES?
I WON'T SQUANDER THE LIVES OF THESE MEN TO HOLD A POSITION WE SHOULDN'T BE IN... NOT EVEN THEIRS.
YOUR ORDERS ARE TO HOLD THIS FORT, CAPTAIN.
THEY'RE BULLSHIT ORDERS FROM POLITICIANS, SITTING ON THEIR ASSES TWO THOUSAND MILES AWAY.
AMERICAN SOLDIERS DON'T TURN TAIL AND RUN!
YOU CAN REGALE US WITH TALES OF YOUR ILLUSTRIOUS FIGHTING CAREER, MR.BENGE. LATER.
RIGHT NOW, WE'VE GOT BUILDINGS IMPOSSIBLE TO DEFEND, NEARLY NO AMMUNITION, MAYBE HALF A KEG OF POWDER--
POWDER'S GONE MISSING, SIR.
SO KEEPING TRACK OF ORDNANCE IS NO MORE YOUR STRONG SUIT THAN MY SUPPLIES!
SEEMS TO ME THAT POURING YOUR SUPPLIES ON OUR PROBLEMS HAS ONLY MADE THEM WORSE. AND WE'RE GOING TO NEED TO BE SHARP TO SURVIVE THIS MESS.
DUMP 'EM OUT, MEN!
ALL OF THEM. EVERY DROP. EVERY BOTTLE.
WHERE, SIR?
RIGHT WHERE YOU STAND, SOLDIERS.

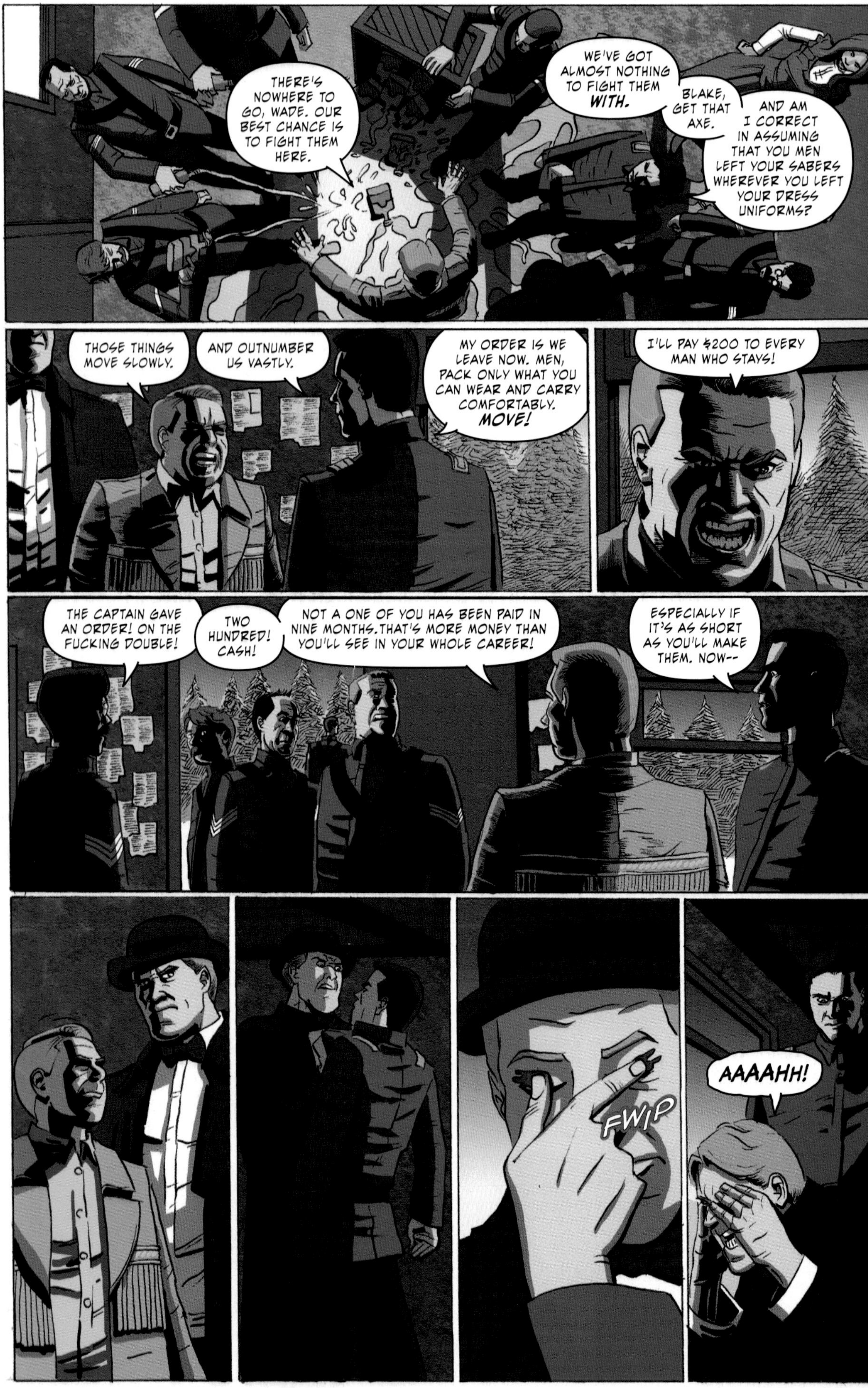
THERE'S NOWHERE TO GO, WADE. OUR BEST CHANCE IS TO FIGHT THEM HERE.
WE'VE GOT ALMOST NOTHING TO FIGHT THEM *WITH.*
BLAKE, GET THAT AXE.
AND AM I CORRECT IN ASSUMING THAT YOU MEN LEFT YOUR SABERS WHEREVER YOU LEFT YOUR DRESS UNIFORMS?
THOSE THINGS MOVE SLOWLY.
AND OUTNUMBER US VASTLY.
MY ORDER IS WE LEAVE NOW. MEN, PACK ONLY WHAT YOU CAN WEAR AND CARRY COMFORTABLY. *MOVE!*
I'LL PAY $200 TO EVERY MAN WHO STAYS!
THE CAPTAIN GAVE AN ORDER! ON THE FUCKING DOUBLE!
TWO HUNDRED! CASH!
NOT A ONE OF YOU HAS BEEN PAID IN NINE MONTHS. THAT'S MORE MONEY THAN YOU'LL SEE IN YOUR WHOLE CAREER!
ESPECIALLY IF IT'S AS SHORT AS YOU'LL MAKE THEM. NOW--
FWIP
AAAAHH!

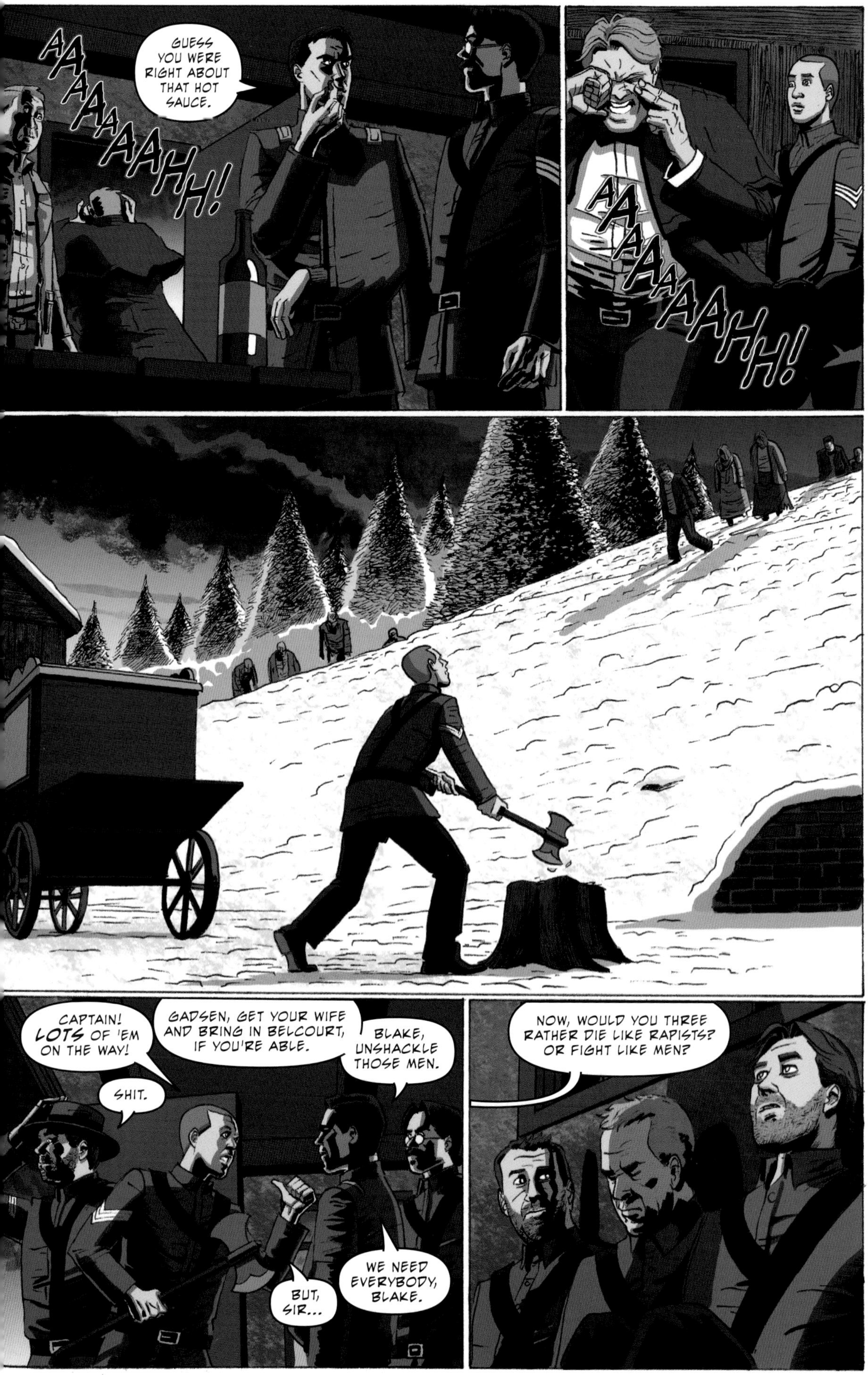
AAAAAAAAHHH!
GUESS YOU WERE RIGHT ABOUT THAT HOT SAUCE.
AAAAAAAAHHH!
CAPTAIN! LOTS OF 'EM ON THE WAY!
SHIT.
GADSEN, GET YOUR WIFE AND BRING IN BELCOURT, IF YOU'RE ABLE.
BLAKE, UNSHACKLE THOSE MEN.
BUT, SIR...
WE NEED EVERYBODY, BLAKE.
NOW, WOULD YOU THREE RATHER DIE LIKE RAPISTS? OR FIGHT LIKE MEN?

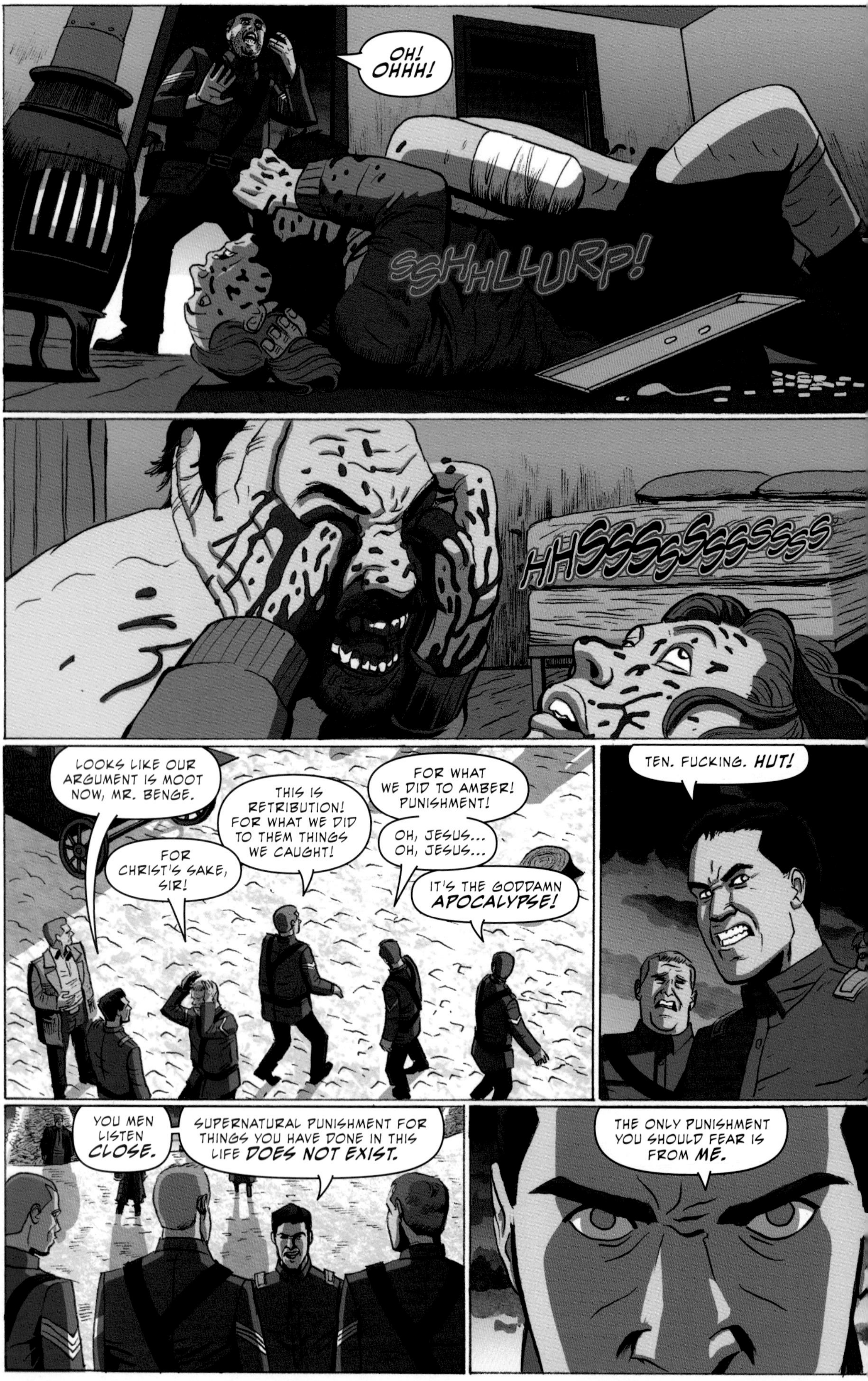
OH! OHHH!
SSHHLLURP!
HHSSSSSSSSSSS
LOOKS LIKE OUR ARGUMENT IS MOOT NOW, MR. BENGE.
FOR CHRIST'S SAKE, SIR!
THIS IS RETRIBUTION! FOR WHAT WE DID TO THEM THINGS WE CAUGHT!
FOR WHAT WE DID TO AMBER! PUNISHMENT!
OH, JESUS... OH, JESUS...
IT'S THE GODDAMN APOCALYPSE!
TEN. FUCKING. HUT!
YOU MEN LISTEN CLOSE.
SUPERNATURAL PUNISHMENT FOR THINGS YOU HAVE DONE IN THIS LIFE DOES NOT EXIST.
THE ONLY PUNISHMENT YOU SHOULD FEAR IS FROM ME.

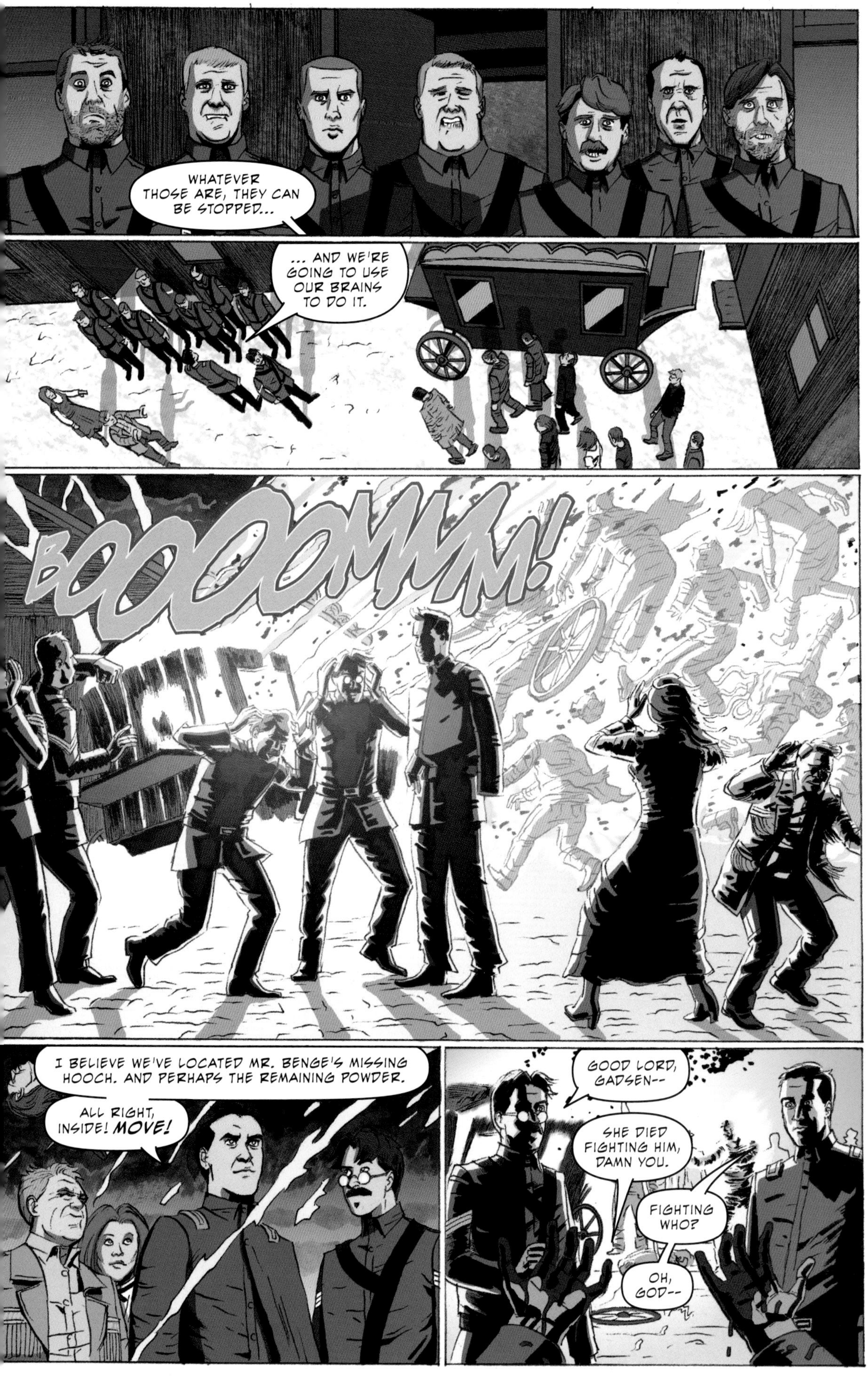
WHATEVER THOSE ARE, THEY CAN BE STOPPED...
... AND WE'RE GOING TO USE OUR BRAINS TO DO IT.
BOOOOMMM!
I BELIEVE WE'VE LOCATED MR. BENGE'S MISSING HOOCH. AND PERHAPS THE REMAINING POWDER.
ALL RIGHT, INSIDE! MOVE!
GOOD LORD, GADSEN--
SHE DIED FIGHTING HIM, DAMN YOU.
FIGHTING WHO?
OH, GOD--

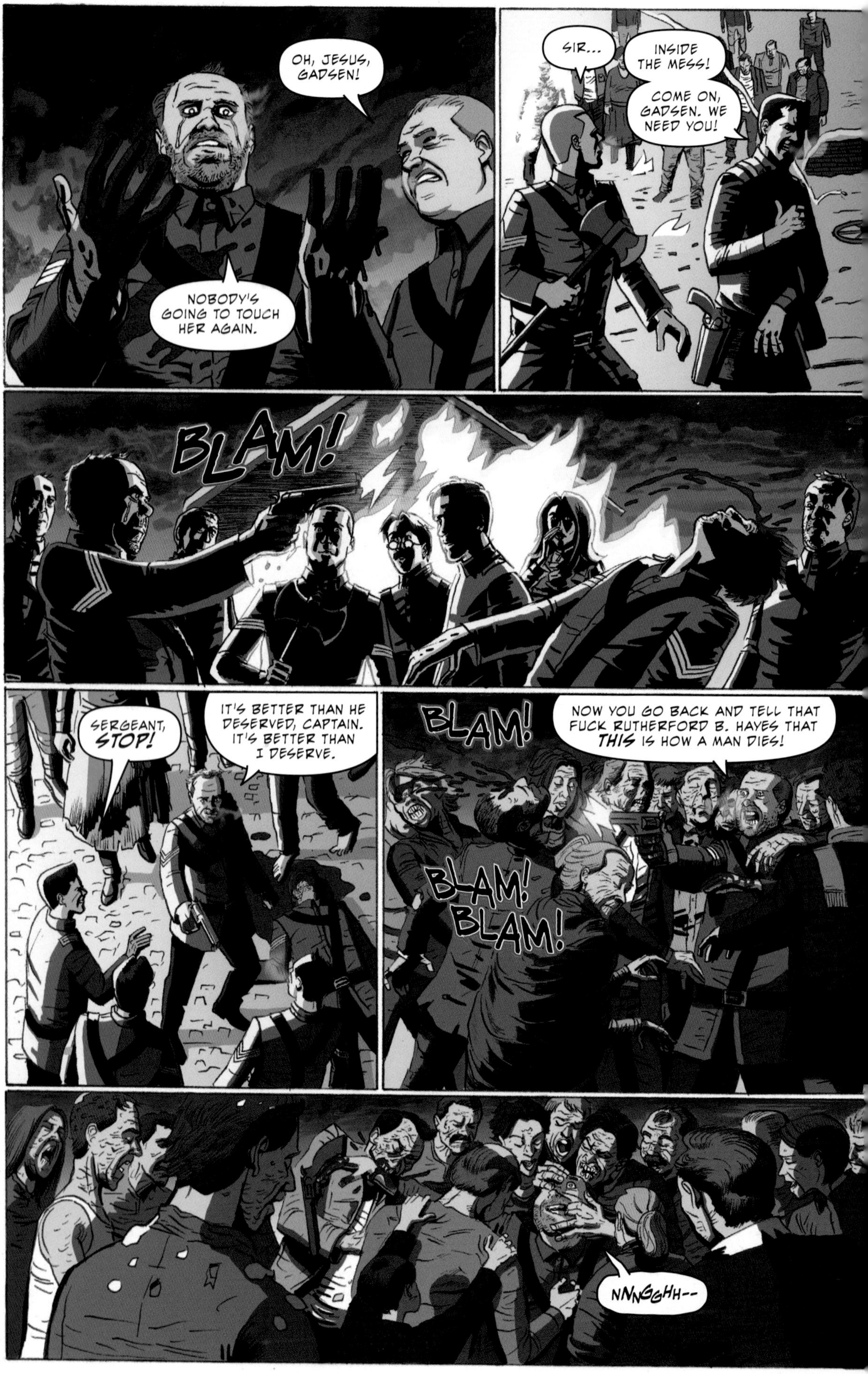
OH, JESUS, GADSEN!
NOBODY'S GOING TO TOUCH HER AGAIN.
SIR...
INSIDE THE MESS!
COME ON, GADSEN. WE NEED YOU!
BLAM!
SERGEANT, STOP!
IT'S BETTER THAN HE DESERVED, CAPTAIN. IT'S BETTER THAN I DESERVE.
BLAM!
NOW YOU GO BACK AND TELL THAT FUCK RUTHERFORD B. HAYES THAT THIS IS HOW A MAN DIES!
BLAM! BLAM!
NNNGGHH--

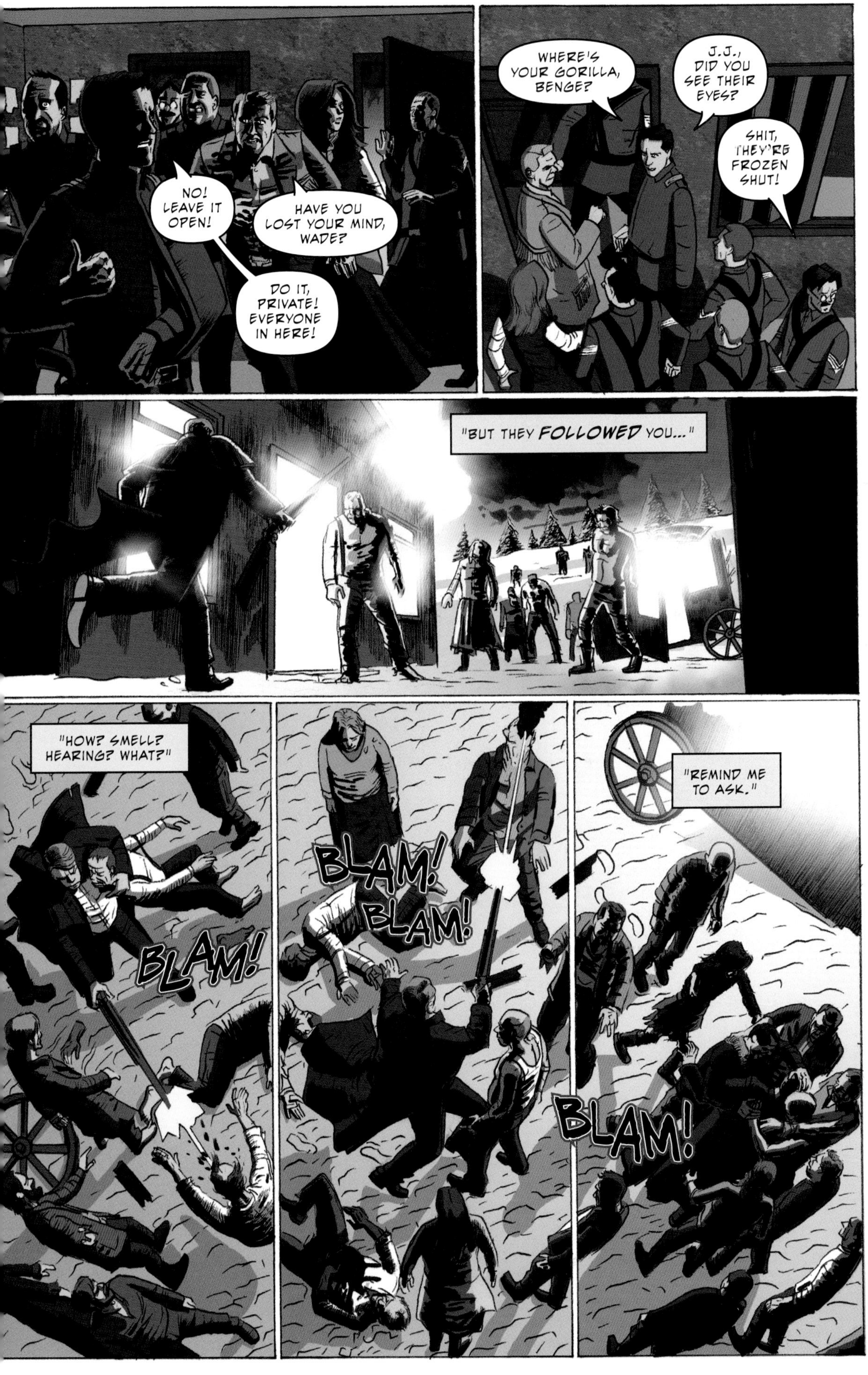
NO! LEAVE IT OPEN!
HAVE YOU LOST YOUR MIND, WADE?
DO IT, PRIVATE! EVERYONE IN HERE!
WHERE'S YOUR GORILLA, BENGE?
J.J., DID YOU SEE THEIR EYES?
SHIT, THEY'RE FROZEN SHUT!
"BUT THEY FOLLOWED YOU..."
"HOW? SMELL? HEARING? WHAT?"
BLAM!
BLAM!
BLAM!
"REMIND ME TO ASK."
BLAM!

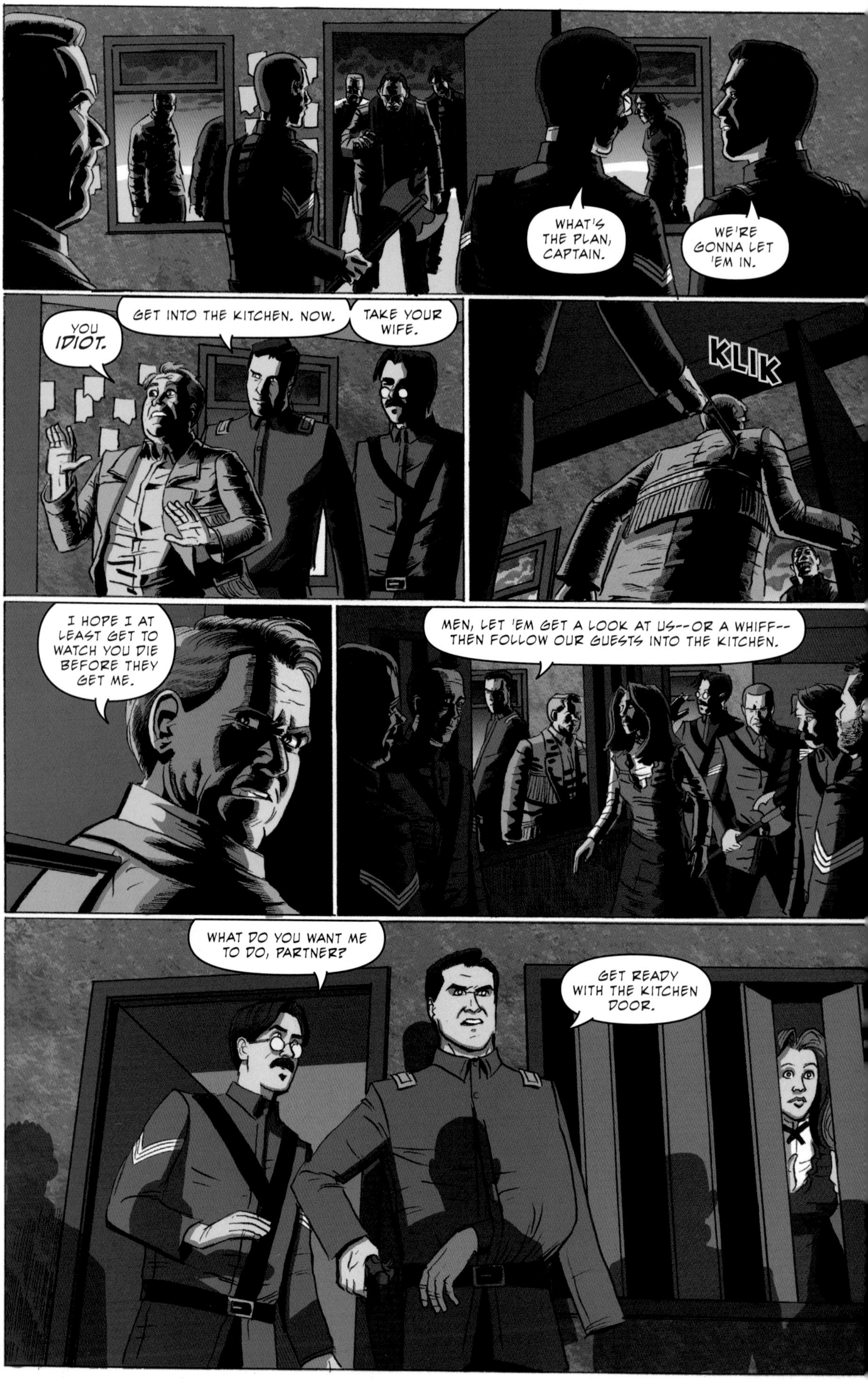
WHAT'S THE PLAN, CAPTAIN.
WE'RE GONNA LET 'EM IN.
YOU *IDIOT.*
GET INTO THE KITCHEN. NOW.
TAKE YOUR WIFE.
KLIK
I HOPE I AT LEAST GET TO WATCH YOU DIE BEFORE THEY GET ME.
MEN, LET 'EM GET A LOOK AT US--OR A WHIFF--THEN FOLLOW OUR GUESTS INTO THE KITCHEN.
WHAT DO YOU WANT ME TO DO, PARTNER?
GET READY WITH THE KITCHEN DOOR.

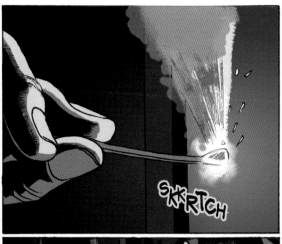

SKKRTCH

WHOOSH

SO THAT'S WHY YOU MADE THEM POUR IT OUT ON THE FLOOR!

IT JUST KEEPS COMING IN HANDY.

WHAT'S YOUR PLAN NOW? TO ESCAPE THOSE THINGS BY BURNING TO DEATH? THERE'S NO WAY OUT OF HERE!

FINISH THE JOB.

KRRRAKK!

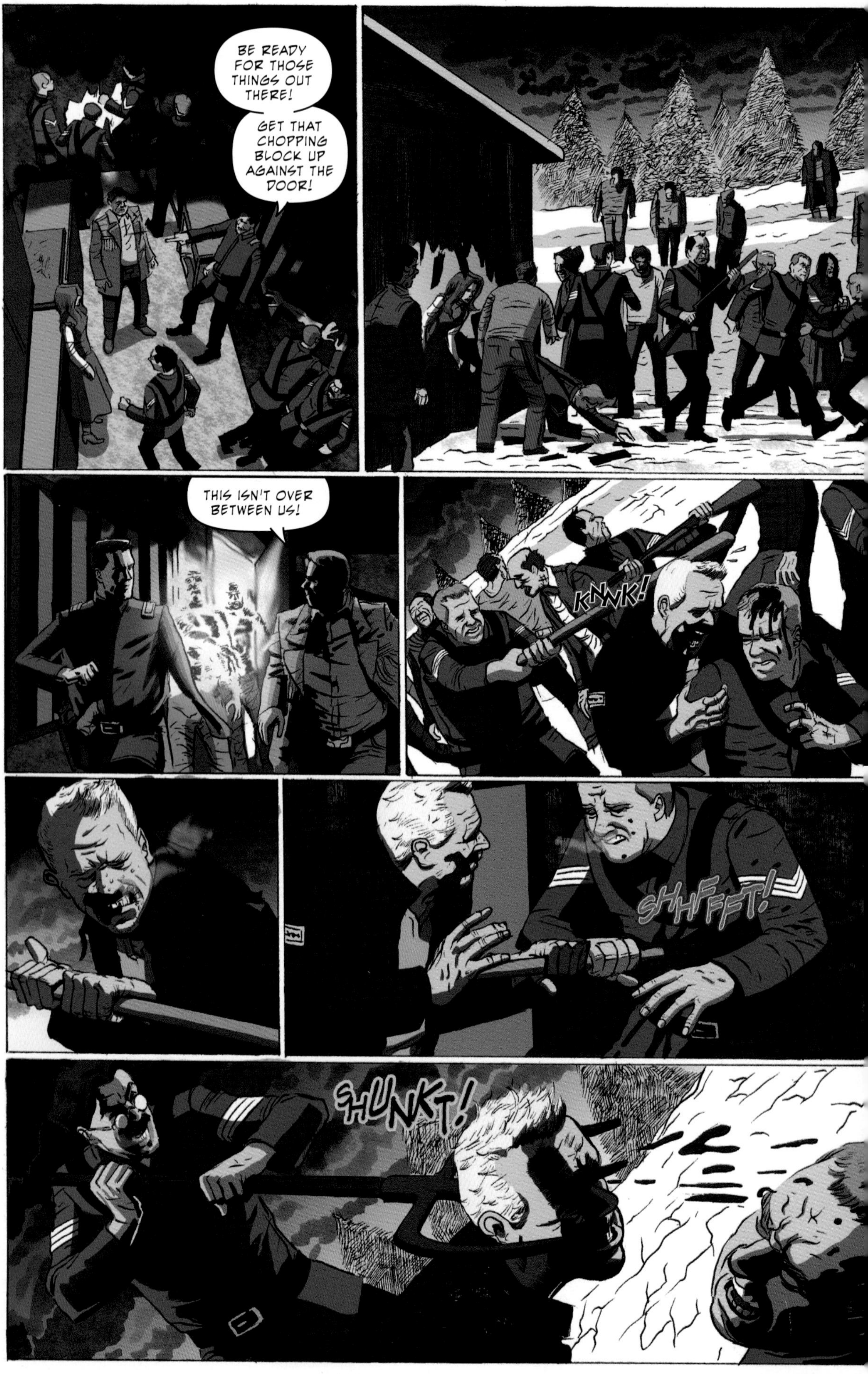
BE READY FOR THOSE THINGS OUT THERE!
GET THAT CHOPPING BLOCK UP AGAINST THE DOOR!
THIS ISN'T OVER BETWEEN US!
KNWK!
SHHFFFT!
SHUNKT!

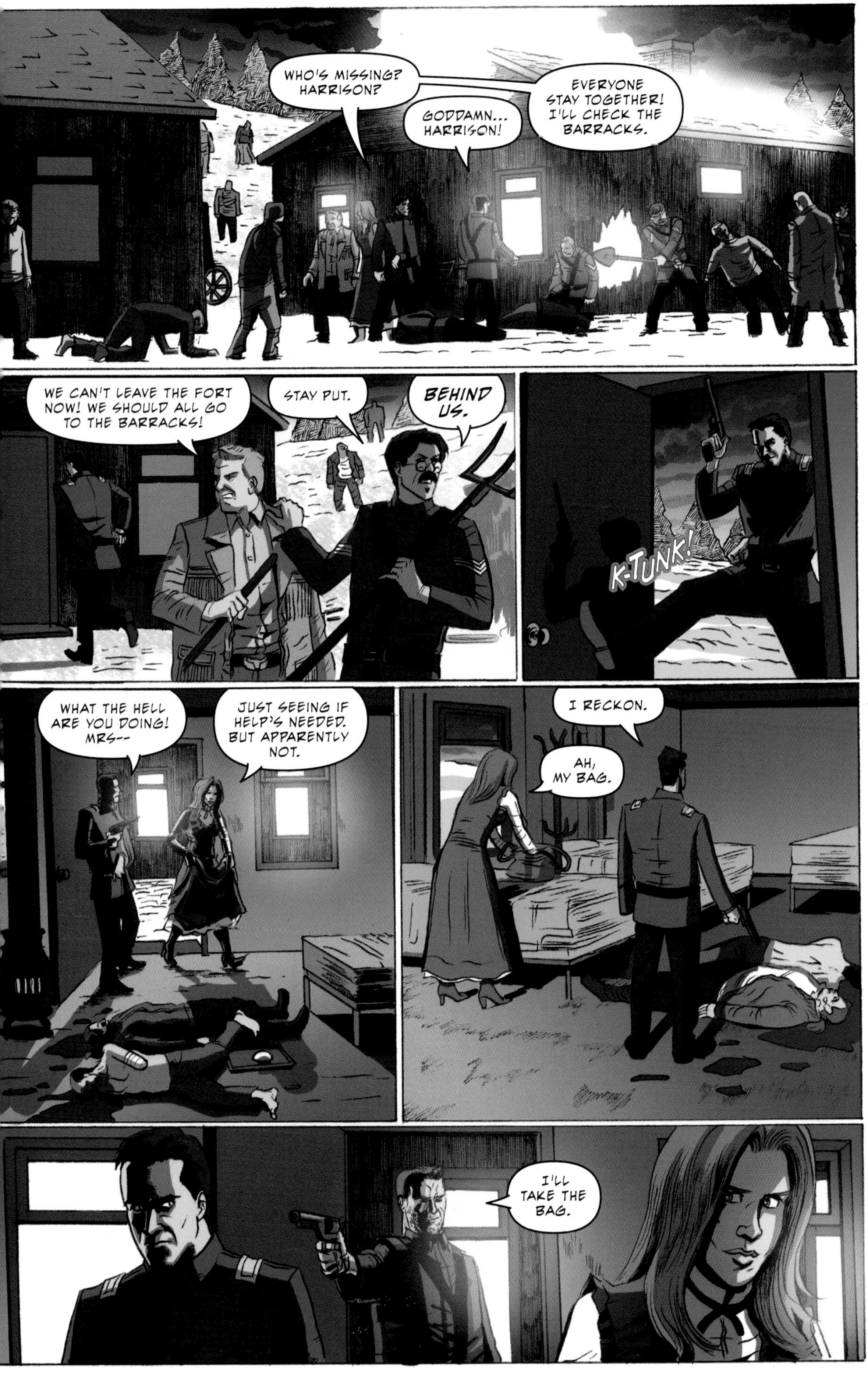
WHO'S MISSING? HARRISON?
GODDAMN... HARRISON!
EVERYONE STAY TOGETHER! I'LL CHECK THE BARRACKS.
WE CAN'T LEAVE THE FORT NOW! WE SHOULD ALL GO TO THE BARRACKS!
STAY PUT.
BEHIND US.
K-TUNK!
WHAT THE HELL ARE YOU DOING! MRS--
JUST SEEING IF HELP'S NEEDED. BUT APPARENTLY NOT.
I RECKON.
AH, MY BAG.
I'LL TAKE THE BAG.

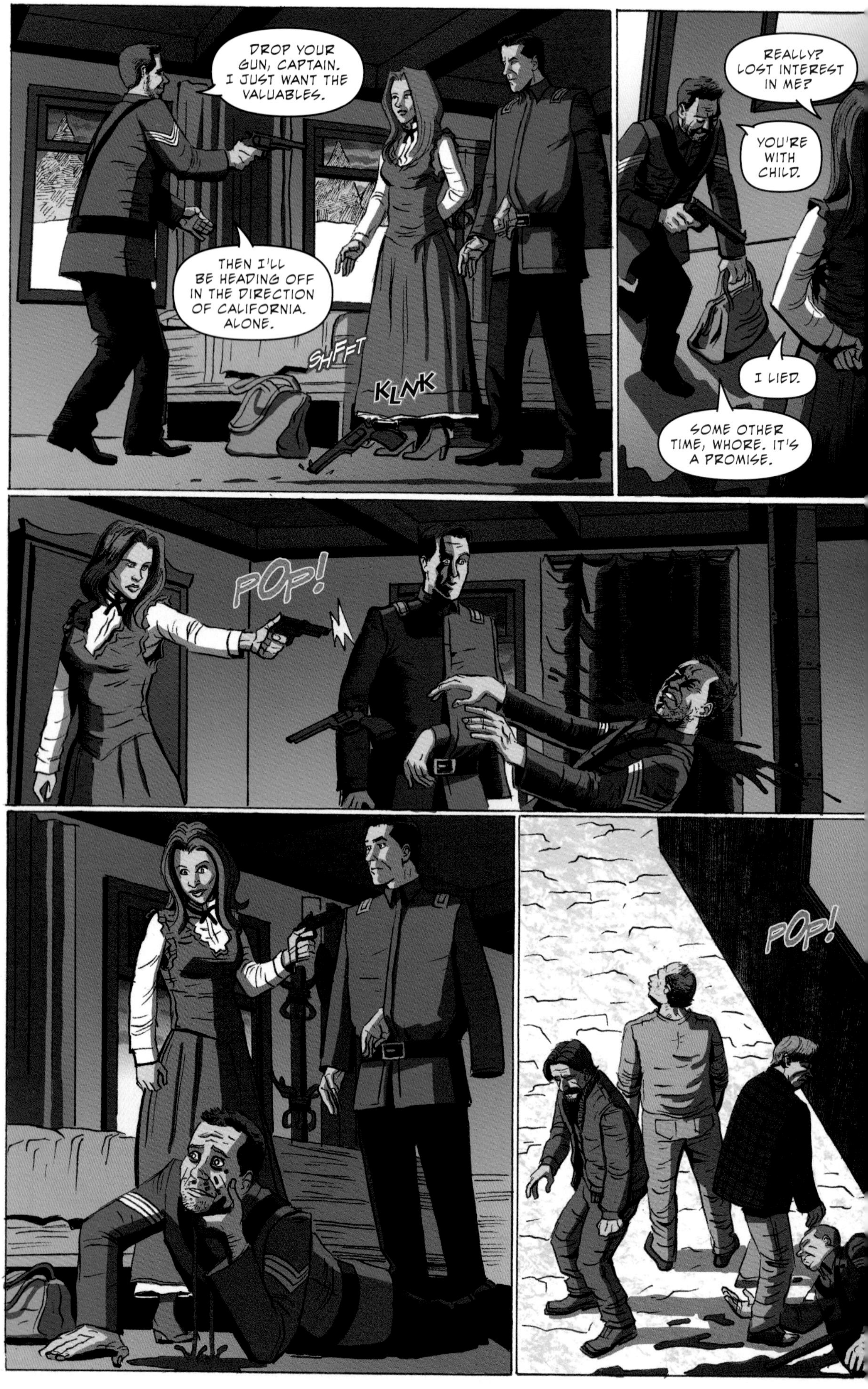
DROP YOUR GUN, CAPTAIN. I JUST WANT THE VALUABLES.
THEN I'LL BE HEADING OFF IN THE DIRECTION OF CALIFORNIA. ALONE.
SHFFT
KLNK
REALLY? LOST INTEREST IN ME?
YOU'RE WITH CHILD.
I LIED.
SOME OTHER TIME, WHORE. IT'S A PROMISE.
POP!
POP!

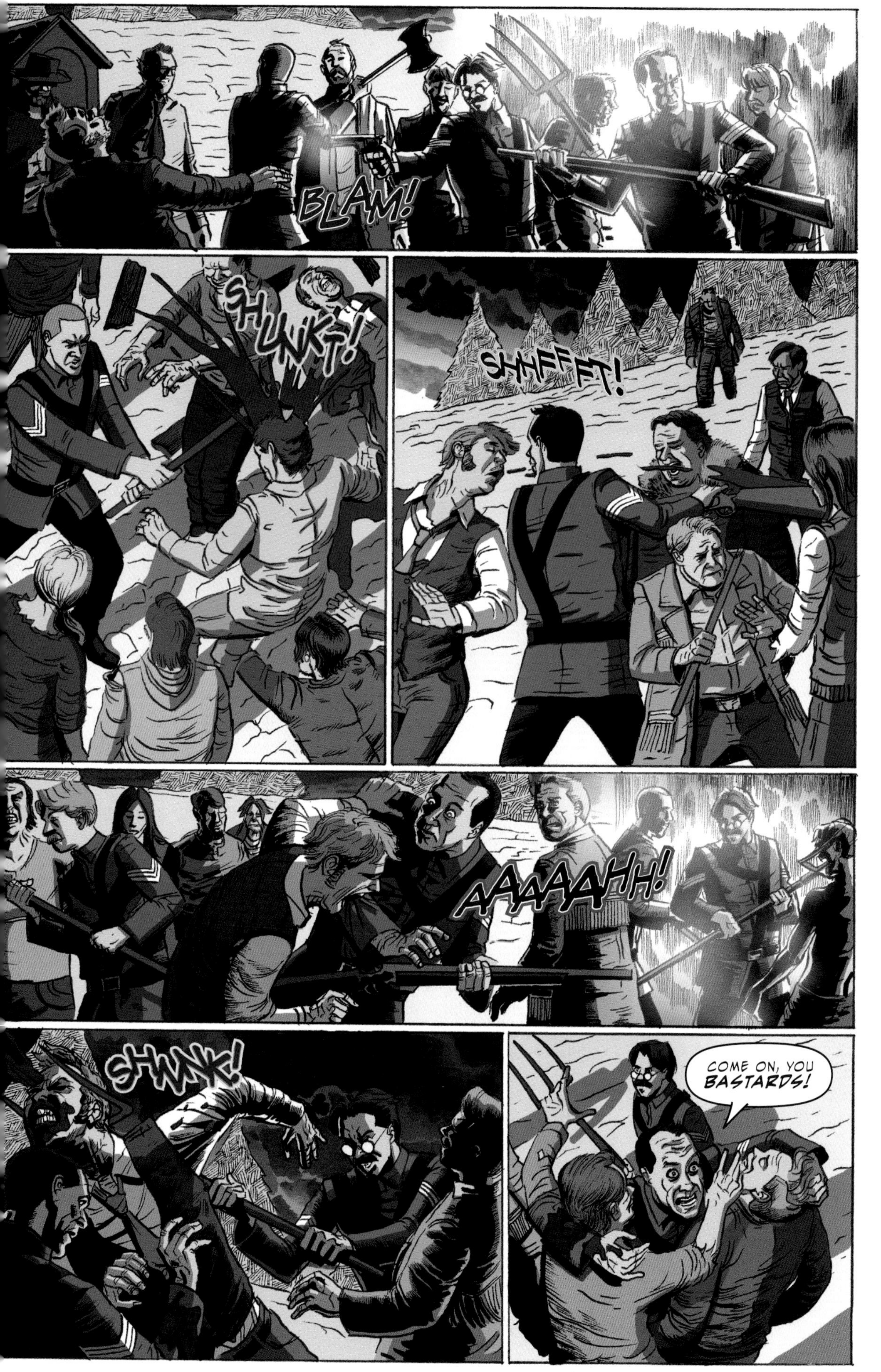
BLAM!
SHUNKT!
SHHFFFT!
AAAAAHH!
SHUNK!
COME ON, YOU BASTARDS!

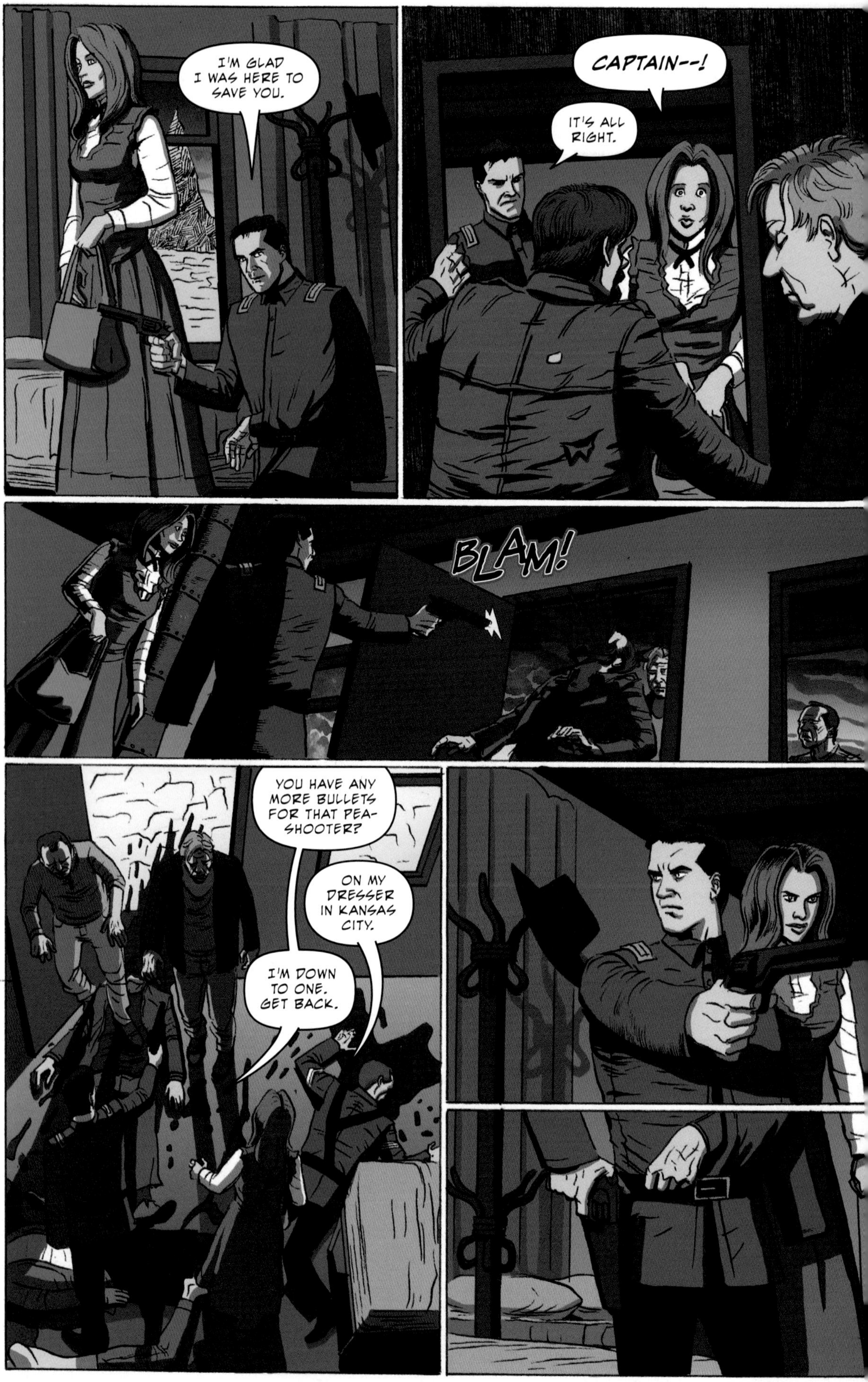
I'M GLAD I WAS HERE TO SAVE YOU.
CAPTAIN--!
IT'S ALL RIGHT.
BLAM!
YOU HAVE ANY MORE BULLETS FOR THAT PEA-SHOOTER?
ON MY DRESSER IN KANSAS CITY.
I'M DOWN TO ONE. GET BACK.

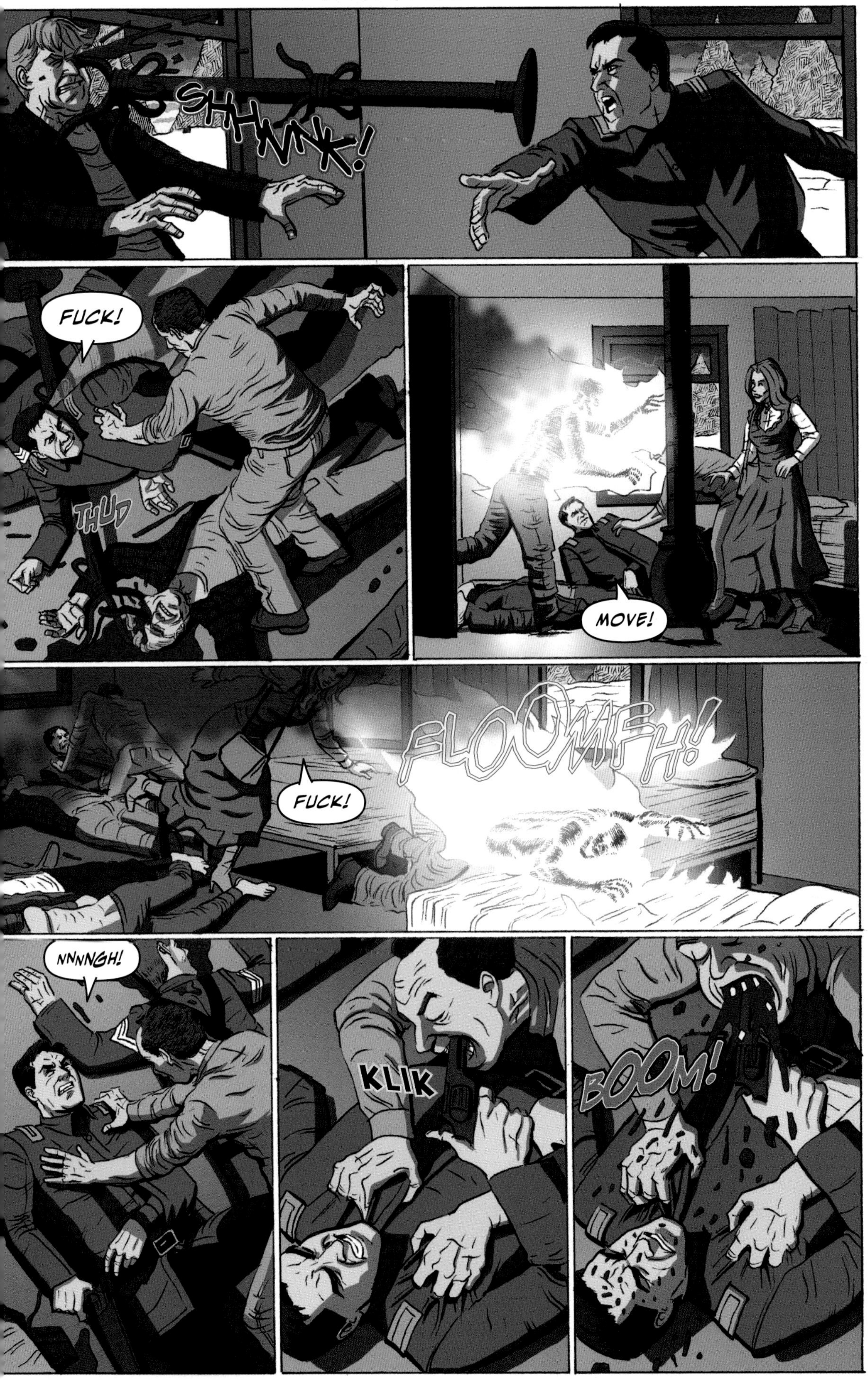
SHHNNK!
FUCK!
THUD
MOVE!
FUCK!
FLOOMFH!
NNNNGH!
KLIK
BOOM!

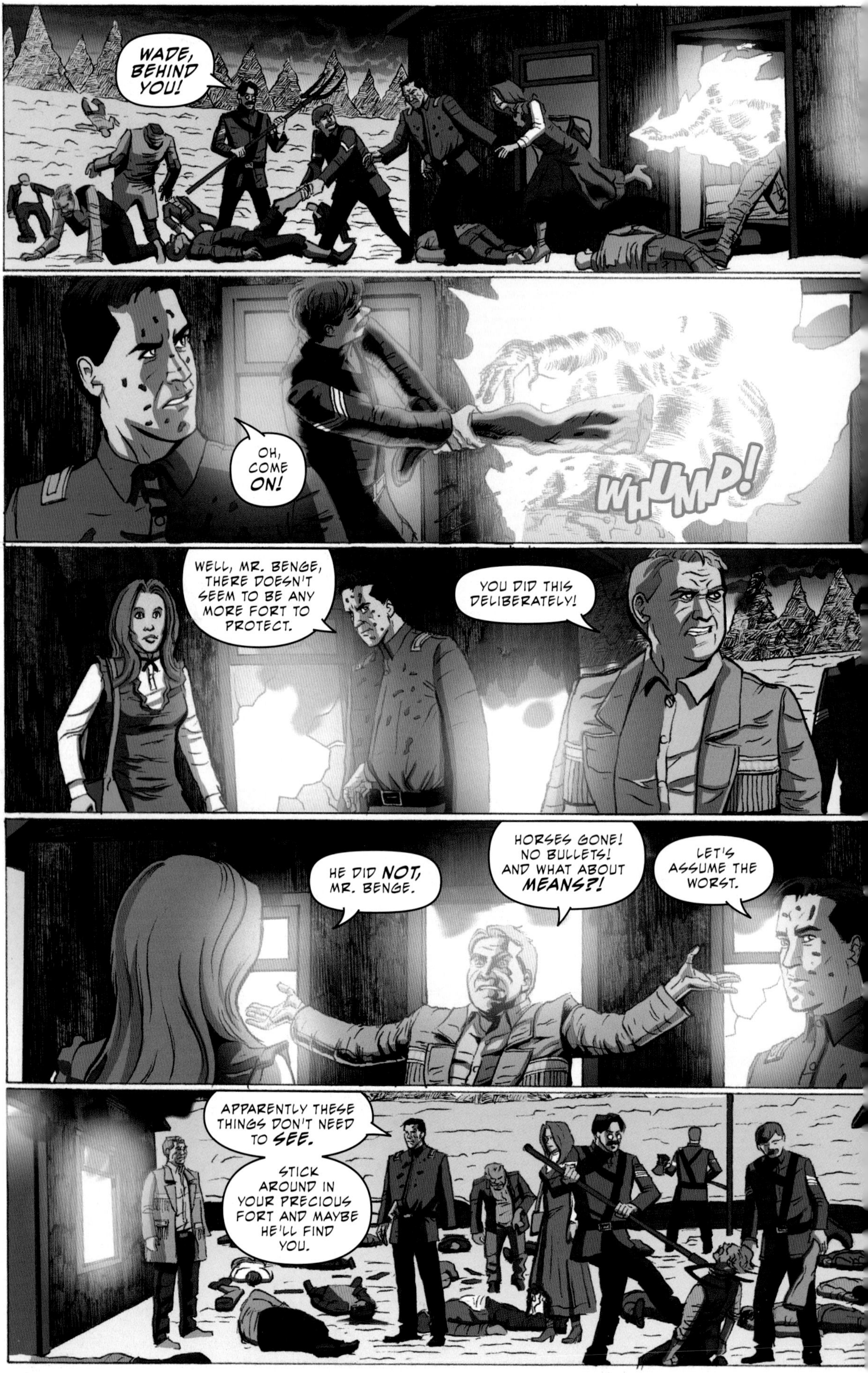
WADE, BEHIND YOU!
OH, COME ON!
WHUMP!
WELL, MR. BENGE, THERE DOESN'T SEEM TO BE ANY MORE FORT TO PROTECT.
YOU DID THIS DELIBERATELY!
HE DID NOT, MR. BENGE.
HORSES GONE! NO BULLETS! AND WHAT ABOUT MEANS?!
LET'S ASSUME THE WORST.
APPARENTLY THESE THINGS DON'T NEED TO SEE.
STICK AROUND IN YOUR PRECIOUS FORT AND MAYBE HE'LL FIND YOU.

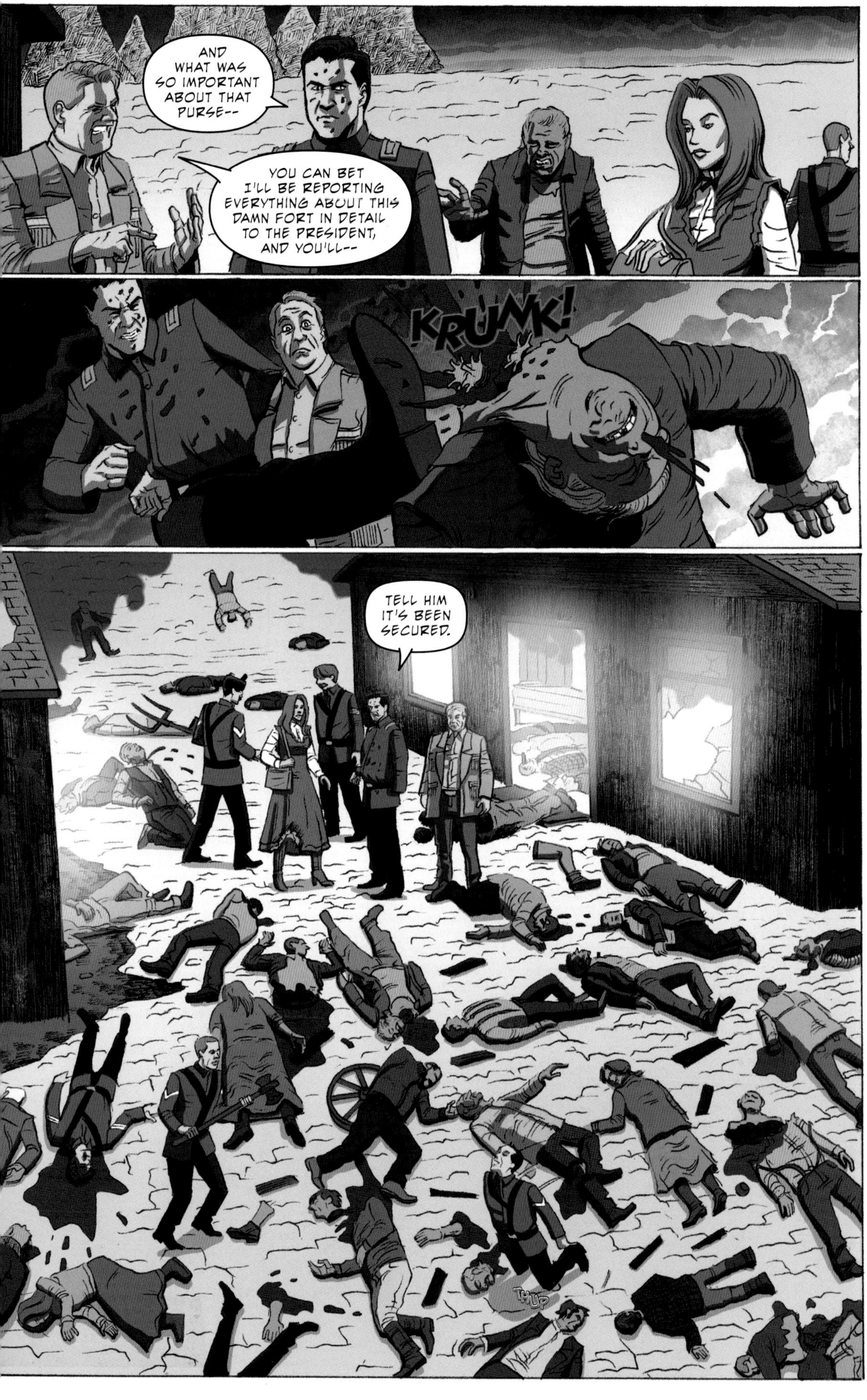
AND WHAT WAS SO IMPORTANT ABOUT THAT PURSE--
YOU CAN BET I'LL BE REPORTING EVERYTHING ABOUT THIS DAMN FORT IN DETAIL TO THE PRESIDENT, AND YOU'LL--
KRUNK!
TELL HIM IT'S BEEN SECURED.
THUP

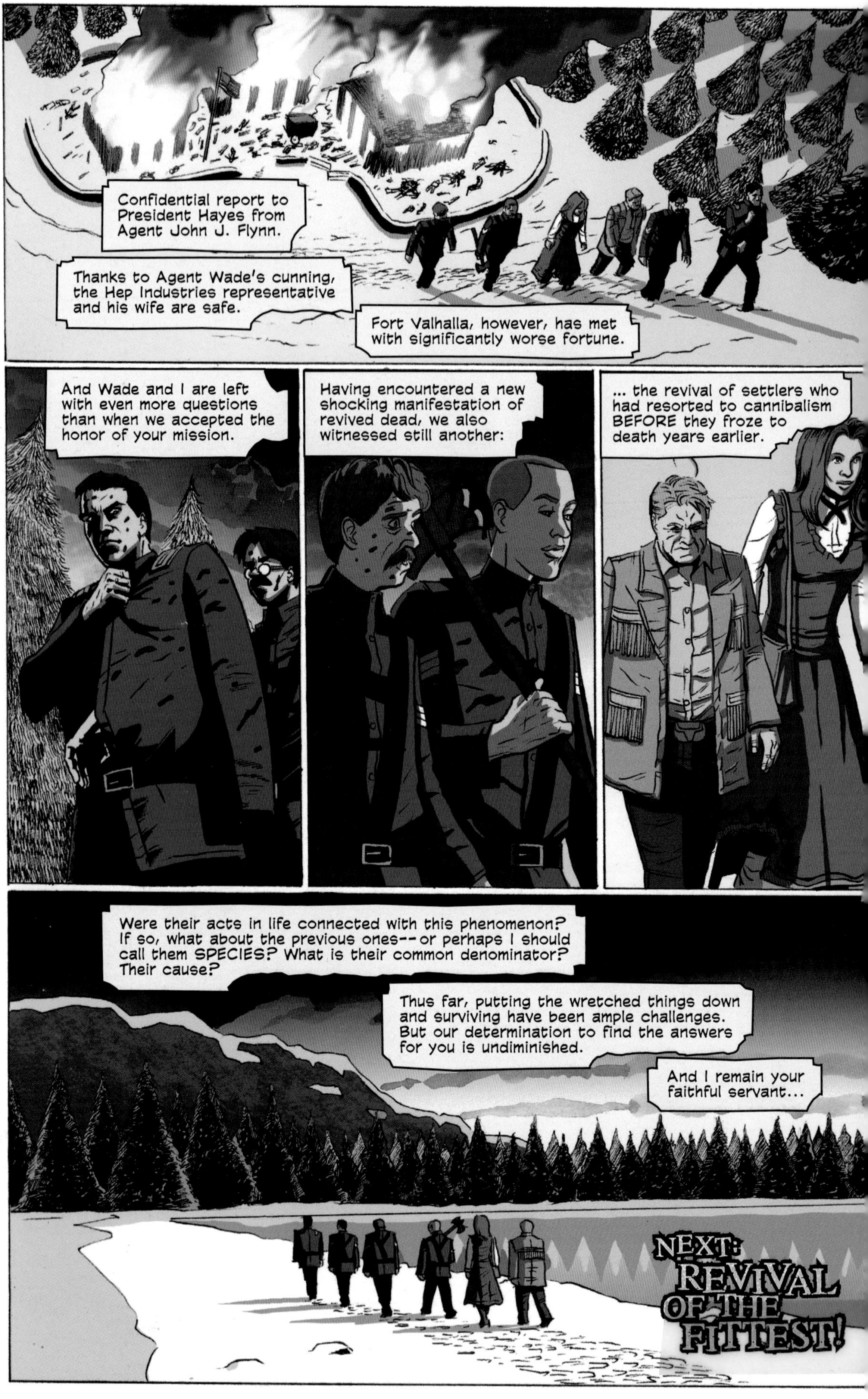
Confidential report to President Hayes from Agent John J. Flynn.
Thanks to Agent Wade's cunning, the Hep Industries representative and his wife are safe.
Fort Valhalla, however, has met with significantly worse fortune.
And Wade and I are left with even more questions than when we accepted the honor of your mission.
Having encountered a new shocking manifestation of revived dead, we also witnessed still another:
... the revival of settlers who had resorted to cannibalism BEFORE they froze to death years earlier.
Were their acts in life connected with this phenomenon? If so, what about the previous ones--or perhaps I should call them SPECIES? What is their common denominator? Their cause?
Thus far, putting the wretched things down and surviving have been ample challenges. But our determination to find the answers for you is undiminished.
And I remain your faithful servant...
NEXT: REVIVAL OF THE FITTEST!